GDPR: General Data Protection Regulation (EU) 2016/679

European Monographs Series Set

VOLUME 107

Editor

Prof. Andrea Biondi is Professor of European Law and Director of the Centre of European Law at King's College London

Introduction & Contents/Subjects

As the process of European integration assumes an increasingly complex character, the EU legal system continues to undergo sweeping changes. The European Monographs series offers a voice to thoughtful, knowledgeable, cutting edge legal commentary on the now unlimited field of European law. Its emphasis on focal and topical issues makes the series an invaluable tool for scholars, practitioners, and policymakers specializing or simply interested in EU law.

Objective

The aim is to publish innovative work appealing to academics and practitioners alike. The result is an original and ongoing library of detailed analyses, theories, commentaries, practical guides, and proposals, each of which furthers the cause of meaningful European integration. Cumulatively, the series may be regarded as a 'work in progress' engaged in building a sharply defined representation of law in Europe.

Readership

Academics and practitioners dealing with EU law.

The titles published in this series are listed at the end of this volume.

GDPR: General Data Protection Regulation (EU) 2016/679

Post-Reform Personal Data Protection in the European Union

Mariusz Krzysztofek

Wolters Kluwer

Published by:
Kluwer Law International B.V.
PO Box 316
2400 AH Alphen aan den Rijn
The Netherlands
E-mail: international-sales@wolterskluwer.com
Website: lrus.wolterskluwer.com

Sold and distributed in North, Central and South America by:
Wolters Kluwer Legal & Regulatory U.S.
7201 McKinney Circle
Frederick, MD 21704
United States of America
Email: customer.service@wolterskluwer.com

Sold and distributed in all other countries by:
Air Business Subscriptions
Rockwood House
Haywards Heath
West Sussex
RH16 3DH
United Kingdom
Email: international-customerservice@wolterskluwer.com

Printed on acid-free paper.

ISBN 978-94-035-0594-7

e-Book: ISBN 978-94-035-0595-4
web-PDF: ISBN 978-94-035-0600-5

Printed in the United Kingdom.

For my wife Justyna and my sons Mariusz and Michał

About the Author

Mariusz Krzysztofek is a Doctor of Science (dr. hab.) in Laws, Ph.D., att., experienced as a Data Protection Officer, expert, auditor, university lecturer and trainer specialising in EU and global privacy and personal data protection laws. He completed postgraduate courses at Georgetown University and the University of Wisconsin – La Crosse in the USA. He has authored six books and dozens of articles on personal data protection and has been an expert for the ministry of justice, the ministry of digital affairs, for data protection regulators, and on business TV channels. He is a member of the programme council of the quarterly 'Information in Public Administration'. He was awarded a medal for educational activity for banks by the Polish Bank Association.

He has worked for major international groups in the financial sector as a global-scale Data Protection Officer as well as an Expert for the Big Four. He is the Director, Privacy Counsel and DPO for EMEA in a global FMCG company.

Table of Contents

INTRODUCTION:

Scope of the Book. Impact of the GDPR on Member State National Personal Data Protection Laws

Regulation (EU) 2016/679 of the European Parliament and of the Council of 27 April 2016 on the protection of natural persons with regard to the processing of personal data and on the free movement of such data, and repealing Directive 95/46/EC (General Data Protection Regulation)[1] (abbreviated in this book as the 'GDPR' or the 'Regulation') regulates the protection of the personal data of natural persons, setting a uniform standard for this protection in the Member States of the European Union (and in the member states of the European Economic Area (EEA), i.e. Iceland, Liechtenstein and Norway). It also ensures free movement of personal data between the Member States, since the data protection level ensured by them is uniform within the EU. The Regulation – as Directive 95/46/EC was before – is the key act of the European Union's secondary law *acquis communautaire* regulating personal data protection.

The GDPR is the first thorough reform of the EU personal data protection regime since the adoption of Directive 95/46/EC of the European Parliament and of the Council of 24 October 1995 on the protection of individuals with regard to the processing of personal data and on the free movement of such data[2] (referred to in this book as 'Directive 95/46/EC').

The GDPR supersedes Directive 95/46/EC. The Regulation entered into force on 25 May 2016, but is to apply and be enforced from 25 May 2018. Directive 95/46/EC was repealed with effect from the same date (Article 94(4) of the GDPR). References to the repealed Directive in other legal acts are to be construed as references to the GDPR (Article 94(2) of the GDPR).

Most of the Member States' existing data protection laws and regulations, implementing Directive 95/46/EC, should be repealed or amended. They are relevant,

1. OJ EU L 119, 4.5.2016, p. 1.
2. OJ EU L 281, 23.11.1995, p. 31.

among others, as the legal basis for the operation of each Member State's supervisory authority (including the qualification requirements for its members, or their terms of service), as Article 54 of the GDPR provides that such legal basis shall be provided for in the Member State's law. Legislators in Germany, Poland and the United Kingdom chose to replace their respective personal data protection laws, applicable thus far, with new laws, which, according to their implementing provisions, repeal and supersede the previous laws. In contrast, the Spanish legislator chose to revise the existing legal act instead of repealing it.

Legal acts which require modification also include laws and regulations which regulate aspects of personal data processing in each of various domains and sectors, such as labour, legal services (e.g. of barristers, solicitors or notaries), public statistics, land and mortgage registers, access to medical files and banking law etc. Each of these laws and regulations, if found to be subject to EU law, must be reviewed and revised as necessary to ensure compliance with the GDPR.

Recital 8 of the preamble to the GDPR states that specifications or restrictions of its rules by Member State law are only possible in areas specified in the GDPR. Thus, the scope of data controllers' and data processors' obligations and data subjects' rights is specified in the GDPR rather than in national legal acts. The GDPR only specifies certain exclusions where discretion is left to national legislators in the Member States.

Maintaining laws or regulations which are in conflict with the GDPR or duplicate its provisions in the areas subject to European Union law is not only prohibited but also ineffective, since the GDPR, as any EU regulation, is directly applicable in the EU Member States (second sentence of Article 99(2) of the GDPR) and also in light of the principle of primacy of binding EU law over the Member States' national laws, whereby the Member States may not apply national law provisions which are in conflict with EU law.[3]

In areas regulated by the GDPR, national acts must not duplicate or modify the key principles of data processing, obligations of data controllers, rights of data subjects or fines (except where this is expressly allowed by the GDPR in areas subject to specific Member State law provisions on personal data processing). They must be restricted to acting as 'triggers', allowing the GDPR to be implemented and applied. Thus, they must regulate issues such as the operation of the national data protection authority, inspection proceedings, procedures for investigating infringements against personal data protection regulations, procedures for imposing administrative fines, accreditation and certification procedures, court procedures in claims related to personal data protection, notifying the appointment of a data protection officer to the supervisory authority, the age of a child in the context of information society services, restrictions on transfers of sensitive data to third countries, data processing in employment

3. Judgment of the Court of Justice of the European Union (CJEU) of 15 July 1964 in Case 6/64 *Costa v E.N.E.L.*, http://eur-lex.europa.eu/legal-content/EN/TXT/HTML/?uri=CELEX:61964CJ0006, and the CJEU judgment of 10 December 1969 in joined Cases 6 and 11-69 *Commission of the European Communities v French Republic*, http://eur-lex.europa.eu/legal-content/EN/TXT/HTML/?uri=CELEX:61969CJ0006.

relations, limitation of fines imposed on public authorities, and restrictions on the rights of data subjects who are customers of small- and medium-sized enterprises.

The reform is being introduced by a regulation rather than an amendment to the Directive. It will thus become applicable directly in all the Member States without the need to be implemented, in accordance with Article 288 of the Treaty on the Functioning of the European Union (TFEU), providing for direct applicability of regulations in all Member States. The repeal of Directive 95/46/EC and application of the GDPR will be a transition from the current harmonisation of personal data protection laws in the EU Member States towards a unification of data protection rules within the EU. This objective was also emphasised by the Court of Justice of the European Union (CJEU).[4]

The GDPR has a direct horizontal effect in the Member States[5]. This means it regulates relations between individual entities and may be invoked by them directly in disputes involving these entities. The GDPR will thus be binding in the same way as national laws of the Member States have been thus far, but will apply uniformly across the European Union.

This will increase legal certainty in this area among data subjects who are customers of multinational corporations, as well as among data controllers operating internationally; it will also enhance the operation of the internal market.[6]

This book is a comprehensive commentary on the GDPR. It offers a broad account of the legal and practical aspects of the European Union personal data protection law following its recent reform, the most extensive since the first EU laws in this area were adopted and implemented into the legal orders of the Member States. In addition, the principle of direct effect of the EU regulation in the Member States and the principle of primacy of EU law over national law means that the GDPR is, at the same time, a national data protection regulation in each Member State and is expected to remain one for years to come.

Subsequent chapters of this book discuss all the principles of personal data processing, the obligations of data controllers and the rights of data subjects (Articles 1 to 50 of the GDPR). This is the core of the personal data protection regime. Other

4. CJEU judgment of 24 November 2011 in joined cases C-468/10 and C-469/10, Asociación Nacional de Establecimientos Financieros de Crédito (ASNEF) and Federación de Comercio Electrónico y Marketing Directo (FECEMD) v Administración del Estado, points 28-29, http://eur-lex.europa.eu/legal-content/EN/TXT/?uri=CELEX:62010CJ0468: '[...] Directive 95/46 is intended [...] to ensure that the level of protection of the rights and freedoms of individuals with regard to the processing of personal data is equivalent in all Member States. [...] [T]he harmonisation of those national laws is not limited to minimal harmonisation but amounts to harmonisation which is generally complete.'

5. As also pointed out by M. Kawecki, 'Wybór rozporządzenia jako instrumentu prawnego unijnej reformy prawa ochrony danych osobowych oraz konsekwencje takiego rozwiązania', (in:) *Ogólne rozporządzenie o ochronie danych osobowych. Wybrane zagadnienia*, ed. M. Kawecki, T. Osiej, p. 2; and M. Wiewiórowski, 'Nowe ramy ochrony danych osobowych w Unii Europejskiej', special appendix to *Monitor Prawniczy*, 2012, No. 7, p. 3.

6. Arguments in favour of the need to harmonise European personal data protection law are presented, among others, in: C. Kuner, Regulation of Transborder Data Flows under Data Protection and Privacy Law: Past, Present, and Future, Tilburg University, Netherlands, TILT Law & Technology Working Paper 2010, No. 016, Version: 1.0, p. 35, http://www.tilburguniversity.edu/research/institutes-and-research-groups/tilt/publications/workingpapers/ckuner16.pdf.

subjects, such as the powers and organisation of supervisory authorities and the European Data Protection Board (Articles 51 to 76 of the GDPR), legal remedies and sanctions (Articles 77 to 84 of the GDPR) and specific processing situations (Articles 85 to 91 of the GDPR), are discussed in chapters focusing on related issues. For instance, the competences of supervisory authorities are discussed, among others, in chapters on approval of BCRs, authorisation by a supervisory authority of a transfer of data to third countries, and certification.

CHAPTER 1

Subject Matter and Objectives of the GDPR and the Nature of Changes Introduced By It; Direct Applicability of the GDPR; The Right to Protection of Personal Data as a Fundamental Right; The Context of Personal Data Protection in the European Union; International Models of Personal Data Protection; Update of the Council of Europe Convention No. 108

§1.01 SUBJECT MATTER AND OBJECTIVES OF THE GPDR AND THE NATURE OF CHANGES INTRODUCED BY IT

The key objectives of the GDPR are listed in its Article 1. These are:

- protection of the fundamental rights and freedoms of natural persons and, in particular, their right to the protection of personal data (as demonstrated further, this right is a specific formulation of the right to privacy, which is one of the human rights and fundamental freedoms[1] and is recognised as a fundamental right following the entry into force of the Charter of Fundamental Rights),

1. P. Craig, G. de Búrca, *EU Law: Text, Cases, and Materials*, Oxford 2008, p. 384; S. Rodotà, 'Data Protection as a Fundamental Right' (in:) *Reinventing Data Protection?*, ed. by S. Gutwirth, Y. Poulet, P. de Hert, S. Nouwt, C. de Terwangne, Dordrecht 2009, p. 77.

- the free movement of personal data within the Union that is neither restricted nor prohibited for reasons connected with the protection of natural persons with regard to the processing of personal data, but at the same time ensures respect of the rights of the citizens of the Member States to have their personal data protected.

As implied by Article 1 of the GDPR, the definitions in Article 4(1) of the GDPR and recital 14 of its preamble, the scope of personal data only covers information on natural persons. It does not cover the data of legal persons and, in particular, undertakings established as legal persons, including the legal person's name, legal form and contact details.

Differences in civil-law and business terms between Member States may lead to uncertainty on whether the data of natural persons operating as businesses (sole proprietors) are protected under the GDPR. My own interpretation of this issue is presented further in the book, in the commentary on the definition of personal data.

The scope of personal data protection is expanded to cover establishments and legal units in the context of electronic communication under the ePrivacy Regulation, which complements the GDPR and is to replace Directive 2002/58/EC. The ePrivacy Regulation is discussed in further chapters of this book, with particular reference to electronic marketing and cookies.

Along with the formulation of the principle of free exchange of personal data within the EU, a uniform data protection standard is established. It prevents the creation of barriers to international economic cooperation within the EU, which could result from the restriction of data transfer between Member States. This objective of economic integration was a key feature of Directive 95/46/EC and remained so in the GDPR, besides the objective of protection of natural persons' fundamental rights and freedoms.

Another purpose of the reform of the EU data protection law was to bring it in line with the current circumstances, dramatically different from those prevalent at the time when Directive 95/46/EC (and national provisions implementing it) entered into force. The existing data protection regulations therefore required an update. The global scale and evolution of information technologies, the ubiquity of online data processing, the popularity of social networking services, online shopping and mass transfers of data are just some factors that require new legal arrangements allowing people to regain control of their personal data, as mentioned in recitals 6 and 7 of the preamble to the GDPR.

The EU model of data protection includes the key principles of personal data processing, common to all EU Member States, and the obligations of data controllers and rights of data subjects. These include the processing of data only on a specified legal basis, e.g. under consent of the data subject or pursuant to the right or obligation provided for in a specified legal provision. In practice, consent for electronic marketing and for the collection of sensitive data are particularly relevant. The principles also include the purpose limitation principle, the data accuracy principle, the data minimisation principle (also referred to as the proportionality or adequacy principle), and the storage limitation principle. It is also crucial for the lawfulness of processing that the data subject be provided with information on the processing of his/her data and of his/her right to access the data, have them rectified, and object to their processing, e.g. to customer profiling. Other requirements include a data processing impact assessment (risk analysis) and the obligation to safeguard data against unauthorised access or modification. The provisions also regulate the appointment, tasks, position and status of the data protection officer and lay down principles of the international transfer of data, in particular the ways of ensuring adequate protection of data subsequent to a transfer to a non-EU country. They also specify the competences of supervisory authorities and the European Data Protection Board, fines for personal data breach and the possibilities of enforcing claims through court litigation.

This book presents the EU personal data protection regime according to the new legal situation following the reform, which is to apply in a multi-annual perspective.

The personal data processing rules, which had been in force for 21 years, have not been replaced, but updated and significantly reinforced. The reformed personal data protection law is based on the previous model.

The data protection regime is still based on the fundamental principles, such as the purpose limitation principle, data minimisation principle or storage limitation principle. The controller is still required to specify the legal basis of the processing; this requirement has been made more stringent in relation to sensitive data. The data subject still has the right to access his/her data, have them rectified, object to the processing thereof, etc. However, the elements of this structure have been modernised to respond to the growing influence of the Internet and new technologies on the protection of personal data.

For example, the right of access to data, previously formulated in Article 12(a) of the Directive, now includes not only the right to information under Article 15 of the GDPR but also the right to portability of data in electronic format under Article 20 of the GDPR. The right to object to the processing of data under Article 12(b) and (c) and Article 14 of the Directive has developed into the right to erasure of data and the 'right to be forgotten' under Article 17 of the GDPR (which, unprecedentedly, includes the 'right to be forgotten' on the Internet, thanks to the earlier CJEU judgment of 13 May 2014 in Case C-131/12 *Google Spain SL and Google Inc. v Agencia Española de Protección de Datos (AEPD) and Mario Costeja González*), and, among others, the right to object to profiling under Article 21 of the GDPR.

§1.02 DIRECT APPLICABILITY OF THE GDPR

Directive 95/46/EC obliged the Member States, pursuant to Article 288 of the TFEU, to achieve the results stipulated therein, but it only defined the minimum required adjustment scope; any Member State could therefore go beyond those minimum requirements in the respective areas while adopting its own regulations, which led to discrepancies between the regulations in each country. Furthermore, the Directive did not impose the legal form or legal means that Member States were to use in order to implement its provisions; recital 8 of its preamble only provided for an approximation of laws (minimum harmonisation). Thus, the Directive did not require full harmonisation, i.e. Member States were not obliged to introduce entirely uniform regulations.

By replacing the Directive with a Regulation, the European Commission removed the discrepancies existing thus far between Member States' national data protection laws. The Regulation is, by the very nature of an EU regulation, directly applicable in the Member States, which ensures uniformity (full harmonisation) and precludes any differences (save for the areas specified below) in the scope of data protection within the EU.

Article 16(2) of the TFEU is the legal basis for adopting a uniform EU data protection law, i.e. laying down rules relating to the protection of individuals with regard to the processing of personal data by EU institutions, bodies, offices and agencies, and by the Member States when carrying out activities which fall within the scope of Union law.

As the GDPR applies uniformly in all Member States, it does not make references, as some national laws did, to separate legal acts (e.g. on bank or insurance secrecy) which introduced data protection going beyond the general level prescribed by personal data protection laws. The GDPR expressly names selected areas in which Member States may introduce specific personal data processing regulations; it does not, however, make a general reference to the possibility of imposing more stringent protection by separate laws. As a result, the GDPR prevails over Member States' national laws, as well as EU laws, regulating personal data processing, with the exception of Directive 2002/58/EC, which lays down the rules of processing data for providing generally available electronic communications services in public networks in the EU, and subsequently the ePrivacy Regulation (Regulation on Privacy and Electronic Communications), which is to replace the Directive.

However, despite the unification of data protection rules within the EU, detailed national laws regulating data processing will still be allowed to differ between Member States in selected areas. This is because, firstly, not all areas are subject to EU law, and secondly, the GDPR itself allows national regulations to differ in certain indicated cases. One area where differing regulations are permitted is data processing in employment relations. (Article 88 of the GDPR: 'Member States may [...] provide for more specific rules to ensure the protection of the rights and freedoms in respect of the processing of employees' personal data in the employment context.')[2]

Member States' laws may also set limits to the transfer of specific categories of personal data to a third country which has not been found, by a European Commission

2. C. Fritsch, 'Data Processing in Employment Relations; Impacts of the European General Data Protection Regulation Focusing on the Data Protection Officer at the Worksite', in: Reforming European Data Protection Law, (ed.) S. Gutwirth, R. Leenes, P. de Hert, Springer 2015, p. 147-167; W.R. Wiewiórowski (Assistant European Data Protection Supervisor), 'Nowe ramy ochrony danych osobowych w Unii Europejskiej', Monitor Prawniczy 2012, no. 7, special appendix 'Ochrona danych osobowych 2012', p. 3; N. Leopold, M. Meints, 'Profiling in Employment Situation (Fraud)', section 'Legal Grounds with Respect to Data Protection in the Working Context', in: Profiling the European Citizen. Cross-Disciplinary Perspectives, ed. by M. Hildebrandt, S. Gutwirth, New York 2008, pp. 217 et seq.

decision, to ensure an adequate level of personal data protection (Article 49(5) of the GDPR).

Another area of exception is the processing of personal data for criminal proceedings, given specific requirements on cooperation between Member States' law enforcement and judicial authorities in criminal cases and the need to introduce rules on the protection and free flow of personal data in that area.[3]

Sectoral provisions, reflecting the distinctive features of certain forms of data processing or sectors where data are processed, will remain necessary but must be consistent with the GDPR. This includes, in particular, laws on privacy in electronic communications as being more specific in relation to the GDPR. To ensure this consistency, Directive 2002/58/EC on privacy in the electronic communications sector (known as the ePrivacy Directive)[4] had to be revised (recital 173 of the preamble to the GDPR and Article 95 of the GDPR).[5] On 10 January 2017 the European Commission submitted a proposal for a Regulation of the European Parliament and of the Council concerning the respect for private life and the protection of personal data in electronic communications and repealing Directive 2002/58/EC (Regulation on Privacy and Electronic Communications, or the ePrivacy Regulation).[6] Initially, the Commission intended the ePrivacy Regulation to become applicable on the same day as the GDPR, i.e. 25 May 2018. However, during the legislation proceedings, this application date of the ePrivacy Regulation was found to be unrealistic. The Regulation now appears unlikely to come into effect until 2020 at the earliest. The GDPR, along with the ePrivacy Regulation, is essential for the introduction of the Digital Single Market. Personal data from electronic communications are simultaneously protected under the GDPR and under the ePrivacy Regulation as a more specific law in relation to the GDPR. The delay in adoption of the ePrivacy Regulation has resulted in interpretation problems concerning the relation between the GDPR and Member States' laws and regulations implementing Directive 2002/58/EC, which will only be repealed by the ePrivacy Regulation.

The two-year *vacatio legis* provided time for analysing the impact that the GDPR would have on different sectors and institutions, as well as for defining the obligations arising therefrom, and introducing arrangements to ensure compliance with the GDPR. This period only seems long: it proved challenging for organisations with complex structures, processing data on a large scale. Any processing of data which started before the GDPR application date (25 May 2018) and continued beyond that date had

3. This area is regulated by Directive (EU) 2016/680 of the European Parliament and of the Council of 27 April 2016 on the protection of natural persons with regard to the processing of personal data by competent authorities for the purposes of the prevention, investigation, detection or prosecution of criminal offences or the execution of criminal penalties, and on the free movement of such data, and repealing Council Framework Decision 2008/977/JHA (OJ EU L 119, 4.5.2016).
4. Directive 2002/58/EC of the European Parliament and of the Council of 12 July 2002 concerning the processing of personal data and the protection of privacy in the electronic communications sector (Directive on privacy and electronic communications), OJ EU L 201, 31.07.2002, p. 37-47.
5. The Article 29 Data Protection Working Party, Opinion 03/2016 on the evaluation and review of the ePrivacy Directive (2002/58/EC), No. WP 240 of 19 July 2016, http://ec.europa.eu/justice/article-29/documentation/opinion-recommendation/files/2016/wp240_en.pdf.
6. http://eur-lex.europa.eu/legal-content/EN/TXT/?uri=CELEX:52017PC0010.

to be brought into compliance during the two-year transition period starting with the GDPR's entry into force on 25 May 2016.

In addition, legislators in the Member States had to review local laws governing the processing of data in various areas and bring those laws in line with the GDPR.

The GDPR also introduces new obligations of supervisory authorities, e.g. to analyse the reported personal data breaches (Article 33 of the GDPR) and to consult data processing impact assessments which indicate a high data processing risk (Article 36 of the GDPR). These obligations will impose significant new burdens on the supervisory authorities. These authorities have already signalled increased staffing demands (e.g. ICO in the UK needs to grow from 451 to 620 staff members; GIODO in Poland – from 150 to 250), which will not be easily met given the shortage of specialists on the market and their growing salary demands. The scale of the problem is illustrated by the number of personal data breaches expected to be reported: before the GDPR entered into force, while the obligation to notify breaches only applied to the telecom sector, the number of breaches was several hundred per year; once the obligation applies across all sectors, the number will grow to tens of thousands.

§1.03 THE RIGHT TO PROTECTION OF PERSONAL DATA AS A FUNDAMENTAL RIGHT

The GDPR defines the right to the protection of personal data as one of the fundamental rights and freedoms of natural persons (Article 1(2) of the GDPR). The right to privacy has been declared as a human right and fundamental freedom by being formulated in acts of international law such as the Universal Declaration of Human Rights, Council of Europe Convention No. 108 for the Protection of Individuals with regard to Automatic Processing of Personal Data, and the Treaties of the European Union, presented in detail later in this book.[7] Upon entry into force of the Charter of Fundamental Rights of the EU (CFR), the right to privacy was accorded the status of a fundamental right.

The level of protection of personal data, or in a broader view, the right to privacy of natural persons, guaranteed by the GDPR, must be interpreted in the context of the CFR. The scope of the right to privacy and to protection of personal data as defined in legal acts of European scope is defined in specific terms in case law, i.e. the body of rulings, of the European Court of Human Rights (ECtHR) and the CJEU, discussed in a separate chapter of this book. The level and uniformity of data protection within the EU also result from interpretations and guidelines, presented in the book, relating to the application of personal data protection laws. These interpretations and guidelines were formulated in particular by the Article 29 Working Party on the Protection of Individuals with regard to the Processing of Personal Data, which was an independent EU advisory body on data and privacy protection, established by Article 29 of Directive 95/46/EC (hereinafter referred to as the 'Article 29 Working Party'). Following the reform, the Article 29 Working Party was replaced by the European Data Protection

7. P. Craig, G. de Búrca, EU Law: Text, Cases, and Materials, Oxford 2008, p. 384; S. Rodotà, 'Data Protection as a Fundamental Right', in: Reinventing Data Protection?, ed. by S. Gutwirth, Y. Poulet, P. de Hert, S. Nouwt, C. de Terwangne, Dordrecht 2009, p. 77.

Board, composed of the head of one supervisory authority of each Member State and of the European Data Protection Supervisor, or their respective representatives (Article 68 of the GDPR).

§1.04 THE CONTEXT OF PERSONAL DATA PROTECTION IN THE EUROPEAN UNION

The global scale and evolution of information technologies have changed the data processing environment and brought new challenges. These result in particular from the widespread online processing of data, the ubiquity of devices with access to the Internet, common use of social networking services, online shopping and online banking, mass transfers of data within multinational corporations, and the growing capacity of data processing hardware and software.[8]

The Internet and mobile telephony, along with other technologies, are indirectly used by third parties to obtain (predominantly, though not exclusively, for commercial purposes) data on their users' location at specific times, their interpersonal relations, professional activities, interests, health, or wealth. New categories of data emerge, such as geolocation data or profiles of Internet users as consumers.[9] The impact of new technologies is growing. Some have existed before, such as the Internet of Things or facial recognition systems, but are increasingly important as they become common. All these developments mean that the threat to the right to privacy grows in proportion to the scale of data redundancy and retention.

These challenges have made it necessary to update the existing data protection regulations to take into account the new conditions of data processing, dramatically different from those prevalent at the time when Directive 95/46/EC entered into force. The 21 years which have elapsed since its adoption is a very long time in the area of digital technology. The right to privacy, consumer rights, and the digital services market all need new foundations in new, updated personal data protection law, adapted to the current situation.

In a Eurobarometer survey published on 16 June 2011 by the European Commission,[10] 75% of the subjects declared they wanted to exercise their 'right to be forgotten' by being able to delete, at any time, the data relating to them from the Internet, and 90% believed it necessary to implement uniform EU-wide regulations in that respect.

8. N.N. Gomes de Andrade and S. Monteleone, 'Digital Natives and the Metamorphosis of the European Information Society. The Emerging Behavioral Trends Regarding Privacy and Their Legal Implications', in: *European Data Protection: Coming of Age*, ed. S. Gutwirth, R. Leenes, P. de Hert, Y. Poullet, Springer Dordrecht 2013, pp. 119 et seq.
9. These arguments in favour of a reform of data protection law have also been voiced by the European Data Protection Supervisor in his opinion of 14 January 2011 on the Communication from the Commission to the European Parliament, the Council, the Economic and Social Committee and the Committee of the Regions – 'A comprehensive approach on personal data protection in the European Union', Section A, point 2, OJ EU C 181, 22.6.2011, p. 1; M.-T. Tinnefeld, 'Jak Internet zmienia prawne ramy prywatności?', in: *Internet. Prawno-informatyczne problemy sieci, portali i e-usług*, ed. G. Szpor, W. Wiewiórowski (Assistant European Data Protection Supervisor), Warszawa 2012, p. 3.
10. http://europa.eu/rapid/press-release_IP-11-742_en.htm?locale=en.

Some 74% of the subjects believed that collecting and processing of personal data online should require explicit consent from the data subject and 43% expressed concern at their data being shared without their consent by companies to which the data had been made available.

Furthermore, in a communication from the European Commission to the European Parliament, the Council, the European Economic and Social Committee and the Committee of the Regions, 'A Digital Agenda for Europe'[11] of 26 August 2010, in point 2.1.3 'Building digital confidence', it was pointed out that one of the main reasons (quoted by nearly 30% of the survey subjects) for choosing not to shop online was privacy concerns.[12] The European Commission has consequently emphasised the need to build the European Single Digital Market.

§1.05 INTERNATIONAL MODELS OF PERSONAL DATA PROTECTION

Interpretations of the right to privacy, including limits of the protection of personal data and laws regulating them in specific terms, vary globally.[13] These differences are a function of history, social and political system, culture, the prevalence of individualism or collectivism.[14] Also important are certain events which, although incidental, are spectacular enough to influence the views and emotions of the general public, such as terrorist attacks, which are invoked as a rationale (often accepted by society) for expanding the powers of national services at the expense of the privacy of individuals.

The EU and other EEA countries have introduced a stringent standard of personal data protection. Noticeably, the European data protection model has also been adopted in some non-EU countries: personal data protection regulations compatible with EU law are in place e.g. in Australia, Argentina, Israel, Canada, New Zealand, Switzerland, Uruguay (countries found to ensure an adequate level of protection, i.e. equivalent to the EU level), and also, to a certain extent, Japan, Singapore, the United Arab Emirates and South Africa. This model, however, is not shared by all the major global players. The scale of trade between the EU and, in particular, the US and China requires finding arrangements which will not stall international trade but at the same time will not make the right to data protection a price to be paid for maintaining the trade. The Council of Europe expressed this concern in its Convention No. 108 for the Protection

---

11. COM(2010)245, http://eur-lex.europa.eu/LexUriServ/LexUriServ.do?uri=COM:2010:0245:FIN:EN:PDF.
12. Eurostat Community Survey on ICT Usage by Households and by Individuals 2009.
13. M. Kirby, 'The history, achievement and future of the 1980 OECD guidelines on privacy', *International Data Privacy Law 2011*, Vol. 1, No. 1, http://idpl.oxfordjournals.org/content/1/1/6.full, points out that the divergent legal nature of personal data protection and privacy protection regimes in different cultures and legal systems makes any international consensus in this area problematic. The need to harmonise privacy protection laws was signalled by P.E. Fischer in Will Privacy Law in the 21st Century be American, European or International?, London 2010, pp. 4–5.
14. P. Trudel, 'Privacy Protection on the Internet: Risk Management and Networked Normativity', in: *Reinventing Data Protection?*, ed. S. Gutwirth, Y. Poullet, P. de Hert, C. de Terwangne, S. Nouwt, Springer 2009, p. 322.

of Individuals with regard to Automatic Processing of Personal Data, done in Strasbourg on 28 January 1981. It emphasised in the preamble to the Convention that 'it is desirable to extend the safeguards for everyone's rights and fundamental freedoms, and in particular the right to the respect for privacy, taking account of the increasing flow across frontiers of personal data undergoing automatic processing'. However, it declared 'at the same time [its] commitment to freedom of information regardless of frontiers'. As a way of preventing any conflict between those two values, it declared that 'it is necessary to reconcile the fundamental values of the respect for privacy and the free flow of information between peoples', i.e. to weigh and balance these values.

This conclusion is important in the context of two objectives of the GDPR, indicated in its Article 1(2) and (3): the protection of natural persons' fundamental rights and freedoms, in particular their right to the protection of personal data, precluding at the same time limitations or prohibitions of the free movement of personal data in the EU for data protection reasons.

Importantly, the GDPR is designed to prevent any conflict between these two objectives, i.e. to ensure the respect of the fundamental right of personal data protection (as expressly provided for in the EU Charter of Fundamental Rights as well as the GDPR itself) while allowing cooperation within the EU, particularly in the economy, but also in science or public interest.

The transfer of personal data across borders, especially between the EU Member States, which have all uniformly adopted the highest data protection standard, does not represent a threat for privacy where it complies with the GDPR requirements. The threat, therefore, is not associated with the international aspect of data transfer, but the processing of data in violation with the basic principles, irrespective of whether the data are transferred. A data transfer may also constitute a breach of data protection principles even if it is within a single country or a single capital group.

§1.06 UPDATE OF THE COUNCIL OF EUROPE CONVENTION NO. 108[15]

Convention No. 108 of the Council of Europe was the first legally binding act of international law to regulate personal data protection (the Council of Europe includes all the European Union Member States). The purpose of the Convention is to secure, in the territory of each Party, for every individual the respect for his/her rights and fundamental freedoms, and in particular his/her right to privacy, with regard to the automatic processing of personal data relating to him/her.[16] The Convention is an international standard of personal data protection for a significant part of the world, since currently half of the countries which adopted personal data protection rights are its signatories.

15. The Council of Europe Convention No. 108 for the Protection of Individuals with regard to Automatic Processing of Personal Data, done in Strasbourg on 28 January 1981, https://www.coe.int/en/web/conventions/full-list/-/conventions/treaty/108.
16. The Council of Europe Convention No. 108 has an Additional Protocol of 8 November 2001 regarding supervisory authorities and transborder data flows.

Articles 6(2) and 6(3) of the Treaty on European Union contain a declaration on the Union's accession to the European Convention for the Protection of Human Rights and Fundamental Freedoms and grant the fundamental rights, as guaranteed in the Convention and as they result from the constitutional traditions common to the Member States, the status of general principles of EU law.

Convention No. 108 has been modernised after almost four decades. On 18 May 2018, in Elsinore, Denmark, the 128th Ministerial Session of the Council of Europe's Committee of Ministers adopted the Protocol (CETS No. 223) amending the Convention and endorsed its Explanatory Report.[17] The Protocol was open for signature on 25 June 2018 in Strasbourg.

Its update was initiated for the same reasons that prompted the introduction of the GDPR: challenges resulting from new data processing technologies and environments, and the global scale of data processing and exchange. The first stage in this revision and update process was the adoption of Resolution No. 3 on data protection and privacy in the third millennium during a Council of Europe Conference of Ministers of Justice in November 2010 in Istanbul.[18]

The key aims of the update process are to enhance privacy protection in the digital environment and to strengthen the follow-up of Convention No. 108.[19]

One mechanism proposed as part of the Convention's update to account for the technological challenges and the need to ensure effective instruments is 'privacy by design', also featuring (as 'data protection by design') as a key requirement in the GDPR.[20]

A draft protocol amending Convention No. 108, reviewed at the final stage of works by the Ad hoc Committee on Data Protection (CAHDATA), composed of representatives of the Council of Europe Member States and observer states, was presented during the meeting on 15 and 16 June 2016.[21]

Given the schedule for approving amendments to the Convention by the Committee of Ministers and the procedure of opening for signature in 2018, the update of Convention No. 108 is expected to become applicable (following its ratification by the parties) in 2020, i.e. two years after the GDPR becomes applicable.[22]

As one of the changes, the scope of the Convention covers data processing without the existing limitation to automatic processing. Furthermore, the data subject's consent is admitted as a basis for data processing, which eliminates the existing

17. https://search.coe.int/cm/Pages/result_details.aspx?ObjectId=09000016807c65bf.
18. Resolution No. 3 on data protection and privacy in the third millennium adopted at the 30th Council of Europe Conference of Ministers of Justice, Istanbul, Turkey, 24–26 November 2010, MJU-30 (2010) RESOL. 3 E.
19. https://www.coe.int/en/web/portal/28-january-data-protection-day-factsheet?desktop=true.
20. S. Kierkegaard, N. Waters, G. Greenleaf, L.A. Bygrave, I. Lloyd, S. Saxby, '30 years on – The Review of the Council of Europe Data Protection Convention 108', *Computer Law & Security Review* No. 27/2011, p. 224.
21. Ad Hoc Committee on Data Protection (CAHDATA) Abridged Report Strasbourg 15–16 June 2016 CAHDATA(2016)RAPAbr.
22. M. Ciechomska, 'Zmiana Konwencji nr 108 Rady Europy o ochronie osób w związku z automatycznym przetwarzaniem danych osobowych szansą na powstanie globalnego instrumentu ochrony danych', *Monitor Prawniczy* no. 16/2017, August 2017.

discrepancy between the Convention and the GDPR (and, previously, Directive 95/46/EC). The Convention also introduces the principle of accountability, requiring the data controller *and* the data processor (another new aspect) to actively ensure compliance with data protection laws, without being prompted to do so by data subjects or supervisory authorities. Another element is the requirement to conduct data protection impact assessments concerning data subjects. The Convention also requires its signatories to establish independent supervisory authorities. Material personal data breaches have to be notified to such authorities.

These and other changes to the Convention will ensure its consistency with the GDPR, whereby the personal data protection standards in countries where the GDPR applies will also be introduced in other countries which are signatories of the Convention.

The amendment of the Convention largely reflects the data protection model adopted in the GDPR. However, it requires minimum standards to be met by the parties and allows more stringent standards to be applied by them.

CHAPTER 2

Definitions of the Right to Privacy; Protection of Personal Data as One Aspect of This Right; Legal Foundations of the Right to Privacy in European Union Law; Scope of the Right to Privacy in European Union Case Law

§2.01 DEFINITIONS OF THE RIGHT TO PRIVACY; PROTECTION OF PERSONAL DATA AS AN ASPECT OF THIS RIGHT

The definition and scope of the right to privacy have been subject to various interpretations. These point to different aspects of privacy in a number of areas of private and family life, economic activity, personal finance, freedom of speech and press, and personal data.[1]

1. K. Motyka, '*Prawo do prywatności*', *Zeszyty Naukowe Akademii Podlaskiej w Siedlcach* 2010, No. 85, pp. 25-35; M. Jagielski, *Prawo do ochrony danych osobowych. Standardy europejskie*, Warszawa 2010, pp. 23-24; C.J. Bennett, C.D. Raab, *The Governance of Privacy. Policy Instruments in Global Perspective*, London 2006, pp. 13 et seq.; L.A. Bygrave, 'Privacy Protection in a Global Context - A Comparative Overview', *Scandinavian Studies in Law* 2004, Vol. 47, pp. 320 et seq.; C. Doyle, M. Bagaric, 'The Right to Privacy: Appealing but Flawed', *International Journal of Human Rights* 2005, Vol. 9, No. 1, pp. 4 et seq.; J.H.F. Shattuck, *Right of Privacy*, New York 1997, pp. 145 et seq.; A. Sakowicz, Prywatność jako samoistne dobro prawne (per se), *PiP* 2006, Vol. 1, pp. 20 et seq.; J. Braciak, *Prawo do prywatności*, Warszawa 2004, pp. 28 et seq.; A. Etzioni, *The Limits of Privacy*, New York 1999, pp. 183 et seq.; S. Crawford, 'Keeping It to Themselves: Bank Privacy Towards 2000', *Ottawa Law Review* 1998, No. 29, pp. 426-475; R. Jay, A. Hamilton, *Data Protection Law and Practice*, London 2003, p. 35; J. Klosek, *Data Privacy in the Information Age*, Westport 2000; D.H. Flaherty, 'Visions of Privacy: Past, Present and Future', in: *Visions of Privacy: Policy Choices for the Digital Age*, ed. by C.J. Bennet, R. Grant, Toronto 1999, pp. 19 et seq.

The date when the right to privacy was first formulated (in American academic literature) is universally considered to be the year 1890, when it was defined as 'the right to be let alone' in the article 'The Right to Privacy' published in the *Harvard Law Review*.[2] The authors invoked the common law principle of protecting the rights of an individual. They also signalled the necessity of periodical verifications and updates of the scope of privacy protection in view of social changes and the extent of public access to information published by the media.[3]

In 1928, L.D. Brandeis, acting as a US Supreme Court judge, again equated the right to privacy with the 'right to be let alone' in his dissent from the judgment in the case *Olmstead v U.S.*[4] He stated it to be the right most valued by civilised men, and every unjustifiable intrusion by the government upon the privacy of the individual to be a violation of the Fourth Amendment to the United States Constitution.

The same idea has been expressed by Marek Safjan, the former president of the Polish Constitutional Tribunal, who stated that 'privacy should be subject to protection precisely and only because everyone is granted the right to exclusively control this area of life that does not concern others, and in this area, freedom from the curiosity of others is a specific *sine qua non* condition for the free development of an individual'.[5] This approach to privacy, which I consider to convey its nature, emphasises the exclusive right of an individual to make decisions concerning his or her private life and to be free from any interference by public authorities and other entities in this respect.[6] However, some limitations of the right to privacy are justified by the privacy of others and necessary for the protection of public interests.

The interpretation of the right to privacy was also substantially influenced by the arguments made by W.L. Prosser in his article 'Privacy', published in 1960 in the *California Law Review*,[7] and then in 1977 in the Second Restatement of Torts in §§ 652A–652I.[8] Prosser distinguished four aspects of the right to privacy, as defined by the following violations of this right:

---

2. S.D. Warren, L.D. Brandeis, 'The Right to Privacy', *Harvard Law Review* 1890, No. 4, pp. 193–220, http://groups.csail.mit.edu/mac/classes/6.805/articles/privacy/Privacy_brand_warr2.html.
3. K. Motyka, *'Prawo do prywatności'*, *Zeszyty Naukowe Akademii Podlaskiej w Siedlcach* 2010, No. 85, p. 11; A. Mednis, *Prawo do prywatności a interes publiczny*, Kraków 2006, p. 59.
4. *Olmstead v. U.S.*, 277 U.S. 438, 478 (1928); quoted in: R.B. Standler, Privacy Law in the USA, 1997, http://www.rbs2.com/privacy.htm, 43 S. Ct. 394; 67 L. Ed. 785; 1923 U.S. LEXIS 2588; 24 A.L.R. 1238.
5. M. Safjan, 'Prawo do ochrony życia prywatnego', in: *Podstawowe prawa jednostki i ich ochrona*, ed. L. Wiśniewski, Warszawa 1997, p. 128, and idem, 'Prawo do ochrony życia prywatnego', in: Szkoła praw człowieka, Helsinki Foundation for Human Rights, Warszawa 2006, pp. 211 et seq.
6. Similarly: J. Braciak, 'Prawo do prywatności', in: *Prawa i wolności obywatelskie w Konstytucji RP*, ed. B. Banaszak and A. Preisner, Warszawa 2002, p. 278. Cf. also: A. Kopff, 'Koncepcja prawa do intymności i do prywatności życia osobistego (zagadnienia konstrukcyjne)', *Studia Cywilistyczne* 1972, vol. 20. The author defined privacy as 'the personal right in the form of private life, covering everything that, due to an individual's justified separation from the community, serves the purpose of development of this individual's physical or mental personality and preservation of his or her social position'.
7. *California Law Review* 1960, Vol. 48, pp. 383–423.
8. W.L. Prosser, 'Restatement (Second) of Torts §§ 652A–652I (1977)', quoted in: R.B. Standler, *Privacy Law in the USA*, 1996, last revision: 24 May 1998, http://www.rbs2.com/privacy.htm.

- unreasonable intrusion upon the seclusion of another: for example, physical invasion of a person's home and violation of confidentiality of correspondence;
- appropriation of a person's name or likeness, including using a person's trademark as an act of unfair competition;
- publication of private facts, for example, photographs of a person in his or her home, income tax data, personal letters, medical treatment;
- defamation.

The third of the above aspects coincides with the scope of personal data protection as one of the fundamental aspects of the right to privacy. Josef Kohler also defined privacy from the perspective of an individual's freedom to use the information concerning him or her.

The above definitions and legal regulations show that the methodology of creating legal definitions of the right to privacy in legal systems and academic literature is based on specifying:

- the areas falling within the scope of the concept, such as family life, domestic peace, confidentiality of correspondence, personal data protection, or bank secrecy,[9] including sensitive data, data concerning intimacy, and data of particular importance for an individual's privacy;
- the types of violations of the right to privacy in the particular areas.

The general legal framework, thus defined, of the right to privacy is subject to further specification in case law and jurisprudence.[10]

§2.02 LEGAL FOUNDATIONS OF THE RIGHT TO PRIVACY IN THE EUROPEAN UNION

The right to privacy is formulated in Article 12 of the Universal Declaration of Human Rights, adopted on 10 December 1948 in Paris by the United Nations General Assembly (http://www.un-documents.net/a3r217.htm), and in Article 17 of the International Covenant on Civil and Political Rights, opened for signature on 19 December 1966 in

9. The Polish Constitutional Tribunal, in its ruling of 24 June 1997, K 21/96 (OTK 1997, No. 2, item 23, p. 15 of the grounds), pointed to the fact that 'the right to privacy also covers the protection of secrecy of data concerning the citizen's financial situation, therefore also covering his or her bank accounts (and similar accounts) and the transactions made by him or her'. Bank secrecy, as one of the aspects of the right to privacy, is discussed by: M. Krzysztofek, Tajemnica bankowa i ochrona danych osobowych w praktyce bankowej, Warszawa 2010, p. 11; M. Krzysztofek, Tajemnice zawodowe i ochrona danych osobowych w instytucjach finansowych, Warszawa 2015, p., 29; A. Mednis, 'Ochrona prawna danych osobowych a zagrożenie prywatności – rozwiązania polskie', in: Ochrona danych osobowych, ed. M. Wyrzykowski, Warszawa 1999, p. 168, and idem, Prawo do prywatności a interes publiczny, Kraków 2006, p. 163, and A. Jurkowska-Zeidler, 'Tajemnica bankowa jako środek ochrony prawa do prywatności', in: Prawa człowieka: wczoraj – dziś – jutro, ed. J. Zajadło, Gdańskie Studia Prawnicze 2005, vol. 13, p. 220.
10. The same view is expressed by J. Hołda, Z. Hołda, D. Ostrowska, J.A. Rybczyńska, *Prawa człowieka. Zarys wykładu*, Warszawa 2008, p. 114.

New York under Resolution 2200A (XXI) of the UN General Assembly. These two articles prohibit unlawful interference with anyone's privacy and grant everyone the right to the protection of the law against such interference.[11]

In addition to these global fundamental acts, the right to privacy is also formulated in European acts,[12] adopted by the Council of Europe and by the European Union (the Council of Europe consists of 47 member states, 28 of which constitute the European Union until the date of Brexit, i.e. the United Kingdom's withdrawal from the EU). The personal data protection principles enshrined in these acts are largely convergent.

The Council of Europe laid down its personal data protection principles in the following provisions:

- Article 8 of the Convention for the Protection of Human Rights and Fundamental Freedoms adopted by the member states of the Council of Europe, drafted on 4 November 1950 in Rome. This Article grants everyone the right to respect for their private and family life, home and correspondence, and prohibits any interference by a public authority with the exercising of this right, except such as is in accordance with the law and is necessary in a democratic society in the interests of national security, public safety or the economic well-being of the country, for the prevention of disorder or crime, the protection of health or morals, or the protection of the rights and freedoms of others.
- Article 1 of Convention No. 108 of the Council of Europe of 28 January 1981 for the Protection of Individuals with regard to Automatic Processing of Personal Data, drafted in Strasbourg. This specifies the purpose of the Convention to be to secure in the territory of each Party for every individual the respect for his/her rights and fundamental freedoms, and in particular his/her right to privacy, with regard to automatic processing of personal data relating to him/her.[13] Convention No. 108 of the Council of Europe was the first legally binding act of international law to regulate personal data protection. Convention No. 108 has been modernised after almost four decades. On 18 May 2018, in Elsinore, Denmark, the 128th Ministerial Session of the Council of Europe's Committee of Ministers adopted the Protocol (CETS No. 223) amending the Convention and endorsed its Explanatory Report.[14] The Protocol was open for signature on 25 June 2018 in Strasbourg.

---

11. Personal data protection is also the subject of the OECD Council Recommendation concerning Guidelines governing the Protection of Privacy and Transborder Flows of Personal Data (first published by the Organisation for Economic Co-operation and Development (OECD) in 1980; revised version adopted on 11 July 2013, http://oecd.org/sti/ieconomy/oecd_privacy_framework.pdf), and Resolution 45/94 of the United Nations General Assembly of 14 December 1990 – Guidelines for the Regulation of Computerized Personal Data Files (http://www.refworld.org/pdfid/3ddcafaac.pdf).
12. L.A. Bygrave, 'International Agreements to Protect Personal Data', in: *Global Privacy Protection. The First Generation*, ed. J.B. Rule, G. Greenleaf, Cheltenham–Northampton 2007, pp. 15 et seq.
13. Convention No. 108 of the Council of Europe has an Additional Protocol of 8 November 2001 regarding supervisory authorities and transborder data flows.
14. https://search.coe.int/cm/Pages/result_details.aspx?ObjectId=09000016807c65bf.

The principles of personal data protection are also laid down in the following legal acts of the European Union:

- the Treaty on the European Union;[15]
- the Treaty on the Functioning of the European Union;[16]
- the Charter of Fundamental Rights of the European Union;[17]
- the General Data Protection Regulation (GDPR, i.e. Regulation (EU) 2016/679) and, before its adoption, Directive 95/46/EC – the two key acts of the European Union's secondary law acts regulating personal data protection;[18]
- Directive 2002/58/EC of the European Parliament and of the Council of 12 July 2002 concerning the processing of personal data and the protection of privacy in the electronic communications sector (Directive on privacy and electronic communications),[19] to be replaced by Regulation of the European Parliament and of the Council concerning the respect for private life and the protection of personal data in electronic communications and repealing Directive 2002/58/EC (Regulation on Privacy and Electronic Communications, or the ePrivacy Regulation);
- Regulation (EC) No. 45/2001 of the European Parliament and of the Council of 18 December 2000 on the protection of individuals with regard to the processing of personal data by the Community institutions and bodies and on the free movement of such data[20] (which, according to recital 17 of the preamble to the GDPR, is to be adapted to the principles and rules of the GDPR);
- Directive (EU) 2016/680 of the European Parliament and of the Council of 27 April 2016 on the protection of natural persons with regard to the processing of personal data by competent authorities for the purposes of the prevention, investigation, detection or prosecution of criminal offences or the execution of

15. The consolidated version in OJ EU C 202 of 7.6.2016, p. 13. Known as the Maastricht Treaty, it was signed on 7 February 1992 and entered into force on 1 November 1993.
16. The origin of the Treaty on the Functioning of the European Union is as follows: the Treaty establishing the European Economic Community (the Treaty of Rome) entered into force in 1958. Under the Treaty of Maastricht in 1992, it was amended into the 'Treaty establishing the European Community'. Its current wording, with the title 'The Treaty on the Functioning of the European Union', was introduced by the Treaty of Lisbon. The Treaty of Lisbon, amending the Treaty on European Union and Treaty establishing the European Community, was signed on 13 December 2007, published in OJ EU C 306 of 17.12.2007, and entered into force on 1 December 2009. The consolidated version of the Treaty of Rome of 1957 and the Treaty of Maastricht of 1992 were published in OJ EU C 115 of 9.05.2008; the consolidated version of the Treaty on the Functioning of the European Union was published in OJ EU C 202 of 7.6.2016, p. 47. For an extensive discussion of the Treaty of Lisbon, see: P. Craig, *The Lisbon Treaty. Law, Politics, and Treaty Reform*, Oxford 2011.
17. The consolidated version in OJ EU C 202 of 7.6.2016, p. 389. The Charter of Fundamental Rights of the European Union was signed on 7 December 2000, during the Nice summit of the European Council, by representatives of the European Parliament, the Council, and the European Commission. After corrections, it was signed again by the presidents of these institutions at the Lisbon summit, on 12 December 2007. The basis for the legal effect of the Charter is the Treaty of Lisbon.
18. The GDPR and, before its adoption, Directive 95/46/EC also cover non-EU countries which are members of the European Economic Area, i.e. Iceland, Liechtenstein and Norway.
19. OJ EC L 201, 31.07.2002, p. 37.
20. OJ EU L 8 of 12.01.2001, p. 1.

criminal penalties, and on the free movement of such data, and repealing Council Framework Decision 2008/977/JHA.[21]

The Treaty on European Union also contains, in Article 6(1), a declaration of recognition by the EU of the rights, freedoms and principles set out in the Charter of Fundamental Rights of the EU of 7 December 2000, as adapted in Strasbourg on 12 December 2007, which has the same legal value as the Treaties. Articles 6(2) and 6(3) of the Treaty on European Union contain a declaration on the Union's accession to the European Convention for the Protection of Human Rights and Fundamental Freedoms and grant the fundamental rights, as guaranteed in the Convention and as they result from the constitutional traditions common to the Member States, the status of general principles of EU law. In Article 8(1) of the Convention, it recognises the right to have one's private life respected, although in Article 8(2) it provides for permissibility of interference by a public authority with the exercise of this right, on certain conditions, including prevention of crime.

Article 16(1) of the TFEU grants everyone the right to the protection of personal data concerning them. Importantly, the standard introduced by this provision applies directly, which means that individuals have the right to the protection of their personal data even in the absence of a secondary law act to that effect.[22] Locating this provision among the generally applicable provisions of the TFEU indicates its status as a self-standing basis for the right to data protection, with a horizontal effect, i.e. affecting public bodies of the EU and its Member States as well as private sector entities.

The Charter of Fundamental Rights of the EU formulates in its Article 8(1) the right of every person to the protection of personal data concerning him or her (similarly to Article 16(1) of the TFEU). Article 8(2) of the Charter contains a principle that such data must be processed fairly for specified purposes and on the basis of the consent of the person concerned, or some other legitimate basis laid down by law. It further provides that everyone has the right of access to data which have been collected concerning him or her, and the right to have them rectified. The preceding Article 7 provides for everyone's right to the respect of their private life, which indicates that the right to the protection of personal data is a specific aspect of the right to privacy. Upon entry into force of the Treaty of Lisbon (including the Charter of Fundamental Rights of the EU) in December 2009, the right to the protection of personal data became a fundamental right.

---

21. OJ EU L 119 of 4 May 2016. The Directive regulates the processing of personal data for criminal proceedings, given specific requirements on cooperation between Member States' law enforcement and judicial authorities in criminal cases and the need to introduce rules on the protection and free flow of personal data in that area. The Directive has replaced Council Framework Decision 2008/977/JHA of 27 November 2008 on the protection of personal data processed in the framework of police and judicial cooperation in criminal matters (OJ EU L 350 of 30 December 2008, p. 60). On the issue of personal data processing in criminal proceedings, see: Council of Europe, Limits to the Use of Personal Data, IRIS plus collection, 2011, No. 6. Directive 2016/680 on the protection of personal data in criminal proceedings is not discussed in this book.
22. P. Litwiński, Barta P., Kawecki M., *Rozporządzenie UE w sprawie ochrony osób fizycznych w związku z przetwarzaniem danych osobowych i swobodnym przepływem takich danych. Komentarz*, Warszawa 2017, p. 11.

As the Treaty of Lisbon abolished the previous three-pillar structure of the European Union, introduced by the Treaty of Maastricht signed on 7 February 1992 (first pillar – economic union; second pillar – political union; third pillar – police and judicial union), its entry into force provided a legal basis for the unification of the personal data protection regimes previously covering areas of the three pillars separately. Article 16(2) of the TFEU empowers the European Parliament and the Council to lay down, according to the ordinary legislative procedure, the rules relating to the protection of individuals with regard to the processing of personal data by EU institutions, bodies, offices and agencies, and by the Member States when carrying out activities which fall within the scope of Union law, and the rules relating to the free movement of such data between Member States.

Article 39 of the Treaty on European Union empowers the Council to lay down rules relating to the protection of individuals with regard to the processing of personal data by the Member States when carrying out activities concerning the common foreign and security policy and rules relating to the free movement of such data. The application of this special procedure, bypassing the European Parliament, has thus been limited in scope in comparison with Article 16(2) of the TFEU.

All of the above Treaties provide that compliance with the rules of personal data protection is subject to control by independent authorities (cf. Article 39 of the TEU, Article 16(2) of the TFEU, and Article 8(3) of the CFR).

The Treaty on European Union, the Treaty on the Functioning of the European Union, and the Charter of Fundamental Rights of the EU are the sources of the right to personal data protection in the EU's primary legislation.

The GDPR is supplemented by Regulation (EC) No. 45/2001 of the European Parliament and of the Council of 18 December 2000 on the protection of individuals with regard to the processing of personal data by the Community institutions and bodies and on the free movement of such data. This regulates the protection of personal data and their free movement between the Member States and the EU institutions and bodies, as well as between the EU institutions and bodies, for purposes relating to the exercise of their powers subject to EU law. It was also in this Regulation that the institution of the European Data Protection Supervisor was established.

Given the specific threats to the right to privacy resulting from information society services and electronic communications, as well as unauthorised access to online data, the GDPR is supplemented by Directive 2000/31/EC of the European Parliament and of the Council of 8 June 2000 on certain legal aspects of information society services, in particular electronic commerce, in the Internal Market (Directive on electronic commerce) (OJ EU L 178 of 17.07.2000, p. 1) and Directive 2002/58/EC of the European Parliament and of the Council of 12 July 2002 concerning the processing of personal data and the protection of privacy in the electronic communications sector (Directive on privacy and electronic communications) (OJ EU L 201 of 31.07.2002, p. 37). Directive 2002/58/EC is to be replaced by the ePrivacy Regulation (on 10 January 2017 the European Commission submitted a proposal for a Regulation of the European Parliament and of the Council concerning the respect for private life and the protection of personal data in electronic communications and repealing Directive 2002/58/EC – known as the Regulation on Privacy and Electronic Communications, or the ePrivacy

Regulation). The scope of application of all these legal acts covers data processing irrespective of the sector or industry in which the data controller operates, if the controller uses the tools, distribution channels or means of communication covered by these provisions.

To ensure consistency of the provisions on privacy and electronic communication with the GDPR, Directive 2002/58/EC had to be revised (cf. recital 173 of the preamble to the GDPR and Article 95 of the GDPR). The Commission intended the ePrivacy Regulation to become applicable on the same day as the GDPR, i.e. 25 May 2018. However, during the legislation proceedings, this application date of the ePrivacy Regulation was found to be unrealistic. The Regulation now appears unlikely to come into effect until 2020 at the earliest. Personal data from electronic communications are simultaneously protected under the GDPR and under the ePrivacy Regulation as a more specific law in relation to the GDPR. The delay in adoption of the ePrivacy Regulation has resulted in interpretation problems concerning the relation between the GDPR and Member States' laws and regulations implementing Directive 2002/58/EC, which will only be repealed by the ePrivacy Regulation.

The GDPR and the ePrivacy Regulation are also essential for the introduction of the Digital Single Market. This vision of EU-wide digital economy, involving digitalisation of entire sectors of industry and services and the full use of technologies such as the Internet of Things or cloud computing, requires safeguards of digital security in line with the privacy and personal data protection standards.

The manner in which the right to privacy is formulated in the above acts of international law accords it the status of one of the human rights and fundamental freedoms[23] and, following the entry into force of the Charter of Fundamental Rights of the EU, the status of a fundamental right.

§2.03 THE SCOPE OF THE RIGHT TO PRIVACY IN EUROPEAN CASE LAW

Privacy is not an absolute right; it is not subject to absolute protection. In Article 8(2), the Convention for the Protection of Human Rights and Fundamental Freedoms allows for interference by a public authority with the exercising of the right to privacy. It is justified in cases provided for by law, where such interference is necessary in a democratic society in view of national security, public safety or the economic well-being of the country, the prevention of disorder or crime, the protection of health or morals, or the protection of the rights and freedoms of others.[24] Similar limitations are permitted in Article 52(1) of the Charter of Fundamental Rights of the European Union, albeit with the reservation that they must be provided for by law and respect the

23. P. Craig, G. de Búrca, *EU Law: Text, Cases, and Materials*, Oxford 2008, p. 384; S. Rodotà, 'Data Protection as a Fundamental Right', in: *Reinventing Data Protection?*, ed. by S. Gutwirth, Y. Poulet, P. de Hert, S. Nouwt, C. de Terwangne, Dordrecht 2009, p. 77.

24. Opinion of Article 29 Working Party No. 1/2014 of 27 February 2014 on the application of necessity and proportionality concepts and data protection within the law enforcement sector, WP 211, http://ec.europa.eu/justice/article-29/documentation/opinion-recommendation/files/2014/wp211_en.pdf.

essence of those rights and freedoms, must be subject to the principle of proportionality, and may be made only if they are necessary and genuinely meet objectives of general interest recognised by the Union or the need to protect the rights and freedoms of others.

The exclusions of the right to privacy determine its actual scope.

The scope of the right to privacy as defined in legal acts of a European reach, listed in section 1 of this Chapter, including the right to personal data protection, is defined in specific terms in case law, i.e. the body of rulings of the European Court of Human Rights and the Court of Justice of the European Union. The European Court of Human Rights (ECtHR) makes sure that the member states of the Council of Europe comply with their obligations under the European Convention of Human Rights. The Court of Justice of the European Union (CJEU) safeguards compliance with EU law.

The rulings of both these courts confirm that the right to privacy is not absolute, and interpret the conditions for its limitation, specified in Article 8(2) of the ECHR and in Article 52(1) of the CFR.

The European Court of Human Rights in Strasbourg has specified the essence and the scope of the right to privacy by adopting Article 8 of the ECHR as the basis thereof and by verifying compliance of the regulations and the bodies of rulings of the Council of Europe's member states with the Convention. The Court evaluates the permissibility of interference of public authorities in the right to privacy in the cases that are in accordance with the law and necessary in a democratic society, as specified in Article 8(2) of the ECHR.

In the case of *Van Oosterwijck v Belgium*,[25] the ECtHR specified the right to privacy to be the right to live in accordance with the will of the individual and the possibility to 'stay in the shadows'. This definition corresponds with perceiving privacy as 'the right to be let alone', as proposed in 1890 by S.D. Warren and L.D. Brandeis.

Furthermore, the ECtHR concluded in the case of *Leander v Sweden* that the mere collection and storage of personal data by public authorities may constitute a violation of Article 8 of the ECHR, even if such data are not sensitive data (except in cases of interference in the right to privacy by public authorities in accordance with the law and necessary in a democratic society).[26] The Court also confirmed that, in the cases specified in Article 8(2) of the ECHR, interference in privacy by processing data obtained through monitoring of correspondence and telephone calls of suspected criminals is permissible, provided that the legal regulations invoked as the basis for such actions are sufficiently clear.[27]

---

25. The judgment in the case of Van Oosterwijck v Belgium, 6 November 1980, Application No. 7654/76, http://hudoc.echr.coe.int/sites/eng/pages/search.aspx?i=001-57549.
26. Judgment in the case of *Leander v Sweden*, 26 March 1987, Application No. 9248/81, 9 EHRR 433; judgment in the case of *Hilton v the United Kingdom*, 6 July 1988, Application No. 12051/86, DR 57/108; judgment in the case of *H. Amann v Switzerland*, 16 February 2000, Application No. 27798/95, 87 ECHR.
27. The European Court of Human Rights related to this aspect in the cases of: *Malone v the United Kingdom* (Application No. 8691/79, 2 August 1984, http://hudoc.echr.coe.int/sites/eng/pages/search.aspx?i=001-57533), *Huvig v France* (Application No. 11105/84, 24 April 1990, http://hudoc.echr.coe.int/sites/eng/pages/search.aspx?i=001-57627), *Kruslin v France* (Application No. 11801/85, 24 April 1990, http://hudoc.echr.coe.int/sites/eng/pages/search.aspx?i=001-5

The ECtHR arrived at the same conclusions in its judgment in the case of *Szabó and Vissy v Hungary*,[28] challenging the Hungarian anti-terrorist services' prerogatives, accorded to them by a law enacted in 2011, to secret intelligence gathering, including secret house search, the opening of letters and parcels, as well as checking and recording the contents of electronic communications. The Court noted that the law in question infringed upon individuals' right to privacy as laid down in Article 8 of the ECHR, as it failed to specify the categories of persons who could be subject to secret surveillance, to make such surveillance contingent on the presence of a terrorist threat, to specify the maximum surveillance period with sufficient precision, or to ensure effective supervision of the surveillance.

The ECtHR reiterated these conclusions in its judgment in the case of *Roman Zakharov v Russia*,[29] in which it challenged the right of telecom operators, the Ministry of Communications and the Federal Security Service to secret interception of mobile telephone communications. The Court held that surveillance based on a law which did not stipulate the conditions for initiating it, its duration, the obligation to discontinue it after the expiry of the circumstances which justified it, and the maximum storage period of the recordings and data, was a violation of Article 8 of the ECHR.

The scope of the right to privacy was also defined by the ECtHR in the case of *Pretty v the United Kingdom*[30] as an individual's physical and psychological integrity and confidentiality of both sensitive information, in particular information concerning health, and non-sensitive information, such as age.

Another example of the limits of the right to privacy being indicated in the ECtHR's rulings is the finding, in the case *M.S. v Croatia*,[31] that Article 8 of the ECHR is potentially violated not only by divesting a person of his or her legal capacity but even by initiating proceedings for divesting such a person of their legal capacity; therefore, for such proceedings to be initiated, all the conditions specified in Article 8(2) of the ECHR must be met.

The CJEU, as part of ensuring that the Member States follow the obligations specified in the Treaties and providing interpretations of EU law at the request of national courts, has defined the right to privacy from the point of view of personal data protection in a manner that coincides with the definition presented in the body of rulings of the ECtHR.

7626), in which the Court found the legal regulations concerning permissible interference in privacy to be insufficiently precise, and in the cases of *Klass and others v Germany* (Application No. 5029/71, 6 September 1978, http://hudoc.echr.coe.int/sites/eng/pages/search.aspx?i=001-57510), Leander v Sweden (Application No. 9248/81, 26 March 1987, http://hudoc.echr.coe.int/sites/eng/pages/search.aspx?i=001-57519), *Lüdi v Switzerland* (Application No. 12433/86, 15 June 1992, http://hudoc.echr.coe.int/sites/eng/pages/search.aspx?i=001-57784), in which the Court found the legal regulations to be sufficiently precise.

28. Judgment of 12 January 2016 in the case of *Szabó and Vissy v Hungary*, application no. 37138/14, http://hudoc.echr.coe.int/eng?i=001-160020.
29. Judgment of 4 December 2015 in the case of *Roman Zakharov v Russia*, application no. 47143/06, http://hudoc.echr.coe.int/eng?i=001-159324.
30. *Pretty v the United Kingdom*, Application No. 2346/02, 29 April 2002, http://hudoc.echr.coe.int/sites/eng/pages/search.aspx?i=001-60448.
31. Judgment in the case of *M.S. v Croatia*, 25 November 2013, Application No. 36337/10, http://hudoc.echr.coe.int/fre?i=001-118736#{'itemid':['001-118736']}.

In its judgment of 20 May 2003,[32] the CJEU emphasised the requirement to demonstrate that data disclosure is necessary for the aim pursued by the legislator – in the case in question, the appropriate management of public funds. Therefore, the CJEU allows the right to personal data protection to be limited by the Member States, but only if such limitations are provided for in statutory regulations or regulations issued on the basis of a statute, and only to the extent necessary to achieve the purposes specified in Article 13(1) of Directive 95/46/EC (Article 23 of the GDPR), such as public security.

In the judgment of 29 January 2008,[33] the CJEU defined the boundaries of personal data protection by means of specifying the relationship between EU laws regarding e-commerce and copyrights[34] and the laws concerning personal data protection. The Court admitted that personal data may be disclosed by the courts of the Member States at the justified request of claimants in the context of proceedings concerning infringement of intellectual property rights. However, in light of the proportionality principle, this does not mean that the Member States are required to lay down an obligation to communicate personal data in the context of civil proceedings in connection with infringements of intellectual property rights.

The Court of Justice of the EU also concluded[35] that it would be a violation of the EU laws on personal data protection to require an Internet service provider to implement a system identifying the persons that use the provider's network to transfer files containing musical or cinematographic work in respect of which the applicant claims to hold intellectual property rights.

In the judgment of 16 December 2008,[36] the CJEU declared that personal data protection may be restricted if necessary for ensuring the freedom of expression as part of journalistic or artistic activities, but only to the necessary extent.

The ECtHR has also signalled the necessity of balancing the right to privacy with that of the freedom of the press.[37]

---

32. The joined cases of *Rechnungshof* (C-465/00) *v Österreichischer Rundfunk et al.* and *Christa Neukomm* (C-138/01), *Joseph Lauermann* (C-139/01) *v Österreichischer Rundfunk*, http://eur-lex.europa.eu/legal-content/EN/TXT/HTML/?uri=CELEX:62000CJ0465.
33. Judgment in Case C-275/06 *Productores de Música de España (Promusicae) v Telefónica de España SAU*, http://eur-lex.europa.eu/legal-content/EN/TXT/?uri=CELEX:62006CJ0275.
34. The subject matter of the case was the interpretation of Directive 2000/31/EC of the European Parliament and of the Council of 8 June 2000 on certain legal aspects of information society services, in particular electronic commerce, in the Internal Market (Directive on electronic commerce) (OJ EU L 178, 17.07.2000, p. 1), Directive 2001/29/EC of the European Parliament and of the Council of 22 May 2001 on the harmonisation of certain aspects of copyright and related rights in the information society (OJ EU L 167, 22.06.2001, p. 10), and Directive 2004/48/EC of the European Parliament and of the Council of 29 April 2004 on the enforcement of intellectual property rights (OJ EU L 157, 30.04.2004, p. 45, as amended), as well as of Article 17(2) and Article 47 of the Charter of Fundamental Rights of the EU.
35. Judgment of 24 November 2011 in case C-70/10 *Scarlet Extended SA v Société belge des auteurs, compositeurs et éditeurs SCRL (SABAM)*.
36. Judgment in case C-73/07 *Tietosuojavaltuutettu v Satakunnan Markkinapörssi Oy, Satamedia Oy*, http://eur-lex.europa.eu/legal-content/EN/TXT/?uri=CELEX:62007CJ0073.
37. Cases: *Axel Springer AG v Germany* of 7 February 2012, Application No. 39954/08, http://hudoc.echr.coe.int/eng?i=001-109034; *Von Hannover v Germany* of 7 February 2012, Applications No. 40660/08 and 60641/08, http://hudoc.echr.coe.int/eng?i=001-109029; *Biriuk v Lithuania* of 25 November 2008, Application No. 23373/03, http://hudoc.echr.coe.int/eng?i=001-89827.

The right to privacy is also being restricted due to its conflict with the right of access to public information. The principle of transparency in the operation of public authorities, introduced in Articles 1 and 10 of the TEU and Article 15(1) of the TFEU, entails access of authorised persons to official documents. Therefore, a conflict with the right to privacy and to protection of personal data must occur whenever such official documents and public information contain personal data. In such cases, these rights must be balanced and an assessment must be made on a case-by-case basis on which of those rights should be more protected.

Access to public information is guaranteed in EU law by virtue of Regulation (EC) No 1049/2001 of the European Parliament and of the Council of 30 May 2001 regarding public access to European Parliament, Council and Commission documents (OJ EU L 145, 31.05.2001, p. 3) and in Article 42 of the CFR and Article 15(3) of the TFEU, which also cover the right of access to the documents of the EU institutions, bodies, offices and agencies.

The CJEU has resolved the conflict between the right to protection of personal data and the right of access to public information.[38]

The background to the case was the following: a German brewery requested a copy of minutes of a meeting of representatives of the European Commission and the UK authorities. The Commission provided the documents, but with the names of five participants removed. This was justified by two of them having objected to the disclosure of their names, and the Commission's being unable to seek the consent of the remaining three. However, the Court of the First Instance ruled that the disclosure of the names of the participants of a formal meeting, who represented a public authority, did not violate their right to protection of privacy.

On the other hand, in the appeal proceedings, the CJEU admitted that the Commission's refusal to disclose the names was justified. The CJEU found that the transparency requirement had been met by the disclosure of the document, and the applicant had not demonstrated the necessity of obtaining the names of the participants. Thus, the CJEU ruled that the right to access public information is not always equivalent to the right to obtain personal data contained therein.

The CJEU also argued that the right to personal data protection is not absolute, and presented the conditions for limiting this right, as specified in Article 8(2) of the ECHR and Article 52(1) of the CFR, in its judgment of 9 November 2010.[39] In the judgment, the Court confirmed that, in a democratic society, the right of the public to obtain information about the use of public funds is a necessary exception from personal data protection. Still, the Court emphasised that the limitations must be provided for by

38. Judgment of the CJEU in case T-194/04 of 8 November 2007, *The Bavarian Lager Co. Ltd. v Commission of the European Communities*, http://eur-lex.europa.eu/legal-content/EN/TXT/HTML/?uri=CELEX:62004TJ0194, and judgment of the CJEU in case C-28/08 P of 29 June 2010, *European Commission v The Bavarian Lager Co. Ltd.*, http://eur-lex.europa.eu/legal-content/EN/TXT/?uri=CELEX:62008CJ0028.
39. Judgment of 9 November 2010 in joined cases C-92/09 and C-93/09, *Volker und Markus Schecke GbR* (C-92/09) and *Hartmut Eifert* (C-93/09) *v Land Hessen*, http://eur-lex.europa.eu/legal-content/EN/TXT/?uri=CELEX:62009CJ0092.

law, respect the essence of the rights in terms of data protection, and be proportionate to the aim pursued by the legislator.[40]

The right to privacy is also formulated in constitutions of the EU Member States, though not all of them, and not always directly. Of the five most populous Member States of the post-Brexit European Union (EU-27), the right is laid down in the Constitution of Poland (Article 47, 'Everyone has the right to the legal protection of his or her private life'), and many aspects of the right, e.g. the confidentiality of correspondence (postal secrecy), are also included in the Constitutions of Germany (Article 10), Italy (Article 15), Spain (Article 18) and Poland (Article 49).

The right to privacy features particularly prominently in the Constitution of Poland. Article 31(1) allows a limitation of this right, but only by statute and only when necessary in a democratic state for the protection of its security or public order, or to protect the natural environment, health or public morals, or the freedoms and rights of other persons. This protection is reinforced with the prohibition of violating the essence of freedoms and rights with such limitations. The limits of interference in privacy are also set in Article 51(1) of the Constitution, which requires that the obligation of a person to disclose data that concerns him or her be specified in a statute, and in Article 51(2), which prohibits public authorities from acquiring, collecting, and making accessible information on citizens to an extent greater than necessary in a democratic state ruled by law. Notably, according to Article 233(1) of the Polish Constitution, the protection of the right to privacy cannot be limited even in times of martial law and states of emergency.

§2.04 THE IMPORTANCE OF PERSONAL DATA PROTECTION FOR THE RIGHT TO PRIVACY

It is important to grasp the essence of personal data protection and its importance for the right to privacy. When a person uses, or merely owns, a mobile phone or a tablet, various entities create registers of his or her calls and collect his/her geolocation data. Customers are profiled while shopping. This means that, irrespective of the original and main purpose of the data controller, the user's place of stay and his or her travels are monitored, the persons he or she contacts using the phone are identified, and information on this person's online activity, his or her preferred books, films, discussion forums, queries on medical websites, leisure activities (flight reservations, hotel bookings) etc. is regularly collected.[41]

---

40. The subject matter of the case was the admissibility of publishing, on the website of the German Federal Office for Agriculture and Food (the Bundesanstalt), the personal data of the recipients of funds from the EAGF and the EAFRD (names, municipalities where they reside or are registered, and the amounts received in a given year).
41. M. Krzysztofek, ''Prawo do bycia zapomnianym' i inne aspekty prywatności w epoce Internetu w prawie UE', *Europejski Przegląd Sądowy* 2012, No, 8, p. 29; idem, 'Prawo do bycia zapomnianym', Part 1 and 2, *Computerworld* 2012, No. 10 and 11; P. Blume, 'Transborder Data Flow: Is There a Solution in Sight?', *International Journal of Law and Information Technology* 2000, No. 8, p. 65.

Given the widespread use of the Internet and smartphones or tablets, the extent of threats to personal data protection is massive, and the data subjects' control over the processing of their data has become very limited. Moreover, the numerous applications used on smartphones or tablets require access to the user's data, which generates further privacy risk.[42]

Cashless payments, made in forms such as bank transfers or by payment cards, mean that information on a bank client's account movements and liabilities may lead to the disclosure of sources and recipients of monies transferred to and from the bank account and, consequently, may indirectly reveal the account owner's financial standing, lifestyle, behaviours, interests, creed, or health status.[43] Such data are sensitive according to not only their definition but also the popular understanding of the word. Wealth status, though not included in the scope of sensitive data according to law, is broadly perceived as sensitive information.

International Working Group on Data Protection in Telecommunications (aka the Berlin Group), Working Paper of 15-16 April 2013: Web Tracking and Privacy: Respect for context, transparency and control remains essential, https://www.coe.int/t/dghl/standardsetting/dataprotection/News/Web%20tacking.pdf. The Working Group mentions these privacy threats and emphasises the significance and binding character of the fundamental rights of Internet users; it points to the need to ensure transparency and monitoring of online activity as well as Privacy by Design.

42. Article 29 Working Party, Opinion 02/2013 on apps on smart devices, 27 February 2013, WP 202, http://ec.europa.eu/justice/article-29/documentation/opinion-recommendation/files/2013/wp202_en.pdf, and Opinion 13/2011 on Geolocation services on smart mobile devices, 16 May 2011, WP 185, http://ec.europa.eu/justice/article-29/documentation/opinion-recommendation/files/2011/wp185_en.pdf.

43. M. Krzysztofek, *Tajemnica bankowa i ochrona danych osobowych w praktyce bankowej*, Warszawa 2010, p. 10; cf. also G. Gorczyński, 'Sąd cywilny a tajemnica bankowa – uwagi na tle uchwały Sądu Najwyższego z 7 grudnia 2006 r.', *Prawo Bankowe* 2007, No. 12, p. 52.

CHAPTER 3

Scope of Protection of Personal Data and Key Definitions

§3.01 SCOPE OF ENTITIES COVERED

The scope of protection of personal data is defined by the types of entities and types of data under protection (Articles 1 and 2 of the GDPR) as well as the territorial scope (Article 3 of the GDPR) in connection with the key definitions (Article 4), in particular the definitions of personal data, data processing, and filing system. The scopes of entities and data, the territorial scope and the definitions which are the key to defining these scopes are discussed in the later sections of this chapter.

The nature and definition of personal data, which define the scope of entities covered by the protection, are discussed in detail below. Crucially, as implied by recital 14 of the preamble to the GDPR, its Article 1 and the definitions in its Article 4(1), the scope of personal data under protection only covers information on natural persons. It does not cover information relating to legal persons and, in particular, undertakings established as legal persons, including the legal person's name, legal form and contact details, or information related to non-incorporated organisational units.

Differences in civil-law and business terms between Member States may lead to uncertainty on whether the data of natural persons operating as businesses (sole proprietors) are protected under the GDPR. My own interpretation of this issue is presented further in the book, in the commentary on the definition of personal data.

Obligations to protect data under the GDPR are binding upon all entities which process personal data as part of their business or professional or statutory activities, e.g. data controllers and data processors, whether they are public sector units (central or local government units or other state-owned or municipal organisational units) or private sector units (legal persons and non-incorporated organisational units, e.g. commercial-law companies and partnerships, cooperatives, associations or foundations). This includes non-public entities carrying out public tasks (for example private hospitals and schools) and natural persons.

Processing of personal data by EU institutions, bodies and organisational units is regulated by Regulation (EC) No 45/2001 of the European Parliament and of the Council of 18 December 2000 on the protection of individuals with regard to the processing of personal data by the Community institutions and bodies and on the free movement of such data,[1] which is to be adapted to the principles and rules formulated in the GDPR.

§3.02 MATERIAL SCOPE

To define its material scope of application (Article 2(1)), the GDPR refers to automated means of data processing as the distinguishing criterion.

Specifically, the processing of data wholly or partly by automated means is covered by the GDPR irrespective of other circumstances. On the other hand, non-automated processing of personal data is covered by the GDPR if the data 'form part of a filing system or are intended to form part of a filing system'. This wording, as well as recital 15 of the preamble to the GDPR, suggests the interpretation that data processed by wholly or partly automated means is protected under the GDPR irrespective of whether it is processed (or intended to be processed) as part of a filing system, whereas non-automated data processing is not covered by the GDPR if the data do not form part, and are not intended to form part, of a filing system. This distinction was already made in Article 3(1) of Directive 95/46/EC and is reiterated in the GDPR.

Whether non-automated data processing is covered by the GDPR or not is thus determined by the controller's intention (or lack thereof) to include such data in a data filing system (cf. the wording 'personal data which form part of a filing system or are intended to form part of a filing system'). Using the example of data sent by a job applicant to a prospective employer, I would therefore distinguish two types of cases.

- The employer maintains, or intends to maintain, a data filing system containing data of job applicants, structured according to specific criteria, and adds an applicant's CV to the filing system, even if only in a paper form. The GDPR does apply to this situation.
- The employer has not published a job vacancy and does not intend to maintain a filing system with applicants' data, or even add the CV it received to an existing filing system, but to dispose of it. The GDPR does not apply to this situation. Otherwise, the entity's status as a data controller, rather than being determined by the processing purpose specified the controller itself (as per Article 4(7) of the GDPR), would result from the mere fact that the entity has unwillingly received personal data. It would, in my view, be unjustified to require such an entity to comply e.g. with the information obligation.

1. OJ EU L 8, 12.1.2001, p. 1.

However, even data which are not covered by the GDPR are not entirely unprotected, for instance, against disclosure to an unauthorised person. Such protection is ensured essentially from the right to privacy, enshrined in the EU Charter of Fundamental Rights.

If this distinction were to be taken literally in every case, data which are processed outside IT systems (non-automated data processing), are not part of a filing system and which the data controller does not intend to form part of a filing system should fall outside the scope of the GDPR. This would leave it to the data controller's discretion whether such personal data were to be covered by the protection. Indeed, it is for the controller to decide whether a filing system should be set up or whether specific data are to be included in it. Thus, the right to the protection of personal data or even, in a broader view, fundamental rights under the EU Charter of Fundamental Rights and constitutions of EU Member States, would only become applicable upon the controller taking a technical action, and their applicability would depend on the controller's intention to include the data in a filing system, which is unacceptable.

Thus, following the above example, I find it appropriate to assume that personal data contained in a CV sent by a job applicant to a company which had not intended to receive it and has no intention to include the data in a filing system but, on the contrary, intends to erase the data, is not covered by the GDPR.

On the other hand, if the company keeps the data for any reason (for instance, as a result of its prior dealing with the data subject), but does not technically include the data in a filing system (e.g. an employee puts the CV in a drawer rather than in a file sorted alphabetically), the data are still protected under the GDPR.

Article 8(1) of the EU Charter of Fundamental Rights and Article 16(1) of the TFEU grant everyone the right to protection of their personal data. Upon entry into force of the Treaty of Lisbon (including the Charter of Fundamental Rights of the EU) in December 2009, the right to protection of personal data became a fundamental right. There is no reason to limit the protection and the scope of that right according to the criteria of the technical means and filing system.

Personal data are subject to legal protection even if they merely may be included in a personal data filing system, irrespective of whether they are eventually included in such a filing system.[2]

According to recital 15 of the preamble of the GDPR, 'in order to prevent creating a serious risk of circumvention, the protection of natural persons should be technologically neutral and should not depend on the techniques used'. Thus, as well as covering automated (or even partly automated) forms of processing, including in IT systems (which is crucial due to the increased leakage risk of data processed in this way), the protection also covers processing in manual and paper-based filing systems (files, indexes, directories and registers). It even covers processing outside filing systems: the fundamental right to privacy cannot be excluded because the data controller has no intention of processing the data in an organised way, and this

2. Decision of the Polish Supreme Court, Penal Chamber, of 11 December 2000, II KKN 438/00, OSNKW 2001 No. 3-4, item 33, p. 101, *Biuletyn Sądu Najwyższego* 2001 No. 2, p. 16, KZS 2001 No. 3, item 11, p. 8.

precisely would be the result of excluding the protection of data which are not intended to form part of a filing system.

Any controversies on automated means of data processing as the criterion of data protection are, anyway, bound to become negligible with time, since the manual processing of data involves, in most cases, at least some degree of automation (e.g. scanning a CV submitted on paper, entering data from paper documents to a computerised system, parallel archiving of paper and digitised documents).

In response to widespread concerns, it is crucial to point out that the GDPR does not curtail anyone's right to use personal data in standard relations or situations, such as calling out the names of schoolchildren receiving awards during a school year closing ceremony. Making a point of not using the pupils' names (which is not unheard of) is absurd, as the children are no longer anonymous to their school colleagues of several months or years.

It should also be borne in mind that the processing of data in non-compliance with the fundamental principles, including without a legal basis as specified in Article 6 of the GDPR, or processing of sensitive data, such as relating to health or criminal convictions, in non-compliance with Articles 9 and 10 of the GDPR, is punishable by a fine of up to EUR 20 million or 4% of the non-compliant undertaking's total worldwide annual turnover of the preceding financial year (Article 83(5)(a) of the GDPR).

CCTV systems which are not structured and which do not enable recordings relating to a specific person to be found according to a specified criterion are not personal data filing systems. CCTV systems, installed in frequented locations such as means of public transport or underpasses, record unspecified persons continuously for the purposes of preventing incidents and providing evidence in case of an offence. However, when associated with other information or databases, they may enable the identification of certain individuals, e.g. based on an offender's image or the number plate of a vehicle. A non-structured continuous recording is not a filing system but contains personal data, which are protected under law.

§3.03 EXCLUSIONS FROM THE SCOPE OF THE GDPR

The GDPR does not, on the other hand, cover the processing of data that is limited, for instance, to a mere inspection of identity documents, i.e. the consultation of data without their subsequent entry in any form to filing systems, or processing outside filing systems. In practice, however, such cases are becoming increasingly scarce and irrelevant: recording such data (such as the identity of the inspected person and the time and location of the inspection), whether manual or automated (such as with a mobile device for recording data from field inspections) amounts to the processing of personal data and is thus covered by the GDPR.

Still, the GDPR does not cover filing systems created on an ad hoc basis, such as for a one-off marketing action (this exclusion is not laid down in Article 2(2) of the GDPR). It should be mentioned as an aside that such cases are different from extractions, which are not separate filing systems but short-lived files extracted from an existing filing system, e.g. submitted to a call centre team.

The GDPR does not apply to the processing of personal data in the course of activities falling outside the scope of EU law (e.g. national security) and the processing of data by the Member States as part of their activities within the scope of the EU's common foreign and security policy (Title V, Chapter 2 of the TEU). The scope of this exemption should be defined by reference to areas of EU competence (Articles 2–6 of the TFEU) but also to the powers, expressly conferred to the EU, to lay down uniform rules relating to the protection of individuals with regard to the processing of personal data and the rules relating to the free movement of such data (Article 16(2) of the TFEU).

Articles 2–6 of the TFEU list areas under the exclusive competence of the EU as well as areas in which the EU shares its competences with Member States. The GDPR applies in all these areas. The TFEU also lists areas under the exclusive competences of the Member States. In these areas, the EU powers are limited to supporting, coordinating or supplementing the actions of the Member States. The exemption of personal data processed in these areas from the scope of the GDPR (as provided for in Article 2(2)(a) of the GDPR) creates areas in which personal data protection rules will not be uniform across the EU, unless Member States unify them on their own initiative. Some of these areas are very broad, such as healthcare, education or administrative cooperation. Article 16(2) of the TFEU seems to aim to extend the uniform EU-wide data protection rules also to the areas only covered by the EU's coordination competences provided for in Article 6 of the TFEU. Still, although Article 16(2), as amended by the Treaty of Lisbon, may be a basis for laying down uniform personal data protection rules across the EU, it also contains a limitation of its own scope to activities covered by EU law. Consequently, competence conflicts are to be expected. One area where the GDPR coverage is excluded beyond doubt (as provided for expressly in its Article 2(2)(b)) is the processing of data by the Member States as part of their activities within the scope of the EU's common foreign and security policy (Title V, Chapter 2 of the TEU).

Also exempt is the processing of personal data by competent authorities for the purposes of the prevention, investigation, detection or prosecution of criminal offences or the execution of criminal penalties, including the safeguarding against and prevention of threats to public security.

§3.04 PROCESSING OF DATA FOR PERSONAL OR HOUSEHOLD PURPOSES AS AN EXEMPTION FROM THE MATERIAL SCOPE OF THE GDPR

More practical discrepancies result from another exemption from the GDPR, relating to the processing of data by a natural person in the course of a purely personal or household activity (Article 2(2)(c) of the GDPR), i.e. unrelated to professional or economic activity. Personal or household activity could include correspondence and the holding of addresses in directories in personal mobile phones, collecting data in personal notebooks or computers, e.g. in emails, social networking and online activity undertaken within the context of such activities (Recital 18 of the preamble to the GDPR). On the other hand, although the use of a social networking service by a user may be personal and, as such, be excluded from the scope of the GDPR, the activities of data controllers or processors (such as social networking service providers) providing means for processing personal data for personal or household activities are covered by the GDPR.

Personal or household data processing activities must be non-commercial, with the exception of activities conducted for material gain but in a limited scope and for personal needs, such as sale of used items on online auction sites on a non-business basis, or trade of items (even valuables) between collectors.

Even the processing of sensitive data, e.g. relating to health or used in pending criminal or civil proceedings, are covered by the 'personal or household' exemption if the processing is outside gainful or professional activities.

One example of processing data for personal or household purposes is CCTV monitoring of a person's own property. The purpose and other aspects of such processing are outside the scope of the GDPR. However, once the monitoring goes beyond this private area, whether deliberately or inadvertently, for example when a CCTV camera is misadjusted and its viewing angle includes part of a neighbouring property or public space (e.g. a street), this exceeds the processing of data for personal or household activities and is therefore covered by the GDPR.[3] Consequently, any such processing of data would require that a legal basis be specified and the required information provided, e.g. the controller, the purpose of the processing, and the rights of the persons being recorded would have to be specified, and the recordings would have to be safeguarded against third party access. It is practically impossible to enforce these requirements in such relations.

However, the CJEU has argued that where a private individual publishes personal data of third persons on the Internet, identifying them by name or by other means, such a publication is covered by personal data protection law. This is because such a publication is not one of a purely personal or household nature. The household exemption, as argued by the CJEU, 'must [...] be interpreted as relating only to activities which are carried out in the course of private or family life of individuals, which is clearly not the case with the processing of personal data consisting in publication on the internet so that those data are made accessible to an indefinite number of people'.[4]

Other than in the processing of data for personal or household activities, the GDPR applies irrespectively of whether the data are used for commercial or professional purposes or for private and non-commercial purposes. Therefore, the GDPR is binding upon foundations and NGOs (non-government organisations) as well as well as on businesses.

3. Judgment of the CJEU of 11 December 2014 in Case C-212/13 *František Ryneš v Úřad pro ochranu osobních údajů*, http://eur-lex.europa.eu/legal-content/EN/TXT/?&uri=CELEX:62013CJ0212.
4. Judgment of 6 November 2003 in Case C-101/01, *Bodil Lindqvist v Aklagarkammaren i Jönköping*, point 47, http://eur-lex.europa.eu/legal-content/EN/TXT/HTML/?uri=CELEX:6200 1CJ0101.

§3.05 TERRITORIAL SCOPE

The scope of the GDPR covers the processing of personal data in the context of the activities (not limited to commercial activities) of the establishment of a controller or a processor in the EU, regardless of whether the processing takes place in the EU or not. The territorial applicability of the GDPR relates to the controller's or processor's registered office (i.e. its main business and decision-making centre) being located in an EU Member State (or another location where the law of an EU Member State is applicable under international public law) but also to an establishment of a third-country institution being located in an EU Member State, in any legal or organisational form. Such establishments include in particular: (i) a branch, i.e. a part, separate and autonomous in terms of its organisation, of a business, maintained by the business owner outside of the location of the registered office or the business or its main operating location, or (ii) a representation, operating in a limited scope focused on advertisement and promotion of a foreign business. Essentially, an establishment operates effectively within stable structures. Whatever its legal form, be it an incorporated subsidiary company, a branch, or a representation, it makes the GDPR apply to the data controller or processor.

A ground-breaking new arrangement introduced in the GDPR is protection of personal data regardless of their processing location. The processing of personal data by the establishment of a controller or a processor in the EU is covered by the GDPR regardless of whether the processing itself takes place in the EU. However, the physical location of an establishment in the EU is not the only factor which determines the applicability of the GDPR. An innovation introduced by the GDPR is its applicability to the processing of personal data of persons in the EU by a controller or processor who is not established (i.e. does not have an establishment) on the EU territory but whose data processing activities include: (a) offering goods or services to persons within the EU, whether or not on a paid basis, or (b) the monitoring of the behaviour of such persons, if this behaviour is within the EU. Thus, large-scale data processing by third-country companies targeting EU citizens is covered by EU data protection rules. Furthermore, in such cases the controller or processor not established within the EU must designate its representative in the EU. The representative must be established in one of the Member States of the location of the data subjects whose personal data are processed in relation to the offering of goods or services to them or whose behaviour is monitored. This includes observing their activities and choices as consumers and using the information from this observation for analysing and forecasting the individual's decisions, preferences or behaviours, i.e. profiling of the person (Article 27 of the GDPR).

Therefore, pursuant to the GDPR, its rules also apply to the processing of EU citizens' and residents' personal data by non-EU-based companies, e.g. providers of services (even unpaid) and companies which monitor their customers, such as web browser providers, social networking service providers and online retailers, including the global market leaders, such as Google, Facebook or Amazon.

The GDPR therefore departs from the rule laid down thus far in Directive 95/46/EC (Article 4(1)(a)), which subjected the processing of data to the local jurisdiction of a Member State only if the data were processed in the context of the controller's establishment on the territory of this Member State. Establishment was defined in recital 19 of the preamble of the Directive as the effective and real exercise of activity through stable arrangements, with a proviso that the legal form of such an establishment, whether simply a branch or a subsidiary with a legal personality, was not the determining factor in this respect. As an alternative to this establishment criterion, the Member State's jurisdiction was also determined in the Directive (Article 4(1)(c)) on the basis of the controller's use, for the purposes of processing personal data, of equipment situated on the territory of the said Member State, unless such equipment was used only for purposes of transit through the territory of the Community. In my opinion, the territorial scope defined in the GDPR still implies, as Article 4(1)(c) of Directive 95/46/EC did, that controllers which are not established in the EU are exempt from the obligation to comply with EU law if they only use the means located in an EU Member State for the transit of personal data through EU territory, as long as the transit does not involve the use or modification of the data. In my opinion, the territorial scope defined in the GDPR implies, as did Article 4(1)(c) of Directive 95/46/EC, that controllers which are not established in the EU are exempt from the obligation to comply with EU law if they only use the means located in an EU Member State for transit of personal data through the EU territory, as long as the transit does not involve the use or modification of the data.

The initial version of Article 29 Working Party's Opinion 8/2010 on applicable law[5] provided an example (Example No. 11) relating to a social network platform having its headquarters in a third country and an establishment in the EU, actively targeting residents of all EU Member States, who constituted a significant portion of its customers and revenues. In this initial version, the applicable law was deemed, pursuant to Article 29 Working Party 4(1)(a) of Directive 95/46/EC, to be the data protection law of the Member State where the company was established within the EU. Still, the supervisory authority of this Member State was required, under Article 28(6) of the Directive, to cooperate with other supervisory authorities, e.g. in order to deal with requests or complaints coming from residents of other EU countries.

Although the GDPR applies to the processing of personal data by companies from outside the EU which offer services to European customers, it would certainly be a misconception to infer that the mere possibility of using, in the EU, goods or services offered by a third-country company makes the GDPR applicable to such a company's business. The fact that the company's website is available in the EU or that the company uses a language that is widespread in the EU but also an official language in a third country or widely used in international trade is not a sufficient criterion for the applicability of the GDPR. On the other hand, if the company targets citizens of an EU Member State and this is clear from the list of languages or countries of residence which the customer can choose from to place the order, or the currency used to quote the prices, then the processing of data falls within the scope of the GDPR. In this way, the

5. Article 29 Working Party, Opinion 8/2010 on applicable law, adopted on 16 December 2010, WP 179, p. 27, http://ec.europa.eu/justice/article-29/documentation/opinion-recommendation/files/2010/wp179_en.pdf.

GDPR was adapted in terms of its territorial applicability to the current situation where services are available online, i.e. the location of a service provider's headquarters or branches (for instance, in the United States) is unrelated to the place of residence (the European Union) of the customers the company targets. This removes many barriers for the enforcement of data subjects' rights.

The principle of data protection regardless of the data processing location, now enshrined expressly in the GDPR, had already been formulated by the Court of Justice of the EU in its judgment of 13 May 2014 in Case C-131/12[6] *Google Spain SL and Google Inc. v. Agencia Española de Protección de Datos (AEPD) and Mario Costeja González*. This judgment was formulated in the context of the interpretation of Directive 95/46/EC before the GDPR was adopted.

The judgment confirmed that Directive 95/46/EC applied (and, consequently, so does the GDPR) where a third-country-based search engine provider had an office or subsidiary in an EU Member State, established in order to direct advertising through that search engine to the residents of that state.

As a result of that judgment, Article 29 Working Party updated, on 16 December 2015, its earlier Opinion No. 8/2010 on applicable law of 16 December 2010.[7]

The CJEU has argued to the same effect in its judgment of 1 October 2015 in Case C-230/14 *Weltimmo s.r.o. v. Nemzeti Adatvédelmi és Információszabadság Hatóság*.[8] The Court ruled that a controller may be deemed to be active in the territory of a Member State, and thus subject to the EU data protection law, even if it merely runs a property dealing website concerning properties situated in the territory of that Member State, written in that Member State's language, and the activity involves the processing of personal data.

The CJEU's arguments in these judgments relate also to the term 'establishment' under the GDPR, after its applicability date. The CJEU's judgments imply a broad scope of the term 'establishment' and a flexible interpretation of economic activity.[9]

§3.06 KEY DEFINITIONS

The scope and modalities of personal data protection are determined by the definitions key to the application of the GDPR. This chapter presents the definitions of personal

6. Case C-131/12 for a preliminary ruling under Article 267 TFEU upon request made by Audiencia Nacional (Spain) by decision of 27 February 2012, received at the Court on 9 March 2012, in the proceedings *Google Spain SL, Google Inc. v. Agencia Española de Protección de Datos (AEPD), Mario Costeja González*, http://eur-lex.europa.eu/legal-content/EN/TXT/?uri=CELEX:62012CJ0131.
7. Update of Opinion 8/2010 on applicable law in light of the CJEU judgment in Google Spain, adopted on 16 December 2015, WP 179 update, http://ec.europa.eu/justice/article-29/documentation/opinion-recommendation/files/2015/wp179_en_update.pdf.
8. https://eur-lex.europa.eu/legal-content/EN/TXT/?uri=CELEX%3A62014CJ0230.
9. An interpretation shared by M. Czerniawski, 'Zakres terytorialny a pojęcie 'jednostki organizacyjnej' w przepisach ogólnego rozporządzenia o ochronie danych – zarys problemu', in: 'Ogólne rozporządzenie o ochronie danych. Aktualne problemy prawnej ochrony danych osobowych 2016', *Monitor Prawniczy*, ed. G. Sibiga, p. 23.

data and other terms such as pseudonymisation and anonymisation, genetic data, biometric data, data concerning health, as well as filing system and processing. Definitions of other key terms, including controller, processor, recipient, consent to processing of data, restriction of processing, profiling, binding corporate rules and standard contractual clauses, are discussed in other chapters of this book, presenting data processing principles.

[A] Personal Data

Personal data are defined (Article 4(1) of the GDPR) by two criteria: (a) they only concern natural persons and (b) they identify or enable the identification of a person to whom they refer (the data subject), which does not mean that they are limited to identification data.

[1] Personal Data as Information on Natural Persons

The scope of personal data is limited to information relating to natural persons (Article 1 of the GDPR, definition in Article 4(1) of the GDPR, and recital 14 of the preamble to the GDPR). It does not cover information relating to legal persons and, in particular, undertakings established as legal persons, including the legal person's name, legal form and contact details. Nor does it cover information related to non-incorporated organisational units and civil-law partnerships, despite their names containing the partners' names (cf. Polish Supreme Court judgment of 13 November 1997, I CKN 710/97, OSNC 1998, No. 4, item 69), as a 'legal person' should be defined in accordance with the Member State law.

On the other hand, protection of information under sectoral professional secrecy arrangements in sectors such as banking, insurance, practice of law, and tax, as well as trade secrets, applies irrespective of the legal form of the entity in question.

[a] Data of Natural Persons Acting on Behalf of Legal Persons

Information on natural persons who represent, or hold positions in, incorporated entities relates to such incorporated entities but also constitutes the personal data of those natural persons which act on their behalf. Such data include the names of the executive board members entered into a business register, or of employees indicated on the company's website as contact persons for placing orders or making complaints (i.e. these data serve the purpose of identifying persons representing the legal person). This does not mean that all data appearing in a public register in relation to the activities of a legal person are exempt from the GDPR. For instance, information on the property arrangements between a member of the company's executive board and his/her spouse is still protected under the GDPR as personal data. Any assessment of whether the data of these persons are processed lawfully must focus on the purpose of such processing. It is entirely permissible to process such data for the purpose and in the scope corresponding to these persons' position in the bodies or structure of the corporation (e.g. sending mail relating to the person's remit within the corporation). On the other hand, using the same data for other purposes, e.g. for marketing of products or services which are intended not for the company represented by these persons but for themselves as consumers, requires that other requirements of lawful data processing be met.

[b] Data of Sole Proprietors

The GDPR does not specify the scope of protection of data relating to sole proprietors, i.e. natural persons conducting business, whose data are publicly available in business registers. The GDPR excludes from its scope (as indicated in recital 14 to its preamble) legal persons, particularly undertakings incorporated as legal persons. The exclusion is thus based on the entity's legal status rather than its status as an undertaking. While there is no EU-wide definition of a legal person and the applicable laws in this respect vary between Member States, there is no doubt that a natural person conducting business is an undertaking but not a legal person. The GDPR thus provides no grounds for excluding sole proprietors' data from its protection, as they are natural persons.

Arrangements introduced in the past in EU Member States' legislations ranged from one extreme, i.e. complete exclusion of sole proprietors' data included in public registers from personal data protection laws, to the other, i.e. full protection of such data. Based on these experiences, an intermediate solution is advisable, taking into account the nature of business and trade and the purposes of public availability of business registers. An approach worthy of recommendation is that adopted in the Polish Freedom of Business Act of 2 July 2004, in its Article 39b, which entered into force on 19 May 2016 but has since ceased to apply, being in conflict with the GDPR. It exempted public data and information made available in the Central Registration and Information on Business (CEIDG) from most provisions of the Personal Data Protection Act, including basic rules such as those relating to the legal basis of data processing (including data on convictions for offences committed in the course of business), the requirements to provide information upon the collection of data, the registration of data filing systems and the transfer of data to third countries. However, data sourced from a business register were still subject to appropriate safeguards and supervision by the data protection authority.

A failure to differentiate the extent of protection of consumers' and business operators' personal data leads to paradoxes, such as in the context of the obligation to inform the data subject that his/her data have been obtained (even if they have been obtained from a publicly available business register) or in the context of marketing, where an offer directed by a company to a sole proprietor (i.e. in a business-to-business relationship) is equated to an offer directed to a consumer.

[c] Personal Data of Deceased Persons

Since the scope of personal data is limited to the data of natural persons, the data of deceased persons are exempt from protection under the GDPR (recital 27 of its preamble), as a person's ability to be the subject of rights and obligations ceases upon the person's death. Thus, the personal data of deceased persons are still personal data, but are not protected under the GDPR. However, Member States may still adopt laws protecting the personal data of deceased persons. Some of them have declared that they do not plan to enact any such laws, as sufficient protection is, in their opinion, ensured through the model described below.

Data of a deceased person may be subject to protection only insofar as they may be used indirectly to identify a living person. Personal data protection rights cannot be inherited. Accordingly, any demands that the inheritor may make, such as for erasure of the data or of photographs of the deceased person which may be detrimental to that person's reputation, may not be justified with the inheritor's right to object to the processing of the deceased's personal data, but only by respect for the deceased's memory, which is a personal good (not of the deceased but of his/her surviving relatives).

On the other hand, protection under, for example, bank secrecy is not limited in time and does not expire upon the death of the person protected. Information covered by bank secrecy, relating to a deceased customer, may only be provided to his/her relatives under certain conditions, e.g. where inheritance has been confirmed by a court or a by notary public through a deed.

[2] Identifiability of a Natural Person as the Qualifying Criterion of Information as Personal Data

[a] Direct or Indirect Identifiability of a Data Subject

Personal data are information relating to a natural person ('data subject') who is directly or indirectly identified or identifiable, in particular, by reference to his/her name, an identification number, location data, an online identifier or factors specific to the physical, physiological, genetic, mental, economic, cultural or social identity of that natural person. These identification means must be assessed in relation to a specific data controller, as its real ability to identify a person based on information it holds may differ depending on the means at its disposal.[10]

Two alternative criteria of the identifiability of a natural person were distinguished in the context of the CJEU proceedings in Case C-582/14 *Patrick Breyer v. Bundesrepublik Deutschland*,[11] specifically in the opinion of Advocate General M. Campos Sánchez-Bordona, relating to this case (point 53).[12] According to the objective identifiability criterion, a person is identifiable (e.g. on the basis of the IP address) regardless of the actual possibility of identifying that person by a specific entity with information at its disposal, or the practical potential availability of information from other sources allowing identification. On the other hand, according to the subjective

10. G. Sibiga, *Postępowanie w sprawach ochrony danych osobowych*, Warszawa 2003, p. 37.
11. CJEU judgment of 19 October 2016 in Case C-582/14 *Patrick Breyer v Bundesrepublik Deutschland*, https://eur-lex.europa.eu/legal-content/EN/TXT/?uri=CELEX:62014CJ0582.
12. https://eur-lex.europa.eu/legal-content/EN/TXT/?uri=CELEX:62014CC0582.

criterion, identification is only possible if data held by a third party may be accessed by a specific entity and used for identifying a person with this entity's own resources. Favouring one of these two conflicting approaches over the other determines the interpretation of the definition of personal data, since personal data relates to an 'identifiable natural person'. This very issue, besides the reference to dynamic IP addresses, was at the core of the CJEU judgment referred to above. Personally, I favour the subjective criterion over the objective one.

The CJEU emphasised in point 46 of its judgment (in line with point 68 of the Advocate General's opinion) that the usability of data at the disposal of another entity for identifying a person could be ruled out 'if the identification of the data subject was prohibited by law or practically impossible on account of the fact that it requires a disproportionate effort in terms of time, cost and man-power, so that the risk of identification appears in reality to be insignificant'. I believe this conclusion to be crucial. Otherwise any information which could merely in theory allow a person to be identified would be deemed personal data, even though it could in practice never be used to identify that person.

I disagree with the opinion that the mere existence of a decryption key to an encrypted database is sufficient to consider such encrypted content to be personal data, regardless of how unlikely it would be to obtain this key by an entity in relation to which the legal nature of the information is being assessed.[13] Adopting this approach would make it illegal for IT companies to provide database hosting services, even if the encrypted data were to be inaccessible to the hosting company, as only selected persons representing the data controller would hold the decryption key. Another example is sending printed medical records via traditional mail. Although any postman is technically able (though not legally allowed) to open the envelope, and this presents a risk of unauthorised access to data, this does not mean that a contract should be concluded with the mail service for the processing of medical data, as the mail service only delivers an unspecified letter rather than specific personal data.

I subscribe entirely to the opinion[14] that the GDPR uses the subjective identifiability criterion. This is reflected in recital 26 of its preamble: a natural person is identifiable if he/she can be identified by means which are 'reasonably likely to be used' (rather than abstract), and the reasonable likelihood reflects factors such as the cost and time required for identification, the available technology and technological developments. Thus, any piece of information relating to a specific individual only constitutes personal data if an entity who can access the data has means to identify the person with the use of such data *and* is likely to use these means. This understanding is consistent with the risk-based approach adopted in the GDPR.[15]

---

13. P. Carey, *Data Protection*, Oxford 2004, p. 15.
14. P. Litwiński, 'Pojęcie danych osobowych w ogólnym rozporządzeniu o ochronie danych osobowych – glosa do wyroku Trybunału Sprawiedliwości z 19.10.2016 r. w sprawie C-582/14 Patrick Breyer', *Europejski Przegląd Sądowy*, No. 5/2017 *Nowe prawo unijne o ochronie danych osobowych*, pp. 53-54.
15. Article 29 Working Party, *Statement on the role of a risk-based approach in data protection legal frameworks*, 30 May 2014, WP 218, http://ec.europa.eu/justice/article-29/documentation/opinion-recommendation/files/2014/wp218_en.pdf.

[b] Scope of Personal Data

The formulation of the scope of personal data is open-ended. This means, first, that no category of information relating directly or indirectly to a natural person is 'personal data' by its mere nature. Isolated data, without additional information, do not necessarily identify a person. For example, different people may have the same first name and surname and their identification may require the addition of other data, e.g. age.

Second, even a piece of information which is a unique identifier does not necessarily constitute personal data for the person who has obtained it. For instance, a number in an electronic population register is not sufficient identification information for a person who cannot access the database of such numbers, although a court or an official institution, capable of accessing the register because of its statutory obligations, may use such information to identify the person concerned. From this institution's standpoint, therefore, such a number is personal data. However, even the identification of an official of a court or an institution must be limited to what is required as part of this official's duties during proceedings, and access to a database for these purposes is supervised.

Third, any information which does not normally identify a natural person may become personal data in specific circumstances. For instance, information on a person's account balance is neutral, but when the amount is very high and unique in a community served by a local bank, it may be associated clearly with a specific member of that community.

Similarly, information displayed in the stairwell of a building, showing the numbers of flats with the amounts owed by the respective residents to the housing cooperative, constitutes personal data. Even if no identification data are provided, the information of the debt amounts can very easily be associated with specific persons, as neighbours know each other personally and each flat is marked with its number.

Fourth, the list of information constituting personal data evolves with technological change. For instance, the GDPR states that geolocation data, collected, for example, by mobile telephone operators, are personal data. The importance of geolocation data ought not to be underestimated. The collection of such data often leads to the identification of specific persons. An entity collecting such data may identify a person by linking location information to other data. Information on several locations visited by an unidentified person at specified times, obtained through geolocation or based on that person's entries on online forums, coupled with information on that person's card payment, allows him/her to be identified (as few as four such pieces of information enabled the identification of 90% of persons in an anonymised database in a study by Yves-Alexandre de Montjoye's team at Massachusetts Institute of Technology.[16]

16. de Montjoye Y.-A., Radaelli L., Singh V. K., Pentland A. S., 'Unique in the shopping mall: On the reidentifiability of credit card metadata', *Science*, 30 January 2015, Vol. 347 no. 6221 pp. 536-539.

Technologies reduce the amount of time, cost, or effort necessary to identify a person based on specified information. They are therefore liable to influence the list of personal data. One example is facial recognition technology, which, together with the widespread use of CCTV cameras in public places, makes it increasingly easy to identify individuals successfully in recordings or photographs.

Even information relating to a third person but enabling the identification of a data subject indirectly may constitute personal data. An example could be the processing of a piece of information stating that Person A occupies a given post in a given institution, whereas in reality the post is occupied by Person B. In this situation, Person B cannot be considered a third party as the data relate to him/her indirectly.

Direct or indirect identification is based on such identifiers as: surname and given names, residence address, identification number in an electronic population register, tax identification number, identity card number, photograph (the face image is also biometric data), surname at birth, parents' given names and surnames at birth, surname, surname at birth and given names of spouse, telephone number, email address, vehicle registration number, specimen of signature, bank account number, credit card number.

Identifying information also includes all other information which, in specific circumstances, may lead to the identification of the person in question. This may include location data or online identifiers of a person (such as those listed in recital 30 of the preamble to the GDPR: IP addresses, cookie identifiers or other identifiers, such as RFID tags, or others, such as nicknames used by Internet forum users). It may also include economic, cultural or social identifiers of a natural person, such as: date and place of birth, gender, citizenship, marital and family status, education status, financial standing, employment status, income and expenditure, number of persons in the household, marital property regime, occupation, profession, criminal convictions and behaviour as a consumer or Internet user.

Other personal data are physical, physiological, genetic or mental identifiers of a natural person. The GDPR has introduced a new definition of genetic data as personal data relating to the inherited or acquired genetic characteristics of a natural person which give unique information about the physiology or the health of that natural person and which result, in particular, from analysis of a biological sample from the natural person in question (Article 4(13) of the GDPR). Therefore, samples of blood or tissues which can be used for DNA analysis or ascertaining consanguinity constitute personal data. The GDPR has also formulated a definition of biometric data as personal data resulting from specific technical processing relating to the physical, physiological or behavioural characteristics of a natural person, which allow or confirm the unique identification of that natural person, such as facial images or dactyloscopic data (Article 4(14) of the GDPR). Thus, fingerprints or retinal scans, increasingly used, for example, in biometric passports, or voice recordings, used for decades in criminal investigations and recently also, on a growing scale, for purposes such as identifying bank customers, are personal data. So are data related to the physical or mental health of a natural person, including the provision of health care services, which reveal information about the person's health status, defined as data concerning health in Article 4(15) of the GDPR.

The definition of personal data may raise doubts as to whether untrue information and opinions on a person are personal data. In my opinion, an untrue piece of information, relating to an objectively non-existent state of affairs, is personal data as long as it can be assigned to a specific and identifiable natural person. For example, information concerning a person's debt which was published in a loan register and was not updated after the person repaid the debt, thus wrongly showing that the person is still a debtor, is personal data which should be rectified.

[c] Telephone Number, Email Address and IP Number as Personal Data

The assessment of whether a piece of information constitutes personal data depends in many cases on the data processing technologies used. One example is diverging views on whether a telephone number is personal data. GIODO, the Polish data protection authority, responded in the affirmative,[17] arguing that the telephone owner may be identified by contacting him/her directly. Other authors have disagreed, pointing out that a telephone number alone, without access to other data, does not allow identification.[18] A piece of information is personal data if it enables a person to be identified without excessive cost or time expense, within the limits of the technology available. Understandably then, the available technology must affect this assessment and the evolution of technology may change it (cf. recital 26 to the preamble of the GDPR). The assumption that a telephone number does not identify its owner was proven wrong by an experiment conducted by Jonathan Mayer and Patrick Mutchler of Stanford University. Their aim was to see whether it was possible to identify the names of the owners of phone numbers solely based on the information these individuals themselves disclosed on the Internet. Using Google Places, Facebook, Yelp and Intelius proved sufficient to find out the names of 91 phone owners, out of a random sample of 100 phone numbers.[19]

There is a similar dispute on whether an email address is personal data. Certainly, addresses of functional mailboxes used by institutions for receiving complaints or objections to marketing are not personal data. On the other hand, an email address made up of the person's name and a domain name which is the company name of his/her employer is personal data. However, even the use of a first name and surname in an email address does not directly enable the identification of the email user (even less so if the initial is used instead of the first name), as the name may be false or repetitive. Conversely, even the use of a nickname rather than a real name does not prevent identification, as the nickname may be easily recognisable in a given community. Where a service provider collects its customers' email addresses, or a court records a person's email address as his/her contact address, the address is undoubtedly

17. Grounds of GIODO decision of 22 January 2008, DIS-DEC0150-42/1511, 1515, 1520/08/08, unpublished.
18. P. Barta, P. Litwiński, *Ustawa o ochronie danych osobowych. Komentarz*, C.H. Beck 2016, Legalis.pl.
19. R.J. Rosen, 'Stanford Researchers: It Is Trivially Easy to Match Metadata to Real People', The Atlantic, 24 December 2013, http://www.theatlantic.com/technology/archive/2013/12/stanford-researchers-it-is-trivially-easy-to-match-metadata-to-real-people/282642/.

personal data, because it is recorded in a database together with the name of the person whose identity has been confirmed. Furthermore, even if the content of an email address does not directly identify its owner, it is the address which the person uses to receive mail; a message sent to that address will still reach the person. In practice, email addresses are tending to replace traditional residential addresses as the key contact data, given the costs and speed of delivery. A growing number of traditional mail services even provide the service of scanning paper letters and sending them to email addresses.

Personal data may also include IP (Internet Protocol) addresses, i.e. numbers assigned to specific individual devices on the Internet and recorded along with the user's entries on online forums or during online shopping. These include permanent IP addresses, assigned by the Internet provider to specific devices, and dynamic IP addresses, assigned for the duration of an Internet connection and changing for each subsequent connection. An IP address constitutes personal data if the Internet service provider or a provider of online services also stores the customer's identification data, e.g. for payment management, and can match those data with the IP address. Fixed IP addresses assigned to an individual device rather than to a group of users of a local area network (LAN) are also personal data: the operator collecting the data does not have, and cannot normally obtain, additional information enabling it to identify the users, but still collects the IP addresses for possible future identification, for instance, at the request of an authorised judicial authority in criminal proceedings.[20] The Article 29 Working Party has even expressed a more rigorous approach, stating that all IP addresses are personal data unless a search engine operator can demonstrate that it is not able to identify a user.[21]

A permanent IP address was confirmed to be personal data in the documents quoted above and also in the CJEU judgment of 24 November 2011 in Case C-70/10 *Scarlet Extended SA v Société belge des auteurs, compositeurs et éditeurs SCRL (SABAM)*. The IP address is personal data from the standpoint of an Internet access provider, as the provider identifies the party of an agreement which it entered into. This, however, is not tantamount to identifying a specific person using, at any given moment, the device assigned the IP address. For other entities, the IP address is personal data as it allows them to identify a specific person, which would not be possible without access to other data relating to that person, accessible through the IP address.

The CJEU, in its judgment of 19 October 2016 in Case C-582/14 *Patrick Breyer v Bundesrepublik Deutschland*,[22] ruled that dynamic IP addresses are personal data as well. According to this judgment, the definition of personal data in Article 2(a) of Directive 95/46/EC (and, consequently, in Article 4(1) of the GDPR as well) should be

20. The Article 29 Working Party, Opinion 4/2007 of 20 June 2007 on the concept of personal data, WP 136, http://ec.europa.eu/justice/article-29/documentation/opinion-recommendation/files/2007/wp136_en.pdf.
21. The Article 29 Working Party, Opinion 1/2008 of 4 April 2008 on data protection issues related to search engines, WP 148, http://ec.europa.eu/justice/article-29/documentation/opinion-recommendation/files/2008/wp148_en.pdf.
22. https://eur-lex.europa.eu/legal-content/EN/TXT/?uri = CELEX:62014CJ0582.

interpreted to mean that the dynamic Internet Protocol address, which the online media services provider (i.e. the website host) records while the user accesses the website, is personal data for this provider, if it has the legal means at its disposal to identify the data subject thanks to additional data of the data subject, available to the Internet service provider. The identification may be justified e.g. by the need to identify the perpetrator of a hacking attack or the dissemination of illegal content.

The judgment may have a practical impact on online profiling and big data.

Still, in my opinion, the treatment of permanent and dynamic IP addresses as personal data in the Article 29 Working Party's opinions and in the CJEU case law underestimates the fact that a private computer may be used by several different persons in a household.

[B] Anonymisation and Pseudonymisation

Anonymisation of data is the removal of elements identifying a person, so that it becomes impossible to identify the person despite reasonable efforts. Anonymisation is permanent and irreversible. Thus, anonymised data are no longer personal data and are not covered by personal data protection legislation.

On the other hand, pseudonymised information (cf. recital 26 of the preamble to the GDPR) is still personal data, as pseudonymisation is reversible. Pseudonymisation is the processing of personal data in such a manner that the data can no longer be attributed to a specific data subject without the use of additional information, provided that such additional information is kept separately and is subject to technical and organisational measures to ensure that it is not attributed to an identified or identifiable person (Article 4(5) of the GDPR).[23] Identifying information is thus masked or replaced with information that is unintelligible for a person who does not have a key to read it. For instance, identifying data may be replaced with a number or code (with the link to the person being stored in a different database, secured against unauthorised access), or a person's name may be replaced with initials, or names of the street and town in an address may be replaced with their initial letters. However, there is a risk of a violation: pseudonymised data can be indirectly used to identify a person where they contain information which, in a specific and restricted environment, e.g. a local community or social group, can characterise and identify an individual.

One example is pseudonymisation of data in court judgments, where the case pending before a local court is publicised and evokes emotions in the community. In such a case, despite the masking of identification data, the individuals involved might still be recognisable.

23. In its Opinion No. 5/2014 of 10 April 2014 on Anonymisation Techniques, WP 216, http://ec.europa.eu/justice/article-29/documentation/opinion-recommendation/files/2014/wp216_en.pdf, the Article 29 Working Party presents a broad selection of anonymisation methods and similar methods leading to analogous effects, as well as mistakes in anonymisation operations, particularly ones that cause the anonymisation to be ineffective, i.e. identification is still possible despite the anonymisation efforts.

Since pseudonymisation is the processing of personal data in such a manner that the data can no longer be attributed to a specific data subject without the use of additional information, provided that such additional information is kept separately and is subject to technical and organisational measures to ensure that it is not attributed to an identified or identifiable person, then pseudonymisation, if applied correctly, allows data processing to be outsourced. Information which, from the data controller's standpoint, continues to be personal data even after pseudonymisation, does not need to be so for the data processor, as long as it cannot access the pseudonymised or encrypted content of the personal information, and the decryption key (or the pseudonymisation reversal key) is only available to selected persons on the data controller's side, but not on the data processor's side. Pseudonymisation also allows the need-to-know principle to be applied in the data controller's structure. The pseudonymised data being processed by the controller remain personal data, as the controller's authorised staff have the decryption key or the pseudonymisation reversal key. However, the data do not allow identification by other employees, who only have access to selected files and applications, excluding the decryption keys.

Importantly, since pseudonymisation is reversible and pseudonymised data remain personal data, pseudonymisation may not be resorted to as an alternative to the erasure of data; only anonymisation may serve as such an alternative solution.

[C] Filing System

The GDPR has abolished the obligation, laid down in Directive 95/46/EC and the implementing national laws, to notify the supervisory authorities of the processing of personal data, in particular, the registration of personal data filing systems (cf. recital 89 of the preamble to the GDPR). This obligation has been shown not to improve the data protection standard to an extent proportionate to the administrative and financial burden it involves. It has consequently been replaced with procedures and mechanisms focusing on processing operations which may involve a high risk of infringement upon natural persons' rights or freedoms. Such operations include, in particular, processing operations which involve new technologies, or have yet to be assessed by the controller for the risk they pose to data protection, or require verification due to the lapse of time.

The filing system has been defined (Article 4(6) of the GDPR) as a set of personal data that has two defining features: (a) it is structured and (b) the personal data contained therein are accessible according to specific criteria, which means that the data of a specific person may be found without the need to perform a time-consuming search through all entries in the set.

The genuine possibility of effectively finding and accessing specific personal data is of key importance. Thus, for example, a data set such as a visual recording of a frequented public place from a CCTV camera is not a filing system if the recording is only sequenced chronologically. Although it is possible, e.g. for the police, to find a section of the recording involving a particular person by knowing the time when the offence was committed, the search is not based on a criterion referring to the features of that specific person but only according to the time sequence. The time is a factor structuring the recording itself, but the crowd on the street, recorded continuously, remains anonymous and the person being searched for will appear on the recording at random, among other people. On the other hand, applying a technology to such a data set which allows the data to be quickly searched and found makes it a filing system, as it meets the criterion of accessibility according to specific criteria.

Files which are not structured according to specific criteria should not fall within the scope of the Regulation (recital 15 of the preamble to the GDPR). The definition of filing system in the GDPR refers to 'specific criteria', rather than 'a specific criterion', of data accessibility. It might be interpreted (and has in fact been interpreted by some authors and courts) to mean that the possibility of finding a specific person using only one criterion is not sufficient for considering a data set a filing system if other criteria need not be used. However, I do not agree with this literal interpretation. Like most authors, I favour a teleological interpretation: in my opinion the use of a plural does not imply that more than one criterion of structuring data in a filing system is required, but merely indicates that the use of different criteria is possible. Arguing to the contrary would lead to pathological interpretations, for instance that a list of school students or hospital patients, structured alphabetically, is not a filing system.[24] Whether a data set is a filing system does not depend on the number of people (data subjects) whose data appear in it. A filing system may even include the data of a single person, and will remain a filing system as the data of further data subjects are added to it.

Whether a data set is a filing system does not depend on whether it is centralised, decentralised or dispersed on a functional or geographical basis. It is therefore irrelevant whether the filing system (be it an IT system or paper files, indexes, or other records) is kept in a single building or room or in separate locations, e.g. on the data controller's servers located, for security reasons, in two offices in different cities, or in an archive of paper documents, maintained under an outsourcing contract by a specialised archiving provider.

Even if a data set is structured and accessible according to a specified criterion, it is not necessarily a filing system. A data set may, for functional reasons, be part of an already existing filing system. This depends on the controller's assessment verified by a data protection authority. For example, a list of job applicants, structured according to identification data and perhaps the characteristics relevant for assessing each candidate, is a filing system, yet lists of applicants for separate posts are not necessarily separate filing systems, but may be parts of an existing filing system of job applicants.

This is especially true when such a sub-set is created on an ad hoc basis, i.e. for a specified short time. A list of the participants at a conference, with data to be removed or anonymised after the conference is completed, is an ad hoc filing system. However, if the list is subsequently used for sending offers of permanent cooperation, invoking the experts' knowledge presented at the conference, it will no longer be an ad hoc filing

24. P. Barta, P. Litwiński, *Ustawa o ochronie danych osobowych. Komentarz*, C.H. Beck 2016, Legalis.pl and J. Barta, P. Fajgielski, R. Markiewicz, *Ochrona danych osobowych. Komentarz*, Kraków 2007, pp. 369–370.

system. Still, it need not be treated as a separate filing system if it is a functional part of a broader list of customers or marketing database.

[D] Data Processing

The GDPR defines processing (Article 4(2)) as an operation or set of operations performed on personal data or sets of personal data, and indicates selected data processing operations, from collection and recording to erasure or destruction of data. The definition of processing includes automated and non-automated operations, using all types of IT tools as well as paper documents.

Processing is defined by providing a list of examples of processing operations because the list must remain open-ended and flexible given the diverse nature of sectors in which data controllers operate and given the technology evolution. The list is very broad and includes all operations, from collecting data and recording them on a physical carrier (whether electronic or paper). Further processing of data includes, but is not limited to, using them actively for the controller's purposes, managing them through organisation, adaptation or alteration, making them available to another controller, i.e. providing them or making them accessible for consultation, and erasure or destruction, including through an outsourced destruction of paper or electronic data carriers. Passive storage of data, including through outsourced file archiving or data hosting, is also data processing.

The GDPR applies to personal data, regardless of the form of their processing: it covers non-automated processing as well. According to recital 15 of the preamble of the GDPR, 'in order to prevent creating a serious risk of circumvention, the protection of natural persons should be technologically neutral and should not depend on the techniques used'.

A very broad definition of data processing, covering its aspects from collection to erasure of data, may lead to problematic situations. One example could be when a debtor requesting a suspension of debt enforcement provides his bank with information on his health (e.g. a copy of his medical record), which constitutes sensitive data (Article 9(1) of the GDPR). In my opinion, it should be assumed that, as long as the institution (e.g. the bank) has obtained the data without intending or attempting to do so and with no intention to process them further, this does not constitute collection of personal data. The bank should not include the debtor's health information in its files because the suspension of debt enforcement only requires a formal confirmation of the preventing circumstances, i.e. the debtor's poor health. On the other hand, the full information on health status goes beyond that purpose. Its inclusion in the files, i.e. in the filing system, would be against the data minimisation principle and would render the processing unlawful. However, a literal interpretation of the law would not allow the conclusion that merely taking note of the data, drawing a conclusion and then destroying them do not constitute data processing. On the contrary: even erasure and destruction of data are classified as processing. In my opinion, though, it should be assumed that the controller's intention in obtaining personal data, i.e. the purpose of the processing, is crucial for the processing. The purpose limitation principle (Article

5(1)(b) of the GDPR) relates to this very purpose, and this purpose should be communicated to the data subject (Articles 13 and 14 of the GDPR). Taking note of the data, making a decision on their basis and destroying the data precludes their further processing, and as such should not be subject to obligations under the GDPR.[25]

25. As also argued by G. Sibiga, *Postępowanie w sprawach ochrony danych osobowych*, Warszawa 2003, p. 50.

CHAPTER 4

Key Principles of Personal Data Processing

§4.01 PRIMACY OF THE PRINCIPLES OF PERSONAL DATA PROCESSING

The personal data processing principles laid down in Article 5 of the GDPR (Article 6(1) of the Directive) are fundamental for the protection of data and the application of the GDPR and the Directive. They are modelled on the principles laid down in Article 5 of the Council of Europe Convention No. 108 for the Protection of Individuals with regard to Automatic Processing of Personal Data of 28 January 1981.[1]

These principles constitute the framework of data protection law. All EU laws regulating personal data protection in detailed terms must conform to these principles. The key principles also serve as guidelines for the interpretation of detailed legal provisions.

The overriding nature of these principles means, among others, that in certain contexts they are not modifiable even with the consent of the data subject. For instance, the maximum permissible scope of data which may be processed in a given case (in accordance with the data minimisation principle, one of the key ones) may in some cases not be expanded even if the data subject has expressed his or her consent for such an expansion.

The key principles of personal data processing, formulated in Article 5(1) of the GDPR (Article 6(1)(a)–(e) of the Directive), include the following:

- The lawfulness, fairness and transparency principle, requiring that personal data are processed in accordance with statutory laws and regulations issued on

1. Convention No. 108 has been modernised: on 18 May 2018, in Elsinore, Denmark, the 128th Ministerial Session of the Council of Europe's Committee of Ministers adopted the Protocol (CETS No. 223) amending the Convention and endorsed its Explanatory Report (https://search.coe.int/cm/Pages/result_details.aspx?ObjectId = 09000016807c65bf).

the basis of such laws, and that such processing respects legitimate interests of the data subjects and is transparent to them.
- The purpose limitation principle, whereby data may only be collected for specified purposes and must not be further processed in a manner that is incompatible with those purposes.
- The data minimisation principle, requiring that the scope of data being processed is limited (in terms of the quantity and content of data) to what is necessary to meet the purposes of the processing.
- The accuracy principle, whereby data must be factually accurate, complete, and kept up to date.
- The storage limitation principle, which prohibits the storage of data, in a form permitting identification of data subjects, for longer than is necessary for the purposes for which the data are processed.
- The integrity and confidentiality principle, i.e. the requirement to ensure security of the personal data by using appropriate technical or organisational measures, including protection against unauthorised processing or accidental loss of data.

These key principles are supplemented with the accountability principle (Article 5(2) of the GDPR, Article 6(2) of the Directive), requiring data controllers to implement arrangements to ensure the lawfulness of data processing, i.e., in particular, its compliance with the key principles of data protection, including data quality principles.[2]

This constitutes an obligation of proactive behaviour, requiring the data controllers to act on their own initiative rather than wait for complaints and requests from customers or the critical remarks and recommendations of supervisory authorities. An example of taking such action is the data controller maintaining records of the implemented safeguards of lawfulness of data processing,[3] including an effective security policy compliant with the legal requirements, and the introduction of a procedure for handling complaints and requests.

§4.02 LAWFULNESS, FAIRNESS AND TRANSPARENCY PRINCIPLE

The key data processing principles, i.e. the purpose limitation principle and the quality principles, are preceded with the lawfulness, fairness and transparency principle (Article 5(1)(a) of the GDPR, Article 6(1)(a) of Directive 95/46/EC). This principle

2. Ch. Raab, 'The Meaning of "Accountability" in the Information Privacy Context', p. 15; C.J. Bennett, 'The Accountability Approach to Privacy and Data Protection: Assumptions and Caveats', p. 33; J. Alhadeff, B. Van Alsenoy, J. Dumortier, 'The Accountability Principle in Data Protection Regulation: Origin, Development and Future Directions', p. 49 – all in: *Managing Privacy Through Accountability*, ed. D. Guagnin, L. Hempel, C. Ilten, I. Kroener, D. Neyland, H. Postigo, Houndmills, Palgrave MacMillan 2012.
3. Article 29 Data Protection Working Party, Opinion 3/2010 on the principle of accountability, 13 July 2010, WP 173, http://ec.europa.eu/justice/policies/privacy/docs/wpdocs/2010/wp173_en.pdf.

requires that personal data are processed in accordance with statutory laws and regulations issued on the basis of such laws, and that such processing respects the legitimate interests of the data subjects and is transparent to them.

The lawfulness and fairness principle encompasses all the other data processing principles and the legal bases and purposes of processing. It is a general principle, expressed in detailed terms in specific legal provisions, case law, and good practices.

The obligation for data to be processed *lawfully* means the requirement to comply with statutory laws and regulations issued on the basis of such laws, substantive and procedural law, and case law. *Unlawful* processing is that which disregards obligations or prohibitions laid down by law; this includes in particular processing of data without legal basis or for unlawful purposes.

The data controller's obligation to ensure that data processing is lawful means that the processing, in all its aspects enumerated in Article 4(2) of the GDPR (Article 2(b) of the Directive), i.e. from collection to erasure, has to conform to at least one of the lawfulness criteria specified in Article 6 of the GDPR (Article 7 of the Directive). This includes the prohibition on collecting data, or processing data collected, in an unlawful manner. For instance, where data are to be processed under the consent of the data subject, such consent must be unambiguous and freely given, with no potential adverse consequences of a refusal. The obligations also include the requirement to specify the purpose of data processing and the data recipients (Articles 12–14 of the GDPR, Articles 10 and 11 of the Directive), to ensure access to the data (Articles 15 et seq. of the GDPR, Articles 12 and 14 of the Directive), to implement measures to ensure the security of processing at an adequate level (Article 32 of the GDPR, Article 17(1) of the Directive), and to comply with other obligations provided for in the GDPR and the Directive as well as other generally applicable legal regulations which apply to individual cases of data processing.

The lawfulness principle is also invoked in the context of the purpose limitation principle laid down in Article 5(1)(b) of the GDPR (Article 6(1)(b) of the Directive) by defining the permissible purposes of data processing as not only specified and explicit but also legitimate.

The conditions of lawful data processing are derived indirectly from the conditions of permissible restriction of the right to protection of personal data, as formulated in Article 52(1) of the Charter of Fundamental Rights of the EU and Article 8(2) of the European Convention of Human Rights. The conditions laid down in the two documents are convergent, as Article 52(3) of the CFR provides that rights contained in the CFR corresponding to rights guaranteed by the ECHR have the same scope and meaning. At the same time, the EU law may grant further-reaching protection, which means that the exclusions of the right to protection of data, listed in Article 8(2) of the ECHR, define the minimum lawfulness standard within the EU law.

Data processing is lawful provided that it is based on a statutory law or a legal act issued on the basis of such a law and is necessary in a democratic society for meeting a legitimate purpose.

The ECtHR has emphasised that interference with the right to privacy is lawful if based on a legal provision which is accessible to the persons concerned and formulated with sufficient precision.[4] Analogously, the ECtHR ruled that in the cases specified in Article 8(2) of the ECHR, interference in privacy by processing data obtained through monitoring of correspondence and telephone calls of suspected criminals is permissible, but with the reservation that the legal regulations invoked as the basis for such actions are unambiguous.[5]

The condition that the interference with privacy must be necessary in a democratic society in order to be lawful was emphasised by the ECtHR in the case of *Leander v Sweden*.[6] The Court defined this necessity as implying that the interference corresponds to a pressing social need and is proportionate to the aim pursued. The ECtHR declared that confidential procedures of assessment of applicants for posts which are important for the national security are permissible if such a procedure is necessary, and that, in individual cases, national security must be protected above the interests of an individual.

The CJEU ruled along similar lines in its judgment of 9 November 2010,[7] confirming that, in a democratic society, the right of the public to obtain information about the use of public funds is a necessary exception from personal data protection. This justifies the publication of personal data of natural persons who benefit from public funds. Still, the Court emphasised that the limitations must be provided for by law, respect the essence of the rights in terms of data protection, and be proportionate to the aim pursued by the legislator. The Court ruled that the publication of beneficiaries' personal data without drawing a distinction as to the amounts obtained or the frequency of receiving them is a violation of the data minimisation principle.

The GDRP also requires in its Article 5(1)(a) (Article 6(1)(a) of the Directive) that data be processed *fairly*. Fair processing of personal data is interpreted as processing which respects the interests and reasonable expectations of data subjects and ensures balance between the data controller's commercial interests and the data subject's privacy.[8] The fairness of data processing is subject to interpretation on a case-by-case basis, and the interpretation may evolve over time, in particular, due to technological changes in data processing and safeguarding means. It may also be influenced by the

4. H. Amann v Switzerland, 16 February 2000, Application No. 27798/95, 87 ECHR.
5. The ECtHR related to this aspect in the cases of: *Malone v the United Kingdom* (Application No. 8691/79, 2 August 1984, http://hudoc.echr.coe.int/sites/eng/pages/search.aspx?i = 001-57533), *Huvig v France* (Application No. 11105/84, 24 April 1990, http://hudoc.echr.coe.int/sites/eng/pages/search.aspx?i = 001-57627), *Kruslin v France* (Application No. 11801/85, 24 April 1990, http://hudoc.echr.coe.int/sites/eng/pages/search.aspx?i = 001-57626), in which the Court found the legal regulations concerning permissible interference in privacy to be insufficiently precise, and in the case of *Klass and others v Germany* (Application No. 5029/71, 6 September 1978, http://hudoc.echr.coe.int/sites/eng/pages/search.aspx?i = 001-57510).
6. Judgment in the case of *Leander v Sweden*, 26 March 1987, Application No. 9248/81, 9 EHRR 433.
7. Judgment of 9 November 2010 in joined cases C-92/09 and C-93/09, *Volker und Markus Schecke GbR* (C-92/09) and *Hartmut Eifert* (C-93/09) *v Land Hessen*, http://eur-lex.europa.eu/legal-content/EN/TXT/?uri = CELEX:62009CJ0092. The subject matter of the case was the admissibility of publishing, on the website of the German Federal Office for Agriculture and Food (the Bundesanstalt), the personal data of the recipients of funds from the EAGF and the EAFRD.
8. P. Barta, P. Litwiński, *Ustawa o ochronie danych osobowych. Komentarz*, Warszawa 2009, p. 263; L.A. Bygrave, *Data Protection Law. Approaching its Rationale, Logic and Limits*, Hague-New York 2002, p. 58. See also R. Jay, A. Hamilton, *Data Protection Law and Practice*, London 2003, pp. 150 et seq.; C. Kuner, *European Data Privacy Law and Online Business*, Oxford-New York 2003, p. 61.

scale of the data controller's activities and the scope of data being processed. For instance, the fairness principle is violated if the clause of consent for the use of data for marketing purposes is included in other clauses, making it impossible for the customer to refuse his/her consent, even though he/she is entitled to do so.[9]

The fairness requirement has been interpreted in this context, for example, by the British Data Protection Tribunal in its judgment of 24 March 1998.[10] The Tribunal ruled that British Gas Trading Limited acted in an 'unfair' manner as the controller of personal data of consumers (gas end users) when it made these data available to other entities for marketing purposes 'without the free and informed consent of such customers', especially as the company was the monopolist in the UK gas sector.

Fair data processing also implies transparency for the data subjects. The reference to the principle in Article 5(1)(a) of the GDPR includes *transparency* alongside lawfulness and fairness, requiring data to be processed 'in a transparent manner in relation to the data subject'.[11]

This includes the data controller's obligation to provide the data subject with information including the processing purpose and the data recipients, if such information is not confidential under law, and to ensure access to the data for the data subject.

The transparency principle is complied with by providing data subjects with information on the processing of their data 'in a concise, transparent, intelligible and easily accessible form, using clear and plain language' (Article 12(1) of the GDPR).

Transparency also requires that public authorities put in place effective means guaranteeing access to the data. One instance of an infringement of this principle was a five-year delay by security services in providing information they had collected on a citizen. The ECtHR challenged the absence of a procedure to ensure access by a citizen to information relating to him/her within a reasonable period.[12]

§4.03 PURPOSE LIMITATION PRINCIPLE

Another principle crucial for the lawfulness of data processing,[13] laid down in Article 5(1)(b) of the GDPR (Article 6(1)(b) of Directive 95/46/EC), is the purpose limitation principle.[14] This makes the purpose of data processing binding. Under this principle,

9. An interpretation shared by M. Jagielski, *Prawo do ochrony danych osobowych. Standardy europejskie*, Warszawa 2010, p. 80.
10. In the case *British Gas Trading Limited v Data Protection Registrar* (DA98 3/49/2; 1998 Info. T.L.R. 393).
11. The transparency principle is discussed in the comments relating to the information requirement principle.
12. ECtHR judgment in the case of *Haralambie v Romania* (Application No. 21737/03, 27 October 2009, http://hudoc.echr.coe.int/eng#{'dmdocnumber':['856690'],'itemid':['001-95302']}.
13. See, e.g., L.A. Bygrave, *Data Protection Law. Approaching Its Rationale, Logic and Limits*, Hague-New York 2002, p. 61; R. Jay, A. Hamilton, *Data Protection Law and Practice*, London 2003, pp. 162 et seq.; C. Kuner, *European Data Privacy Law and Online Business*, Oxford-New York 2003, p. 59.
14. Opinion of Article 29 Working Party No. 3/2013 of 2 April 2013 on purpose limitation, WP 203, http://ec.europa.eu/justice/article-29/documentation/opinion-recommendation/files/2013/wp203_en.pdf, pp. 15–19.

data may only be collected for specified, explicit and legitimate purposes and must not be further processed in a manner that is incompatible with those purposes.

The principle is binding upon both the controller which originally collected the data and the controller to which the data were subsequently made available.

The data processing purposes are determined by the data controller, whose role is defined by this right. However, for controllers who are public entities, data processing purposes must result directly from law, which corresponds to the requirement of them being specified and lawful. For private-sector controllers, data processing purposes must correspond to, and be justified by, the scope of their lawful activities.

The data controller must specify the data processing purpose prior to commencing the data processing. Processing of data for purposes which are not specified, or are specified imprecisely to the point of being unlimited or vague, renders the processing unlawful.

The processing purpose must be specified in the internal documentation maintained by the controller, which need not be notified to, but is subject to inspection by, the supervisory authority (records of processing activities).[15]

The obligation to notify the data subject of the processing purpose should not be equated with the obligation to obtain the data subject's consent, or to comply with his/her objection, to data processing. Not all data processing purposes require the data subject's consent or are affected by his/her objection, but even for those who do not, the data subject must be aware of the controller's intended purpose of the processing.

The requirement that the data be collected for 'specific' purposes corresponds with the information obligation laid down in Articles 12 to 14 of the GDPR (Article 10(b) and Article 11(1) of the Directive), whereby the data subject must be provided with the information, among others, as to the intended purpose of data processing. The GDPR provisions imply that the information obligation is met if the information specified in those provisions has been presented by the controller to the data subject in a sufficiently transparent, intelligible and easily accessible form; written form is not compulsory.

Among the possible ways of demonstrating compliance with the information obligation are: the data subject's signature on the form provided by the controller, confirming that he/she has read the information clause; ticking the required box on a website, to the same effect; the controller's demonstrating that the web page is laid down in such a way that the customer must read the information before proceeding to the product details. Another way of demonstrating compliance with the information obligation is available through a telephone conversation with the controller's call centre. The proof that the required information has been provided is then available in the archived records of conversations or thanks to the controller having implemented a binding conversation scenario, including the appropriate clause. On the other hand,

15. The GDPR has abolished the obligation, laid down in Directive 95/46/EC and the implementing national laws, to notify the supervisory authorities of the processing of personal data, in particular, the registration of personal data filing systems (cf. recital 89 of the preamble to the GDPR).

the information obligation cannot be discharged through an announcement made in the press or on the Internet, as it is not directed to the specific data subject.

Under the purpose limitation principle, data must not be further processed in a way which is incompatible with the purposes for which the data were collected (the initial purposes). The assessment of whether the controller has complied with this prohibition relates to the controller's prior declaration as to the processing purposes, i.e. there is a link to the information obligatorily provided to the data subject. Without that reference it would be impossible to verify the purpose compatibility.

However, further processing of data in a way *incompatible* with purposes for which the data were collected should be distinguished from further processing of data for purposes *different* from those originally specified. Article 5(1)(b) of the GDPR (Article 6(1)(b) of the Directive) does not prohibit further processing of data for different purposes, but only for purposes incompatible with those originally specified. Therefore, processing of data for purposes different from, but compatible with, those initially specified is not precluded.[16] If the purpose of data processing is to be changed, provided it remains compatible with the initial purpose, the data subject must be informed of the new purpose. If the new purpose is incompatible with the original purpose, the data subject's consent must be obtained, or a different legal basis for the processing invoked. The purposes of processing must be specified in the records of processing activities. Their scope specified therein may include further processing purposes, which are not incompatible with the initial purpose.

If the original purpose of data processing declared by the controller was marketing, then targeting the company's customers with promotion of its new products which were not in its product range at the time when the original purpose was declared is certainly a purpose compatible with the original one. On the other hand, promotion and sale of products of other companies, or providing the customers' personal data to another company for its own marketing purposes, is usually a new purpose and requires a new legal basis.

The consent of the person being targeted by a marketing communication is not required when such a communication is made for the data controller's legitimate purpose. For instance, the legitimate purpose is direct marketing of the data controller's own products or services. However, this does not mean that a bank, for example, may not process personal data for the purposes of marketing its services as an insurance agent or distributor of investment fund participation units on the basis of the justified purpose clause, without the consent of the data subject. On the contrary: despite the fact that these are not the bank's own products and the bank only acts as an external service provider in distributing them, their sale is still a service provided by it. Therefore, the marketing of these services is the bank's justified purpose and does not

16. J. Barta, P. Fajgielski, R. Markiewicz, *Ochrona danych osobowych. Komentarz*, Kraków 2007, p. 504; P. Barta, P. Litwiński, *Ustawa o ochronie danych osobowych. Komentarz*, Warszawa 2009, p. 268; C. Kuner, *European Data Privacy Law and Online Business*, Oxford-New York 2003, p. 60; M. Jagielski, *Prawo do ochrony danych osobowych. Standardy europejskie*, Warszawa 2010, p. 90. It should be noted that, according to certain opinions, processing data for purposes different from the purpose for which the data were collected is unacceptable; cf. E. von Ehmann, M. Helfrich, *EG-Datenschutzrichtlinie: Kurzkommentar*, Köln 1999, p. 111.

require the consent of the person targeted. However, an objection of the person must be complied with.

On the other hand, marketing the controller's products among its employees would constitute a purpose incompatible with the original one. Data collected for recruitment or employment purposes should not be used for commercial purposes without appropriate conditions having been met, i.e. only because such data are stored in the controller's database and because the controller can use its corporate email. The employees' data have been collected for the purposes of human resource management, payment of salaries, keeping the required documentation, payment of taxes and social security contributions. Any sale of products is a different purpose.

Targeting employees as potential customers requires that the same conditions be met towards them as towards any other customers.

Article 5(1)(b) of the GDPR (as well as Article 6(1)(b) of the Directive) expressly provides for certain activities as not being incompatible with the initial purposes of processing, provided that appropriate safeguards of the data subject's rights and freedoms are provided. These activities are processing for archiving purposes in the public interest, scientific or historical research purposes or statistical purposes.

The inclusion of statistical purposes is important for business activities. A company may use its customer database for statistical analysis in order to research its customers' preferences or decisions on purchasing goods or services. This does not require the data subjects' consent. On the other hand, such data may be provided to another company for statistical purposes without the data subjects' consent only if appropriate safeguards are provided. The pseudonymisation of data is such a safeguard, as statistical analyses do not require the identification of persons within a group.

However, there is a risk of a violation: pseudonymised data can be used indirectly to identify a person where they contain information which, in a specific and restricted environment, e.g. a local community or social group, can characterise and identify an individual.

Article 29 Working Party distinguishes the two concepts (though they are closely related): the purpose of data processing and the interest (of the data controller or a third party) serving as a basis for data processing. The *purpose* of data processing is the specific reason why the data are processed; an *interest*, on the other hand, is a broader concept referring to the benefits that the data controller or a third party derives from data processing.[17]

§4.04 DATA MINIMISATION PRINCIPLE

Other key principles which define the framework of the data protection law are collectively known as data quality principles. They include: the data minimisation principle, the data accuracy principle, and the storage limitation principle.

17. Opinion 6/2014 on the notion of legitimate interests of the data controller under Article 7 of Directive 95/46/EC, 9 April 2014, WP 217, http://ec.europa.eu/justice/article-29/documentation/opinion-recommendation/files/2014/wp217_en.pdf, Chapter III.3.

The overriding nature of these principles means, among others, that in certain contexts they are not modifiable even with the consent of the data subject. For instance, the maximum permissible scope of data which may be processed in a given case in accordance with the data minimisation principle may in some cases not be expanded, even if the data subject has expressed his or her consent for such an expansion. Where consent may be the basis for expansion of the scope of processed data, this scope must be assessed for its proportionality to the processing purpose.

The data minimisation (data proportionality) principle is formulated in Article 5(1)(c) of the GDPR (Article 6(1)(c) of Directive 95/46/EC) as the obligation to ensure that personal data are 'adequate, relevant and limited to what is necessary in relation to the purposes for which they are processed' (or, as in the Directive, 'adequate, relevant and not excessive in relation to the purposes for which they are collected and/or further processed').

The Regional Court (Landgericht) in Bonn, Germany, confirmed the interpretation of the data minimisation principle set forth in Art. 5 (1) lit. c) GDPR.[18] The Court's decision is dated 29 May 2018, only a few days after the GDPR became applicable, which probably makes it the first GDPR court judgment worldwide.

Therefore, the data minimisation principle prohibits processing of data in a way that exceeds the scope necessary for the processing purpose. The Polish Constitutional Tribunal argued likewise in its judgment of 20 November 2002 (K 41/02)[19] by pointing out that any interference in the right to privacy must be *necessary* (*indispensable*) for achieving the purposes referred to in Article 31(3) of the Constitution of Poland, and not merely *conducive to*, or *facilitating*, their achievement. Furthermore, the burden of such an interference for the person whose freedoms or rights are being limited must be kept to a minimum.

In practice, an adequate scope should be understood as such as is necessary for achieving the purpose (recital 39 of the preamble to the GDPR). In the context of the data minimisation principle, I believe these two concepts to be synonymous: data exceeding the scope necessary for the processing purpose would not be adequate (proportionate), since the purposes of processing could be met with a narrower scope of data, i.e. a lesser compromise to privacy. The Polish Supreme Administrative Court shared such an interpretation of the principle in its judgment of 10 October 2006 (I OSK 1353/05)[20] and its judgment of 19 December 2001 (II SA 2869/00).[21]

Therefore, if the purpose of the processing can be met without identifying the person, only by resorting to pseudonymised data, then any processing of identification data should be considered as exceeding the necessary scope and breaching the data minimisation principle. For instance, if it is sufficient to combine the information of a payment having been made, or a service having been used, with only the card entitling its holder to use the service, rather than with the person him/herself, then only such a

18. *The Internet Corporation for Assigned Names and Numbers (ICANN) v Registrar EPAG Domainservices GmbH*, 10 O 171/18, https://www.icann.org/de/system/files/files/litigation-icann-v-epag-request-court-order-prelim-injunction-redacted-30may18-de.pdf (in German only).
19. OTK-A 2002, No. 6, Item 83.
20. LEX No. 281325, CBOSA.
21. ONSA 2003, No. 1, item 29, CBOSA.

minimum scope of information should be used, i.e. the service should be recorded as having been provided, without specifying the person who used it. This is all the more relevant as redundant identification leads to the collection of further data, such as geolocation data.

The permissible scope of data may be defined expressly in a statutory law or a legal provision issued on the basis of a statutory authorisation. Its proportionality may also be assessed on a case-by-case basis. The scope of data that is indicated in a legal provision was, prior to the adoption of the GDPR, *lex specialis* in relation to the data minimisation principle. The scope of personal data which was in line with such a list, laid down in a statutory law or a regulation issued on the basis of such a law, was deemed adequate to the processing purpose. This is the case in many countries, e.g. for labour law, laws on enforcement of claims from bank accounts or real property, and laws on processing data of gas or power consumers. Where no such list existed, the data minimisation principle had to be interpreted by assessing whether the scope of data to be processed only contained data necessary for the purpose.

However, the GDPR does not provide for any exception from the data minimisation principle; nor does it include any reference to separate laws which could provide more stringent protection. It must therefore be considered whether defining the data scope in legal acts as *lex specialis* in relation to the data minimisation principle is compatible with the GDPR. Some authors argue that where a national legal provision of a Member State specifies a positive scope of data which may legally be processed as an exemption from the data minimisation principle, this is non-compliant with the GDPR. I subscribe to this view insofar as it relates to the positive scope of data and goes beyond the cases where the data must be processed to comply with a legal obligation binding upon the data controller, or to perform a task carried out in the public interest or in the exercise of official authority (recital 45 of the preamble to the GDPR).

I believe that the absence of a general exemption in the GDPR from the data minimisation principle does not mean that laying down positive scopes of personal data in legal acts is, in principle, incompatible with the GDPR. It only becomes incompatible if such a positive scope exceeds the scope necessary to meet the processing purpose. However, any processing carried out in accordance with a legal obligation to which the controller is subject, or necessary for the performance of a task carried out in the public interest, or in the exercise of official authority, should have a basis in EU or Member State law (recital 45 of the preamble to the GDPR). Accordingly, national laws may specify the scope of data which must be processed to meet legal obligations relating e.g. to the prevention of money laundering, VAT and medical files etc. The scope of data thus defined will meet the data minimisation requirement, since it results from a legal obligation and it is necessary to meet it.

I also believe it entirely permissible to introduce laws specifying negative scopes of data, i.e. defining data which must not be processed, regardless of whether the data controller believes the scope of data to be compliant with the data minimisation principle. One example may be labour law provisions which may specify a negative scope of data on grounds of the inequality of parties and the risk of discrimination.

The data minimisation principle can be illustrated by different scopes of data being collected by a bank, e.g. for accepting a deposit and for granting a loan. To grant a loan, the bank first needs to assess the customer's creditworthiness, which makes it necessary to collect and analyse an extensive body of personal data. On the contrary, no such assessment is necessary for accepting a deposit. If the scopes of data to be processed were identical in these two cases, that would be in conflict with the data minimisation principle.

The data minimisation principle may be complied with in practice by using alternative identification numbers of a single person. For instance, the account of an insured person is identified with his/her tax identification number only if the person does not have an identification number in the population registration system. Such personal data should not be duplicated; data should only be used in a scope allowing identification.

A similar problem was decided upon by the Polish data protection authority, GIODO (Generalny Inspektor Ochrony Danych Osobowych – Inspector General for Personal Data Protection) (DIS/DEC-170/16/14463, DIS/DEC-622/15/67982). GIODO challenged the practice of copying identity documents by telecom operators, which it considered to be collecting personal data without a legal basis. The permissible scope of data which could legally be collected without the customer's consent was then laid down in Article 161(2) of the Polish Telecommunications Law. Prior to being amended to bring it in line with the GDPR, the Telecommunications Law defined an exhaustive scope of data to be used for concluding a telecom services agreement. Following the said amendment, the Telecommunications Law does not specify the permissible scope of personal data but subjects the processing of a telecom user (a natural person) to the GDPR. This means that the scope of data which may legally be processed depends on what the operator can demonstrate to be proportional to the purpose. Prior to the amendment, the scope of data included the customer's name, date and place of birth, place of residence and mailing address, PESEL (Polish population register number) and the number of an identity document. GIODO (the supervisory authority) ruled that any processing of the personal data of a natural person beyond this scope would be permissible subject to the person's consent (provided for in Article 161(3) of the Telecommunications Law). By copying (photocopying or scanning etc.) the customers' ID documents, the operator also obtained his/her image and the information on his/her height, eye colour, or the number and validity date of his/her driving licence.

GIODO also found that, in certain cases, the conclusion of a contract was made contingent upon the customer's consent to the processing of personal data contained in the copied documents. In such cases, the consent is only valid if it is freely given.

Notwithstanding the decision by GIODO, it is worth mentioning that the Polish Telecommunications Law provides for the possibility of processing additional data under the data subject's consent without specifying the exhaustive scope of such data, but referred in particular to the bank account number or bank card number, email address and contact phone numbers. The collection of these types of data is justifiable for concluding a contract. On the other hand, the collection of data such as height, eye colour, or driving licence validity date in the context of a telecom service contract should also be assessed against the purpose limitation principle and the data minimisation principle.

The decision by GIODO was confirmed by the Provincial Administrative Court in Warsaw in its judgments of 18 February 2016 (ref. no. II SA/Wa 1655/15) and 28 March 2017 (ref. no. II SA/Wa 779/16).

The Polish data protection authority has been consistent in this approach, including in its past decisions the denouncement of the PZU insurance company's practice of copying customers' ID cards. GIODO ordered the insurer to limit the scope of the processed personal data of customers making claims for compensation under a non-compulsory vehicle insurance contract to only cover the person's name, address, and personal identification number or date of birth. Accordingly, GIODO forbade the insurer from copying customers' ID cards, as they also contained other personal data under the law applicable at that time. Ultimately, the problem of redundant data in ID cards was solved by introducing new ID cards which contain only basic identification data, not even including the residence address.

Copies of individuals' ID cards may be processed in accordance with a legal obligation to which the controller is subject. One example is Directive (EU) 2015/849 of the European Parliament and of the Council of 20 May 2015 on the prevention of the use of the financial system for the purposes of money laundering or terrorist financing, which requires that obliged entities, such as banks and insurers, ensure that the customer provides upon request relevant copies of identification data and other relevant documentation on the identity. Thus customers of banks and other financial institutions may be obliged to provide a copy of ID card or other official document of identity. However in many legislations analogous provisions have not been adopted in other sectors, for example, for mobile operators.

On the other hand preventing frauds by identifying customers may be necessary to meet the data controller's legitimate interest. Thus, for example, sending a scanned copy of ID card can be justified in online contracts, if the transfer is secured against unauthorised access. But the storage limitation principle prohibits the storage of copies of ID cards for longer than is necessary for the purpose of identification.

Still, there is a growing problem connected with using copies of individuals' ID cards to steal their identity in order to incur debts or perpetrate fraud. Therefore, the practice of copying, scanning or photographing ID documents by data controllers, such as hotels or sports equipment rentals, should also be assessed in the context of this risk.

The principles formulated in Article 5 of the GDPR (Article 6(1) of the Directive), including the data minimisation principle, have an overriding character. This has raised diverging opinions about situations where an exhaustive list of types of data to be processed is laid down in the legal provision regulating the data controller's activities. The controversy is over whether this scope of data can be expanded on the basis of the data subject's consent. Some authors[22] express the opinion that such an interpretation is indeed acceptable, since the data subject is free to make use of his or her data. A different interpretation, though, was formulated by GIODO (The Polish Data Protection Authority) in its intervention concerning the content of a questionnaire used by PZU Życie SA, a Polish life insurance company, for concluding and prolonging

22. J. Barta, P. Fajgielski, R. Markiewicz, *Ochrona danych osobowych. Komentarz*, Kraków 2004, p. 498.

a group employee insurance contract. GIODO opposed PZU Życie collecting data on the education status, marital status, and occupation of their customers, and requiring their consent to process information on their health status. GIODO argued that the scope of data which could lawfully be processed under the Data Protection Act could not be expanded upon obtaining the data subject's consent.[23]

In my view, the collection of data beyond the scope provided for by law, based on the data subject's consent, should be permissible, provided that the scope of data is proportional to the processing purpose and, crucially, that the consent is indeed freely given. In many cases, such as contracts with the person's employer, or when the provision of services is made contingent on giving consent, this freedom of consent is problematic.

Another application of the data minimisation principle is the definition of limits of permissible interference in privacy by public administration bodies. The constitutions of EU Member States (e.g. the Constitution of Poland, in its Article 51(2) and (5)) limit the possibility of collection of information on citizens and making such information available. Limits on the right to privacy may only be introduced in cases provided for in law, and only where such limitations are necessary in a democratic state for the protection of its security or public order. The inevitable conflict between the right to privacy and the powers of authorities such as the police has been made subject to universal standards of proportionality assessment, defined in the context of Article 8 of the ECHR.[24] Not only must the interference with privacy be necessary for the public interest, but the infringement upon the individual's rights and the burden of such an infringement must not be excessive. The intrusion into the right to privacy must be necessary for achieving the objectives specified in the Constitution, rather than merely facilitate their achievement.[25]

§4.05 ACCURACY PRINCIPLE

The accuracy principle, formulated in Article 5(1)(d) of the GDPR (Article 6(1)(d) of Directive 95/46/EC), is the second of the three data quality principles. It requires the data being processed to be accurate and, where necessary, kept up to date. The data controller must therefore ensure that data are correct, factually accurate, complete, and up to date. Article 5(1)(d) of the GDPR requires every reasonable step to be taken to ensure that personal data which are inaccurate are erased or rectified without delay. This must take into account the purposes for which the data are processed.

The measures must be selected to account for the extent to which the data are inaccurate and the credibility of the data source. Inaccurate information might have been provided by the very person concerned, or the error might be in the external data

23. E. Kulesza, 'Ankieta, która budzi poważne wątpliwości', *Rzeczpospolita*, 13 August 1999.
24. Judgment of the Polish Constitutional Tribunal of 12 December 2005, K 32/04, OTK-A 2005, No. 11, item 132.
25. Judgment of the Polish Constitutional Tribunal of 20 December 2002, K 41/02, OTK-A 2002, No. 6, item 83, and judgment of the Polish Constitutional Tribunal of 28 September 2006, K 45/04, OTK ZU No. 8/A/2006, item 111).

source from which the controller has obtained the data, or the error might have been made by the controller itself. The controller should also take into account the adverse consequences of inaccurate data for the data subject and, potentially, for the execution of legal obligations, e.g. compulsory reporting to tax authorities or prevention of money laundering.

Article 5(1)(d) of the GDPR requires every reasonable step to be taken to ensure that personal data which are inaccurate are erased or rectified without delay. This does not imply, however, that the data controller is required to verify constantly and actively, on its own initiative, whether all the data in the filing systems are accurate and up to date. It is crucially at the data collection stage that the data accuracy must be ensured, namely by collecting data from verified and reliable sources. Subsequently, the controller does not have the means, for example, to constantly monitor changes in its customers' residence or their marital or family status. It should, however, put in place a procedure to erase or rectify data at the request of the data subject (compliant with the time limit requirement in Article 12(3) of the GDPR) or whenever the controller finds, based on the information held or obtained from credible external sources, that the data in its control require rectification. The controller is also obliged to notify third parties to which it transfers the data if they require rectification.[26]

The requirement for data to be kept up to date, expressed in the data quality principles, is to be understood to mean that data relate to a specified point in time. This, therefore, does not mean that data must be updated if the documentation serves the purpose of maintaining information about the situation in a specified time in the past.

For instance, a lender who has changed her name as a result of marriage cannot require it to be changed in the original loan agreement which she signed before getting married. On the other hand, an update is necessary where maintaining inaccurate data resulting from past findings could harm the person concerned. Data which must be constantly monitored for their accuracy and kept up to date include, for instance, information about a bank customer's indebtedness, maintained in loan registers. These data are used to assess lenders' creditworthiness (repayment of past debts); any inaccuracies may thus be very detrimental to them.

The data quality principle is also violated by the collection of data from sources of unverified reliability. One example is profiling customers based on data which are unconfirmed, inaccurate or incomplete, and classifying persons on that basis. Projecting the characteristics and behaviours of a person on the basis of unconfirmed information, e.g. obtained from social networking services, may lead to completely erroneous conclusions.

§4.06 STORAGE LIMITATION PRINCIPLE

Another key data processing principle is the storage limitation principle, which prohibits the storage of data in a form permitting identification of persons (i.e. personal data) for longer than is necessary for the purposes for which the data are processed

26. S. Singleton, Data Protection: The New Law, Bristol 1998, p. 19.

(Article 5(1)(e) of the GDPR, Article 6(1)(e) of the Directive).[27] This principle serves the purpose of preventing the storage of data for an indefinite time where this is not based on a legal regulation or justified by the execution of a contract with the data subject. Such data storage has no purpose and often results from deficiencies on the data controller's part: a lack of systematic knowledge on data storage systems and forms available in its business sector; lack of technical functionality permitting the erasure of data from certain systems; maintaining data in systems which have been replaced by other systems; or other similar circumstances which must be considered non-compliant with the data protection by design principle as well as the storage limitation principle.

Thus, the storage limitation principle requires the data controller to make an internal analysis of the purposes for which it processes data, and the related data retention periods. Following this analysis, the controller should specify the timeframe of erasure or periodic review of the data. The envisaged time limits for erasure of the different data categories must be indicated directly, or at least by reference to the criteria used for defining them, and must be specified in the records of processing activities (Article 30 of the GDPR) and in the information clauses presented to the data subject during the collection of data (Articles 13 and 14 of the GDPR).

Data stored in the same filing system do not necessarily have the same retention periods. For example, information relating to employment and salaries (employees' files concerning their employment period and remuneration, serving as a basis for establishing pension rights) are obligatorily archived even for decades (depending on local laws). However, other data of employees, such as those collected through the employer's monitoring activities (GPS tracking in company cars, history of websites visited), should only be retained for short periods, adequate to legitimate purposes defined by the employer. Such data, relating to workplace discipline, are not normally needed for a longer time than is necessary to take disciplinary measures towards employees.

Such a list of the controller's purposes of data processing and the corresponding data retention periods is used for monitoring whether the maximum retention period is exceeded, and for erasing obsolete data. However, drawing up such a list is a complicated task: not all processing purposes are regulated by law, and therefore retention periods must be specified arbitrarily by the controller. One example of a widely used data processing method which is not directly regulated in all countries is closed-circuit television (CCTV). In the absence of direct regulations, the rules of using CCTV are interpreted in the context of the constitutional right to privacy, personal interest, or labour law, but if neither of which define the data retention period precisely, this period must therefore be established through case-by-case analysis. Installing CCTV cameras on streets, in court buildings or in schools is justified by data controllers on the grounds of safety and security considerations; rightly so in many, though not all cases. However, the commonplace practice of storing CCTV recordings

27. ECtHR, judgment in the case of S. and *Marper v the United Kingdom*, 4 December 2008, Applications No. 30566/04 and 30566/04, http://hudoc.echr.coe.int/eng?i=001-90051#{'item id':['001-90051']}.

for a period of, for example, one year, merely because the controller's system has sufficient storage capacity, is wrong. If, during such a period, there has been an incident, the recording of which could be used as evidence, the storage is indeed justified. If no such incident has taken place, though, security considerations must not be invoked for the storage of recordings which do not document any incident. Such storage is pointless, and the recordings may contain scenes that are potentially embarrassing or humiliating for the persons depicted. The security considerations have been reconciled with the storage limitation requirement e.g. by some regulation authorities, which have accepted the 30-day or 90-day recording storage period in cases where the recordings are not used as evidence.

There is room for potential conflict between the data storage periods under law and the controller's business needs. Moreover, data processed in a common IT system within a corporate group may be subject to different retention periods in different countries, in accordance with local laws.

The definition of personal data implies that the storage limitation principle also applies to data which allow an indirect identification of their subjects. It also implies that erasure of all data is not required. To meet the obligation provided for in Article 5(1)(e) of the GDPR (Article 6(1)(e) of the Directive), it is sufficient to anonymise data, i.e. to permanently remove the elements permitting the identification of a person, whereby other data relating to that person cannot be attributed to him/her despite reasonable efforts. As anonymisation is irreversible, anonymised data are no longer personal data.

Therefore, data which are to be erased must be erased irreversibly, without the possibility of retrieving them from fragments left over in the applications in which they were used (such fragments might still be usable in combination with other data of the person).

Importantly, pseudonymisation may not be resorted to as an alternative to the erasure of data. Pseudonymisation is the processing of personal data in such a manner that the data can no longer be attributed to a specific data subject without the use of additional information, provided that such additional information is kept separately and is subject to technical and organisational measures to ensure that it is not attributed to an identified or identifiable person (Article 4(5) of the GDPR). Thus, pseudonymised data remain personal data.

One of the key purposes of processing data as part of business is performing a contract or actions leading to a conclusion of a contract at the request of the data subject (Article 6(1)(b) of the GDPR, Article 7(b) of the Directive). This purpose of data processing is referred to, for example, in the judgment of the Provincial Administrative Court in Warsaw of 22 February 2005 (II SA/Wa 2030/04). According to this judgment, once a bank loan is repaid in full or a bank account is closed and, consequently, the purpose of data processing is achieved, any legal basis for processing the data of the account holder ceases to exist. This view should be specified more precisely. It is true only insofar as the performance of the contract to which the data subject is party is the sole basis for data processing. On the other hand, where there are other grounds for data processing as specified in Article 6(1)(a)–(f) of the GDPR (Article 7(a)–(f) of the Directive), the termination of a liability does not result in a lack of a legal basis for further data processing, as the performance of a contract is not necessarily the sole purpose for data processing. For instance, in the cases of data processing for purposes provided for in law (Article 6(1)(c) of the GDPR, Article 7(c) of the Directive), the obligation to erase or anonymise data does not arise immediately upon completion of the original processing purpose (i.e., for instance, upon the expiry of the contractual obligation under the contract concluded with the bank), but upon expiry of the period which is laid down in legal regulations. These include, for example, accountancy regulations, which require accounting documents to be archived for 5 years, or anti-money laundering regulations,[28] which provide for the obligation to retain information for 5 years.

Likewise, even if a contract between the controller and the customer has expired, the controller may still target marketing activities at the customer if the customer has given his/her consent for processing his/her data for that purpose, has not withdrawn that consent, and the consent was not limited to the duration of the contract. Still, an assessment should be made of the period when invoking such consent after the expiry of the contract is proportional.

Personal data are also often archived to enable the controller to react to possible complaints by data subjects during the claims prescription period, which depends on local law and the nature of the relationship with the customer. Furthermore, data relating to suspicions which may, in the future, be the subject of criminal proceedings may be retained for the period in which the controller still has legitimate reasons to hold the suspicions and a legal basis for processing the data.

An exemption from the storage limitation principle is formulated in Article 5(1)(e) of the GDPR, which allows data to be stored, in a form permitting direct or direct identification of data subjects, for longer than is necessary for the initial purposes of the processing, but only for archiving purposes in the public interest, scientific or historical research purposes or statistical purposes in accordance with Article 89(1) of the GDPR. Such storage requires the implementation of appropriate technical and organisational measures in order to safeguard the rights and freedoms of the data subject: the data must be minimised, i.e. their scope must be limited to what is necessary to meet the purposes. One such measure which may be introduced, unless it precludes the achievement of the processing purpose, is pseudonymisation, e.g. such modification of data that they can no longer be attributed to a specific person without the use of additional information kept separately and subject to measures preventing identification. However, importantly, if the archiving, scientific, historical or statistical purposes can be met with the use of anonymised data, the processing should be limited to such data.

28. Regulation (EU) 2015/847 of the European Parliament and of the Council of 20 May 2015 on information accompanying transfers of funds and repealing Regulation (EC) No 1781/2006 and Directive (EU) 2015/849 of the European Parliament and of the Council of 20 May 2015 on the prevention of the use of the financial system for the purposes of money laundering or terrorist financing.

§4.07 ERASURE OF DATA FROM BACKUP COPIES

The storage limitation principle also applies to processing of data in backup copies. Once a data controller loses the legal basis for processing data, for example because of an objection of the data subject, the controller is obliged to erase data including the backup copies. This is because the data stored therein are an element of the personal data filing system and the backup copies are part of the IT system.[29]

In my view, the introduction of the risk-based approach under the GDPR allows a less stringent interpretation of the applicability of the storage limitation principle to backup copies. Specifically, I believe that data need not be erased from backup copies as soon as they are erased from the main system. The risk-based approach consists essentially of taking action to safeguard the data under processing, in line with the priorities and timeframe resulting from the findings of the risk analysis. A risk-based assessment would, in my opinion, show that the increase in data security resulting from a stringent application of the storage limitation principle to backup copies is disproportionate to the costs of the obligation to erase data from backup copies immediately, irrespective of the circumstances. The risk for the data subject's rights resulting from restoring data lost from the main system is negligible and affects a minor proportion of data subjects. Conversely, the financial, organisational and technological costs of erasing data from backup copies immediately after their erasure from the main system are bound to be substantial for an organisation processing data on a large scale.

It should also be taken into account whether the process of monitoring and erasing data stored in backup copies is reasonably within the controller's technical capacities, for instance, where the erasure is only possible by destroying the backup copy carriers or by retrieving the content of the copy in an IT system, modifying it and making a new copy.

Moreover, a backup copy may only serve its purpose if its integrity is maintained; erasing individual records may preclude this. The person exercising his/her right to the erasure of data is not the only data subject requiring protection. The integrity of backup copies safeguards the security of processing the data of all persons whose data are in the system; the relative weight of these potentially conflicting rights must be taken into account. In addition, the storage of data in backup copies may be necessary to meet the data controller's legitimate interest or legal obligation, e.g. to enable it to analyse the causes of personal data breaches and to notify those breaches to the supervisory authority. According to statistics, the average time lag between the occurrence of an incident and its detection is 86 days.[30]

I will argue that the risk-based approach permits the controller to temporarily maintain, in backup copies, data that have been removed from the main system. Standard backup copying procedures, anyway, mean that old data will be erased in a reasonable time by being overwritten by new data.

---

29. Polish Supreme Administrative Court judgment of 3 July 2009, I OSK 633/08.
30. 2015 Trustwave Global Security Report, https://www2.trustwave.com/rs/815-RFM-693/images/2015_TrustwaveGlobalSecurityReport.pdf, pp. 23-26.

CHAPTER 5

Legal Bases for the Processing of Personal Data

§5.01 GENERAL REMARKS

The processing of ordinary personal data is lawful when at least one of the six equivalent substantive conditions (five for public authorities in the performance of their tasks) listed in Article 6 of the GDPR is met by the data controller. Therefore, the precondition for the lawfulness of the processing (lawfulness principle of Article 5(1)(a) of the GDPR) is for the data controller to demonstrate having met at least one of these conditions as a legal basis for the processing of data. This means that, for instance, the mere fact that the data were obtained from a publicly available source is not sufficient to meet the condition of lawful data processing.

The conditions listed in Article 6 of the GDPR are equivalent: the processing of data is lawful if any of these conditions is met. Demonstrating compliance with one of them is therefore sufficient. However, data processing by a controller may be based (and in practice often is) on more than one of these conditions simultaneously. This may be relevant when one of them is no longer met but the fulfilment of another still makes the data processing lawful. Still, the impact of any such change on the purpose of the processing and the permissible scope of data processed should be considered, in line with the data minimisation principle formulated in Article 5(1)(c) of the GDPR.

A legal basis for data processing must be demonstrated by each data controller collecting and subsequently processing data or making them available to another controller, as well as by the controller to which data have been made available. The lawfulness and fairness principle (Article 5(1)(a) of the GDPR) prohibits any processing of data coming from illegal sources or unlawfully collected, which is particularly relevant where the data source is not the data subject.

The substantive grounds provided for in Article 6 of the GDPR constitute a legal basis for the processing of ordinary data (as distinguished from special categories of personal data, as discussed below, i.e. sensitive data listed in Article 9 of the GDPR and personal data relating to criminal convictions and offences, referred to in Article 10 of the GDPR). This is a positive formulation: the processing of ordinary data is lawful in the circumstances described in Article 6 of the GDPR. One of those circumstances is the existence of legitimate interests pursued by the controller or by a third party. The scope of legitimate interests is open-ended and defined by the controller. This means that the processing of ordinary data is generally allowed (since a provision specifying the exception of a rule must be formulated and interpreted strictly).

In contrast, the rules applicable to sensitive data and personal data relating to criminal convictions and offences are far more stringent given the particular relevance of these data for the right to privacy. The conditions for the lawful processing of sensitive data are reversed in relation to those applicable to ordinary data. The processing of sensitive data is generally prohibited and this prohibition does not apply where one of the conditions listed in Article 9(2) of the GDPR is met. This is, therefore, a negative formulation: the conditions for the lawful processing of sensitive data are formulated as exceptions from the general prohibition. Unlike for ordinary data, the legitimate interest of the data controller is not one of these exceptions, i.e. it is not a sufficient justification for the processing of sensitive data.

The new rule formulated in the GDPR (Article 6(4)) allows data to be processed for a purpose different from the initial purpose, even without the consent of the data subject and without another purpose being specified in EU or Member State law; still, the data may not be processed for a purpose which is incompatible with the initial purposes. Further processing of data for purposes *different* from the initial purpose should be distinguished from the processing of data for purposes *incompatible* with those originally specified. This is discussed in more detail in Chapter 4 in relation to the purpose limitation principle.

§5.02 PROCESSING OF DATA UNDER CONSENT OF THE DATA SUBJECT

[A] Consent of the Data Subject

The first type of circumstance of lawful data processing is consent given by the data subject (Article 6(1)(a) of the GDPR). Consent to data processing is an unambiguous indication of the data subject's wishes, expressed by a statement or by a clear affirmative action, signifying the data subject's agreement to the processing of personal data relating to him/her (Article 4(11) of the GDPR).

The content of consent to data processing, as a declaration of will, is subject to interpretation under civil law rules. Unambiguous consent may be given expressly, through an oral or written statement or, for example, selection of an option in an online form, or may be inferred from the circumstances.

The definition of consent formulated in the GDPR requires consent to be unambiguous. This includes any clear action sufficiently indicative of the data subject's intention to express consent. This requires that the circumstances in which the data subject is expressing this intention be taken into account, as well as the ways of communication used habitually in the given sector and the behaviours unambiguously indicative of consent.

An employer whose corporate structure includes several branches and which wants to put photos of its staff on a corporate intranet database in order to streamline cooperation of staff between branches may send a message to internal email addresses, encouraging staff to send their photos. If an employee uploads his/her own photo to the database and there is no doubt as to his/her voluntary action, this is equivalent to valid consent.

Consent to data processing is not unambiguous where the declaration of consent is added to another obligation, e.g. relating to the use of a service, which does not include information on the purpose and scope of data processing. The condition of unambiguous consent is also not met when the clause of consent refers to information published in the data controller's branches, advertisements, or general contractual terms and conditions or policy statements. This implies too that data may not be lawfully processed where the data subject merely did not object after being informed by the controller of its intention to process data. Furthermore, even if the data subject has accepted an offer, this is not equivalent to consent to data processing if the offer does not indicate that the data subject has been informed that acceptance of the offer means giving consent to processing of data for a specified purpose. Also, if the data subject's consent does not relate expressly to the intended transfer of data to third countries but only to general contractual terms or regulations where the transfer of data is indicated as a possible aspect of data processing, this does not meet the condition that the consent be specific or unambiguous. The fact that data processing is defined broadly and also includes making data available does not mean that consent to processing allows data to be made available to another controller or to be transferred to third countries. A transfer of data to third countries exceeds the scope of processing that a data subject may expect as part of the services provided to him/her or the execution of other contracts. These aspects of data processing require specific consent.

Neither can the requirement of unambiguous consent be met by using a clause formulated in obscure language or using jargon. This is implied by the unambiguity requirement, but an intelligible and easily accessible form and clear and plain language are also required expressly (Article 7(2) of the GDPR). Where the data subject's consent is to be given in the context of a written declaration which also concerns other matters, the request for consent must be presented in a manner which is clearly distinguishable from the other matters. Any part of the data subject's declaration which does not comply with this rule is not binding (Article 7(2) of the GDPR).

The rules on consent are often breached when different and unrelated purposes of data processing are put together in one clause, which prevents the data subject from distinguishing the purposes which are necessary from those which merely serve the controller's interest. It is also frequent but unacceptable to formulate clauses in a way which implies that consent is automatic and inevitable. Different purposes of data processing require separate consents and should not be put together in a way preventing the data subject from making a selection between them. This does not mean that consent is required for each and every purpose of data processing: for many of the purposes, the processing is based not on consent but, for example, on a legal obligation or the execution of a contract.

In Section 3.2 of its opinion no. WP 90 of 27 February 2004 concerning the interpretation of Article 13 of Directive 2002/58/EC of the European Parliament and of the Council of 12 July 2002 concerning the processing of personal data and the protection of privacy in the electronic communications sector (Directive on privacy and electronic communications), the Article 29 Working Party points out that if a data controller uses pre-ticked boxes on its website to obtain a data subject's consent online, this consent is not a specific indication and thus cannot serve as a basis for a transfer of data.

The controller should only request the data subject's consent to the processing of data for a specified purpose if the consent is to be the only legal basis of the processing. It should not be suggested to the data subject that he/she has the right to refuse consent and thus to prevent the processing of data where in fact the data controller is legally required or authorised to process the data or the processing is necessary for the performance of a contract, i.e. the data is processed on a different legal basis, irrespective of the data subject's consent. Therefore, where consent is sought, the data subject should have a genuine rather than an illusory possibility of a refusal.

[B] Conditions for Valid Consent

The definition of consent in the GDPR and civil law principles require that consent (in addition to being unambiguous, as discussed above) be freely given, specific and informed.[1] These conditions of consent as a valid basis of data processing imply the following:

(a) Freely given consent: the data subject must be free to decide. He/she must not be subject to pressure or compulsion, whether resulting from the circumstances, direct, social, financial, psychological, or other. The data subject must not risk any adverse consequences of refusing consent (recital 42 of the preamble to the GDPR).[2]
Consent cannot be invoked as a legal basis for data processing where there is a significant imbalance between the position of the data subject and the controller, justifying doubt as to whether the consent is indeed freely given. This assessment must, however, be on a case-by-case basis and depend on the circumstances. Even an employment relation cannot be seen as necessarily precluding the freedom of consent, since the consent of an employee is

1. The conditions of valid consent have been defined by the Article 29 Working Party in its Guidelines on Consent under Regulation 2016/679 of 28 November 2017, last revised and adopted on 10 April 2018, WP 259 rev.01, point 3, pp. 5 et seq.
2. Article 29 Working Party, Opinion 15/2011 of 13 July 2011 on the definition of consent, WP 187, p. 12.

included as a possible basis for data processing in recital 155 of the preamble to the GDPR.[3]

The need for consent to be freely given was also referred to, in the context of employers processing their employees' biometric data, by the Article 29 Working Party in the Working document on biometrics of 1 August 2003.[4] The Working Party stated that the data subject's consent may serve as a basis for processing biometric data only if the data subject had full freedom of expressing consent and was not threatened with any consequences in the event of refusal.

The requirement for consent to be freely given to be valid means that the data subject must not risk any adverse consequences of refusing consent. However, adverse consequences must not be understood to include loss of benefits, such as those offered in standard commercial relations, for example when a retailer gives a discount to a customer in exchange for consent to processing of his/her data for direct marketing.

On the other hand, it is unacceptable to make the performance of a contract (including the provision of a service) conditional on obtaining consent to processing data for direct marketing, as processing data for direct marketing is not necessary for the performance of the contract (Article 7(4) of the GDPR).

Whenever consent is requested from a data subject (a customer), he/she has the right to refuse consent. The technique of developing forms and consent clauses must allow for the requirement to include the refusal option alongside the consent option.

One way of ensuring this is including two boxes, 'consent' and 'refusal', in the online or paper form. This condition is also met if the box relating to statements necessary for the conclusion of the contract (e.g. acceptance of the sale policy) is marked with an asterisk, but expressing consent to direct marketing is separate and voluntary. Where a default printed form to be signed by the customer has the consent boxes pre-ticked, this constitutes a breach of the consent rules. Consent may also be expressed by selection of technical settings in information society services.

(b) Specific consent: another condition of consent as a valid basis of data processing is its specificity. The purpose of data processing to which the consent relates must be indicated clearly, in a way making it correctly understandable by an average customer in specific circumstances typical of the given sector.

Any blank consent is void, as consent must not relate to an unspecified scope of data and purpose of processing.

3. An interpretation shared by the Article 29 Working Party in its Opinion 8/2001 of 13 September 2001 on the processing of personal data in the employment context.
4. Working document on biometrics, 1 August 2003, WP 80, http://ec.europa.eu/justice/policies/privacy/docs/wpdocs/2003/wp80_en.pdf.

It is acceptable to restrict consent by relating it only to selected and specific personal data, processing purposes, processing operations, period or territory, or making consent contingent on meeting a condition. However, in the practical circumstances of most organisations which process many categories of data for different purposes, it is not technically practicable to make such distinctions; standard clauses of consent for data processing must be used (but only for the processing of data which is not based on other legal grounds, such as the exercise of a legal provision).

It should also be verified whether the circumstances of the processing consented to by the data subject changed after the consent was granted. If data are processed under consent, whenever the purpose of the processing changes, the controller must obtain the data subject's consent in relation to the changed circumstances.

(c) Informed consent

For consent to be valid, the data subject must be aware of all the aspects of the planned processing, i.e. the information obligations under Article 13 or 14 of the GDPR must have been duly met.

The key aspects of data processing which should be assessed by the data subject and are liable to influence his/her decision to give or refuse consent include: the data controller's identity, the purposes of processing of personal data, the data recipients, any intention to transfer data to third countries and the level of data protection subsequent to the transfer, the envisaged data storage period, the consequences of data processing for the data subject, and the potential consequences of refusing consent.

Where a data subject gives consent to the processing of data in the conditions of a material error, having received misleading or incomplete information from the controller as part of the controller's information obligations, in particular where the information relates to the purpose and scope of the planned data processing, the data subject may avoid the legal effects of consent expressed as a result of this material error.

[C] Validity of Consent Obtained Prior to the GDPR Application Date

One issue which is especially relevant to the entry of the GDPR into practical application is the validity of consent obtained before 25 May 2018. The GDPR contains no transitory provisions. Any conditions of the validity of consent given prior to the GDPR application date are to be found in recital 171 of the preamble to the GDPR. As stated therein, where the processing is based on the data subject's consent, it need not be reobtained provided that 'it is in line with the conditions laid down in the GDPR'. This has been confirmed by the Article 29 Working Party in its Guidelines on Consent under Regulation 2016/679 of 28 November 2017, last revised and adopted on 10 April 2018.[5]

5. Article 29 Working Party document no. WP 259 rev.01, point 8, pp. 30 et seq.

According to the GDPR, consent is valid provided that it is a freely given, specific, informed and unambiguous indication of the data subject's wishes, whether through a statement or through a clear affirmative action.

These conditions are not newly introduced by the GDPR: they had already been laid down in Directive 95/46/EC, national Member State laws implementing it and generally applicable civil law principles. Therefore, it may be assumed (although individual clauses must be assessed on a case-by-case basis) that where consent obtained by a data controller before 25 May 2018 complied with the conditions applicable at the time it was given, then it also complies with the conditions formulated by the GDPR and, as such, remains valid as the processing basis.

Admittedly, whether consent was informed depends on the scope of information relating to data processing that was provided to the data subject – and the scope of data required to be provided has been largely expanded by Articles 13 and 14 of the GDPR (e.g. information on the revocability of consent and on the data retention periods was added). However, whether the information obligation has been met must be assessed against the requirements applicable on the date when the information was provided. The expanded information as required by the GDPR (e.g. on the revocability of consent) may be provided gradually as part of communication directed to the data subject; a mechanism allowing him/her to revoke consent must also be provided, e.g. through a website.

[D] Form of Expressing Consent

The GDPR provisions relating to consent do not require a written form or any other specific form of expressing consent. There is only a proviso in Article 7(1) that where processing is based on consent, the controller must be able to demonstrate that the data subject has expressed consent. This means that consent may be expressed in any clear form, using any tool or carrier enabling the controller to demonstrate that it has indeed obtained consent. It may therefore be obtained through the customer's signature on a paper form, an online form with tick boxes, an email message, a recorded telephone conversation or answering 'yes' to a clear oral request. The Article 29 Working Party, in its Guidelines on Consent under Regulation 2016/679 of 28 November 2017, last revised and adopted on 10 April 2018,[6] also allows for the expression of consent by making a gesture on the touchscreen of a mobile device or moving the device itself in a way that clearly is not coincidental (e.g. swiping on a screen, turning the device clockwise or in a figure 8 motion, which must then be repeated to confirm) and the information provided to the user indicates clearly that the specified gesture expresses consent to data being used for the specified purpose.

6. Article 29 Working Party document no. WP 259 rev.01, section 3.4.. Unambiguous indication of wishes, p. 17, example 15, http://ec.europa.eu/newsroom/article29/item-detail.cfm?item_id=623051,.

[E] Withdrawing Consent

The data subject has the right to withdraw his/her consent to data processing at any time (Article 7(3) of the GDPR). The withdrawal of consent does not affect the lawfulness of processing based on consent before its withdrawal. Consent ceases to serve as the basis of data processing only upon its withdrawal (*ex nunc* effect).

A customer gave his/her consent to a retailer to send him/her promotional newsletters via email in exchange for providing him/her with discount coupons. If the customer then withdraws his/her consent, this does not affect the lawfulness of data processing under the consent prior to its withdrawal. Neither will the customer be required to reimburse the discounts already obtained. The retailer must, however, stop sending any further promotional newsletters to this customer. The withdrawal of consent must not cause the customer to be charged with any additional payments; otherwise consent would not be freely given. On the other hand, I believe that the loss of discounts, which were given by the retailer to the customer in exchange for the right to direct marketing, is justified and does not compromise the voluntary nature of the consent.

Withdrawal of consent does not automatically mean that there is no basis for further processing of data. This occurs only if consent was the sole basis for the processing. Where there have been different grounds for processing of data, such as the legal requirement to archive data under accountancy, tax, or anti-money laundering laws, the withdrawal of consent does not affect those other grounds. Similarly, where the processing serves the purpose of performing a binding contract between the controller and the data subject, the latter's withdrawal of consent and his/her demand to erase the data would be virtually equivalent to terminating the contract. The admissibility thereof would have to be verified under laws governing contractual obligations, rather than data protection laws. Thus, while the withdrawal of consent makes it unlawful to continue any processing of data which was previously carried out under consent (such as electronic marketing), the controller is still authorised, or obliged, to process data under a legal provision or for the performance of a contract.

The data subject's right to withdraw consent to processing of data was not clearly formulated in Directive 95/46/EC before being laid down expressly in the GDPR. However, while this deficiency was pointed out, it did not lead to conflicting interpretations; the data subject's right to withdraw consent was never questioned.[7]

It must be as easy to withdraw as to give consent. The practice of creating artificial unjustified obstacles to data subjects withdrawing consent or objecting to data processing, such as accepting such statements only on the controller's forms or in its branches, is unacceptable (still, the data subject must be identified). The GDPR requires the data subject to be informed, prior to giving consent, of his/her right to withdraw consent at any time, without affecting the lawfulness of processing based on consent before its withdrawal (Article 7(3), Article 13(2)(c), and Article 14(2)(d)).

7. M. Krzysztofek, 'Zmiana przepisów o zgodzie na przetwarzanie danych osobowych', PPH 2011, no. 4, p. 57.

The data subject's right to withdraw consent makes it risky to resort to consent as the basis for a system of data processing, for example systematic transfers of data within corporate groups using common global databases. Where the data controller has no other legal grounds for the processing of data, such as a legal provision, the controller's processing system may be rendered inoperable even if only one data subject whose personal data are processed withdraws his/her consent. There is also a risk of the consent validity being challenged for other reasons indicated in this chapter: the consent not being freely given or the data subject not being aware of all the aspects of the planned processing.

[F] A Child's Consent for the Provision of Information Society Services

Children are subject to a higher level of personal data protection, as they may be less aware of the risks, consequences and safeguards concerned and their rights in relation to the processing of personal data. Such specific protection applies in particular to the use of children's personal data for the purposes of marketing or creating personality or user profiles or providing services offered directly to a child (recital 38 of the preamble to the GDPR).

For this reason, where information society services are offered directly to a child under the data subject's consent, it is legally permissible to process the data of children aged at least 16 based directly on their consent. For children below the age of 16, such processing is only lawful if consent is given or authorised by the holder of parental responsibility over the child, and only within the scope of consent (Member States may provide by law for a lower age for those purposes, but not below 13 years). The age of a child defined in the national law of a Member State shall correspond to the age of limited legal capacity according to the national civil law. This correspondence is important since Article 8 of the GDPR does not relate to declaring the intention to conclude a contract on information society services, but a unilateral statement of consent for the processing of personal data, e.g. for marketing purposes.

Information society services (Article 4(25) of the GDPR) are all services normally provided 'for remuneration, at a distance, by electronic means and at the individual request of a recipient of services'.[8] This includes numerous and rapidly growing categories of services such as online financial services (online banking, online insurance), sale of other services, e.g. tourist services, online retailing, e.g. sale of books, music, electronic appliances, clothing or cosmetics in online shops, online news subscription, sale of mobile applications. Annex I to Directive (EU) 2015/1535 lays down an indicative list of services which are not covered by this term because they are either not provided 'at a distance' (e.g. consultation of an electronic catalogue in a shop with the customer on site), or not provided 'by electronic means' (e.g. automatic cash or ticket dispensing machines), or not provided 'at the individual request of a recipient

8. Services defined in Article 1(1)(b) of Directive (EU) 2015/1535 of the European Parliament and of the Council of 9 September 2015 laying down a procedure for the provision of information in the field of technical regulations and of rules on Information Society services (OJ EU L 241, 17.9.2015, p. 1).

of services' but transmitted for reception by an unlimited number of individual receivers (e.g. television broadcasting services).

The GDPR does not lay down precise criteria to ascertain whether an information society service is offered to a child directly. One indication may be the content of the service, e.g. the type of films or games being offered, clearly indicating children as the intended target group, despite not excluding access by adults. This criterion might be misleading, though, as children might, in line with changing trends, consider themselves to be the target of content which adults find unsuitable for them. On the other hand, certain services clearly unintended for children and explicitly prohibiting children's access, e.g. a portal sharing recipes for alcoholic beverages, might not include any technical access restrictions and only rely on the user's declaration of age.

Whether the holder of parental responsibility over the child has expressed or authorised consent to the processing of data of a child below a specified age limit is to be verified by the controller. Given the nature of information society services, consent for their provision is given online; whether consent was indeed given by the authorised person is often probable rather than proven. Article 8(2) of the GDPR therefore requires reasonable efforts to be made to verify this, taking into consideration the available technology. The same requirement is also formulated in the US Children's Online Privacy Protection Rule ('COPPA').[9]

Practical arrangements developed by controllers must result from the available IT tools (which are bound to evolve) and the specific nature of each controller. Some solutions used include: blocking the account on a social networking service until age is confirmed by sending a scan of an ID card or credit card details and a confirmation of the parent's consent in an email message originating from the parent's email address. I find the first solution to be a breach of the data minimisation principle. It also carries an additional risk: if these scans are lost, unauthorised persons might find out the user's password or steal his/her identity. On the other hand, the confirmation of the identity of the child's parent or legal guardian through his/her email address, i.e. a confirmation that the consent has not been given by the child him/herself, is recommended in the US Children's Online Privacy Protection Rule ('COPPA').[10] Age verification technologies are likely to progress in the future. One solution now being tested is inferring age from a self-portrait photograph sent to the controller.

However, any practical solution of this kind only increases the probability (rather than being an absolute proof) that the consent was given by the parent or guardian and not by the child him/herself. The requirement to provide an email address for the data

9. §6501. Definitions: (9) 'The term 'verifiable parental consent' means any reasonable effort (taking into consideration available technology)…', https://www.ftc.gov/enforcement/rules/rulemaking-regulatory-reform-proceedings/childrens-online-privacy-protection-rule.

10. §6501. Definitions: '(12) Online contact information: The term 'online contact information' means an e-mail address or another substantially similar identifier that permits direct contact with a person online.'

controller to send the registration confirmation link constitutes reasonable diligence on the controller's part, but does not ensure that the email address was not created by the child him/herself for this purpose.

There are paradoxical consequences of the fact that a child may directly enter into a contract which does not relate to an information society service, but the child's parent's consent must be obtained for the child to be offered information society services. For instance, a child may decide to purchase a cinema ticket but not to subscribe to the cinema's marketing newsletter. This may seem even more baffling if, for instance, national law allows a 13-year-old to purchase a ticket, but the GDPR requires a 16-year-old to prove his/her parent's consent online. However, while the purchase of a ticket is a one-off occurrence without far-reaching consequences, a child trading their personal data for (potentially illusory) benefits may expose themselves to more serious consequences. Far from wishing to deny this, one must realise that, given the scale of children's online activity, the requirement for the child's parents to express consent every time the child wants to play a game online or join a social networking service might be scarcely enforceable.[11]

The 'right to be forgotten' (Article 17 of the GDPR) is an additional protection of a child who might have made his/her data (e.g. photos) available without the experience-based awareness of how this might adversely affect his/her life, e.g. career, in the long-term. An essential element of the 'right to be forgotten' is the right to demand that personal data put on the Internet by the data subject or third parties be erased therefrom. The right to erasure of data on the Internet is crucial for the protection of data, considering the effects of the ease with which everyone can access and share data on the Internet today. The Court of Justice of the EU focused on this particular aspect in its judgment of 13 May 2014 in Case C-131/12, a crucial judgment for the right in question, discussed in detail later. This judgment, predating the GDPR by two years, formulated the 'right to be forgotten' by inferring it directly from Articles 7 and 8 of the Charter of Fundamental Rights and from the right to erasure of data, stipulated in Directive 95/46/EC. However, the right to erasure should also be seen in relation to data processing in all other forms and environments.

The requirement to obtain consent or authorisation of consent from the holder of parental responsibility over a child to the provision of information society services directly to the child does not affect the general contract law provisions of the EU Member States regulating validity, conclusion, or effects of contracts involving children (who, depending on the age limit defined in national laws, might have no legal capacity or restricted legal capacity).[12]

11. I wish to thank my sons Michał and Mariusz for their consultation on methods of age and consent verification for the purposes of information society services.
12. Article 29 Working Party, Opinion 2/2009 on the protection of children's personal data (General Guidelines and the special case of schools), 11 February 2009, WP 160, http://ec.europa.eu/justice/article-29/documentation/opinion-recommendation/files/2009/wp160_en.pdf.

§5.03 PROCESSING OF DATA FOR THE CONCLUSION OR PERFORMANCE OF A CONTRACT

Another circumstance permitting the processing of data is the processing necessary for the performance of a contract entered into with the data subject or for taking steps at the request of the data subject prior to entering into a contract.

It is incorrect to seek the consent of the data subject (e.g. a customer or an employee) to processing of his/her data for the purpose of performing a contract, thereby suggesting that the data subject has the right to refuse consent, where in fact the data processing is a necessary condition for performing the contract binding upon the controller and must take place irrespective of the data subject's consent. If the request to conclude a contract, or the performance of the contract, was to be made contingent on the customer's consent to the processing of his or her data (rather than merely on his/her expression of intention concerning the contract itself), this would defy logic: no contract can be performed for the benefit of an anonymous customer, employee or an anonymous party in general; payments cannot be made to an anonymous recipient, etc. Resorting to the data subject's consent would also be incorrect because the data subject has the right to withdraw consent at any time and unconditionally. Withdrawal of consent and demanding erasure of data would be virtually equivalent to terminating the contract. The admissibility thereof would have to be verified under laws governing contractual obligations, rather than data protection laws.

Processing of data for the performance of a contract by the controller is a typical situation in commerce. It is the basis to be invoked, for instance, when a tour operator provides the list of the tour participants to its local subcontractor organising an optional trip, or where an online newspaper provides the list of its subscribers to an online bookshop which offers them discounted e-books. It is also the basis for processing personal data of a company's staff, e.g. when the employer provides its business partner with the data of persons authorised to represent it for performing a contract (they might be people authorised to access a transaction system or to make decisions on accepting a portion of work). In both these areas, i.e. service contracts and employment contracts, data are also processed under statutory obligations, such as issuing an invoice to a customer or keeping employees' files, and archiving data for tax and social security purposes.

On the other hand, the Article 29 Working Party has criticised the commonplace practice whereby multinational corporate groups process employees' data in the group's joint IT system provided by the parent company, claiming that this is necessary for the performance of the employment contract. Such systems are often used for centralised handling of information on employees' absences or for periodic evaluation of employees. According to the Working Party, presenting such transfers as necessary for the performance of an employment contract between the data subject and the controller is a misinterpretation. The Working Party has argued that transferring data to a joint IT system accessible to the parent company and, in many cases, also other companies of the group is not directly and objectively linked to performance of an employment contract. On the other hand, a transfer of data by a tour operator to hotels and other commercial partners organising the tourists' stay is one which can be justified; so is the transfer of payment information to a third country for the execution of a bank transfer. However, such a transfer may not go beyond what is necessary; it may not, for instance, include data to facilitate direct marketing in the future.

Crucially, the initiative to enter into a contract must be on the data subject's part; the precontractual measures invoked as the justification of the data processing may not be taken on the controller's initiative. The processing of data is also permissible as part of actions taken at the clear request of the data subject prior to the conclusion of a contract; my opinion is that this criterion is met by an unambiguously favourable reaction (one which is clearly equivalent to a declaration of will) by a potential customer in response to an offer made under legal direct marketing activities.

This reference to the data subject's initiative precludes, for example, the practice of issuing bank cards, and opening accounts connected with such cards, for potential holders selected by the bank from among its customers according to criteria adopted by the bank, where the issuance of the card and opening of the account is not at the customer's request, but on the initiative of the bank, as part of its marketing and sale activities. This goes beyond marketing: the customer is not merely targeted with the offer of issuing a bank card for him/her – the card has already been issued and the corresponding bank account has already been opened. None of these should take place before the contract is concluded. Actions taken by the controller in order to enter into a contract may not include any marketing actions, and much less aggressive marketing, such as in this case. Such marketing efforts may be made under the data subject's consent or for the purposes of the legitimate interest pursued by the controller (Article 6(1)(a) or (f) of the GDPR). On the other hand, invoking an alleged intention to conclude a contract in the absence of the data subject's initiative, i.e. in non-compliance with Article 6(1)(b) of the GDPR, is not a permissible way to circumvent the admissibility conditions of electronic marketing.

Data may be processed for the purpose of entering into or performance of a contract only when the data are *necessary* for that purpose. This term may not be subject to a broad interpretation whereby 'necessary' could be considered synonymous with, for example, 'useful', 'justified', 'facilitating' or 'economical'. The processing necessary should be defined to mean that the purpose (i.e. the performance of a contract or of actions leading to the conclusion of a contract) cannot possibly be achieved without the processing of personal data. The Article 29 Working Party stressed, on page 13 of its working document no. WP 114 of 25 November 2005, that the ''necessity test' here requires a close and substantial connection between the data subject and the purposes of the contract'.

The data minimisation (data proportionality) principle is also applicable: not only must the data processing itself be necessary but the scope of data processed must be adequate to the purpose of the processing. The controller must specify the scope of data without which the scope of the processing cannot be achieved.

One example of invoking, wrongly, the necessity of data processing for the performance of a contract is the practice of multinational corporations which outsource their corporate payroll management, and consequently provide the data of their employees to such outside service providers. Indeed, payroll management is, by law, the data controller's responsibility; if the controller outsources it in order to optimise its administration costs, this is in the interest of the controller rather than the data subject.

The provision discussed here refers directly only to the personal data of a party to the contract or a person which has requested the conclusion of such a contract. It does not refer to third parties who are not party to the contract or whose data are being provided by a person requesting the conclusion of the contract. Such third parties may include spouses or guarantors. I believe, however, that Article 6(1)(b) of the GDPR, despite this restriction implied by its literal wording, may be interpreted to allow the data of such third parties to be processed where this is necessary for the conclusion or performance of a contract. The Provincial Administrative Court in Warsaw argued to the same effect in its judgment of 3 October 2006 (Case II SA/Wa 871/06).

§5.04 PROCESSING OF DATA FOR COMPLIANCE WITH A LEGAL OBLIGATION

Data may also be lawfully processed where this is necessary for compliance with a legal obligation to which the controller is subject (Article 6(1)(c) of the GDPR). The controller's obligation justifying the processing of data must result directly from applicable law but also, importantly, the processing of data in the specified scope must be necessary to comply with that obligation.

Legal obligation does not necessarily need to be provided for in a legislative act adopted by a parliament (recital 41 of the preamble to the GDPR). A 'legal obligation' should be considered as such also where it is provided for by regulations of a lower status, but such regulations may only serve as a basis for the processing of personal data if they have been issued under a statutory delegation and do not exceed its scope. Regulations issued to implement a statutory law may, in particular, lay down detailed scopes of personal data which must necessarily be processed to comply with a statutory obligation, such as keeping medical records or employees' files, the recovery of liabilities from a bank account or other property, or publishing invitations to tender. Such a legal obligation may be defined e.g. by the model form to be filled in with the data which must be collected. A legal basis for data processing may also be provided for in an international agreement ratified by a parliament, where this is allowed for in the constitution of the Member State in question.

The requirement to specify a legal basis means that a general reference to a legal act regulating the controller's business, without invoking a specific provision imposing the given legal obligation on the controller, is insufficient. This does not mean, though, that every single operation of personal data processing must refer to a separate legal basis. A legal regulation may serve as 'a basis for several processing operations based on a legal obligation to which the controller is subject' (recital 45 of the preamble to the GDPR).

The provision requiring the processing to be 'necessary for compliance with a legal obligation' must be interpreted strictly and not in a broadening manner: the processing of data must not be merely *useful* for the purpose. This must include an assessment against the data minimisation principle, i.e. whether the legal obligation can be met without the processing of data in the specified scope or whether the legal provision introducing the obligation specifies a limited scope of categories of personal data. For example, if a law regulating the auction of property requires the bailiff to make a public announcement of the location and time of the auction and the type and estimated value of items to be auctioned, but not personal data of the debtor, then including data identifying the debtor in such an announcement would lack a legal basis.

The basis of processing data, referred to in Article 6(1)(c) of the GDPR, is the processing being necessary for compliance with a legal *obligation* to which the controller is subject. There is no reference to exercise of a legal *right* to which the controller is entitled. A similar limitation was also present, prior to the adoption of the GDPR, in Directive 95/46/EC (Article 7(c)) and has been maintained in some national Member State laws, such as the British Data Protection Act 2018[13] (Schedule 9.3: 'The processing is necessary for compliance with a legal obligation to which the data controller is subject, other than an obligation imposed by contract.'). On the other hand, some pre-GDPR national laws of Member States were more liberal, allowing data to be processed not only to comply with a legal obligation but also to exercise a legal right of the controller. One example was the Polish Personal Data Protection Act (Article 23(1)(3).

Indeed, legal provisions, as well as imposing obligations (such as to collect a specified scope of legal data and other information and to notify any suspicions resulting from these data for the prevention of money laundering, or to archive certain categories of personal data for tax or pension purposes), also introduce rights whose exercise requires the processing of personal data. Examples include an employer's right to use CCTV for security purposes or a bank's right to use automated data processing, including profiling, to assess a customer's creditworthiness.

A natural solution to this problem would be to revise all national laws regulating data processing in such a way as to provide for legal bases expressly allowing data to be processed for specified purposes. Importantly, though, Article 6(1)(c) of the GDPR requires that processing be necessary for compliance with a legal obligation, rather than for the exercise of a legal right to which the controller is entitled. The use of CCTV by an employer for security purposes or profiling by a bank for creditworthiness assessment are their respective rights as controllers; there is no way data processing can be seen as an obligation in these contexts. This, however, does not mean that the use of CCTV is prohibited, either. A solution which I would suggest is to assume that, for instance, the use of CCTV for security is based on the controller's legitimate interest, and the processing of data, for example in CCTV, is based on a legal provision allowing such a legitimate interest to be pursued. For instance, the basis for the use of CCTV in a workplace is the legal provision enabling the controller to pursue its legitimate interest and specifying the conditions thereof.

The circumstances of lawful data processing specified in Article 6(1) of the GDPR are equivalent and alternative; however, if the lawfulness of data processing results

13. http://www.legislation.gov.uk/ukpga/2018/12/pdfs/ukpga_20180012_en.pdf.

directly from a legal obligation of the controller, this basis of data processing should be invoked before the others.

§5.05 PROCESSING OF DATA FOR PROTECTION OF VITAL INTERESTS

Data may also be processed if necessary in order to protect the vital interests of the data subject or of another natural person (Article 6(1)(d) of the GDPR).

A 'vital interest' is a critical one, essential for a person's physical integrity, life or health. Only in exceptional circumstances may this include economic interests. An example of vital interests justifying the transfer of data is the monitoring of the spread of an epidemic, or a natural disaster (recital 46 of the preamble to the GDPR).

Unlike in analogous circumstances allowing the processing of sensitive data (Article 9(2)(c) of the GDPR) and transfer of data to a third country (Article 49(1)(f) of the GDPR), invoking the necessity for the protection of vital interests is not made contingent in Article 6(1)(d) on the data subject's physical or legal incapability of giving consent. However, I believe that this condition should be applied in relation to this provision as well. Assuming otherwise would mean that the controller would be free to determine the data subject's vital interests without the data subject's knowledge and against his/her will.

The necessity for the protection of vital interests should be restricted to cases where the data subject cannot give consent (and the processing cannot be manifestly based on another legal basis, cf. recital 46 of the preamble to the GDPR) and the processing of data is necessary, such as when the immediate transfer of medical data, without waiting for consent, is essential for saving a person's life or health or for making a quick diagnosis (document no. WP 114 of the Article 29 Working Party). Circumstances where obtaining the data subject's consent is not possible include loss of consciousness due to an illness or an accident, or the data subject being in an unknown location and beyond reach. However, a decision on processing of data should only be made for the data subject when it may be reasonably assumed that the data subject would make the same decision.

It may also include temporary situations where consent cannot be given in the time when the peril to vital interests may still be avoided. If, however, once these circumstances pass, the data subject is able to give consent, then the protection of vital interests may no longer be invoked as the basis for data processing. Consent should be sought or the processing should cease. As an example of an emergency where it is justified to invoke the need to process personal data to protect the data subject's vital interests, consider a situation where a pharmacist has sold the wrong medication to a patient and is contacting the patient's doctor, asking for the patient's telephone number in order to warn him/her in time. The context of the conversation and the reference to a specified prescription provides assurance that the person asking to be given the patient's number is the pharmacist.

Data may only be processed where this is *necessary*. This means that the processing may not be justified only, for example, by the controller's organisational considerations, but must result from the conclusion that vital interests cannot be effectively protected without the processing of data, e.g. providing them to another controller, despite the impossibility to obtain the data subject's consent. The data minimisation (data proportionality) principle must also be applied: not only must the data processing itself be necessary, but the scope of data processed must be adequate to the purpose of the processing.

Such protection of vital interests may benefit not only the data subject but also other natural persons whose life or health may be in danger due to a lack of information on the data subject. Processing, including transfer, of data in such a situation is not conditional upon the impossibility of obtaining the consent of the data subject. However, information necessary for the protection of vital interests of a third person may relate, for example, to the fact that the data subject is infected with a dangerous contagious disease and might have infected another person. This is information on health, thus belonging to a special category of data, i.e. sensitive data. The basis for processing of such data, when necessary for the protection of vital interests, is Article 9(2)(c) of the GDPR, which covers sensitive data, whereas the analogous Article 6(1)(d) of the GDPR covers ordinary data. However, according to Article 9(2)(c) of the GDPR, providing sensitive information is contingent upon the data subject's physical or legal incapability to give consent. If interpreted literally, this provision would imply that where a doctor is able to make contact with the data subject but this person, either lacking good will or afraid of possible stigmatisation, is unwilling to give consent to warning other people whom he/she might have infected, then those people – whose health or life may depend on an early diagnosis – become hostage to the data subject's right to privacy.

It would be wrong to resolve in this way the conflict between the data subject's right to privacy and a third person's right to protection of health or life. While all circumstances of lawful data processing are equivalent and alternative, the vital interest of another natural person should only be invoked as the legal basis of personal data processing where the processing cannot be manifestly based on another legal basis (recital 46 of the GDPR). In certain cases, such as the example presented here, the processing of data may serve an important public interest as well as the vital interests of a natural person, such as where it is necessary for the monitoring of an epidemic. In such a case, processing, including transfer, of data may be based on Article 9(2)(i) of the GDPR, which allows the processing of data when necessary for reasons of public interest in the area of public health, such as protecting against serious cross-border threats to health.

§5.06 PROCESSING OF DATA IN THE PUBLIC INTEREST

Another basis for lawful processing of personal data is the processing being necessary for the performance of a task carried out in the public interest or in the exercise of official authority vested in the controller.

The public interest (i.e. that held valuable by the society, such as public security and order) should be recognised in the EU or Member State law applicable to the controller (working document no. WP 114 of the Article 29 Working Party). It might be, for example, international data exchange between competition authorities, tax or customs administrations, financial supervisory authorities, or services competent for social security matters or for public health, for example in the case of contact tracing for contagious diseases or in order to reduce and/or eliminate doping in sport (recital 112 of the preamble to the GDPR).

On the other hand, as expressed in Opinion 6/2002 of 24 October 2002 (document no. WP 66)[14] and in document no. 114, the Article 29 Working Party argued that routine and wholesale transfer of personal data is not acceptable where it is justified by a unilateral decision taken by a third country for reasons of its own public interest.

There is no clear division between the scope of applicability of Article 6(1)(e) of the GDPR, i.e. data processing being necessary for the performance of a task carried out in the public interest, and Article 6(1)(c) of the GDPR, i.e. data processing being necessary for compliance with a legal obligation to which the controller is subject. In many cases, the legal obligation binding upon the controller is also a task carried out in the public interest or in the exercise of official authority.

The difference is that, under Article 6(1)(c) of the GDPR, legal regulations are a direct basis of processing of data, whereas Article 6(1)(e) relates to cases where legal regulations do not explicitly allow for processing of data but the processing is necessary for the performance of a task in the public interest.

The 'tasks carried out in the public interest' have been defined in literature as 'actions taken in the 'public interest' using non-authoritative means', vested in the data controller under law.[15] Article 6(1)(e) of the GDPR expands the scope of the task carried out in the public interest to include the exercise of official authority vested in the controller, i.e. the restrictions to 'non-authoritative means' seems to no longer apply. However, recital 45 of the preamble to the GDPR confirms that, where processing is carried out in accordance with a legal obligation to which the controller is subject or where processing is necessary for the performance of a task carried out in the public interest or in the exercise of official authority, the processing should have a basis in Union or Member State law and its purpose should also be indicated in law. I believe it wrong, though, to assume that the processing of data in any form or for any purpose should have a direct basis in a legal provision. The provision discussed here relates to public tasks, which means that CCTV surveillance in a court or a public institution, for example, may be used on the basis of legitimate interest rather than by direct reference to a legal provision (cf. recital 47 of the preamble to the GDPR).

I believe that, for example, anti-money laundering measures taken by banks and other institutions subject to this requirement, although certainly important for the public good, are not a task carried out in the public interest as referred to in Article 6(1)(e) of the GDPR. Banks and other such institutions are bound by requirements specified in anti-money laundering regulations. This means that, under such measures,

14. Opinion 6/2002 on transmission of Passenger Manifest Information and other data from Airlines to the United States, http://ec.europa.eu/justice/article-29/documentation/opinion-recommendation/files/2002/wp66_en.pdf.
15. J. Barta, P. Fajgielski, R. Markiewicz, *Ochrona danych osobowych. Komentarz*, Kraków 2007, p. 509.

data are processed on the basis of being necessary for the performance by the controller of a legal obligation binding upon it. The Provincial Administrative Court in Warsaw argued to the same effect in its judgment of 7 November 2006 (Case II SA/Wa 1289/06), stating that the security of deposits and effective operation of the banking system are not a 'public good' and purposes of this type must be explicitly provided for by law.

The necessity of data processing for the performance of a task carried out in the public interest should only be invoked by controllers operating in the public sector or exercising official authority vested in them. It does not apply to private sector controllers or even to public entities in the scope of their commercial activities, such as holding shares in commercial companies (cf. Polish Supreme Administrative Court judgment of 6 December 2000 in Case I SA/GD 1977/99).

Data may be processed on the basis in question if the processing is *necessary* for the performance of a task carried out in the public interest or in the exercise of official authority. This term may not be subject to a broad interpretation whereby 'necessary' could be considered synonymous with, for example, 'useful', 'justified', 'facilitating' or 'economical'. The processing being necessary should be defined to mean that the purpose cannot possibly be achieved without the processing of the personal data. The data minimisation (data proportionality) principle must also be applied: not only must the data processing itself be necessary but the scope of data processed must be adequate to the purpose of the processing. The controller must specify the scope of data without which the scope of the processing cannot be achieved.

§5.07 PROCESSING OF PERSONAL DATA FOR THE LEGITIMATE INTERESTS OF THE DATA CONTROLLER; MARKETING AND COOKIES

[A] Processing of Personal Data for the Legitimate Interests

Article 6(1)(f) of the GDPR, formulating the legitimate interest clause, allows the data controller (including a controller to whom data may be disclosed, or a third party) to process data, including making them available, where none of the other circumstances listed in Article 6(1) of the GDPR can be invoked as a legal basis for the processing of data. Also in this case, the data subject's consent need not be sought, but the data subject's objection must not be disregarded. On this basis, data may be processed if this is necessary for the purposes of the legitimate interests pursued by the controller or by a third party, except where such interests are overridden by the interests or fundamental rights and freedoms of the data subject which require protection of personal data, in particular where the data subject is a child.

Therefore, the legitimate interest may be invoked as the basis for data processing provided that the following conditions are met: the processing purpose is correctly found to be legitimate, the data processing is necessary for achieving this purpose, and the legitimate interest pursued through the processing of data is demonstrably not subordinate to the interests or fundamental rights and freedoms of the data subject.

The 'legitimate interest' basis does not apply to the processing of data by public authorities in the performance of their tasks (cf. the second sentence of Article 6(1) of the GDPR). Any legal basis for the processing of personal data by public authorities should be specified in a legal provision specifying an obligation of the controller, or the necessity to perform a task carried out in the public interest (Article 6(1)(c) and (e) of the GDPR). This, however, does not mean (as I argued above) that, for example, CCTV surveillance of public areas in a court or a public institution cannot be used on the basis of legitimate interest. This is because the provision discussed here relates to public tasks rather than auxiliary or logistic activities, which include CCTV surveillance.

Ascertaining whether the interests in question are legitimate requires an individualised case-by-case assessment of whether a data subject can reasonably expect at the time and in the context of the collection of the personal data that his/her data may be processed for the specific purpose. The assumption that the data subject may expect the processing of his/her data for the specific purpose may result in particular from the existence of a contractual relation between the data subject and the controller, such as where the data subject is a client or in the service of the controller (recital 47 of the preamble to the GDPR). The processing purpose pursued by the controller or the third party is legitimate where it is within the scope of their business, professional, or statutory activity.

The assessment is also based on the criterion of the type of activity pursued by the controller or recipient. Furthermore, interests may only be considered legitimate if they comply with the law, social conventions and public morals.[16]

Legitimate interests typically include the processing of data for direct marketing and the prevention of fraud detrimental to the controller or its customers (recital 47 of the preamble to the GDPR). Another example could be CCTV surveillance for security purposes.

The list of legitimate purposes is open-ended, but the scope of processing must be *necessary* for the purposes resulting from the legitimate interests, i.e. it must not exceed what is sufficient to achieve the purpose, in line with the data minimisation principle.

Since direct marketing is a legitimate interest, the processing of data for this purpose does not require the consent of the data subject. This does not apply to electronic marketing communication, which is subject to specific rules. Therefore, as long as the controller does not intend to go beyond the processing of data for marketing of its own products or services targeted to its existing customers or persons who have requested an offer from the controller, and the controller is not using electronic means of communication, the controller is not required to seek consent for marketing efforts within these limits.

In practice, however, marketing requires consent since excluding former customers or refraining from the use of email or telephone[17] would render the marketing effort ineffective and costly. Although marketing is the controller's legitimate interest and,

16. J. Barta, P. Fajgielski, R. Markiewicz, *Ochrona danych osobowych. Komentarz*, Kraków 2007, p. 513.
17. Opinion of GIODO (Polish data protection authority) of 15 January 2010, http://www.giodo.gov.pl/332/id_art/3320/j/pl/ (in Polish).

consequently, the processing of data for this purpose does not require consent, it must finally include sending marketing communications, which, in practice, are sent by electronic means and this does require consent.

Although the mere processing of data for marketing purposes and sending marketing materials in the form of paper leaflets to specified persons without their consent is allowed and lawful (as this does not constitute electronic communication), this does not mean that this can be done against such persons' will.

It is possible without the customer's 'active' consent, i.e. his/her statement accepting the sending of marketing materials to him/her. However, the data subject has the right to object to direct marketing, including to profiling for direct marketing (Article 21(2) of the GDPR). This right is unconditional, and the objection does not require a justification. This applies both to objection made upon the collection of personal data by selecting the 'no consent' option on a form containing the 'consent' and 'no consent' options, as well as made in response to marketing mail received, or made in any other form and time. Moreover, when a data subject refuses consent upon request, this should be considered an objection. An objecting customer may no longer be the target of marketing; this is effective immediately upon the objection. The objection must be registered in the IT system to make sure that the requesting data subject is not targeted with direct marketing communications or subject to profiling.

An objection to marketing includes all channels and aspects of marketing, i.e. paper advertisements, such as those distributed through leaflets or printed on the customers' bank account statements,[18] as well as electronic marketing via telephone, text messages and email. It also requires the discontinuation of any activities which are not advertising in the strict sense but constitute direct marketing in a broad sense, such as customer satisfaction surveys, in relation to the data subject in question.

It seems permissible to remind customers who have objected to marketing that they may withdraw their objection. In cases such as the introduction of a new newsletter containing practical advice on using the controller's product, it is not prohibited to inform customers of its periodic publication. However, as a key requirement, such communication must be restricted to such a justified exception. It must not take the form of a marketing action on a scale justifying claims that the controller disregards its customers' objection to marketing. The message should therefore be only a side element of a communication which would anyway be directed to the data subject, e.g. as part of an obligatory periodic statement of transactions.

The scope of direct marketing of the data controller's own products or services falling within the notion of legitimate interest as a basis of data processing also includes marketing relating e.g. to a bank's insurance agency services or distribution of investment fund participation units. While these are not the bank's own products provided for in its statutory documents, and the bank only acts as an external service provider in distributing them, their sale is still a service provided by the bank. On the other hand, although recital 47 of the preamble to the GDPR specifies direct marketing as a legitimate interest, and Article 6(1)(f) of the GDPR also allows data to be processed

18. Opinion of GIODO (Polish data protection authority) of 18 October 2010, http://www.giodo.gov.pl/332/id_art/3779/j/pl/ (in Polish).

for the purposes of legitimate interests pursued by third parties, I will argue that invoking this right as justifying marketing activities for a third party may be a breach of the purpose limitation principle laid down in Article 5(1)(b) of the GDPR. This is because the scope of such marketing activities, serving the business interests of the controller and third parties collaborating with it, could deviate too far from the scope and purposes of data processing which the data subject could expect in the specified context. Indeed, as pointed out in recital 47 of the preamble to the GDPR, it should be assessed 'whether a data subject can reasonably expect at the time and in the context of the collection of the personal data that processing for that purpose may take place'.

Furthermore, the draft ePrivacy Regulation (Article 16(2)) only allows customers' email addresses to be used without the customers' consent for the direct marketing of the provider's own products or services, with an opt-out possible (limitations applicable in this context are presented in this chapter as part of the commentary on electronic marketing in the ePrivacy Regulation).

Data may only be processed for the purposes of the legitimate interest if the interests or fundamental rights and freedoms of the data subject which require protection do not override the legitimate interest of the data controller. The data subject's fundamental rights and freedoms are formulated, in particular, in the Charter of Fundamental Rights of the EU: the freedoms are laid down in Title II (and include, in particular, the right to respect for private and family life and the right to the protection of personal data) and the citizens' rights are laid down in Title V, and in Member States' constitutions.

As also specified in Article 6(1)(f) of the GDPR, the legitimate interest clause may not be invoked for the processing of children's personal data, as their interest and their fundamental rights and freedoms are expressly defined in this article as being superior to the controller's or a third party's interest.

Children's personal data have been covered with particular protection especially with regard to the processing of such data for marketing or for the creation of personality or user profiles. This is because children may be less aware of the risks, consequences and safeguards concerned and their rights in relation to the processing of personal data (recital 38 of the preamble to the GDPR).

In court judgments allowing the transfer of claims under the clause of legitimate interest[19] it has been emphasised that Article 7(f) of Directive 95/46/EC (which corresponds to Article 6(1)(f) of the GDPR) requires the interests of both sides to be weighed on a case-by-case basis and, in principle, allows the processing of data which is necessary for the performance of the controller's legitimate purposes, unless a comparison of the interests of the two sides shows that the fundamental rights and freedoms of an individual prevail over the specific interest of the controller.

The processing of a debtor's personal data by a creditor for the purpose of sending a payment reminder to the debtor is an element of the performance of a contract (cf. Article 6(1)(b) of the GDPR). However, as pointed out by the Article 29 Working

19. Polish Supreme Administrative Court judgment of 6 June 2005 (I OPS 2/05), ONSAiWSA 2006, no. 2, p. 38, *Prokuratura i Prawo* 2005, no. 11, p. 45, *Palestra* 2005, Vol. 11–12, p. 259.

Party,[20] any further action, such as the outsourcing of debt enforcement, may be conducted, depending on the national law, under the legitimate interest clause. Nevertheless, I consider it crucial that debt enforcement would not take place if the debtor had met his/her payment obligation according to the contract, which makes the debt enforcement part of the creditor's activities to make the debtor perform the contract, which meets the criterion of Article 6(1)(b) of the GDPR. This is also because the right to object to the processing of data under the legitimate interest clause may not be invoked as an alternative to an anti-enforcement suit by the debtor.

[B] Electronic Marketing in Directive 2002/58/EC

Marketing itself is the controller's legitimate interest (cf. recital 47 of the preamble to the GDPR) and, therefore, the processing of data for its purposes does not require consent, though an objection must be respected (the controller must allow an opt-out and respect it). However, the processing of data for marketing purposes must finally include sending marketing communications, which, in practice, are sent by electronic means. Electronic marketing is subject to far more stringent rules, laid down in Directive 2002/58/EC of the European Parliament and of the Council of 12 July 2002 concerning the processing of personal data and the protection of privacy in the electronic communications sector (Directive on privacy and electronic communications) (OJ EC L 201, 31.7.2002, p. 37). This Directive is to be replaced with the Regulation on Privacy and Electronic Communications, or the ePrivacy Regulation, according to information on the progress of legislative work, available during the preparation of this book.[21] The Directive regulates electronic forms of marketing, such as email, telephone calls, text messages and automated calling systems, and associated forms, such as cookies.

The Directive prohibits the sending of spam. Under European law, the definition of spam is limited to unsolicited commercial communications or marketing communications (including direct or indirect advertisement of a company's products, services, or image), directed to a specified recipient via electronic communication means, in particular email. Beyond the scope of this definition, spam is a broader term covering all unsolicited electronic communications, in particular emails and text messages, sent without the recipient's consent.

Commercial communications are considered to be solicited if the recipient has given consent to receiving them (Article 13 of Directive 2002/58/EC). According to Article 2(f) of Directive 2002/58/EC, consent by a user or subscriber corresponds to the

20. Opinion 6/2014 on the notion of legitimate interests of the data controller under Article 7 of Directive 95/46/EC, 9 April 2014, WP 217, http://ec.europa.eu/justice/article-29/documentation/opinion-recommendation/files/2014/wp217_en.pdf, p. 61.
21. On 10 January 2017 the European Commission submitted a proposal for a Regulation of the European Parliament and of the Council concerning the respect for private life and the protection of personal data in electronic communications and repealing Directive 2002/58/EC (Regulation on Privacy and Electronic Communications, or the ePrivacy Regulation). Initially the Commission intended the ePrivacy Regulation to become applicable on the same day as the GDPR, i.e. 25 May 2018. The Regulation now appears unlikely to come into effect until 2020 at the earliest.

data subject's consent in Directive 95/46/EC. Therefore, since the GDPR requires Directive 2002/58/EC to be consistent with it, consent for electronic marketing is subject to the rules applicable to consent, laid down in Article 7 of the GDPR. The regulation requires that consent be freely given (unforced) and allows it to be given in any clear form. This may in particular include making one's email address available, as long as it is for this specific purpose. It should therefore be understood that the same applies to a mobile telephone number, where commercial information is to be sent via text messages.

Consent may also be given by accepting an online message appearing on the screen, or in a telephone conversation. The controller must be in a position to demonstrate having obtained consent.

The requirement to obtain consent for electronic marketing communication is sometimes circumvented in practice, in an inept way, by addressing recipients with communications disguised as questions, but in fact containing information on the cost of products or links to websites; thus, such communications are in fact commercial information and constitute intentional advertisement.

Any use, for direct marketing purposes, of automated calling systems (without human intervention) or email or fax (the latter falling out of use) requires the recipient's prior consent (Article 13 of Directive 2002/58/EC).

It is expressly prohibited to conceal, in electronic marketing communications, the sender's identity and contact details for expressing objection.

According to the response from the Information Commissioner's Office (1 September 2018, case reference number PEC0760512) the PECR [the Privacy and Electronic Communications (EC Directive) Regulations 2003 No. 2426 (as amended: 2004 No. 1039, 2011 No. 1208, 2015 No. 355, 2016 No. 524] 'state that if you are sending a marketing email to an individual subscriber, then in almost all circumstances you must have obtained their consent. If you are sending a marketing email to a corporate subscriber such as firstname.lastname@company.com, then you do not need prior consent before you send the marketing email. (…) You may be able to rely on legitimate interests to justify some of your business to business marketing'.

However in my opinion – to avoid a misinterpretation of the ICO's statement - any assessment of whether email addresses of employees of companies are processed lawfully for e-marketing must focus on the nature of such communication. It is entirely permissible to send such offer for the purpose and in the scope corresponding to these persons' position in the bodies or structure of the corporation (for example an audit or IT services offer letters). On the other hand, using the same email address for marketing of products or services which are intended not for the company represented by these persons but for themselves as consumers, requires that other requirements of lawful data processing be met. The ICO rightly distinguishes corporate subscriber and individual subscribers. Marketing of products or services which are intended not for the company but for employees as consumers is marketing to an individual subscriber. It is not B2B, but B2C e-commerce, thus it requires consent.

While the use of automated calling systems without the recipient's consent is prohibited, the rules concerning the permissibility of live marketing calls are not uniform within the EU: Article 13(3) of Directive 2002/58/EC allows the Member States to choose whether their respective legislations provide for the requirement of consent (opt-in) or the possibility to object (opt-out) to live marketing.

One example of the more liberal opt-out option is the British regulation PECR (the Privacy and Electronic Communications Regulations (Regulation 21 'Unsolicited calls for direct marketing'). This prohibits the use of electronic means, including marketing calls, for making unsolicited direct marketing communications to subscribers who have entered their numbers on one of the central opt-out registers: the Telephone Preference Service list (for natural persons) or the Corporate TPS (CTPS) list (for businesses), unless such subscribers, despite their general opt-out, have given their direct consent to marketing communications to the specific caller. On the other hand, no consent is required to send electronic marketing communications in these forms to a recipient whose number is not on the TPS or CTPS list, i.e. who has not made a public general objection to processing of data for marketing by all potential callers or an individual objection relating to a specific caller. Thus, electronic marketing requires consultation of the public opt-out lists, TPS and CTPS, and the internal opt-out list kept by each controller.

The more stringent opt-in approach to the permissibility of live marketing calls has been adopted, for example, in Polish law. The Act on Providing Services by Electronic Means (*Ustawa o świadczeniu usług drogą elektroniczną*), in its Article 10, prohibits the sending, by electronic communications means, of unsolicited commercial information addressed to a specified recipient who is a natural person. Electronic marketing is also subject to other more stringent restrictions introduced by the Consumer Rights Act (*Ustawa o prawach konsumenta*) of 30 May 2014, which, upon its entry into force on 25 December 2014, amended Article 172(1) of the Telecommunications Act (*Ustawa Prawo telekomunikacyjne*) of 16 July 2004.[22]

The previous wording of Article 172(1) of the Telecommunications Law prohibited the use of automated calling systems for direct marketing without prior consent of the subscriber or end user. The amendment expanded the scope of the prohibition to include telecommunications terminal equipment. According to the definition in Article 2(43) of the Telecommunications Law, telecommunications terminal equipment is telecommunications equipment intended for connection directly or indirectly to network termination points. This includes telephones, but also computers, tablets, or other devices which connect to the Internet. An important difference between Article 172 of the Telecommunications Act and Article 10 of the Act on Providing Services by Electronic Means is that the former applies to a wider range of entities: the protection also covers legal persons and organisational units, including businesses.

22. Act implementing Directive 2002/65/EC of the European Parliament and of the Council of 23 September 2002 concerning the distance marketing of consumer financial services and amending Council Directive 90/619/EEC and Directives 97/7/EC and 98/27/EC (OJ EU L 271, 9.10.2002, p. 16) and supplementing the implementation of Article 13 of Directive 2002/58/EC of the European Parliament and of the Council of 12 July 2002 concerning the processing of personal data and the protection of privacy in the electronic communications sector (Directive on privacy and electronic communications) (OJ EU L 201, 31.7.2002, p. 37).

[C] Electronic Marketing in ePrivacy Regulation

Since the ePrivacy rules are being amended by means of a new regulation rather than a revision of ePrivacy Directive 2002/58/EC, then, pursuant to the principle of direct applicability of EU regulations in all Member States (laid down in Article 288 of the TFEU), the electronic marketing rules will thus be made uniform across the EU. This will mean that Member States will no longer have the freedom, allowed thus far in Article 13(3) of Directive 2002/58/EC, to choose whether their national laws provide for an opt-in (consent) or opt-out (objection) towards electronic marketing. However, the current draft of the ePrivacy Regulation may still be subject to changes in the legislative process prior to its adoption.

The draft ePrivacy Regulation (Article 16(1), as the ePrivacy Directive before it, allows electronic communications to be sent for the purposes of direct marketing to end users who are natural persons only if they have previously given their consent (opt-in).

However, the draft Regulation also allows the goods or services provider to use the electronic mail contact details for direct marketing, but only if the provider has obtained the contact details from the customer in the context of the sale of a product or a service. Moreover, an opt-out possibility must be ensured. Only the provider's own products or services may be marketed with the use of such contact details; thus, no third-party products or services may be marketed by email without the customer's consent. Furthermore, only products or services similar to those sold earlier to the same customer may be marketed in this way. The customer must be given clearly and distinctly, at the time of collection and each time a message is sent, the opportunity to object (opt-out), free-of-charge and in an easy manner, to such use of data. As examples of permissible opt-out methods, the draft mentions a link in the email message, or an email address, which can be used to express objection (the admissibility of such methods, already used in practice, is thus confirmed).

Article 16(2) only refers to email, without mentioning phone calls or text messages. Article 16(4), on the other hand, gives Member States the freedom to allow natural person end users to be targeted with voice-to-voice calls for marketing purposes, unless they have objected to receiving such communications. This will therefore require a filtering of objections in the controller's system, but also in publicly accessible records of marketing objections. Article 16(3) of the draft ePrivacy Regulation also includes the obligation to use a code or a prefix identifying the call as a marketing call.

Unlike the GDPR, the ePrivacy Regulation extends its protection not only to natural persons but also to the legitimate interests of legal persons (which relates e.g. to electronically sourced information constituting a business secret).[23]

---

23. CJEU judgment of 14.2.2008 in Case C-450/06 *Varec SA v. Belgian State*, ECLI:EU:C:2008:91, point 48; ECtHR judgment of 2.4.2015 in the case of *Vinci Construction et GTM Génie Civil et Services v. France*, Application No. 63629/10, and judgment of 2.4.2015, Application No. 60567/10, point 63, http://hudoc.echr.coe.int/eng?i=001-153318.

[D] Interpretation of '*Prior* Consent'

In business activities, varying interpretations may be observed as to how the requirement of obtaining 'prior explicit consent of the recipients' before addressing marketing communications to them (recital 40 of the preamble to the ePrivacy directive) should be understood. Companies engaging e.g. in telephone marketing evidently tend to interpret this prior consent requirement in lax terms. In practice, for instance, the customer is asked for consent before the full offer is presented to him/her, but this happens during a telephone call that has been made despite the (prospective) customer not having given consent for electronic marketing in the first place.

I find this practice to be a breach of the principle whereby electronic marketing is only allowed under consent of the data subject. The nature of the telephone conversation is determined by its factual purpose: the prospective customer has been called in order to be presented a marketing communication over the telephone. Seeking consent during the call, before presenting the offer, is irrelevant: the requirement of obtaining consent is a prerequisite for making the marketing telephone call in the first place, rather than for merely presenting the offer during the conversation.

This is also evident, in my view, from the legal rationale of the ePrivacy directive being to protect people from spam and unsolicited marketing communications. The nuisance of receiving a multitude of unwanted telephone calls is not alleviated by being merely asked, during each of these calls, for consent to hear a full marketing offer. On the other hand, a customer's consent may be sought during a telephone call if the call was made for a different customer-service-related purpose, e.g. to verify the customer's data.

This view is corroborated by administrative proceedings initiated in September 2017 by UOKiK, the Polish anti-trust and consumer protection authority, against Netia, a telecom operator[24] (without prejudice to the eventual result of the proceedings). The proceedings related to Netia's practice of obtaining contact data from third parties and using the data to contact people despite not having their prior consent. The purpose of the calls was to present marketing offers, and Netia sought the customers' consent only during the telephone call.

An anti-spam solution tested in many countries and worthy of support is the Mail Preference Service list, also known as the Robinson list. This is either implemented as part of self-regulation introduced by associations of direct marketing operators or regulated by law.

[E] Cookies

The protection of Internet users was enhanced thanks to Directive 2002/58/WE requiring, in its Article 5(3),[25] the data subject's consent (a cookie banner linked to a

24. https://uokik.gov.pl/aktualnosci.php?news_id = 13718 (in Polish).
25. As a result of the amendment introduced by Directive 2009/136/EC of the European Parliament and of the Council of 25 November 2009, OJ EU L 337, 18.12.2009, p. 11, http://eur-lex.europa.eu/legal-content/EN/TXT/?uri = CELEX:32009L0136.

privacy and cookie policy) for sending cookies, saving them in the user's device, and tracking the user's online behaviour for targeting advertisement.[26] A cookie is defined as a 'piece of text stored by a user's web browser and transmitted as part of an HTTP request'.[27] Before giving consent, the data subject must be provided with clear and comprehensive information, including on the purposes of the processing (it is crucial to specify the types of cookies, the consequences of their installation on the user's device, and the possibility of removing them).[28]

Under the same provision, though, consent is not required where cookies are only used for carrying out the transmission of a communication over an electronic communications network or where the installation of a cookie on the user's device (storing of data and access thereto) is necessary for providing a service explicitly requested by the subscriber or user, i.e. where the service requested by the user cannot be completed without the use of cookies.

The Article 29 Working Party, in its Working Document of 7 June 2012, WP 194 (Opinion on Cookie Consent Exemption)[29] indicates the types of cookies which do not require the user's consent to be installed on his/her device and the criteria for judging whether a given cookie belongs to one of these categories.

The types of cookies include user-input cookies used for tracking data entered by the user while filling in online forms or adding items to his/her online shopping basket, or for saving the user's language preference (session-ID cookies, multimedia player session cookies, user interface customisation cookies, including language preference cookies).

Cookies are also categorised into session cookies or persistent cookies, as well as third-party cookies. Session cookies are automatically erased once the user closes the browser, whereas persistent cookies remain stored in the device for a predefined time. An exemption from the requirement of obtaining consent for installing cookies is justified where the installation of a cookie is directly related to its purpose and its storage time does not exceed the time necessary to meet that purpose.

Thus, the conditions for exemption from the requirement to obtain the user's consent, specified in Article 5(3) of the Directive on privacy and electronic communications, are met by session cookies, as these are deleted once they are no longer directly necessary for the purpose they serve. On the other hand, the data subject's consent is necessary for using cookies for behavioural advertisement.

26. G. Skouma and L. Léonard, '*On-line Behavioral Tracking: What May Change After the Legal Reform on Personal Data Protection*', in: Reforming European Data Protection Law, (ed.) S. Gutwirth, R. Leenes, P. de Hert, Springer 2015, p. 46; D. Karwala, 'Nowe zasady przechowywania informacji w telekomunikacyjnych urządzeniach końcowych (uwagi na temat znowelizowanego art. 173 PrTelekom)', Monitor Prawniczy 2013, no. 8 – special appendix 'Aktualne problemy prawnej ochrony danych osobowych 2013', pp. 15 et seq.
27. ENISA, Privacy considerations of online behavioural tracking, (October 2012) available at http://www.enisa.europa.eu/activities/identity-and-trust/library/deliverables/privacy-considerations-ofonline-behavioural-tracking, p. 6.
28. The Article 29 Working Party published guidance on obtaining consent for cookies in its Working Document 02/2013 of 2 October 2013, WP 208, http://ec.europa.eu/justice/article-29/documentation/opinion-recommendation/files/2013/wp208_en.pdf.
29. See http://ec.europa.eu/justice/article-29/documentation/opinion-recommendation/files/2012/wp194_en.pdf.

This approach, adopted previously by the Article 29 Working Party in its Working Document WP 194 of 7 June 2012, was also upheld in the draft ePrivacy Regulation. It allows cookies to be installed without the user's consent e.g. where such cookies do not interfere with the user's privacy but only allow or facilitate his/her use of a website, for instance, by storing the user's language choice, the content of his/her shopping basket and his/her contact data for placing the order etc. (session-id cookies, language preference cookies). Nor will consent be required under this draft for using cookies for the statistical analysis of customers' visits on a website.

On the other hand, the user's consent will be required under the ePrivacy Regulation, as it has been under the ePrivacy Directive, for storing cookies for marketing purposes or using them for targeted advertisement (Article 8(1)(b) of the draft ePrivacy Regulation).

As the entry into force of the ePrivacy Regulation has been delayed in relation to the application date of the GDPR, certain authors have argued that, under the applicable laws, the use of cookies for the data controller's legitimate interests covered not only cookies allowing the statistical analysis of website visits, but also cookies used for targeted advertisement. I disagree with this view. Indeed, legitimate interests may only be invoked if 'a data subject can reasonably expect at the time and in the context of the collection of the personal data that processing for that purpose may take place' (recital 47 of the preamble to the GDPR). Where no links exist between the data subject and the data controller, in particular, where the data subject is not the controller's customer but only visited its website incidentally, it would be unjustified to claim that the data subject should expect that files might be saved on his/her device for the purpose of tracking his/her online activity merely for the controller's business purposes.

The draft ePrivacy Regulation (Article 9(2) provides for expressing consent by using the appropriate settings of the Web browser or other applications enabling access to the Internet. Still, privacy by design and privacy by default principles should be adhered to. The draft also includes the obligation (Article 9(3) to enable users to withdraw their previously given consent at any time, in accordance with Article 7(3) of the GDPR, and to remind them of this possibility every six months throughout the processing period.

CHAPTER 6

Processing of Personal Data of Employees

§6.01 AN EMPLOYEE'S CONSENT AS A BASIS FOR PROCESSING HIS OR HER PERSONAL DATA IN EMPLOYMENT RELATIONSHIPS

The processing of data of employees in the employment context is one of the areas where the GDPR (Article 88) allows Member States to adopt specific rules. Such rules may regulate the processing of data, in particular for the purposes of recruitment and performance of the employment contract, including the discharge of obligations laid down by law or by collective agreements, management, planning and organisation of work, equality and diversity in the workplace, health and safety at work, protection of employer's or customer's property and for the purposes of exercise and enjoyment, on an individual or collective basis, of rights and benefits related to employment, and for the purpose of the termination of the employment relationship.

This means that, despite a transition from harmonisation towards a unification of data protection rules within the EU, more specific rules on the processing of employees' personal data may still differ between the Member States. For instance, specifying the retention periods for the data of former employees or job applicants, or the legal basis for collecting biometric data or the use of CCTV, may require that differences resulting from local laws be taken into account. Consequently, where a multinational capital group (with each member company being a separate employer) attempts to adopt a uniform group-wide policy, this must be made compliant with the most stringent of different local legislations regulating the collection of biometric data or the use of CCTV. Different retention periods must also be taken into account, as the longest one permissible under the national law of one country might be non-compliant with another country's legislation.

In addition, recital 155 of the preamble to the GDPR states that the consent of the employee may be a basis for processing his or her data, subject to conditions discussed in this chapter.

An example of a Member State's legislation that can be amended by virtue of Article 88 of the GDPR and recital 155 of its preamble is the Polish Labour Code, (draft of 7 June 2018). Now, it expressly allows the processing of the personal data of employees based on their consent. It does not, however, include all types of data: the processing of sensitive data covered by Article 9(1) of the GDPR and data relating to criminal convictions and offences covered by Article 10 of the GDPR is only permissible if necessary for the purposes of carrying out the employer's obligations under law. Sensitive data includes biometric data. The processing of employees' biometric data is also allowed where such data must be disclosed to enable the employer to control access to its particularly important information, whose disclosure may be detrimental to the employer, or to control access to premises requiring particular protection. Sensitive data and data relating to criminal convictions and offences, due to their sensitive nature and higher risks for the rights and freedoms of data subjects, are discussed below as a good example illustrating the legal aspects of data processing in the employment context.

Although the above-mentioned provision expressly allows the employee's consent to be invoked as a basis for processing his/her data, I warn against treating this basis as sufficient and unconditional.

The Polish Supreme Administrative Court, in its judgment of 6 September 2011 (I OSK 1476/10), challenged the data subject's consent being invoked as a basis for processing data beyond the scope specified in law. However, the judgment concerns the legal status before the GDPR entered into force. The Court ruled that the use of employees' fingerprints for supervising their working time is disproportionate to this purpose of data processing. A similar view on the principle of data minimisation and the use of fingerprints in the Labour Law was expressed by the Italian data protection authority, Garante per la protezione dei dati personali.[1]

The Supreme Administrative Court's ruling was justified by the Polish Labour Code containing an exhaustive list of personal data which an employer may collect. The list allowed the employer to demand other personal data, but only if the requirement to present those specific data resulted from other legal provisions. If the data subject's consent was a sufficient basis for data processing, the limitation of categories of personal data allowed to be processed by an employer under law would be ineffective.[2] However, this point of view is changed by recital 155 of the preamble to the GDPR, which has introduced the employee's consent as an alternative basis for processing his or her data, unless the local labour law provisions continue to expressly

1. Garante per la protezione dei dati personali (the Italian Data Protection Authority), Uso delle impronte digitali per i sistemi di rilevamento delle presenze nei luoghi di lavoro (Use of Fingerprints for Assiduity Control at the Workplace), 21 July 2005 doc. web n. 1150679, http://www.garanteprivacy.it/web/guest/home/docweb/-/docweb-display/docweb/1166892.
2. E. Kulesza, 'Przesłanki przetwarzania danych osobowych pracowników przez pracodawcę', *Monitor Prawniczy* 2012, no. 7, special appendix 'Ochrona danych osobowych 2012', p. 30; T. Wyka, 'Rola Kodeksu pracy w systemie przepisów dotyczących ochrony danych osobowych pracownika' (in:) *Internet. Prawno-informatyczne problemy sieci, portali i e-usług*, ed. G. Szpor, W. Wiewiórowski, Warszawa 2012, p. 59; G. Sibiga, 'Przetwarzanie i ochrona danych osoby ubiegającej się o zatrudnienie w świetle przepisów prawa pracy', *Radca Prawny* 2005, No. 2, p. 67.

prohibit the processing of sensitive data covered by Article 9(1) of the GDPR and data relating to criminal convictions and offences covered by Article 10, where the processing of these categories of data is not necessary for the purposes of carrying out the employer's obligations under law.

Still, the data subject's consent may not be considered as a basis for processing the employees' data in isolation from the crucial data protection principles: the data minimisation requirement and the voluntary nature of the consent.

The scope of data processing may not go beyond the employee's personal data regarding his/her employment relationship. Even if consent was freely given in a particular case, which must be proven by the employer, it does not invalidate the minimisation requirement. The same applies to the principle of purpose limitation. For instance, it is entirely permissible to use fingerprints for controlling access to protected rooms or critical systems, but using the same data for supervising employees' working time and assessing their effectiveness may be disproportionate in the given context.[3]

Furthermore, depending on the Member State's legislation, it was allowed in most EU Member States to collect information on job applicants' criminal records in the recruitment process, yet not on the same basis. Depending on the country, this could take place upon the applicant's consent (e.g. in Spain and the Netherlands), under legal provisions (e.g. in Belgium and Germany) or in connection with the nature of the job being applied for (e.g. in Romania and Greece). In Poland, there was a particularly rigorous approach before the GDPR application date. The consent itself could not be a basis for the collection of information on the criminal records of job applicants. The collection of such data was only permitted by legal provisions which required that candidates for specific posts (e.g. members of management boards of banks) or in specific sectors (such as judiciary) could not have been convicted for any offences or special categories of offences.

Information on the criminal records of job applicants and employees is particularly important in sectors where the risk of employing persons without adequate verification is high, e.g. in the financial sector. Draft laws currently pending in connection with the GDPR in some Member States respond to those needs and expressly introduce a legal basis for the collection of such data, e.g. in the case of jobs allowing access to data regarding a bank or clients of the bank.

Article 88 of the GDPR also allows Member States to adopt laws specifically authorising banks (given a higher risk of possible data infringement in that sector) to demand biometric data from their employees, including fingerprints, voice recordings, iris patterns and finger vein patterns (that list is going to develop as new technologies become available) if providing such data is necessary for controlling access to information processed by the bank and special rooms.

Another factor influencing the permissibility of the processing of the employee's data upon his/her consent is the freedom of consent. National legislation on the processing of employees' personal data usually allows, for example, employees' pictures to be published online upon their consent which, however, must be freely

3. Opinion 2/2017 of the Working Party of 8 June 2017, p. 22.

given. A subordination of the employee to the employer is one of the fundamental features of each employment relationship. The employee might feel informally pressured to give his/her consent when requested by the employer, which means that the voluntary nature of the employees' consent might be called into question. Consent given by a data subject is only effective if it is entirely voluntary and refusal has no potential adverse consequences. The absence of consent may not be a basis for the adverse treatment of job applicants or employees, nor may cause any other negative consequences for them. In particular, it may not justify a refusal to employ someone or the termination of an employment relationship by the employer upon or without notice.

The Article 29 Data Protection Working Party recommends a reserved approach to treating consent as a basis for the processing of employees' data due to the risk of lacking a voluntary character (Opinion 2/2017 of the Working Party of 8 June 2017 on data processing at work, which is complementary to the earlier Opinion 8/2001 of the Working Party of 13 September 2001 on the processing of personal data in the employment context, pp. 3, 4 and 27).[4] The Polish Supreme Administrative Court gave an analogous ruling in its judgment of 1 December 2009 (ref. no. I OSK 249/09) and emphasised that 'an imbalance between the employer and the employee puts into question the voluntary character of giving consent for collecting and processing personal (biometric) data'.

However, a reserved approach does not mean that giving consent freely is impossible. The factual circumstances of each individual case are crucial for assessment. Firstly, when adopting the GDPR, the EU legislator dropped the statement initially present in the legislative proposal (recital 34 of the preamble) that a situation of dependence, and the resulting clear imbalance, between an employer and an employee affects the freedom of the employee's consent, and, consequently, its validity. At the same time, recital 155 was introduced, which allows personal data to be processed on the basis of the employee's consent, subject to conditions specified in the GDPR. Secondly, certain national labour law provisions provide for giving consent by the employee, which implies its voluntary character; e.g. a pregnant employee or an employee caring for his/her child until the child's fourth birthday must give their consent to working under special working time rules.

Therefore, the content of requests for consent will be important. The employee should be clearly notified of, among others, the purpose of giving consent and its voluntary character. The content of consent clauses should be equally important but, crucially, it should be proven that, for instance, a refusal to give consent to provide biometric data does not cause any discrimination in establishing annual bonuses or regarding the employee's scope of duties. However, it might be impossible to entirely avoid any negative consequences of an employee's refusal to give consent, namely if

4. Opinion 2/2017 adopted on 8 June 2017 on data processing at work, WP 249, pp. 3–4: 'Consent is highly unlikely to be a legal basis for data processing at work, unless employees can refuse without adverse consequence', 'It is important to state that employees are seldom in a position to freely give, refuse or revoke consent, given the dependency that results from the employer/employee relationship.'

the employee's consent was sought (and refused) for introducing special arrangements facilitating the employee's work. For example, if the employer introduces fingerprint entry gates in order to shorten the time employees spend waiting to enter or leave the company (provided that the processing of biometric data is not prohibited under local laws), the employees who do not use the system are more likely to be late, e.g. because a person waiting in a queue before them is looking for a magnetic card. It is a practical problem in many institutions which employ hundreds of people starting and finishing work at the same time.

§6.02 SURVEILLANCE OF THE EMPLOYEES' ACTIVITIES

The widespread use and functionality of new technologies, which were not known or used at the beginning of the 21st century and which make the surveillance of employees possible or are developed especially for this purpose, is a great challenge for the right to privacy. For this reason, it was necessary to update the previous recommendations of the Article 29 Working Party (Opinion 2/2017 of the Working Party of 8 June 2017 on data processing at work (WP 249), complementary to the earlier Opinion 8/2001 of the Working Party of 13 September 2001 on the processing of personal data in the employment context (WP 48))[5] and the working document of 29 May 2002 on the surveillance of electronic communications in the workplace (WP 55).[6]

The Article 29 Working Party addresses its recommendations contained in the opinion 2/2017 to the 'employees', whereas the scope of this term is not restricted merely to persons with an employment contract recognised as such under labour laws, but it also refers to other forms of employment, particularly employment on a freelance basis (Opinion 2/2017, p. 4).

Currently, monitoring is not limited to video monitoring systems (CCTV) but also includes ICT system operations. The former are clearly widespread and popular, and their efficiency and ease of access to collected data are increasing; yet it is the surveillance of ICT systems and the monitoring of email which are crucial e.g. for the prevention of data leakages. Widely used forms of monitoring include recording email recipients and the times of sending messages, numbers, times and duration of phone calls, browsing histories, identification of email attachments meeting specified criteria, recording phone calls, GPS tracking in company cars and 'mystery clients'. This is not an exhaustive list of the surveillance methods which may be expected in future.

However, the awareness of employees regarding the forms and scope of the monitoring of ICT systems is lower than the awareness of CCTV monitoring. Security cameras are visible unless they are miniature and hidden; buildings under surveillance are marked with video surveillance signs, and the scope of information obtained by recording is relatively narrow. On the other hand, due to the different forms of monitoring of ICT systems, the scope of collected information and a possible lack of awareness of the persons under surveillance, this kind of monitoring requires that they

5. http://ec.europa.eu/newsroom/document.cfm?doc_id=45631.
6. http://ec.europa.eu/justice/article-29/documentation/opinion-recommendation/files/2002/wp55_en.pdf.

be informed of more issues and consequences for their privacy. Thus, before introducing such monitoring, the employer must inform the employees accordingly: for CCTV, the area under surveillance must be clearly marked; for recording telephone conversations, a voice warning must be used; for any other type of monitoring, information clauses must be included e.g. in employee handbooks.

This is especially true because many employers allow their employees to use their private electronic devices, such as computers, tablets and mobile phones, for business purposes (BYOD), i.e. within the employer's ICT system. This raises concerns that employers might gain access to data (e.g. pictures) stored in the memory of private devices while these are logged into the corporate network.

Arrangements that are popular due to their working flexibility also include working from home or teleworking (e.g. on a business trip) using devices and systems of both the employer and the employee (such as home Internet access), allowing the employee the same access to the employer's network, systems and resources as they have in their office.

The ECtHR ruled in its judgment of 9 January 2018 in the case of *López Ribalda and Others v Spain* (applications no. 1874/13 and 8567/13)[7] that hidden cameras recording cashiers in a supermarket had breached their right to the protection of their privacy, even though the cameras had been installed following a theft and their purpose was to prevent further thefts and to find the offenders. Only some of the cameras were visible, while others were hidden. The employees had only been informed of the visible ones. Video recordings from the hidden cameras showed that the monitored cashiers did commit theft, which was a reason for their dismissal on disciplinary grounds. However, the Court found that the employer had been obliged to inform the employees of the video surveillance prior to using it. It emphasised that the video surveillance was not a result of suspicions against specific employees.

Therein lies the difference between this case and the case of *Karin Köpke v. Germany* (decision of the ECtHR of 5 October 2010, application no. 420/07),[8] which was also related to covert video surveillance. However, the Court found that the surveillance measure was limited to two suspected cashiers who were handling the same till, it lasted two weeks and was carried out in order to determine which of the two was responsible for recurring thefts. Interference in privacy was thus limited to the minimum necessary.

The ECtHR, in its judgment of 12 January 2016,[9] allowed the surveillance of an employee's private messages sent during working hours via email or Internet messengers. The case was initiated by an application lodged with the ECtHR on 15 December 2008 by Bogdan Bărbulescu, a Romanian national. Part of the applicant's work was contacting his customers via Yahoo Messenger. His employer informed him that his account on Yahoo Messenger had been monitored between 5 and 13 July 2007, which

7. https://hudoc.echr.coe.int/eng?i=001-179881#{'itemid':['001-179881']} [retrieved on 10 March 2018].
8. http://hudoc.echr.coe.int/app/conversion/pdf/?library=ECHR&id=001-101536&filename=001-101536.pdf [retrieved on 10 March 2018].
9. *Bărbulescu v Romania*, 61496/08, http://hudoc.echr.coe.int/eng?i=001-159906.

showed that Mr Bărbulescu had also used his office computer for private communications, which was contrary to the employer's internal regulations and the applicant's written statement. The employer gave this as the reason for terminating Mr Bărbulescu's employment contract. The applicant lodged a complaint for annulment of the employment termination on the grounds of a breach of privacy through unauthorised monitoring of private communications.

The ECtHR ruled that the applicant's right to privacy under Article 8 of the ECHR had not been violated. The Court found it justified for the employer to verify whether its employees fulfilled their duties during working hours. The employer's regulations prohibited the employers from engaging in any private activities or making private communications during working hours with the use of the office equipment. Therefore, the employer had the right to check the history of the employees' communications and expect to find only work-related communications there (although, in this particular case, they turned out to contain private messages as well). The ECtHR also found the employer's examination to have been proportionate, as it was limited to Yahoo Messenger.

It is not only crucial that the monitoring is proportionate to the legitimate aim, but also that the employee is clearly informed in advance that the employer might monitor his/her communications for specific purposes, including to ensure workplace discipline and work efficiency and to prevent any abuse or wrongdoing to the detriment of the employer or its customers.

The ECtHR also emphasised the significance of information on the intended monitoring and the scope thereof in its judgment of 3 April 2007.[10] The dispute between Lynette Copland, an assistant, and Carmarthenshire College, her employer, related to the monitoring of Ms Copland's telephone, email, and Internet connections during her employment. The monitoring was intended to verify whether the applicant was using the College's equipment for her private purposes. The employer claimed that it had only analysed the numbers dialled and the dates, times, duration and costs of the phone calls, the URLs of websites visited and the dates and durations of the visits, and the addresses of the email recipients and the dates and times of sending the messages. During this monitoring, which lasted for many months, the College did not have any internal regulations in place to provide the employees with information on the monitoring or its scope. The Court ruled that monitoring without informing the person affected is a breach of privacy under Article 8 of the ECHR.

The Polish Supreme Administrative Court also emphasised the requirement that monitoring should be made known to the employee (which, certainly, means not that the employee must be informed before each check which the employer plans to make, but only that they be made aware that the rules in place allow monitoring).[11] The Court confirmed that automated collection of information on connections between the internal network and the public network amounts to monitoring of the employee in the workplace as it allows the employer to check the list of websites visited by the

10. *Copland v the United Kingdom*, 62617/00, http://hudoc.echr.coe.int/eng?i=001-79996.
11. Judgment of 13.2.2014, I OSK 2436/12, http://orzeczenia.nsa.gov.pl/doc/A2B1C2D069 (in Polish).

employee, the time and duration of the connection, and the URLs of the websites visited or files downloaded. Such a monitoring activity must therefore meet the requirements of being lawful, made for a legitimate purpose, proportionate, and transparent, where transparency means that the employees are aware of being monitored. Consequently, the Court requires the employer to define precise rules of monitoring and communicate them to the employees.

Recital 155 of the preamble to the GDPR expressly allows an employee's consent to be invoked as the basis for the processing of his/her personal data, subject to conditions referred to in this chapter, particularly subject to a genuinely voluntary nature of consent. However, it should be assumed that the employee's consent should not be a basis for data processing in order to monitor the employees' activities, except for special circumstances, mostly due to reasonable doubts whether giving such consent by the employee in such a case would be entirely voluntary and not subject to any pressure.

In most cases, an appropriate legal basis for data processing for monitoring purposes should be a necessity to pursue the legitimate interests of the employer (Article 6(1)(f) of the GDPR).

Another basis may be a legal provision allowing data processing for monitoring purposes by employers in order to ensure the security of their activities, or by institutions operating in a sector which is particularly exposed to information security risks, e.g. allowing banks to verify the criminal records of their employees in public registers. Another example is recording telephone communications in order to document activities, e.g. to gather evidence for the performance of obligations, which is required by Directive 2014/65/EU of 15 May 2014 on markets in financial instruments (MiFID II).[12]

A legitimate interest of the employer, the pursuit of which requires the monitoring of employees' activities, i.e. which is a legal basis for data processing for monitoring purposes, may be, for instance, ensuring the security of data or other assets, preventing any abuse or wrongdoing to the detriment of the employer or its customers, surveillance of work quality and discipline, as well as documentation of circumstances of particular transactions.

The legitimate interests of the employer may be invoked only if they override the interests or fundamental rights and freedoms of the employee. It is implausible that an employee had an equally legitimate or an overriding interest in comparison to those of the employer if these would include e.g. preventing any abuse perpetrated by employees and the protection of customers' assets. However, the rights and freedoms of the employees derived from the EU Charter of Fundamental Rights, such as the right to the protection of personal data (Article 8), the right to respect for their private and family life (Article 7), the freedom of expression and information (Article 11) and the freedom of assembly and of association (Article 12), may override the legitimate interests of the employer.

12. OJ L 173, 12.6.2014, p. 349.

The assessment of the proportionality of monitoring to the purpose of processing must be related to the specific circumstances. Moreover, interpretation will be subject to evolution resulting from technological developments, also in the context of the social acceptance of new practices in labour relations. For instance, electronic monitoring of body temperature or frequency of eye squinting may prevent accidents caused by driver fatigue, so they are likely to find public approval when they are used in public transport. However, the same technologies may also become a surveillance tool if they are used, for example, for automated analysis of office workers' activity. According to the Article 29 Working Party, such forms of monitoring (e.g. automated analysis of facial expressions and face recognition technology) are disproportionate to common monitoring purposes and may thus interfere with the rights and freedoms of employees so they are, save for some special exceptions, unlawful (Opinion 2/2017, p. 22).

A required analysis of the proportionality of forms and scope of monitoring in relation to the pursuit of legitimate interest and methods of reducing risk regarding breaches of the right to privacy and secrecy of communications may be included in a data protection impact assessment (Article 35 of the GDPR).

The employer is allowed to use, during the recruitment process, information published by job applicants in social media (unless local labour law restricts this possibility), yet not due to the mere fact that such information has been published, but based on legitimate interest, subject to the adequacy of such data to a given job and its profile. Therefore, the employer should assess if the nature of information on the job applicant, which is publicly available, is professional or private (regarding his/her beliefs, interests, family and social life, in some cases sensitive data) and limit the scope of using such information only to what is directly related to the type of job being applied for. An example of the monitoring carried out by the employer, e.g. on LinkedIn, for the pursuit of its legitimate interest, could be the verification of compliance of non-competition clauses by former employees (Opinion 2/2017, pp. 12–13).

A legitimate interest of the employer may also be the GPS tracking of company cars during the working hours of their users and in connection with their work. However, if cars are also made available to employees outside their working hours, the car tracking system should not enable the employer to gain and collect information on, for example, the location of the employee at night. This could be, for instance, prevented by disabling the tracking function by the employee during his/her time off work.

In its Opinion 2/2017 (p. 17), the Article 29 Working Party recommends that the monitoring of outgoing emails in terms of data leakage risk should be systematically based on a statistical analysis and specified alert categories. It should concentrate on the alleged infringer only after the initial automated analysis has detected a possible infringement. The monitoring of email must not infringe upon the confidentiality of correspondence and other personal goods of the employee. However, indiscriminate exclusion of correspondence or files marked in the employer's information system as private from monitoring would be a pathological exposure to a data leakage risk under the pretext of sending private emails. It is good practice to prohibit in the employer's regulations to use an official email for private purposes and to make employees aware that emails are archived in the system even under passive monitoring.

§6.03 THE DATA MINIMISATION PRINCIPLE IN THE EMPLOYMENT CONTEXT

National rules on the processing of personal data of employees, adopted as permitted by Article 88 of the GDPR, must include suitable and specific measures to safeguard the data subject's human dignity, legitimate interests and fundamental rights, with particular regard to the transparency of processing, the transfer of personal data within a group of undertakings, or a group of enterprises engaged in a joint economic activity and monitoring systems at the work place.

Therefore, legislators and employers must consider whether the recruitment process complies with the data minimisation principle, which may be infringed upon by, for instance, questions about maternity plans or the age of the job applicant's children.

The protection of the rights and freedoms of employees (in national laws adopted in accordance with Article 88 of the GDPR, but also, irrespective of such laws, in employers' practices) may also be ensured by the determination of a negative list of the employees' data, i.e. indication of categories of data prohibited from collection, even upon the employee's consent, due to the risk of discrimination. Those could include certain categories of sensitive data, e.g. on health status or addictions. However, it should be pointed out that this applies only to cases where the processing of data on health is not based on legal provisions, e.g. regulating the procedure regarding work-related accidents. Furthermore, practical consequences of the ban on the processing of data regarding, for example, addictions should be taken into account if employees smoking on a regular basis are recorded by the CCTV surveillance of the area outside the workplace carried out for security purposes, although gaining such information is only a side effect of monitoring activities.

CCTV surveillance must not include certain locations, such as sanitary facilities, changing rooms, canteens, smoking rooms and rooms made available to trade unions, unless CCTV is essential for ensuring the security of employees, customers or property, or for maintaining the company's trade secrets while not jeopardising employees' rights and the independence of trade unions. Surveillance of such locations should be prohibited regardless of whether local laws ban it, as it would be contrary to the data minimisation principle.

If the legislator of a Member State does not make use of the option provided for in Article 88 of the GDPR to adopt national laws regulating the protection of employees' data, the status of those data will be the same as that of other kinds of data and thus the employees' data will be subject to general principles specified in the GDPR, including the principles of data minimisation and purpose limitation. Only the processing of the employees' sensitive data is directly regulated by the GDPR (Article 9(2)(b) of the GDPR – processing is necessary for the purposes of carrying out the obligations and exercising specific rights of the controller or of the data subject in the field of employment). Restrictions on the processing of the employees' data in the labour codes of Member States will cease to have effect due to being contrary to the GDPR unless the Commission is notified that a given legal provision has been adopted pursuant to Article 88 of the GDPR.

CHAPTER 7
Sensitive Data and Criminal Records

§7.01 SENSITIVE DATA

The scope of the term 'personal data' is an open one; it depends on the specific nature of each controller and data subject and it evolves with technological progress (the definition, categories, and other aspects of personal data are discussed in the chapter relating to Article 4 of the GDPR). However, the term also covers a closed subset 'special categories of personal data', i.e. sensitive data. This category of data has been separated and covered with enhanced protection in comparison with other (ordinary) data because of their particular importance for the protection of the right to privacy and the risk to fundamental rights and freedoms. Sensitive data belong to a sphere which is not merely private but intimate. Their disclosure may expose the data subject to significant and irreparable harm by violating his/her dignity, stigmatising him/her, or causing him/her to be shunned in his/her environment. It may also lead to discrimination against the data subject in areas important for him/her, for example influence decisions on employment, lending, or life insurance.

The closed scope of sensitive data (referred to in the GDPR as special categories of personal data) includes personal data revealing racial or ethnic origin, political opinions, religious or philosophical beliefs, or trade union membership, as well as genetic data, biometric data uniquely identifying a natural person, and data concerning health or a person's sex life or sexual orientation (Article 9(1) of the GDPR).

This definition is not fully in line with what is commonly considered sensitive data, or with the real consequences of data processing. For instance, a person's salary or financial standing are not within the legal scope of sensitive data, but are commonly believed to be data of high sensitivity. In many countries or communities, asking a person about their salary is considered tactless; in others still, such data are publicly available. Information on a person's health is included in the legal definition of sensitive data, but depending on its nature, it may either be one of the person's intimate secrets (such as information on being infertile or infected with a dangerous virus) or be fairly neutral (e.g. when it relates to the person's brief absence from work due to an injury).

Still, in point 51 of its judgment of 6 November 2003 in Case C-101/01,[1] the CJEU stated that 'reference to the fact that an individual has injured her foot and is on half-time on medical grounds constitutes personal data concerning health within the meaning of Article 8(1) of Directive 95/46'.

Information on addictions is not part of sensitive data. However, due to the problematic character of such information (from the perspective of the persons directly affected), it should arguably be treated as information concerning health. Information on addictions was not listed as sensitive data in Directive 95/46/EC (Article 8(1)), but was expressly included in sensitive data, for instance, in the Polish Data Protection Act (Article 27(1)).

The conditions for lawful processing of sensitive data are reversed in relation to those applicable to ordinary data. The processing of ordinary data is generally lawful, as long as the circumstances described in Article 6 of the GDPR are met (positive formulation). One of these circumstances is the existence of legitimate interests pursued by the controller or by a third party. The scope of legitimate interests is open-ended and defined by the controller. This means that processing of ordinary data is generally allowed, since a provision specifying the exception of a rule must be formulated and interpreted strictly.

By contrast, the special categories of data, enumerated in Article 9 of the GDPR, are subject to far more stringent principles, due to their particular importance for the right to privacy. The processing of sensitive data is generally prohibited – except where one of the conditions listed in Article 9(2) of the GDPR is met, but these conditions do not include the legitimate interests of the controller or a third party. Thus, the conditions for the lawful processing of sensitive data are formulated in a negative way, as exceptions from the general ban on the processing of such data, and these exceptions must be interpreted strictly.

The prohibition on processing of sensitive data does not apply where one of the following alternative conditions is met (Article 9(2) of the GDPR):

(a) The data subject has given explicit consent (by an action leaving no doubt as to the person's intention) to the processing of those personal data for one or more specified purposes, unless EU or Member State law prohibits the processing of sensitive data even with the consent of the data subject.
(b) Processing is necessary for the purposes of carrying out the obligations and exercising specific rights of the controller or of the data subject in the field of employment and social security and social protection law in so far as it is authorised by EU or Member State law or a collective agreement pursuant to Member State law providing for appropriate safeguards for the fundamental rights and the interests of the data subject.

1. CJEU judgment of 6 November 2003 in case C-101/01, *Bodil Lindqvist v Aklagarkammaren i Jönköping*, http://eur-lex.europa.eu/legal-content/EN/TXT/HTML/?uri=CELEX:62001CJ0101.

(c) Processing is necessary to protect the vital interests of the data subject or of another natural person where the data subject is physically or legally incapable of giving consent.
(d) Processing is carried out in the course of its legitimate activities with appropriate safeguards by a foundation, association or any other not-for-profit body with a political, philosophical, religious or trade union aim and on condition that the processing relates solely to the members or to former members of the body or to persons who have regular contact with it in connection with its purposes and that the personal data are not disclosed outside that body without the consent of the data subjects.
(e) Processing relates to personal data which are manifestly made public by, or under the explicit consent of, the data subject; the processing of sensitive data is still prohibited where the data were made public without the data subject's explicit consent, even if with his/her knowledge.
(f) Processing is necessary for the establishment, exercise or defence of legal claims or whenever courts are acting in their judicial capacity.
(g) Processing is necessary for reasons of substantial public interest, on the basis of EU or Member State law which must be proportionate to the aim pursued, respect the essence of the right to data protection and provide for suitable and specific measures to safeguard the fundamental rights and the interests of the data subject.
(h) Processing is necessary for the purposes of preventive or occupational medicine, for the assessment of the working capacity of the employee, medical diagnosis, the provision of health or social care or treatment or the management of health or social care systems and services on the basis of EU or Member State law or pursuant to contract with a health professional and subject to the conditions and safeguards referred to in Article 9(3) of the GDPR, referring to the obligation to maintain professional secrecy.
(i) Processing is necessary for reasons of public interest in the area of public health, such as protecting against serious cross-border threats to health or ensuring high standards of quality and safety of health care and of medicinal products or medical devices, on the basis of EU or Member State law which provides for suitable and specific measures to safeguard the rights and freedoms of the data subject, in particular professional secrecy. However, public interest considerations may not be invoked for the processing of health data by employers, insurance companies or banks (recital 54 of the preamble to the GDPR).
(j) Processing is necessary for archiving purposes in the public interest, scientific or historical research purposes or statistical purposes in accordance with Article 89(1) based on EU or Member State law which must be proportionate to the aim pursued, respect the essence of the right to data protection and provide for suitable and specific measures to safeguard the fundamental rights and the interests of the data subject.

Noticeably, circumstances allowing the processing of sensitive data (i.e. exceptions from the ban on their processing) do not include the processing being necessary for the conclusion of a contract with the data subject at his/her request, or for the performance of a contract entered into with a data subject, which are some of the key grounds for the processing of ordinary data. This means, for example, that the use of biometric data for identifying a bank's customer, even when it is part of the performance of a contract for a bank account, still requires the customer's consent.

For a discussion of the key circumstances allowing an exemption from the prohibition of processing sensitive data, from those presented above, see the comments relating to the legal bases of processing personal data under Article 6(1) of the GDPR (including consent under Article 7 of the GDPR and the performance of a legal obligation) and derogations under Article 49(1) of the GDPR from the prohibition of the transfer of personal data to third countries despite the lack of adequate levels of protection. These comments apply to the above exemptions as well, hence they will not be reiterated here in relation to Article 9(2) of the GDPR.

§7.02 PERSONAL DATA RELATING TO CRIMINAL CONVICTIONS AND OFFENCES

Personal data relating to criminal convictions and offences are subject to particular protection, despite not being sensitive data as covered by Article 9(1) of the GDPR (although they were previously listed as special categories of data in Article 8(5) of Directive 95/46/EC). Uncontrolled processing of such data could expose such convicts or offenders to stigmatisation and rejection in their environments as well as to discrimination, such as in the context of employment or lending. For this reason, they are mentioned in the GDPR alongside sensitive data, for example, in recital 75 in the preamble, citing, among others, the risk of discrimination, identity theft or fraud, financial loss, damage to reputation, or breach of professional secrecy as a result of the processing of sensitive data or data relating to criminal convictions and offences.

The classification of data on criminal convictions and offences as ordinary data is indicated by the relevant provisions being located outside the articles regulating special categories of data (unlike in Directive 95/46/EC), but also expressly by Article 10 of the GDPR, stipulating that these data are processed based on Article 6(1) of the GDPR.

Thus, the processing of personal data on criminal convictions and offences is based on substantive circumstances formulated positively (as opposed to the circumstances justifying the processing of sensitive data, formulated as exceptions from the general prohibition).

Besides the circumstances specified in Article 6(1) of the GDPR, the processing of personal data relating to criminal convictions and offences is based on EU or Member State law providing for appropriate safeguards for the rights and freedoms of data subjects. Article 10 of the GDPR provides for the processing of such data if 'authorised' by law. Thus, where a legal basis meets the condition of providing for appropriate safeguards, the processing is possible not only for 'compliance with a legal obligation to which the controller is subject', as in Article 6(1)(c) of the GDPR, but also for exercising a legal right.

Therefore, personal data relating to criminal convictions and offences or related security measures, where its processing is not expressly allowed under EU or Member State law, may only be processed under the control of an official authority. As the admissibility of processing is not limited to public authorities, private entities may also process such data, provided that the control of an official authority is ensured. This also relates to any comprehensive registers of criminal convictions, including, in particular, national criminal records. On the other hand, when the processing is authorised by EU or Member State law providing appropriate safeguards for the rights and freedoms of data subjects, no control by public authorities is required.

Data on convictions relate to the judgments of courts; furthermore, the term 'convictions' does not include acquittals or judgments of the conditional or unconditional discontinuation of proceedings. However, crimes which have not resulted in convictions, as well as minor offences (punishable e.g. by fines) may arguably be classified as 'offences'.

As far as the interpretation of 'related security measures' is concerned, within the context of the distinction between penalties and other security measures, also taking into account that security measures must be related to the judgment, they may, depending on the national law, include disfranchisement; loss of the right to occupy specified official positions, practise a specified profession or conduct a specified business; a ban from selected locations, environments or events, or house arrest; a restraining order; driving ban; public announcement of a judgment; or electronic monitoring, addiction therapy, or committal to a mental health institution.

One example of where Member State law may allow for the processing of data relating to a criminal conviction is making the conviction public as part of the punishment, provided for in the penal procedure. Such a measure reinforces the effect of the main penalty, influencing the criminal's status in his/her environment and dissuading potential followers.

CHAPTER 8

The Obligation to Provide Information on Data Processing. Privacy Notices

§8.01 BASIS OF THE INFORMATION OBLIGATION; THE EXTENSION OF INFORMATION CLAUSES

One of the data controller's key obligations is to provide data subjects with information on the key aspects of the processing of their data. Each data subject must know, inter alia, who is responsible for the regularity of the processing of his/her data, for what purpose the data have been collected, to whom they are or can be subsequently transferred, and how long they are going to be stored. With this information, the data subject may verify whether the data are processed in accordance with the purpose declared and may exercise his or her rights, e.g. the right to object to data processing.

The requirement to provide data subjects with information on the processing of their data is provided for in both the GDPR (Articles 12 to 14) and the Directive (Articles 10 and 11). However, the scope of information required under the GDPR (Articles 13 and 14) to be provided to the data subject, relating to data processing and the data subject's rights, is far broader than laid down in the Directive.

The scope of some information has been broadened; other categories of information have been introduced for the first time. For instance, the information required currently includes not only the specification of the controller but also contact data of the data protection officer, if one has been designated; not only the purposes of data processing but also the legal basis therefor; not only information on the data subject's right to access the data, rectify them or object to their processing, but also on his/her right to withdraw consent to processing where the consent is the basis for the processing, and on the right to lodge a complaint with a supervisory authority. It has also been made compulsory to inform the data subject on profiling, since a data subject's unawareness of being profiled (which may lead to conclusions being made which are statistically probable but erroneous in relation to the specific data subject) is one of the key threats. The GDPR has also introduced a requirement which will substantially reinforce the data subject's position: an obligation to specify the intended period for which the data is to be stored, or at least the criteria used to determine that period. This enables the data subject to verify, and consequently to challenge, the controller's practices.

As the scope of information required to be provided to data subjects has been expanded, information clauses used in data collection forms (both in paper and online) will have to be modified. This, however, will not be limited to a simple addition of new elements. Indeed, the new information to be provided must be established first. For instance, in order to specify precisely the intended period of storage of data, or the criteria used to determine that period, the categories of data must be established first, along with the legal bases and purposes of their processing, and an appropriate storage period, with a legal basis, must be assigned to each category.

This is a substantial reinforcement of the data subjects' rights, enabling them to control the regularity of the processing. Even the information on the controller's specific legitimate purposes and on the data retention periods brings new challenges. Thus far, a data subject could at times have been unaware of those aspects of data processing. Now, he/she will be able to verify and question them. On the other hand, from the controller's point of view, the obligation to make those aspects clear and to submit them to the data subjects' scrutiny will require an analysis of the data processing procedures. This will not be an easy task as, for instance, data stored in the same filing system do not necessarily have the same retention periods.

Article 13 of the GDPR (Article 10 of the Directive) and Article 14 of the GDPR (Article 11 of the Directive) specify different scopes of information required for the data controller to provide to the person whose data are being collected. These scopes differ depending on the source from which the data relating to a data subject have been obtained by the controller. Thus, Article 13 of the GDPR (Article 10 of the Directive) applies to personal data collected from the data subject (e.g. in direct contact in the controller's branch office, over the telephone, via a website, via an entity processing data for and on behalf of the controller), whereas Article 14 of the GDPR (Article 11 of the Directive) applies to personal data collected from other sources (e.g. from other data controllers, companies compiling marketing databases, or public telephone and address directories). Therefore, these provisions cover jointly all cases of collection of personal data, divided by source.

The collection of data (which has not been defined in the GDPR) means obtaining data, regardless of their source, with the intention of further processing thereof, regardless of the type of processing, technical form of data or the existence of a filing system. This includes online forms in which a customer enters his/her contact data; personal data forms signed by a customer when entering into an agreement; as well as the purchase of a licence for using a marketing database, or obtaining the data of a person from his/her spouse who has indicated him/her as the beneficiary under an insurance contract.

Additionally, Article 15 of the GDPR (and Article 12(a) of the Directive) introduces the right of the data subject to obtain information at his/her request, in a scope compatible with Articles 13 and 14 of the GDPR (Article 10 and 11 of the Directive). However, the information referred to in Article 15 of the Regulation (Article 12(a) of the

Directive) must be provided by the data controller at the request of the data subject, whereas the requirement to provide information under Articles 13 and 14 of the GDPR (Article 10 and 11 of the Regulation) is automatically binding under law upon data collection by a controller. Thus, the information obligations provided for in Articles 13 and 14 of the GDPR and those under Article 15 of the GDPR are independent and not mutually exclusive.

§8.02 THE RELATIONSHIP BETWEEN THE INFORMATION ON PROCESSING AND THE LAWFULNESS OF PROCESSING

One of the fundamental principles of data processing listed in Article 5 of the GDPR (Article 6(1) of the Directive) is the lawfulness of processing. The information obligations specified in Articles 13 and 14 of the GDPR (Articles 10 and 11 of the Regulation) are part of data controllers' key obligations. Therefore the lawfulness of data collection is contingent, among other things, on due compliance with the information obligations. However, if the controller fails to duly comply with the information obligation towards the data subject, this does not necessarily mean that the data processing by the controller is not lawful.[1] The information obligation is one of the key conditions of lawfulness of data processing, and is crucial for the data subject's right to control the processing of his or her data. However, there are also other conditions. These comprise in particular the legal bases of data processing (listed in Article 6 of the GDPR and Article 7 of the Directive), including, for example, data processing being necessary for the performance of a contract entered into with the data subject, or necessary in light of legitimate interests of the data controller. They also include the purpose limitation principle, the data minimisation principle and others.

Failure to duly comply with the information obligation may result in unlawfulness of data processing where data processing is contingent on the data subject's consent or non-objection. This is because for the consent to be valid, the data subject has to be aware of all the aspects of the planned processing.[2] Furthermore, failure to provide information, or providing misleading information, on the purpose of data processing is considered a breach of the fairness principle, formulated alongside the lawfulness principle in Article 5(1)(a) of the GDPR (Article 6(1)(a) of the Directive).[3]

However, appropriate information on data processing, enabling the data subject to scrutinise the processing and to exercise his or her rights, is crucial for the controller's liability. A breach of the data subject's right to be informed on the

1. The opposite view was expressed in: J. Barta, P. Fajgielski, R. Markiewicz, *Ochrona danych osobowych. Komentarz*, Kraków 2007, p. 480: the authors consider compliance with the obligation provisions to be a precondition for the lawfulness of data collection. P. Barta and P. Litwiński argue against this view in: *Ustawa o ochronie danych osobowych. Komentarz*, Warszawa 2009, p. 248.
2. Judgment of the Polish Supreme Administrative Court of 4 April 2003, II SA 2135/02 (Wokanda 2004, No. 6, p. 30).
3. P. Barta, P. Litwiński, *Ustawa o ochronie danych osobowych. Komentarz*, Warszawa 2009, pp. 249-250; P. Carey, *Data Protection*, Oxford 2004, p. 66.

processing of his/her data is subject to an administrative fine (Article 83(5)(b) of the GDPR).

Information obligations are also binding on a controller which has not collected the data by its own action, but has acquired a filing system (a database) from another entity which had failed in its information obligation while collecting the data. Thus, acquisition of a database under a civil law contract is also considered a data collection process.[4]

§8.03 SCOPE OF THE INFORMATION REQUIRED

The scopes of information which the controller is required to provide to the data subject upon collecting the data directly from him/her, e.g. upon providing a service at the controller's branch or via a website, or upon obtaining the data from a different source, e.g. from a marketing company compiling a database, are partly identical (Article 13(1) and (2) and Article 14(1) and (2) of the GDPR). In both cases, the information scope includes the following:

- The name and contact data of the controller and of the controller's representative, if one exists.
  The scope of the contact data must allow the data subject to exercise his/her rights, e.g. to request information on the processing of his/her data or withdraw consent for data processing.
- The contact details of the data protection officer, if one has been designated.
  The scope of data must effectively enable the data subject or the supervisory authority to contact the data protection officer. Thus, depending on the organisation, this may be an email address, provided that the mail is checked regularly. On the other hand, the relevant article does not require the identity of the data protection officer to be communicated to the data subject (e.g. as part of the institution's privacy policy). In addition, communicating the officer's identity would lead to complications in the event of his/her replacement. It is therefore reasonable for the data protection officer to use an email address permanently assigned to the position (such as DPO@, privacy@...) rather than the specific person. Using such an address does not mean that the supervisory authority will be deprived of information on the data protection officer's identity.
- The intended purposes of the data processing and the legal basis therefor.
  For instance, the requirement to specify the purposes of data processing is deemed to be met only if the information is given with sufficient detail. The required precision of formulating the purposes of data processing is enhanced by the new requirement to inform the data subject of the controller's legitimate interests where those are invoked as the legal basis for the processing. However, the scope of processing purposes includes numerous and diverse

4. Judgment by the Polish Supreme Administrative Court of 13 July 2004, I OSK 507/04.

operations, including: marketing, answering contact requests, risk assessment, concluding contracts, entering payments, the distribution of products or services, processing complaints, the enforcement of payments and claims, the payment and reporting of salaries, taxes and social security contributions, archiving, the recruitment of staff and keeping staff files etc. These are only examples of purposes to be met by the data controller. When the legal obligation to provide information on processing purposes is enforced by supervisory authorities, a question arises on how detailed or general the information should or may be and how the legal bases should be invoked (should a specific provision be provided as a basis for processing the data for a specific purpose, or is it sufficient to provide information that the data is collected to enable the controller to meet its legal obligations or perform a contract, or under the data subject's consent).

- The legitimate interests pursued by the controller or by a third party, if they have been invoked as the legal basis for the processing.
  Legitimate interests may include the processing of data for marketing (bearing in mind that electronic marketing communication is subject to more rigorous rules), or for protecting the company and its customers against fraud, including the monitoring and enforcement of claims.
- The recipients or categories of recipients of the personal data.
  The recipients or categories of recipients of the personal data are to be specified subject to the definition of recipient (Article 4(9) of the GDPR). According to this definition, a recipient is a natural or legal person, public authority, agency or another body to which the personal data are disclosed. However, public authorities which may receive personal data in the framework of a particular inquiry in accordance with EU or Member State law (e.g. courts, public prosecutor offices, the police or court bailiffs) are excluded from the definition of recipients. One important change introduced in the GDPR in comparison to some national laws is expanding the definition of recipients to include data processors. An indication of categories of data recipients should not be regarded as sufficient where the controller is able to specify the recipients at the time of performing its information obligation. Such a detailed specification should, however, not be required where it is not realistically feasible, e.g. with a high number of processors, or even not permissible, e.g. if it were to include the names of all staff who may access the system. In practice, information clauses only specify categories of recipients. More detailed information is provided by specifying areas or purposes where the processing of data has been entrusted to such recipients. Individual recipients are only specified if they are, for example, loan registers cooperating with the institution on a regular basis.
- Information on the controller's intention to transfer personal data to a recipient in a third country or an international organisation, if the controller plans to do so, and of the level of data protection subsequent to the transfer outside the EU (i.e. information whether the European Commission has found the level of protection in the target country to be adequate to the EU standard, or – where

the Commission has not issued such a decision and the transfer is made under Article 46, 47, or 49(1) – information on data safeguards provided by the exporter itself subsequent to the transfer, such as BCRs or standard contractual clauses, and the means by which to obtain information on such safeguards).

- The period for which the personal data will be stored, or, if it is not possible to specify this, the criteria used to determine that period.
  The period of data storage following the expiry of a contract (where the data are stored to meet a legal obligation, e.g. under tax regulations) may be specified in years. On the other hand, where the data are processed under the data subject's consent, the data storage period is determined by the withdrawal of consent by the data subject.
- Information on the data subject's right to access the data, rectify or erase them, restrict or object to their processing, and to data portability.
- Where the data (whether normal or sensitive) are being processed on the basis of the data subject's consent, information on the data subject's right to withdraw consent at any time.
- Information on the right to lodge a complaint with a supervisory authority (the competent supervisory authority, its contact details or the applicable procedure need not be specified).
- Information on any automated decision-making, including profiling referred to in Article 22(1) and (4) of the GDPR, and other meaningful information about the logic involved, as well as the significance and the envisaged consequences of such processing for the data subject.

Information on profiling must only be provided if the profiling meets the conditions of Article 22(1) and (4) of the GDPR, i.e. if it provides input to a decision which is based solely on automated processing and produces legal effects concerning the data subject or similarly significantly affects him or her, or the profiling includes the processing of sensitive data. The GDPR does not specify the level of detail which must be provided with the information on making such decisions, e.g. whether it must specify the criteria of a positive or negative decision, defined in the system. The impact of information on other consequences of profiling for the data subject, going beyond data protection and extending to business effects, such as higher prices for selected customers, should also be taken into consideration.

Besides this common scope of information, Article 13(1) and (2) and Article 14(1) and (2) of the GDPR also indicate information required only where information is either obtained directly from the data subject or collected from other sources. This relates to the fact that, where the data have not been obtained from the data subject him/herself, he/she is not aware of their processing; whereas if the data subject has provided his/her own data to the controller, he/she may not be aware of the processing only to a certain extent.

Informing the data subject of whether the provision of personal data is a statutory or contractual requirement, or a requirement necessary to enter into a contract, as well as whether the data subject is obliged to provide the personal data, and of the possible consequences of the failure to provide such data, is only required where the data are collected from the data subject. If data are collected from other sources, i.e. the data subject has not provided them, the information may not be applicable.

When the data subject is informed about whether the provision of data is mandatory or optional, one should bear in mind that the right to privacy, one of the personal rights and freedoms, may only be restricted under a statutory law or regulations issued on the basis of a statutory delegation.[5] Therefore, a legal basis should be specified for the requirement to provide data and for the possible consequences of a refusal. For data to be provided on a voluntary basis, the benefits of providing them may be specified.

Information required to be provided only where data are being obtained from a source other than the data subject includes: the categories of personal data concerned and the source of the data, including whether it is a publicly accessible source (such as a publicly available telephone and address directory).

In order to comply with the information obligation, the controller must provide the required information fully. The questions on how detailed the information must be in the cases listed above will be answered in practice by the enforcement of the information obligation by supervisory authorities.

The scope of information previously required to be provided to the data subjects under the Directive (in its Articles 10 and 11) and Member States' laws was far smaller than formulated in the GDPR (Articles 13 and 14).

The common scope of information required irrespective of whether data were collected from the data subject or from other sources included:

- the identity of the controller and of its representative, if any
- the purposes of data processing
- the recipients or categories of recipients of the data
- the existence of the data subject's right of access to, and the right to rectify, the data concerning him/her.

Where data were collected from the data subject, the Directive also required him/her to be informed whether the provision of data was obligatory or voluntary, as well as on the possible consequences of failure to provide data. Where data were obtained from another source than the data subject, categories of data had to be indicated.

The scope of information on data processing and on the data subject's rights, required to be provided to the data subject under the GDPR, is far broader. The scope of some information has been expanded; other categories of information have been introduced for the first time. For instance, the information required currently includes not only the specification of the controller, but also contact data of the data protection officer, if one has been designated; not only the purposes of data processing, but also the legal basis therefor; not only information on the data subject's right to access the data, rectify them or object to their processing, but also on his/her right to withdraw

5. One example of a legal provision formulating this principle is Article 51(5) of the Constitution of Poland, which states that principles and procedures for collection of and access to information shall be specified by statute.

consent to processing where the consent is the basis for the processing, and on the right to lodge a complaint with a supervisory authority. Also the data subject's rights have been expanded by adding the right to data portability, not included thus far in legal regulations on data protection. It has also been made compulsory to inform the data subject on profiling. This obligation could be inferred from the law existing thus far, but it was not formulated explicitly or broadly practiced. This is important since a data subject's unawareness of being profiled (which may lead to conclusions being made which are statistically probable but erroneous in relation to the specific data subject) is one of the key threats.

The GDPR has also introduced requirements which will substantially reinforce the data subject's position: an obligation to specify the legitimate interests pursued by the controller or by a third party, if they have been invoked as the legal basis for the processing, and an obligation to specify the intended period for which the data is to be stored, or at least the criteria used to determine that period. Finally, and importantly in the context of risks associated with transfers of data outside the EU, often to countries whose legislations do not ensure protection of data at a level adequate to the EU standard, a controller is now required to inform the data subjects of its intention to transfer personal data to a third country, if the controller plans to do so, and on the safeguards of an adequate level of protection of data subsequent to the transfer.

This new scope of required information will necessarily lead to a significant expansion of information clauses used by controllers on their websites or in their paper questionnaires. On the other hand, complying with the information obligation while collecting data during a telephone conversation will become impracticable.

Such a broad scope of information provides data subjects with tools to scrutinise data processing and exercise their rights. For instance, the controller's obligation to specify its legitimate purposes and the data storage periods gives the data subjects the possibility to verify, and consequently challenge, the controller's practices – a possibility which has thus far been incomplete due to the lack of this information.

§8.04 CIRCUMSTANCES GIVING RISE TO THE INFORMATION OBLIGATION

As indicated in Articles 13 and 14 of the GDPR, the information obligation arises upon collection or obtaining of data.[6] Unlike Articles 13 and 14 of the GDPR, Directive 95/46/EC does not specify expressly in Article 10 the moment when the information obligation arises in case of collection of data from the data subject. However, the indication of the moment in GDPR should be considered a mere clarification. The information provided to the data subject, particularly the information on the purpose of

6. Data collection is not defined in the Regulation. It is mentioned as one aspect of personal data processing in Article 4(2). It should be defined, as in P. Barta, P. Litwiński, *Ustawa o ochronie danych osobowych. Komentarz*, Warszawa 2009, p. 240, as each instance of coming into possession of personal data, including consulting them, with the intention of their further processing, irrespective of whether the processing is to be carried out in the personal data filing system.

processing and the recipients of data, may influence the data subject's decision to agree or refuse to make data available. For this reason, where the source of data is the data subject, the information should be provided to the data subject prior to, or at the time of, collecting the data;[7] such an interpretation is in line with the principle also formulated expressly in Article 13 of the GDPR. It could also be inferred from the title of Article 10 of the Directive, indicating that the information obligation is the direct result of data collection, and from the use of the expression 'data subject from whom data relating to himself are collected', rather than 'from whom data ... have been collected' or 'whose data ... have been recorded'.

Where data are collected from sources other than the data subject, the information obligation does not arise upon the obtaining of data. Rather, under Article 14(3) of the GDPR, it arises within a reasonable period after obtaining the data, taking the specific circumstances into consideration, but at the latest within one month.

This Article states further that if the data are to be used for communication with the data subject, the controller must provide the required information to the data subject at the latest at the time of the first communication to that data subject, or, if a disclosure to another recipient is envisaged, at the latest when the personal data are first disclosed. This does not relieve the controller of the information obligation until the time of the first communication or disclosure, if this were to occur in the unreasonably distant future. That would give the controller the freedom of decision on when the information obligation arises and would in essence postpone its performance; consequently, the data subject would be deprived for an unspecified period of the possibility to exercise his or her rights.[8] It therefore seems that, even where the controller envisages a transfer of data to a third party, the information obligation arises within a reasonable period after their collection, but not later than upon the first disclosure of the data.

By allowing the information to be provided 'within a reasonable period after obtaining the personal data', the provision of Article 14(3) responds to justified cost and organisational considerations on the part of data controllers, while not jeopardising legitimate rights of data subjects to obtain information which is necessary for controlling the processing of their data.

Prior to the adoption of the GDPR, the need for this was illustrated by the information obligation stipulated in the Polish Data Protection Act for the collection of data from sources other than the data subject (Article 25(1)). The obligation arose 'directly upon the registration of the collected [personal] data'. Complying exactly with this requirement in a situation of, for example, a bank acquiring the right to use a database from its producer for a single marketing action, would require substantial costs of separate correspondence for the sole purpose of providing the information on data processing. The obligation set out in this provision is therefore usually performed

7. An interpretation shared by: P. Barta, P. Litwiński, *Ustawa o ochronie danych osobowych. Komentarz*, Warszawa 2009, p. 245; J. Barta, P. Fajgielski, R. Markiewicz, *Ochrona danych osobowych. Komentarz*, Kraków 2007, p. 485.
8. The Polish Supreme Administrative Court in its judgment of 13 July 2004 (OSK 507/04) emphasised that it is the immediate performance of the information obligation that enables the beneficiaries to exercise their statutory rights.

in practice in the marketing correspondence for which the right to use the database was acquired by the bank. The Polish Supreme Administrative Court condemned this practice by declaring, in its judgment of 13 July 2004 (OSK 507/04), that 'failing to directly provide information on the acquisition of data prior to sending the first marketing offer' was a breach of Article 25(1) of the Polish Data Protection Act.

The GDPR has substantially expanded the scope of information required to be provided to data subjects in comparison to Directive 95/46/EC and Member State laws. Thus the information should have been provided again to data subjects whose data were collected before 25 May 2018, when the Regulation became applicable.

Where changes or additions are made to privacy policies, 'controllers should make it clear to data subjects that these changes have been effected in order to comply with the GDPR'. Article 29 Working Party recommends[9] that 'at a minimum controllers should make [have made] this information publicly available (e.g. on their website)' prior to 25 May 2018. 'Material or substantive' changes 'should be actively brought to the attention of the data subject'.

I believe that bringing information actively to the attention of the data subject need not require sending direct communication; it may be done, as a minimum, by a conspicuous banner announcing that the privacy policy has been updated and providing a link to the new policy.

§8.05 EXEMPTIONS FROM THE INFORMATION OBLIGATION

The simple fact of obtaining data from publicly available sources, e.g. public telephone and address directories, is not grounds for exemption from the information obligation.

The information obligations laid down in Articles 13 and 14 of the GDPR (Articles 10 and 11 of Directive 95/46/EC) are subject to exemption under those provisions (Article 13(4) and Article 14(5)(a) of the Regulation) where the data subject already has the information that is required to be provided. The exemption may therefore be full or limited to the selected categories of information, specified in those provisions, depending on the extent of information that the data subject has already obtained previously. The reasons why the data subject may already have had the information may be, for instance, that the controller continues to process the data in the same scope and for the same purpose as previously, under the same contract. It is for the controller to demonstrate that the data subject has previously obtained the information in the required scope and that the circumstances of data processing have not changed to the extent that would make it necessary to provide the information again in a modified scope. The intention to process data for a different purpose than the one for which they have been obtained requires providing information to the data subject beforehand on the changed purpose, along with other required information (Article 13(3) and Article 14(4) of GDPR).

9. Article 29 Working Party, *Guidelines on transparency under Regulation 2016/679*, WP 260 rev1, adopted on 29 November 2017, last revised and adopted on 11 April 2018, http://ec.europa.eu/newsroom/article29/item-detail.cfm?item_id=622227, point 3 of the Introduction, p. 5.

Exemption from the information obligation in cases where data are not collected directly from the data subject is also justified (Article 14(5)(b) of the GDPR, Article 11(2) of the Directive), where the provision of the required information would involve a disproportionate effort. It is specified in the provisions that this refers in particular (but not exclusively) to processing for archiving purposes in the public interest, scientific or historical research purposes or statistical purposes, but subject to the condition of ensuring appropriate safeguards for the rights and freedoms of the data subject.

The GDPR and the Directive also provide for an exemption from the information obligation where providing information on the processing of data proves impossible. This addition seems redundant though; given that disproportionate effort constitutes grounds for an exemption, so should impossibility. Failure to provide information directly to the data subject (in cases where data are not collected directly from the data subject) may be partly compensated by placing easily accessible information (privacy policy), in the scope corresponding to Article 14 of the GDPR, on the data controller's website.

In order to fulfil, when data are being recorded, the information obligation towards persons whose data are contained in a database acquired by the controller from its producer for a single marketing action, one is confronted with significant costs of separate correspondence for the sole purpose of providing the required information. The reference to disproportionate effort may therefore refer, among others, to this type of situation. Sending separate correspondence for the sole purpose of providing information on the processing of data seems in such a situation to require disproportionate, excessive cost, time or effort.[10] One may argue that, if the required information is provided only in the marketing correspondence whose sending was the purpose intended by the controller at the time of acquiring the right to use the relevant data base, this entails compliance with the information obligation. However, this requires a proviso that the data subject must be informed of his/her data having been collected from a different source in the first marketing correspondence but, as required by Article 14(3)(a) of the Regulation, within a reasonable period not exceeding one month.

The information obligation in a situation where the data have not been obtained from the data subject is also exempt where the obtaining or disclosure of data is expressly laid down by EU or Member State law to which the controller is subject and which provides appropriate measures to protect the data subject's legitimate interests (Article 14(5)(c) of the GDPR, Article 11(2) of the Directive). This exemption must, however, not be expanded to the obtaining or disclosure of data which is not required by law, but only by personal data exchange policies agreed upon between public administration institutions.[11]

---

10. Cost can be considered excessive if the cost of action necessary to provide the information to the data subject exceeds the negative consequences that might be suffered by the data subject upon failure to be provided with such information; cf. J. Barta, P. Fajgielski, R. Markiewicz, *Ochrona danych osobowych. Komentarz*, Kraków 2007, p. 498.
11. CJEU judgment of 1.10.2015 in Case C-201/14 *Smaranda Bara and Others v Casa Națională de Asigurări de Sănătate and Others*, http://eur-lex.europa.eu/legal-content/EN/TXT/?uri=CELEX:62014CJ0201.

This exemption applies to public sector controllers (central and local government bodies, other State and local organisational units and non-public entities performing public tasks) as well as non-public sector controllers[12] (e.g. financial institutions required to collect and report data under anti-money laundering laws).

Importantly though, the exemption laid down in Article 14(5)(c) of the GDPR is limited to cases where the data being processed were obtained from a source other than the data subject. No such exemption applies under the GDPR where the data are collected directly from the data subject by public administration conducting proceedings (Article 13(4) of the GDPR provides only that the data subject already has the information). Still, the failure to provide the required information is a common breach by public institutions (unless Member State laws regulating the activities of certain institutions provide for limitations of information provided to data subjects). Such information is often lacking e.g. in data collection forms, which are intended for data subjects and should allow them to obtain information on the processing of their data. The information obligation cannot be deemed to have been met by putting the appropriate information clause on a website, in accordance with laws on the access to public information. In such a case, although the information is publicly available, it cannot be demonstrated to have been provided directly to the person whose data are being collected.

Another exemption from the information obligation in a situation where the data have not been obtained from the data subject is professional secrecy under EU or Member State law (Article 14(5)(d) of the GDPR). Such professional secrecy arrangements exist in such professions as lawyers (barristers, solicitors, attorneys at law etc.), notaries, journalists, doctors (physicians), tax authorities, and mail and telecommunication service providers. Thus, a journalist who has obtained the data of a third party from his or her source for an investigation, or a barrister who has obtained the data from his client for the purpose of defending him/her in court, is exempt from the information obligation.

Other secrecy arrangements regulated by law and influencing the information obligation towards the data subject are bank secrecy and insurance secrecy. Bank secrecy may, depending on the regulations in force in the particular EU Member State, lead to a conflict, for example, in a case where a bank has received a loan application containing the personal data of the applicant's spouse. A conflict would occur between the bank's information obligation as the data controller (requiring it to provide information to the applicant's spouse) and its obligation to maintain bank secrecy (to protect the applicant).

Professional secrecy also leads to an exemption of the information obligation where the provision constituting grounds for data processing allows the data to be processed without disclosing the processing or its purpose, or prohibits such disclosure. One example is the prohibition of informing the data subject by a financial

12. P. Barta, P. Litwiński, *Ustawa o ochronie danych osobowych. Komentarz*, Warszawa 2009, p. 260; X. Konarski, G. Sibiga, Zmiany w ustawie o ochronie danych osobowych w świetle Dyrektywy 95/46/WE, M. Praw. 2004, No. 12, p. 551.

institution that it had notified a competent authority about suspected money laundering by the data subject.

Failure to comply with the information obligation towards the data subject from whom data have been collected by the controller cannot be justified by the fact that the data subject initiated the provision of the data, e.g. by requesting the controller to enter into a service contract.[13] The information obligation arises upon collection of data. According to the provisions, the information obligation or its scope does not depend on whether the collection of data was at the initiative of the controller or the data subject. An exclusion or restriction of the information obligation where data is collected at the data subject's request may only be due to the fact that (and only apply to the extent to which) the data subject has already had the information (Article 13(4) of the GDPR). It is the controller's obligation to demonstrate that this is indeed the case, however. In practice, though, differentiating the information clauses included in the forms which the controller uses would be an excessive complication and a redundant effort. In such a situation, the most advisable solution would be to provide the data subject with information according to a standard clause, i.e., in some cases, to provide more information than required.

§8.06 MANNERS OF PERFORMING THE INFORMATION OBLIGATION; TRANSPARENCY PRINCIPLE

Articles 13 and 14 of the GDPR (Articles 10 and 11 of Directive 95/46/EC) do not specify the manner and forms of complying with the information obligation. The obligation should therefore be considered met if the information required under these regulations has been provided to the data subject by the controller in any clear form. The wording of these provisions implies that the information must be effectively provided to the data subject and the burden of proof of complying with that requirement rests with the controller.

The information obligation, met in practice e.g. by publishing information clauses in online contact forms (via links to 'privacy notices' or 'privacy and cookie policies') is a crucial obligation enabling the data subject to control the lawfulness of the processing of his/her data.

Article 12(1) of the GDPR allows the information on the processing of data to be provided in writing but also in other different forms, including electronically, or, if the data subject so requests, orally. Upon the provision of information, the data subject's identity must be confirmed. The GDPR requires a concise, transparent, intelligible and easily accessible form and the use of clear and plain language, in particular where information is addressed to a child.

13. J. Barta, P. Fajgielski, R. Markiewicz (*Ochrona danych osobowych. Komentarz*, Kraków 2007, p. 478) have voiced an opinion that information obligation does not apply in cases of data collection at the request of the data subject. However, P. Barta and P. Litwiński (*Ustawa o ochronie danych osobowych. Komentarz*, Warszawa 2009, p. 240) and A. Drozd, *Ustawa o ochronie danych osobowych. Komentarz*, Warszawa 2004, p. 133) have argued to the contrary.

These requirements may be met in the clauses accompanying the data collection forms through the use of standardised icons (graphical symbols) to give a legible and meaningful overview of the intended processing (icons presented electronically should be machine-readable). The European Commission is empowered to determine the information which should be presented by the icons and to standardise them (Article 12(7) and (8) of the GDPR).[14]

Effective performance of the information obligation may be demonstrated through the data subject's signature on the form provided by the controller, ticking the required box next to the information clause on a website, or sequencing information on the website in such a way that the customer must read the information on data processing before proceeding to the product details. The required information may also be provided in a telephone conversation with the controller's call centre. The controller can then prove having provided the information by presenting a recording of the conversation or demonstrating that it has implemented a binding telephone conversation scenario including the appropriate clause. The information obligation can only be deemed duly complied with if the information is directed at, and directly provided to, the data subject. This excludes such forms as displaying the information on a notice board in the controller's business location or its publication in the press or on the Internet.

Information on data processing may also be provided through 'push' or 'pull' notices. Push notices involve the provision of 'just-in-time' information notices while 'pull' notices facilitate access to information by methods such as permission management or 'learn more' tutorials.[15]

The information obligation is linked with the transparency principle. It is defined in recital 58 of the preamble to the GDPR as requiring that information presented to the data subject or to the public (particularly to children) is concise, easily accessible and easy to understand, including through the use of clear and plain language and,

---

14. The GDPR, in its draft wording adopted by the European Parliament in the first reading on 12 March 2014, even contained a template of such icons in its Article 13a and in the Annex. They related to information whether the data were collected and stored beyond the scope, and for longer periods, than the minimum necessary to meet the processing purposes, whether the data were processed for purposes other than those for which they were collected, whether the data were made available to commercial third parties, sold or leased out, and whether they were stored in an encrypted form. The information on data being stored in an encrypted form ('No personal data are retained in unencrypted form') was misleading for the data subjects and was likely to create excessive expectations on their part, as it implied that encrypted storage was a mandatory safeguard, or at least a recommended one. In reality, it is neither required under law nor necessary. The misunderstanding was due to the use of the expression 'encrypted data', defined in Article 4(2b) of the GDPR in its draft wording of 12 March 2014 as data which through technological protection measures was rendered unintelligible to persons not authorised to access them. Certainly, this description applied to data encryption as well. However, the aim described in the definition is usually attained in practice without resorting to data encryption, through restricted and protected access, including by defining authorisations to process data and to access the relevant IT system and using unique user names and passwords in accordance with a password policy.
15. Article 29 Working Party, Guidelines on transparency under Regulation 2016/679, WP 260 rev1, adopted on 29 November 2017, last revised and adopted on 11 April 2018, http://ec.europa.eu/newsroom/article29/item-detail.cfm?item_id=622227, p. 20.

potentially, through visualisation.[16] This requires use of a language which is comprehensible to the average recipient in the specific context, i.e. avoiding excessively technical language or jargon which is clear to the data controller but not its customers. This principle is also violated by hiding key information in other content or by using fine print (expressly prohibited by consumer protection laws in some countries). The GDPR puts particular emphasis on the relevance of clear and transparent information in situations where technological complexity makes it difficult for the data subject to know and understand by whom and for what purpose his/her personal data are being collected, such as in the case of online advertising.

These proposed standards have been put into law in Article 12 of the GDPR, which defines the principles of transparent information and communication, not only relating to information clauses in the context of data collection (Articles 13 and 14 of the GDPR) but also to situations where the data subject requests information (Article 15 of the GDPR), where the data controller makes automated decisions significantly affecting the data subject, including profiling (Article 22 of the GDPR), and where a personal data breach is communicated to the data subject (Article 34).

16. This relates, among others, to the Resolution on International Standards for the Protection of Personal Data and Privacy, adopted at the 31st International Conference of Data Protection and Privacy Commissioners in Madrid on 5 November 2009: http://www.privacyconference2009.org.

CHAPTER 9

The Rights of Access, Rectification, Erasure ('Right to Be Forgotten'), Restriction of Processing, Data Portability, and Objection to Processing for Direct Marketing and Profiling (Subject Access Requests, Data Subject Rights)

§9.01 PROCESSING WHICH DOES NOT REQUIRE IDENTIFICATION – EFFECT ON THE RIGHTS OF DATA SUBJECTS

Article 11 will not be discussed in accordance with the order of articles in the GDPR but alongside the comments on the rights of data subjects, specified in Articles 15-20 of the GDPR, which are the subject of this chapter, because Article 11 affects their application.

In cases where the purposes for which a controller processes personal data do not require the identification of a data subject by the controller from the very beginning, or no longer require such identification, the GDPR (Article 11(1)) exempts the controller from the obligation to maintain, acquire or process additional information in order to identify the data subject for the sole purpose of complying with the GDPR (rather than for achieving the objectives of the activities carried out by the controller).

This provision may be considered as a reflection of the data minimisation principle specified in Article 5(1)(c) of the GDPR, which limits the scope of the processed data to what is necessary in relation to the purposes for which they are processed. Furthermore, recital 9 of the preamble to Directive 2002/58/EC on privacy and electronic communications obliges Member States and service providers to introduce and develop technological guarantees of minimising data and of using anonymised or pseudonymised data where possible. This also corresponds with the principle of data protection by design specified in Article 25 of the GDPR.

The condition specified in Article 11(1) of the GDPR – that purposes of processing do not or no longer require the identification of a data subject – is not only a basis for the exemption from the obligation to maintain data identifying the data subject, but even a basis for the erasure of such data ('the right to be forgotten') referred to in Article 17(1)(a) of the GDPR – 'the personal data are no longer necessary in relation to the purposes for which they were collected or otherwise processed'.

Since it is impossible to identify a data subject in the above-mentioned cases referred to in Article 11(1) of the GDPR, after his/her data have been removed or anonymised, the provision of Article 11(2) of the GDPR exempts the controller from its obligation to meet claims of the data subject specified in Articles 15-20 of GDPR. However, the controller is obliged to inform the data subject, if possible, for example by email address used by the sender, that it is not in position to identify him/her, and so in consequence that it is not able to meet his/her claims specified in Articles 15-20 of the GDPR (although, essentially, only if the request does not entail the risk of disclosing data to an unauthorised person or redirecting the data subject's mail to an unauthorised address, or other similar risks). However, the controller is obliged to accept the data subject's claims if he/she provides the controller with additional information enabling his/her identification.

§9.02 LEGAL BASES AND SCOPES OF DATA SUBJECTS' RIGHTS

Articles 15 to 22 of the GDPR formulate the rights of data subjects towards the data controller. They correspond to the principles of personal data processing, i.e. the data minimisation or storage limitation principles, as well as the requirement to invoke a legal basis for processing data and to provide information to the data subject. The requirement to invoke a legal basis, the basic data processing principles and the information obligations applicable upon collection of data are all binding upon the controller under law. On the other hand, Articles 15 to 22 of the GDPR indicate data subjects' rights which correspond to those obligations but are exercisable at the request of the data subjects.

Data subjects' rights include:

- information rights: the right to access data, including the right to data portability;
- correction rights: the right to the rectification of data; and
- restrictive rights: the right to erasure ('right to be forgotten'), the right to the restriction of processing and the right to object to processing.

This triad of types of rights enables data subjects to control the processing of their data. The right of access and the right to rectification are self-standing rights, but may also be exercised as the initial stages prior to objecting to the processing of data or demanding erasure or restriction of the processing of data.

The right of access to data includes the right to be informed on the processing of data (Article 15 of the GDPR) and the right to data portability (Article 20 of the GDPR), the latter having been newly introduced in the GDPR. The right to rectification also covers the right to have the data updated and completed (Article 16 of the GDPR). The right to object to processing (Article 21 of the GDPR) may deprive the controller of a legal basis for direct marketing and/or profiling. The data subject's objection to the processing of data may also result, alternatively, in an erasure of data (Article 17 of the GDPR) or a restriction of processing (Article 18 of the GDPR), which also feature as the data subject's self-standing rights.

These rights, formulated by Directive 95/46/EC, are upheld by the GDPR but also significantly expanded and reinforced through legal arrangements designed to restore their practical effectiveness, particularly by taking into account the evolution of data processing technologies. All information rights, correction rights and restrictive rights are presented in detail later in this chapter.

The information, correction and restrictive rights are reserved solely for the data subject. They cannot be exempted from by an agreement between the controller and the data subject, nor are they transferrable by the data subject to a third party, whether during the data subject's lifetime or in contemplation of death.[1] Thus, they may not be claimed, for example, by the data subject's inheritor. Accordingly, any demands that the inheritor may make, such as for erasing the data or a photograph of the deceased person which may be detrimental to that person's reputation, may not be justified with the inheritor's right to object to the processing of the deceased's personal data, but only by respect for the deceased's memory, which is a personal good (not of the deceased but of his/her surviving relatives).

I believe it permissible, however, for a person to entrust the enforcement of his/her correction or restrictive rights following his/her death to his/her inheritors by means of a letter of instruction. The rights are thus not conferred upon the inheritors, but they take action to fulfil the deceased's wishes. I expect such cases to be of increasing relevance, particularly in view of the growing popularity of social networking services. For instance, the number of Facebook profiles of deceased people is estimated to exceed the number of living people's profiles by 2098.

A person's wish that the intimate details of his/her life are not at risk of disclosure through the continued existence of his/her social networking profile following his/her death, where he/she is no longer in a position to control it, ought to be respected. The deceased's acquaintances might find out or guess his/her password, whereupon his/her secrets may be revealed.

Facebook has already made a 'Memorialisation request' form available which may be submitted by a deceased's close relative or the executor of his/her will. When such a request is made and granted, the deceased's profile becomes frozen as a memorialisation vehicle, with no-one able to log on to it. However, I find this a partial solution: the deceased's data are not erased and the possibility to re-access the account cannot be completely ruled out. One relevant example is a highly publicised lawsuit

1. As also argued by J. Barta, P. Fajgielski, R. Markiewicz, *Ochrona danych osobowych. Komentarz*, Kraków 2007, p. 573.

brought against Facebook in Germany by the mother of a teenage girl who died tragically.[2] The mother demanded access to her daughter's social networking account to verify or dispel her suspicions that the girl could have committed suicide as a result of bullying. The Federal Constitutional Court in Karlsruhe ruled on 12 July 2018 that a contract for an account with a social network, as a part of a user's legacy, should be passed on to the mother, with full access to her daughter's posts and private messages.

Any request under the rights of access, rectification, completion, erasure or similar rights must be made to the data controller, not to a supervisory authority. However, a data subject may request that the supervisory authority initiates administrative proceedings if the controller fails to meet its obligations.

The controller is obliged (Article 12(3) of the GDPR) to provide information to the data subject, without undue delay and in any event within one month of receipt of the request, on any action taken on the data subject's request made under Articles 15 to 22. (I find this wording awkward and potentially misleading, as it might suggest that the controller must provide information on the internal procedure activated in response to the data subject's request. In my view, it should rather be understood as an obligation to provide the only information relevant to the requesting data subject, i.e. whether the request was granted and, if not, what the grounds for refusal are.) The GDPR allows this period to be extended by two further months where this is necessary given the complexity and number of the requests. However, the controller must then, within one month of receipt of the request, inform the data subject of any such extension together with the reasons for the delay. In my opinion, the complexity or high number of requests can only be invoked by the data controller in relation to requests made by the same data subject. I do not believe it justified for a controller to cite organisational problems caused by a multitude of similar requests resulting only from the controller's large-scale operation.

If the controller does not take the action requested by the data subject it must inform the data subject without delay, and at the latest within one month of receiving the request, of the reasons for not taking action and on the possibility of lodging a complaint with a supervisory authority and seeking a judicial remedy (Article 12(4) of the GDPR).

The GDPR is flexible as to the form of making, and responding to, requests: they may be made in writing or in other forms (including orally, provided that this is justified by the nature of the request, in which case the data subject's identity must be confirmed by other means). The request may also be made by electronic means, whereupon the controller must reply in an electronic form as well, where possible and unless otherwise requested by the data subject (Article 12(1) and (3) of the GDPR). However, the data controller is responsible for implementing procedures to prevent information being provided to, or action being taken at the request of, a person who is not entitled thereto but is using the data subject's identity, e.g. is sending the request from an email address he/she has set up using the name of the data subject. Providing information or taking other action imprudently upon a request which was ostensibly

2. https://www.theguardian.com/technology/2017/may/31/parents-lose-appeal-access-dead-girl-facebook-account-berlin.

made by the data subject might not only lead to a personal data breach, but also enable the perpetrator to steal the data subject's identity, facilitate phishing (i.e. using the data subject's data to impersonate him/her and obtain his/her email or e-banking login credentials), or cause harm in other ways.

For this reason, a reply may only be sent to an email address once it has been ascertained to belong to the data subject, i.e. if this address was given by the data subject upon signing the agreement in the data controller's office, after his/her identity was checked. The same principle applies to giving an oral reply, which is allowed if the data subject has requested it and provided that the data subject's identity has been confirmed.

This type of situation is referred to in Article 12(2) of the GDPR. According to this provision, where the controller is not in a position to identify the data subject, it shall not refuse to act on the request of the data subject to exercise his or her rights under Articles 15 to 22 (although, essentially, only if the request does not entail the risk of disclosing data to an unauthorised person or redirecting the data subject's mail to an unauthorised address, or other similar risks). The controller may, however, refuse to act on a request for access to data, modification of data or other actions if there is a risk of a breach of the data subject's rights and the controller demonstrates that it is not in a position to identify the data subject (although, if the controller has reasonable doubts concerning the identity of the requesting person, it may request additional information necessary to confirm the person's identity).

However, as far as objection to processing data for marketing is concerned, I do not believe it justified to refuse to grant such objection sent from an unverified address. If, in a specific situation, there is no risk of revealing information on a customer and no grounds for suspicion that the request is part of a fraud, the objection should in my opinion be complied with. Where it is not possible to identify the person making the request, Article 11(2) exempts the application of Articles 15 to 20 of the GDPR, but not Article 21. This means that an unidentified requesting person may not be given access to the data of the data subject or have such data rectified. This is justified, since otherwise an unauthorised recipient could access protected information or, for instance, change the data subject's contact address and subsequently receive the information addressed to the data subject. However, Article 21 of the GDPR does not provide for such exemption. Therefore it is permissible to grant an objection to processing data for marketing purposes if this does not entail the risk of disclosing personal data and the circumstances do not suggest an attempted wrongdoing or offence.

It is recommended in recital 63 of the preamble to the GDPR that data subjects be provided with direct remote access to their personal data via a secure IT system. This solution is widely used by banks, telecoms, or schools. It also includes in practice the possibility for the controller's customers to edit their own data or manage their own payments. This not only ensures transparency but also relieves the controllers of certain actions, as it becomes redundant to make direct requests to controllers for access to data. However, allowing customers to edit their own data carries a risk that must also be taken into consideration. Modifying contact details (which are not verified anyway, but are accepted as communicated) does not entail a significant risk; a change of ID card number, on the other hand, may lead to errors or a security breach.

Pursuant to Article 12(5) of the GDPR, the performance by the controller of its information obligation upon collecting data (Articles 13 and 14) and other actions specified in Articles 15–22 and 34 (e.g. ensuring access to data being processed, erasure of data, or communicating a personal data breach to the data subject) must be free of charge. There is, however, a proviso that if requests from a data subject are manifestly unfounded or excessive (the burden of proving that this is the case rests with the controller), in particular because of their repetitive character, the controller may charge a reasonable fee (taking into account the costs) or refuse to act upon the request. Still, I believe that a refusal should not be seen as a simple alternative to charging a fee. In my opinion, it should only be permissible in relation to blatantly excessive and persistent requests, e.g. those evidently intended to stall the controller's activities by engaging its employees and resources rather than to obtain the information or exercise the rights that the data subject is entitled to. Data subjects' rights provided for in Articles 15–22 and 34 of the GDPR are crucial for the protection of data and compliance with the GDPR. I therefore believe that the requesting person should first be informed of the applicable fees and their justification; only where the data subject refuses to pay may the controller refuse to act upon the request. Another solution might be for the controller to suggest providing the information in a manner or form which is different from the costly form demanded by the requesting person; e.g. if the person asks for information on paper, which would require copying of many pages, the controller may suggest sending it via email or on a compact disc instead. On the other hand, it is not permissible for a controller to set fixed prices based on hourly wages of employees engaged in processing and providing information on behalf of the controller, since providing information is one of the controller's key obligations.

Directive 95/46/EC also did not preclude charging the data subject with the costs of providing him/her with the required information. However, the charge could not be excessive, i.e. it was not to exceed the real cost of providing the information, as justified for the type of action and the characteristics of the controller. The costs could result in particular from the frequency of requests for information (Article 12(a) of the Directive required information to be provided at reasonable intervals and without excessive expense; Article 32(5) of the Polish Personal Data Protection Act, for example, therefore allowed data subjects to obtain information not more often than once every six months).

The information, correction and restrictive rights are reserved solely for the data subject. This does not mean, however, that the demands specified in the relevant legal provisions may only be made by the persons to whom the personal data relate directly. In some particular cases, those rights also cover persons indirectly affected by the personal data in question, especially on the grounds of factual inaccuracy of the data. An example could be the processing of a piece of information stating that Person A occupies a given post in a given institution, whereas in reality the post is occupied by Person B. In such a situation, Person B cannot be considered a third party as the data contained in the filing system relate to him/her indirectly. Thus, Person B should be deemed to have the right to make claims under his/her information, correction and restrictive rights.

§9.03 RIGHT OF ACCESS TO DATA

The data subject's right of access to data (Article 15 of the GDPR, Article 12(a) of Directive 95/46/EC) corresponds with the information obligations of the data controller, specified in Articles 13 and 14 of the GDPR (Articles 10 and 11 of the Regulation), i.e. information clauses used when collecting data (e.g. on paper or online forms used for collecting data). However, the information referred to in Article 15 of the GDPR (Article 12(a) of the Directive) must be provided by the controller at the request of the data subject (who may specify the categories of requested information, within the limits of Article 15 of the GDPR), whereas the requirements to provide information under Articles 13 and 14 of the GDPR (Articles 10 and 11 of the Regulation) result directly from those provisions and arise upon data collection by a controller. The information obligations provided for in Articles 13 and 14 of the GDPR and those under Article 15 of the GDPR are independent and not mutually exclusive.

Information on the key aspects of data processing, such as the categories of collected data, the purposes of processing thereof, the data recipients, and the envisaged period of storage of data, enable the data subject to verify whether the data are processed in accordance with the purpose declared, to control the processing in other aspects, and to exercise his or her rights, e.g. the right to object to data processing.

The data subject's right of access under Article 12(a) of Directive 95/46/EC included the right to obtain from the data controller:

- confirmation of whether one's data were being processed and information at least as to the purposes of the processing, the categories of data concerned, and the recipients or categories of recipients of the data;
- communication in an intelligible form of the data undergoing processing and indication of their source;
- information on the logic involved in any automatic processing of the data subject's data; such information was mandatory in the case of the automated decision making referred to in Article 15(1) of the Directive.

The scope of information required to be provided to the data subject on request, specified in Article 15(1) of the GDPR, is far broader compared to the scope in Article 12(a) of the Directive. The list of information to be provided in information clauses upon the collection of data has been expanded accordingly (Article 13 and 14 of the GDPR).

The scope of information to be provided at the data subject's request includes the elements previously indicated in Article 12(a) of the Directive, i.e. a confirmation of the data subject's data being processed, indication of the purposes of processing, categories of data, and the recipients or categories of recipients to whom the data have been, or are to be, disclosed, particularly in the case of transfers of data outside the EEA (Article 15(1)(a)–(c) of the GDPR).

However, the list has been expanded in the GDPR by adding new elements (Article 15(1)(d)–(h) and Article 15(2)):

- the envisaged storage period of the personal data, or if it is not possible to specify this, the criteria used to determine that period;
- the data subject's right to request from the controller rectification, erasure, or restriction of processing, of his or her data and the right to object to the processing of such data;
- the data subject's right to lodge a complaint with a supervisory authority;
- the source of data, where they have not been collected from the data subject;
- information on any automated decision making, including profiling, referred to in Article 22(1) and (4), and other meaningful information about the logic involved, as well as the significance and the envisaged consequences of such processing for the data subject;
- where personal data are transferred outside of the EEA (to a third country or to an international organisation) – information on the appropriate safeguards of data protection subsequent to the transfer, ensured by the data exporter (including BCRs and standard contractual clauses).

The requirement to specify the purposes of processing of data is deemed to be met provided that the information is given with sufficient detail. This corresponds to the purpose limitation principle laid down in Article 5(1)(b) of the GDPR, whereby data may only be collected for specified purposes and must not be further processed in a way incompatible with those purposes.

The scope of processing purposes includes numerous and diverse operations, including: marketing, answering contact requests, risk assessment, concluding contracts, entering payments, the distribution of products or services, processing complaints, the enforcement of payments and claims, the payment and reporting of salaries, taxes and social security contributions, archiving, the recruitment of staff and keeping staff files etc. These are only examples of the purposes to be met by the data controller. The question on how detailed or general the information should or may be will necessarily be answered in practice when the legal obligation to provide information on processing purposes is enforced by supervisory authorities. When information is provided at the request of the data subject, Article 15 of the GDPR only requires information to be provided on the purposes of data processing. No information need be given on the legal basis of data processing, in contrast to information obligations applicable upon the collection or obtaining of data. However, in my opinion, information on the legal basis of the processing of data should also be given in response to a request for information, as such a request implies, in practice, a challenge to the lawfulness of data processing, e.g. upon expiry of a contract; in such a case, another legal basis, for instance an obligation under tax regulations, should be invoked.

The data subject also has the right to be informed on the categories of his/her personal data being processed. Furthermore, since the data subject is entitled to access his/her data, it is not sufficient to specify the categories of his/her personal data being processed. The content of the data must also be presented, which enables the data subject to verify whether the data are accurate, up-to-date and adequate. (The requirement to present such data is laid down expressly in Article 15(3) of the GDPR, with a proviso in Article 15(4) that presenting the data must not adversely affect the rights and freedoms of others; this implies, in particular, that the data provided must not contain third parties' data unless necessary). Therefore, the controller must not confine itself to informing the data subject that it processes his/her address, but must present the address to the data subject. The information obligation also includes the requirement to provide information in an intelligible form, i.e. to provide it as a full description, without the use of abbreviations, codes, or symbols. If a data system uses abbreviations or symbols (e.g. to denote marital status or age group) for service optimisation, they need to be rendered in full in the information provided to the data subject.

The recipients or categories of recipients of the personal data are to be specified subject to the definition of recipient (Article 4(9) of the GDPR). According to this definition, a recipient is a natural or legal person, public authority, agency or another body to which the personal data are disclosed. However, public authorities which may receive personal data in the framework of a particular inquiry in accordance with EU or Member State law (e.g. courts, public prosecutor offices, the police or court bailiffs) are excluded from the definition of recipients. One important change introduced in the GDPR in comparison to some national laws is expanding the definition of recipients to include data processors. An indication of categories of data recipients should not be regarded as sufficient where the controller is able to specify the recipients at the time of performing its information obligation. Such a detailed specification should, however, not be required where it is not realistically feasible, e.g. with a high number of processors, or even not permissible, e.g. if it were to include the names of all staff who may access the system. In practice, information clauses only specify categories of recipients. More detailed information is provided by specifying areas or purposes where the processing of data has been entrusted to such recipients. Individual recipients are only specified if they are, for example, loan registers cooperating with the institution on a regular basis.

The GDPR requires that the data subject be informed on the correction rights and restrictive rights that he/she is entitled to (i.e. the right to demand rectification or erasure of data or restriction of processing, and to object to data processing). The information on data subjects' rights should not be limited to a reference to the legal act serving as a basis of these rights, which would require the data subject to consult that legal act in order to find out what his/her rights are; rather, the data subject's rights should be spelled out precisely.[3] The obligation to specify the data subject's rights towards the controller has furthermore been expanded by the requirement to inform the data subject of his/her right to lodge a complaint with the supervisory authority

3. P. Barta, P. Litwiński, *Ustawa o ochronie danych osobowych. Komentarz*, Warszawa 2009, pp. 254-255; E. von Ehmann, M. Helfrich, *EG-Datenschutzrichtlinie: Kurzkommentar*, Köln 1999, p. 162.

(the competent supervisory authority, its contact details or the applicable procedure need not be specified).

The information on the source of data enables the data subject to control the processing and to exercise his or her rights where the data have been obtained by the controller from a source other than the data subject. The scope of information which is required to be provided to the data subject under Article 15 of the GDPR is not differentiated according to the source from which the controller has obtained the personal data in question, i.e. whether they have been obtained directly from the data subject, e.g. upon providing service at the controller's office or through its website, or from a different source, e.g. a marketing company creating databases or a public telephone and address directory. Even if the source of the data is publicly available, this does not relieve the controller from the obligation to specify it.

The GDPR has largely expanded the scope of the data subjects' right of access to information. It has been made compulsory, for example, to inform the data subject on profiling, since a data subject's unawareness of being profiled (which may lead to conclusions being made which are statistically probable but erroneous in relation to the specific data subject) is one of the key threats. Also, automated decisions, including profiling, based on algorithms which create a statistical profile (not necessarily an accurate one) of a person may lead to stigmatisation and discrimination and may influence positive or negative decisions in matters such as lending, insurance, or employment. The information obligation also includes specifying the importance and the predicted consequences of such automated decision making, including profiling, i.e. a risk assessment requirement. The Directive, in its Article 12(a), third indent, gave the data subject the right to demand to have the logic of making automated individual decisions presented.

Information on profiling must only be provided if the profiling meets the conditions of Article 22(1) and (4) of the GDPR, i.e. if it provides input to a decision which is based solely on automated processing and produces legal effects concerning the data subject or similarly significantly affects him or her, or the profiling includes the processing of sensitive data. The GDPR does not specify the level of detail which must be provided with the information on making such decisions, e.g. whether it must specify the criteria of a positive or negative decision, defined in the system. The impact of information on other consequences of profiling for the data subject, going beyond data protection and extending to business effects, such as higher prices for selected customers, should also be taken into consideration.

There is also a new obligation to specify the envisaged storage period of the personal data, or, if this is not possible, the criteria used to determine that period. For this to be done, the categories of data must first be established, along with the legal bases and purposes of their processing, and an appropriate storage period, with a legal basis, must be assigned to each category. In this context, it should be pointed out that data stored in the same filing system do not necessarily have the same retention periods. The period of data storage following the expiry of a contract (where the data is stored to meet a legal obligation, e.g. under tax regulations) may be specified in years. On the other hand, where the data is processed under the data subject's consent, the data storage period is determined by the withdrawal of consent by the data subject.

Information rights under Article 15 of thc GDPR (Article 12(a) of the Directive) are not excluded where the data subject already has the information specified in those provisions. In such a situation, the data controller is only exempt from the information obligations applicable upon collection of data (Articles 13 and 14 of the GDPR, Articles 10 and 11 of the Directive). No such exemption is provided for in Article 15 of the Regulation (Article 12(a) of the Directive), despite the fact that part of the information to be provided under this article at the request of the data subject must also be provided prior, under Articles 13 and 14 of the GDPR (Articles 10 and 11 of the Regulation). Therefore, the information rights are designed to safeguard the data subject's right to information in the event that the data controller fails to comply with its obligations upon collection of data.

No exemption from the information obligation is laid down to account for professional secrecy provided for in EU or Member State law, despite such an exemption having been made in Article 14(5)(d) of the GDPR concerning information clauses in cases where the data have not been obtained from the data subject. I find this incomprehensible, as the lack of such an exemption requires e.g. a journalist who has obtained the data of a third party from his or her source for an investigation, or a barrister who has obtained the data from his client for the purpose of defending him/her in court, to reveal the source of the data (Article 15(1)(g) of the GDPR).

Neither the GDPR nor Directive 95/46/EC limit the right of access to data to a specified period in the past. There certainly is no justification for a controller to limit this period arbitrarily to, for instance, one year. The CJEU ruled to this effect in its judgment of 7 May 2009,[4] referring to such a limitation of access to information (relating to recipients and content of data) to one year preceding the request. The Court emphasised that '[...] that right must of necessity relate to the past. If that were not the case, the data subject would not be in a position effectively to exercise his right to have data presumed unlawful or incorrect rectified, erased or blocked or to bring legal proceedings and obtain compensation for the damage suffered.'

Since the GDPR does not specify the period in the past to which the right of access to data may relate, the storage limitation principle must be applied in this context. This principle prohibits the storage of data in a form permitting identification of persons for longer than is necessary for the purposes for which the data are processed (Article 5(1)(e) of the GDPR, Article 6(1)(e) of the Directive).

§9.04 RIGHT TO RECTIFICATION OF DATA

The data subject's right to obtain from the controller the rectification of his/her data refers to the immediate correction of data that are inaccurate, i.e. incompatible with reality, and the completion of data which are accurate but incomplete (Article 16 of the GDPR). The choice between rectification and completion is dictated by the nature of the incompatibility or incompleteness (Article 16 of the GDPR).

4. C-553/07, *College van burgemeester en wethouders van Rotterdam v M.E.E. Rijkeboer*, http://eur-lex.europa.eu/legal-content/EN/TXT/?uri=CELEX:62007CJ0553.

The rectification or completion of data stipulated in Article 16 of the GDPR should be distinguished from similar activities covered by separate provisions, such as in administrative proceedings.

Where a data subject demands the rectification or completion of data, he/she must demonstrate that the data need rectification or completion. For instance, in order to have an ID card number rectified, the data subject must present proof that the number in the controller's files is erroneous or that a new ID card with a different number has been issued.

The right to the rectification or completion of data is one of the fundamental rights of the data subject, provided for in Directive 95/46/EC as well (Article 12(b) and (c)). The Directive required the data controller to provide the data subject with a possibility of rectifying data where their processing did not comply with the provisions of the Directive, in particular because of the incomplete or inaccurate nature of the data. It also involved the obligation to inform third parties to whom the data had been disclosed of such a rectification, unless this proved impossible or involved a disproportionate effort.

Unlike Article 12(b) of the Directive, Article 16 of the GDPR only formulates the right to rectify or complete data, without combining it with the right to demand erasure. Thus, Article 16 of the GDPR, specifying the correction rights, does not reiterate the imperfect wording of Article 12(b) of the Directive. While granting the data subject the right to demand rectification of data, it specifies that rectification can be demanded if data are inaccurate, whereas the right to demand completion concerns data that are incomplete. The restrictive rights formulated in Article 12(b) of the Directive also included the right to demand rectification of data, but further rights were added, namely to demand erasure or blocking of data whose processing did not comply with the provisions of the Directive, in particular because of the incomplete or inaccurate nature of the data. This provision, linking the right to demand rectification or erasure or blocking of data to the incompatibility of their processing with the Directive, did not specify whether the requesting person could choose between exercising his/her correction or restrictive rights, i.e. whether the incompleteness or inaccuracy of data could justify the demand to erase them or only to rectify them. This could lead to disputes between controllers and data subjects, and claims that the data subjects' requests were excessive.[5]

The right to rectification also results from one of the key principles of data processing, i.e. the accuracy principle formulated in Article 5(1)(d) of the GDPR (Article 6(1)(d) of Directive 95/46/EC), requiring every reasonable step to be taken to ensure that data which are inaccurate in the context of the purposes for which they are processed are erased or rectified without delay. It should therefore be concluded that the controller's obligation to rectify data arises not only at the request of the data subject but also irrespective of any such request, wherever the controller finds, based on information in its possession or obtained from external sources, that a situation requiring data rectification has occurred.

5. An interpretation shared by J. Barta, P. Fajgielski, R. Markiewicz, *Ochrona danych osobowych. Komentarz*, Kraków 2007, p. 584.

Typical examples of data rectification include change of contact details (address, telephone number) or change of surname as a result of marriage. The right to rectification of data is held by the data subject. Still, a request for rectification of data may sometimes be binding even if made by a third party. This may happen, for example, if a request for erasure of a customer's mailing address is made not by the customer but by a person who demonstrates having purchased that customer's house. Certainly, such a third person may not give the customer's address and subsequently receive his/her mail. However, in this example, this person is not giving the customer's new address, but only notifying the service provider that an obsolete address of the customer is being kept in the service provider's database and that, consequently, the third person is receiving the customer's mail while not being entitled to receive it, or obliged to preserve it.

Another example of a rectification being necessary is when information on a person's alleged offence is maintained in his/her files as a result of a police investigation whereas the person has not been convicted.[6] The same applies when the information does not serve the public interest, in particular due to it relating to the distant past.[7]

§9.05 THE RIGHT TO ERASURE (THE 'RIGHT TO BE FORGOTTEN')

[A] The 'Right to Be Forgotten': The Nature, Scope and Conditions

The right to the erasure of data, which has existed since the entry into force of Directive 95/46/EC, has been developed into the 'right to be forgotten' (Article 17 of the GDPR).[8] An essential element of the 'right to be forgotten', in the context of the purpose of the reform, is the right to demand that personal data put on the Internet by the data subject or third parties be erased therefrom. The right to erasure of data on the Internet is crucial for the protection of data, considering the effects of the ease with which everyone can access and share data on the Internet today. The Court of Justice of the EU focused on this particular aspect in its judgment of 13 May 2014 in Case C-131/12, a crucial judgment for the right to erasure, discussed in further detail later in this chapter. This judgment, predating the GDPR by two years, formulated the 'right to be forgotten' by inferring it directly from Article 7 and 8 of the Charter of Fundamental Rights and from the right to erasure of data, stipulated in Directive 95/46/EC. However, the right to erasure should also be seen in relation to data processing in all other forms and environments.

The work on introducing the 'right to be forgotten' was inspired by the observation that the Internet knows no equivalent of the right offered by developed legal

6. ECtHR judgment of 18.11.2008, *Cemalettin Canli v Turkey*, Application no. 22427/04, http://hudoc.echr.coe.int/eng?i=001-89623.
7. ECtHR judgment of 6.6.2006, *Segerstedt-Wiberg and others v Sweden*, Application no. 62332/00, http://hudoc.echr.coe.int/eng?i=001-75591.
8. G. Zanfir, 'Tracing the Right to be Forgotten in the Short History of Data Protection Law: The 'New Clothes' of an Old Right', in: *Reforming European Data Protection Law*, (ed.) S. Gutwirth, R. Leenes, P. de Hert, Springer 2015, pp. 227 et seq.

systems to perpetrators of even the most serious crimes: the right to expungement after a specified period following the crime. Any statement, picture or record of any act which finds its way onto the Internet becomes indelible and is liable to influence the life, including the professional and political career, of the person in question for years, and without any time limit.[9] The 'right to be forgotten' is particularly relevant where the data subject made his/her data available, or gave consent to the processing of his/her data, while still a child, i.e. without the experience-based awareness of how this might adversely affect his/her life, e.g. his/her career, in the long-term.

In each of the stages of the legislative process on the GDPR, the right to erasure was always present in its Article 17, as it had been considered one of the key rights since the entry into force of Directive 95/46/EC. On the other hand, the approach to the 'right to be forgotten' evolved. In the European Commission's proposal (draft) of 25 January 2012, it was one of the flagship rights proposed, and featured in Article 17 alongside (and before) the right to erasure. However, in the first reading of the GDPR at the European Parliament on 12 March 2014, the 'right to be forgotten' was dropped, and only the right to erasure remained. The version of the GDPR approved by the EU Council on 15 June 2015 again formulated both rights. In the GDPR, finally adopted on 27 April 2016 as Regulation (EU) 2016/679, Article 17 includes the two terms as referring to the same right rather than separate rights.

As the European Commission declared, the 'right to be forgotten' was to go further than the right, formulated in the Directive, to have data erased or destroyed. The European Commission considered the existing right to demand erasure of data to be insufficient given the scale of data processing on the Internet; consequently, the Commission believed that it should be supplemented by the 'right to be forgotten', consisting in particular of the right to have personal data removed from online circulation. In 1995, when Directive 95/46/EC was adopted, less than 1% of Europeans used the Internet.[10]

It turned out, however, that in its judgment of 13 May 2014 in Case C-131/12 the Court of Justice of the EU had already confirmed that the 'right to be forgotten' in Web search engines could be inferred from Article 7 and 8 of the Charter of Fundamental Rights and from the right to erasure of data, stipulated in Directive 95/46/EC. Still, Article 17 defined the general framework of the 'right to be forgotten', partly drawing from this ground-breaking and outstanding judgment. Rather than providing for a full erasure of data in their source, the judgment focused on erasing them from Web search engines, which essentially meets the objective of the said right.

9. As also pointed out by: Ch. Markou, 'The 'Right to Be Forgotten': Ten Reasons Why It Should Be Forgotten', in: *Reforming European Data Protection Law*, (ed.) S. Gutwirth, R. Leenes, P. de Hert, Springer 2015, pp. 203 et seq.; I. Lipowicz, *Uwagi do strategii poprawy skuteczności unijnych przepisów dotyczących ochrony danych osobowych, przedstawionej przez Komisję Europejską*, prepared by Stowarzyszenie 'Naukowe Centrum Prawno-Informatyczne', Warsaw, January 2011, p. 7, http://ec.europa.eu/justice/news/consulting_public/0006/contributions/not_registered/ncpi_pl.pdf (in Polish); V. Mayer-Schoenberger, Delete: *The Virtue of Forgetting in the Digital Age*, Princeton 2009; G. Bell & J. Gemmell, *Total Recall: How the E-Memory Revolution Will Change Everything*, New York 2009.
10. Opinion of 26 February 2013 by the Industry, Research and Energy Committee for LIBE on the General Data Protection Regulation, p. 3.

The fact that both the 'right to be forgotten' and the right to erasure were included in Article 17 of the initial draft of the GDPR means that they were not seen as synonymous at that stage of the legislative work. However, in the first reading of the GDPR of 12 March 2014, the term 'right to be forgotten' was deleted, whereas in the final version it was put in parentheses next to the term 'Right to erasure'. This means that the 'right to be forgotten' is now synonymous with the right to erasure. Article 4(2) of the GDPR does not include the actions taken to ensure the exercise of the 'right to be forgotten' as data processing forms, but includes 'erasure or destruction'. Both data erasure and the exercise of the 'right to be forgotten' (as well as data anonymisation, being equivalent) are irreversible; otherwise they would have to be referred to as a cessation of data processing for a particular purpose only, for example ceasing to use data for marketing purposes, while other actions on the data, such as data archiving, would still be allowed.

The data subject's right to request that the controller erase personal data (and the controller's obligation to do so) applies in the following cases (Article 17(1)(a)–(f) of the GDPR):[11]

(a) The data have become unnecessary in relation to the purposes for which they were collected or subsequently processed. This corresponds to one of the key principles of personal data processing: the storage limitation principle (Article 5(1)(e) of the GDPR, Article 6(1)(e) of the Directive), which prohibits the keeping of data, in a form permitting identification of data subjects, for longer than is necessary for the purposes for which the data are processed. This requires the controller to specify the envisaged maximum data retention periods in relation to each category of data and the corresponding legal basis, and also to systematically erase data upon finding that they are no longer necessary for the purposes of the processing. This approach is also at the core of the CJEU's judgment of 13 May 2014 in Case C-131/12, in which the CJEU granted the 'right to be forgotten' on the Internet where the initial publication of data was lawful but subsequently, as time passed, any further processing of the data became groundless.

(b) The data subject withdraws his/her consent which has been the basis for the processing of data and there are no other legal grounds for the processing of the data. Article 7(3) of the GDPR explicitly grants the data subject the right to withdraw his/her consent to data processing at any time. This right was not provided for expressly in Directive 95/46/EC, although, in my opinion, it could be inferred from the Directive.[12] Where performance of a contract between the controller and the data subject is not the only purpose of data processing, in particular where the processing is necessary for the controller

11. P. Korenhof, J. Ausloos, I. Szekely, M. Ambrose, G. Sartor, R. Leenes, '*Timing the Right to be Forgotten: A Study into 'Time' as a Factor in Deciding About Retention or Erasure of Data*', in: Reforming European Data Protection Law, (ed.) S. Gutwirth, R. Leenes, P. de Hert, Springer 2015, pp. 171 et seq.
12. M. Krzysztofek, 'Zmiana przepisów o zgodzie na przetwarzanie danych osobowych', *PPH* 2011, no. 4, p. 57.

to meet its legal obligations (e.g. data archiving under accountancy, tax, or anti-money-laundering laws), the request for erasure of data is to be refused by the controller. Similarly, where the processing serves the purpose of performing a binding contract between the controller and the data subject, the latter's withdrawal of consent and his/her demand to erase the data would be virtually equivalent to terminating the contract. The admissibility thereof would have to be verified under laws governing contractual obligations, rather than data protection laws. Hence, the obligation to erase data only applies where the data subject withdraws consent which has been the sole basis for processing his/her data. The same rule should, in my opinion, apply where the data processing period for which the data subject expressed consent has elapsed, as there are no reasons why consent could not be expressed for a limited period (as is the practice in recruitment proceedings).

(c) The data subject objects to the processing of his/her data. An objection to the processing of data, or the withdrawal of consent for processing, results in either the erasure of data (Article 17(1)(b) and (c) of the GDPR) or the restriction of processing (Article 18(1)(d) of the GDPR). The objection may be on grounds relating to the data subject's particular situation (Article 21(1) of the GDPR), in particular where the data are processed for the purposes of the legitimate interests of the controller or a third party, including profiling. In such a case, the obligation to comply with the objection and to erase the data depends on whether the data subject is indeed found to be in a situation different from others and whether there are legitimate grounds for processing of his/her data which prevail over the data subject's right to object or his/her interests. The objection may also relate to the processing of data for the purposes of direct marketing, including profiling for direct marketing (Article 21(2) of the GDPR). In such a case, the right to object is unconditional. The obligation to erase data arises where there are no other grounds for the processing. For instance, where the data subject has objected to processing of his/her data for direct marketing purposes, the controller may no longer use the data for these purposes. However, if there continues to be a binding contract between the data subject and the controller, then there can be no objection to processing of data for other purposes and on other grounds, such as the performance of the contract or archiving of transactions.

(d) The personal data have been processed unlawfully. The obligation for data to be processed lawfully means the requirement to comply with statutory laws and regulations issued on the basis of such laws, substantive and procedural law, and case law. Unlawful processing is that which disregards obligations or prohibitions laid down by law; this includes in particular processing of data without legal basis or for unlawful purposes. The data controller's obligation to ensure that data processing is lawful means that the processing, in all its aspects enumerated in Article 4(2) of the GDPR (Article 2(b) of the Directive), i.e. from collection to erasure, has to conform to at least one of the lawfulness criteria specified in Article 6 of the GDPR (Article 7 of the Directive). This includes the prohibition on collecting data, or processing data collected, in an unlawful manner. For instance, where data are to be processed on the basis of the consent of the data subject, such consent must be unambiguous and freely given, with no potential adverse consequences of a refusal. The obligations also include the requirement to specify the purpose of data processing and the data recipients (Articles 12-14 of the GDPR, Articles 10 and 11 of the Directive), to ensure access to the data (Articles 15 et seq. of the GDPR, Articles 12 and 14 of the Directive), to implement measures to ensure the security of processing at an adequate level (Article 32 of the GDPR, Article 17(1) of the Directive), and to comply with other obligations provided for in the GDPR and the Directive as well as other generally applicable legal regulations which apply to individual cases of data processing. Data processing is lawful provided that it is based on a statutory law or a legal act issued on the basis of such a law, and is necessary in a democratic society for meeting a legitimate purpose. Article 17(1)(d) of the GDPR does not specify the types of unlawfulness which justify the erasure of data. It does not say, for instance, whether the fact that the information obligations upon collection of data (Articles 13 and 14 of the GDPR) are part of the controller's key obligations means that non-performance of these obligations necessitates the erasure of the data at the request of the data subject. I do not believe that such an irregularity, serious though it is, always requires the erasure of the data. In my opinion, erasure of data may be required as a result of failure to duly comply with the information obligation as long as the data processing is contingent on the data subject's consent or non-objection, because for the consent to be valid, the data subject has to be aware of all the aspects of the planned processing.

(e) The personal data have to be erased for compliance with a legal obligation stipulated in Union or Member State law to which the controller is subject. One example is where the acceptable data storage period, specified in law or in the data subject's consent, has elapsed. The erasure of data may also be ordered by a data protection authority or a court. This ground for data erasure may seem redundant since the erasure is a legal obligation binding upon the controller, i.e. the data should be erased by the controller on its own initiative, without the data subject's request. Thus, in my view, the provision should be seen as a means to guarantee that the data subject can control the lawfulness of data processing and enforce the exercise of the controller's legal obligation.

(f) The personal data have been collected in the context of offering information society services directly to a child, under the consent to data processing. Information society services (Article 4(25) of the GDPR) are all services 'normally provided for remuneration, at a distance, by electronic means and at the individual request of a recipient of services'.[13] This includes numerous and

13. Services defined in Article 1(1)(b) of Directive (EU) 2015/1535 of the European Parliament and of the Council of 9 September 2015 laying down a procedure for the provision of information in the field of technical regulations and of rules on Information Society services (OJ EU L 241, 17.9.2015, p. 1).

rapidly growing categories of services such as online financial services (online banking, online insurance), sale of other services, e.g. tourist services or development of photos sent electronically, online retailing, e.g. sale of books, music, electronic appliances, clothing or cosmetics in online shops, online news subscription, sale of mobile applications. Annex I to Directive (EU) 2015/1535 lays down an indicative list of services which are not covered by this term because either they are not provided 'at a distance' (e.g. consultation of an electronic catalogue in a shop with the customer on site), they are not provided 'by electronic means' (e.g. automatic cash or ticket dispensing machines), or they are not provided 'at the individual request of a recipient of services' but transmitted for reception by an unlimited number of individual receivers (e.g. television broadcasting services). It is legally permissible to process the data of children at the age of at least 16 based on their consent, for the purpose of offering information society services directly to them. For children below the age of 16, such processing is only lawful if consent is given or authorised by the holder of parental responsibility over the child (Member States may provide by law for a lower age for those purposes, but not below 13 years). Linking the 'right to be forgotten' in the context of information society services with an age limit is relevant for the essence of this right, which is designed to protect people who were children when they gave their consent to data processing, i.e. were not sufficiently aware of the possible consequences. On the other hand, where an information society service is provided as part of an obligation which is still binding, it would be excessive to apply the 'right to be forgotten' to adult customers. Signed contracts should be subject to civil law and consumer protection laws, and the customer should receive appropriate information on the service and have the possibility of duly expressing his/her consent. However, once the customer has used the service and paid for it and there are no further claims, but the account created by the customer, including his/her personal data, still exists in the service provider's system and might be used for future services, the customer has the right to delete this account. In practice, companies make it possible for their customers to edit or delete their accounts on their own. The reference to Article 8(1) of the GDPR indicates that the obligation to erase data on request is unconditionally binding in relation to information society services offered directly to a child.

The GDPR does not lay down precise criteria to ascertain whether an information society service is offered to a child directly. One indication may be the content of the service, e.g. the type of films or games being offered, clearly indicating children as the intended target group, despite not excluding access by adults. This criterion might be misleading, though, as children might, in line with changing trends, consider themselves to be the target of content which adults find unsuitable for them. On the other hand, certain services clearly unintended for children and explicitly prohibiting children's access, e.g. a portal sharing recipes for alcoholic beverages, might not include any technical access restrictions and only rely on the user's declaration of age.

For a broader discussion on information society services and the conditions of giving consent for the processing of personal data when such services are offered directly to a child, see Chapter 5 of this book ('Legal Bases for the Processing of Personal Data').

[B] Informing Subsequent Controllers of the Data Erasure Request

A controller who has made data public and is then obliged to erase such data for reasons specified in Article 17(1) of the GDPR must also take steps to inform other controllers of the data subject's request to erase all links to, or copy or replication of, those personal data. Any data published on the Internet is available to an unlimited and unspecifiable pool of recipients and further controllers; other users may download the data to their devices and send them further. It is impossible to find all such data and their respective further controllers. The GDPR therefore requires that efforts be taken to achieve a practicable effectiveness of the 'right to be forgotten', i.e. taking steps, including technical measures, which are 'reasonable' taking into account the available technology and costs of implementation (Article 17(2) and recital 66 of the preamble). This implies a requirement to take reasonable efforts rather than to achieve a result irrespective of the possibilities. However, providing information on the data subject's request to the data controllers who are known to the initial controller, e.g. to loan registers by a bank, is compulsory.

The evolving concept of the 'right to be forgotten' at successive stages of work on the GDPR resulted in formulating this right in more realistic terms. For instance, in the GDPR's version of the first reading in the European Parliament of 12 March 2014, Article 17(2) required the controller to 'take all reasonable steps to have the data erased', i.e. not only to pass on the information on the data subject having made the request. This might lead to disagreements between data subjects and data controllers, e.g. as to whether the controllers were required under this provision to take legal steps against further controllers, for instance by lodging complaints with the supervisory authority, if the further controllers disregarded the notification of an erasure of data.

Furthermore, the first reading version of the GDPR provided for an exemption from the controller's obligation to have the data erased by further controllers where the data had been made public under Article 6(1) of the GDPR, i.e. on legal grounds such as the data subject's consent, performance of a contract entered into with the data subject, or processing being necessary for compliance with a legal obligation binding on the controller. In fact, these circumstances are the prerequisites of lawful data processing, which makes all other data processing unlawful. The controller's obligation to erase the data previously made public by that controller (in practice, their erasure from the Internet) would thus be limited to those cases where the data were made public unlawfully in the first place. This would have been equivalent to dropping the 'right to be forgotten' altogether from the GDPR in the first reading, as this law should apply not only if the data were made public without a legal basis, but also if the publication was legal but, for example, the data had become unnecessary over time. This would indeed be a contradiction of the 'right to be forgotten', if it were to become merely an instrument of remedying data controllers' mistakes having led to data being made public in the first place, but would not apply to data made public with the data subject's consent given at the age when the data subject did not have the experience-based awareness of the possible consequences of his/her decision. The final version of the GDPR is free from such mistakes.

[C] Exemptions from the Obligation to Erase Data

The obligation to erase personal data and to inform further controllers processing such data that the data subject has demanded their erasure does not apply insofar as the processing is necessary (Article 17(3) of the GDPR), e.g. for exercising the right of freedom of expression and information or for scientific or historical research. The GDPR proposes (recital 153 of the preamble, Article 85) that the processing of personal data be exempt from the general rules laid down by the GDPR if this is necessary for maintaining balance between the right to data protection and the right to freedom of expression and information. Moreover, the term 'journalism', for example, is open to broad interpretations, as nowadays it is not institutionalised and also includes blogs run by activists, which have become a sort of local press. Thus, as also implied by the CJEU judgment in Case C-131/12, the 'right to be forgotten' is not available, for example, for perpetrators of well-publicised terrorist attacks or political scandals.

The ECtHR arrived at the same conclusions in its judgment in the case of *M.L. and W.W. v. Germany*.[14] The ECtHR ruled that the right to privacy under Article 8 of the ECHR had not been violated by the refusal to prohibit media from allowing Internet users access to information concerning the applicants' conviction for the murder of a famous actor and mentioning their names in full. The Court found it justified as a matter of journalistic freedom, provided that it corresponded to the profession's ethical norms.

The obligation to erase data is also exempt where the processing of such data is necessary for archiving purposes in the public interest or statistical purposes, i.e. where the erasure of data would preclude meeting these purposes. In such cases, though, technical and organisational safeguards to ensure data minimisation or pseudonymisation are required.

A further exemption from the obligation to erase data occurs if the processing is necessary for compliance with a legal obligation under EU or Member State law to which the controller is subject (for instance, a demand to erase data cannot be granted if the controller is obliged to archive data under accounting, tax or anti-money-laundering legislation) or for the performance of a task carried out in the public interest or in the exercise of official authority by the controller. This includes public interest in the area of public health (e.g. universal health care, social security and social care).

Neither does the obligation to erase data apply where processing is necessary for the establishment, exercise or defence of legal claims. Therefore, in my opinion, the

14. Judgment of 28 June 2018 in the case of *M.L. and W.W. v. Germany*, applications no. 60798/10 and 65599/10, https://hudoc.echr.coe.int/eng/#{%22itemid%22:[%22001-184438%22]}.

storage of data for potential future enforcement of civil law claims, for the duration of the prescription period of such claims, is justified, as it serves the purpose of keeping information and evidence which is essential in potential court proceedings or the processing of complaints. The storage of data during the prescription period of tax obligations is likewise justified, while also being required under a separate legal basis, i.e. the processing of data for the exercise of a legal obligation.

[D] 'Right to Be Forgotten' of Company Board Members Whose Personal Data Have Been Entered in Public Registers

The EU Court of Justice, in its judgment of 9 March 2017 in Case C-398/15 *Camera di Commercio, Industria, Artigianato e Agricoltura di Lecce v Salvatore Manni*, determined a relation between 'the right to be forgotten' and the guarantee of business certainty.[15]

The Court ruled that the right to demand the erasure or blocking of data which has been laid down in Directive 95/46/EC (Article 12(b) and subparagraph (a) of the first paragraph of Article 14), read in conjunction with Article 3 of the First Council Directive 68/151/EEC of 9 March 1968 on co-ordination of safeguards which (...) are required by Member States of companies (...), must be interpreted as meaning that, it is for the Member States to determine whether the natural persons referred to in Article 2(1)(d) and (j) of the Council Directive 68/151/EEC, particularly persons authorised to represent the company and liquidators, 'may apply to the authority responsible for keeping, respectively, the central register, commercial register or companies register to determine, on the basis of a case-by-case assessment, if it is exceptionally justified, on compelling legitimate grounds relating to their particular situation, to limit, on the expiry of a sufficiently long period after the dissolution of the company concerned, access to personal data relating to them, entered in that register, to third parties who can demonstrate a specific interest in consulting that data'.

Importantly, the Court confirmed that the data relating to members of bodies of the company and liquidators in a company register constitute personal data (point 34 of the judgment) and the authority maintaining that register processes personal data as a data controller by entering and storing the data as well as disclosing them in the register (point 35 of the judgment).

The Court emphasised that Member States cannot guarantee that natural persons, such as company board members, have the right to the automatic erasure of personal data or blocking of that data from the public, after a certain period of time from the dissolution of the company (point 56 of the judgment). Personal data contained in company registers shall not be erased or anonymised but the access to personal data in the register may be limited after a certain period of time to persons who can demonstrate a specific interest in gaining access to such data.

Comparing the public interest, i.e. business security reflecting the principle of publicity, with the private interest, i.e. the right to privacy, the Court held, rightly, that the former is of more importance in this specific context. In the judgment it was stated

15. https://eur-lex.europa.eu/legal-content/EN/TXT/?uri=CELEX:62015CJ0398.

that 'the basic documents of the company concerned should be disclosed in order that third parties may be able to ascertain (...) especially particulars of the persons who are authorised to bind the company' (point 49 of the judgment). The purpose of Directive 68/151/EEC is 'to protect in particular the interests of third parties in relation to joint stock companies and limited liability companies, since the only safeguards they offer to third parties are their assets'. Effective measures should be ensured to prevent using companies to commit irregularities to the detriment of members of the trade, particularly creditors.

[E] 'Right to be Forgotten' on the Internet as Illustrated by the Judgment of the Court of Justice of the EU of 13 May 2014 in Case C-131/12

As pointed out above, even before the GDPR entered into force, the provisions of Directive 95/46/EC implied a right to erasure of data from the Internet. This was confirmed by the Court of Justice of the EU in its judgment of 13 May 2014 in Case C-131/12,[16] ruling that data subjects have the 'right to be forgotten' in Web search engines, which essentially, albeit not fully, meets the objective of the said right.

The dispute was initiated by a Spanish citizen, who demanded that Google (Google Spain SL and Google Inc.) erase outdated information. This information was published in 1998 by the Spanish daily *La Vanguardia* in its 19 January and 9 March 1998 issues, which were much later also made available on the Internet, as an announcement of the complainant's real property being put up for auction in order to recover overdue social security contributions. The overdue payment was subsequently made, but in 2009 the complainant found out that information on his past indebtedness had remained on the Internet: entering his name in the Google search engine returned a link to the newspaper announcement. The newspaper refused to erase the information, arguing that, although the objective of its publication had expired, the announcement had first been published pursuant to a legal provision, namely an order by the Ministry of Labour and Social Policy.

The complainant approached Google Spain in 2010 with a demand to erase the links directing to the newspaper announcement upon entering his name. Google Spain forwarded this demand to Google Inc., with its registered office in California, as the Web search engine provider.

The data subject also lodged an objection with the Spanish personal data protection authority, Agencia Española de Protección de Datos (AEPD), against the processing of his data by both the newspaper and Google. AEPD ruled that the newspaper was not obliged to erase the information since it had been published on the basis of a legal provision, but that Google, on the other hand, was obliged to erase it

16. Case C-131/12 for a preliminary ruling under Article 267 TFEU upon request made by Audiencia Nacional (Spain) by decision of 27 February 2012, received at the Court on 9 March 2012, in the proceedings *Google Spain SL, Google Inc. v Agencia Española de Protección de Datos (AEPD), Mario Costeja González*, http://eur-lex.europa.eu/legal-content/EN/TXT/?uri=CELEX:62012CJ0131.

from its search indexes. Google Spain and Google Inc. appealed against this decision. The Spanish court Audiencia Nacional stayed the proceedings and referred the following questions to the CJEU for a preliminary ruling: (i) whether the processing of personal data by a search engine provider's office or subsidiary in a Member State was carried out within the context of the activities of the data controller's establishment within the meaning of the Directive, (ii) whether the search engine provider was the data controller and its operation constituted processing of personal data within the meaning of the Directive, and (iii) whether the right to object to data processing, as stipulated in the Directive, could be invoked by the complainant to demand that the search engine provider cause his data not to be visible in the search results.[17]

In his opinion of 25 June 2013,[18] Advocate General of the Court Niilo Jääskinen proposed that the search engine provider should not be considered a personal data controller, except for the data processed in its search engine index, as long as the provider did not index or archive personal data contrary to the instructions of the publisher of the web page. Thus the Advocate General arrived at the conclusion that the search engine provider was not responsible for the contents of web pages to which the search engine directed. The Advocate General recommended that the Court refuse to conclude that, based on the Directive provisions formulating the right to erasure and to blocking of data (Article 12(b)) and the right to object to processing of data (Article 14(a), data subjects were entitled to a 'right to be forgotten' in a search engine in cases when the information in question had been published lawfully on third parties' web pages.

The CJEU, in its judgment of 13 May 2014, ruled that Directive 95/46/EC does apply to search engines, even if the servers used for data processing are located in third countries but the search engine provider has an office or a subsidiary in an EU country.

The Court pointed out that the activity of search engines consisting in finding information placed on the Internet by third parties, indexing it automatically, storing it temporarily and making it available to Web users according to criteria they specify constitutes processing of personal data within the meaning of Article 2(b) of the Directive when this information contains personal data. The Court also ruled that a search engine provider is the controller of these personal data and is responsible for their processing.

17. The Article 29 Working Party had already contributed to specifying questions requiring clarification in this case by formulating conclusions, e.g. that a search engine provider's operation in EEA countries, including the targeting of advertisements to the inhabitants in those countries, is part of activities carried out by an establishment within the meaning of Article 4(1)(a) of Directive 95/46/EC. See Opinion 1/2008 on data protection issues related to search engines, formulated by Article 29 Working Party on 4 April 2008, WP148, http://ec.europa.eu/justice/article-29/documentation/opinion-recommendation/files/2008/wp148_en.pdf. Also cf. P. Fajgielski, 'Funkcjonowanie portali internetowych – wybrane problemy prawne', in: *Internet. Prawno-informatyczne problemy sieci, portali i e-usług*, ed. G. Szpor, W. Wiewiórowski (Assistant European Data Protection Supervisor), Warszawa 2012, p. 133.

18. Opinion of Advocate General Niilo Jääskinen delivered on 25 June 2013 in Case *Google Spain SL and Google Inc. v Agencia Española de Protección de Datos (AEPD) and Mario Costeja González*, C-131/12, http://eur-lex.europa.eu/legal-content/EN/TXT/?uri=CELEX:62012CC0131.

The Court pointed out that, although web search engines direct to information made public by third parties, e.g. media, these operations too should be classified as processing of personal data, since exempting them, widespread as they are, from the scope of the Directive would render its data protection provisions largely ineffective.

The judgment also confirmed that the said processing of personal data is carried out within the context of the activities of the data controller's establishment on the territory of a Member State, where the search engine provider has created an office or subsidiary in that State in order to direct advertising through that search engine to the inhabitants of that State. Therefore, the governing law is to be specified by reference to the location of the data subject rather than that of the data controller's registered office. A search engine provider whose registered office is in a third country is bound by the EU personal data protection provisions and administrative decisions of the data protection authority in the Member State whose inhabitants are the target customers of the services that the provider advertises.

Thus, contrary to the recommendation of the Advocate General, the Court ruled in favour of the data subjects' 'right to be forgotten' on the Internet. This is a milestone as the 'right to be forgotten' was to be introduced by the GDPR, according to its initial draft, as a ground-breaking enhancement of data protection. It was to respond to the challenges resulting from the processing of data in the Internet, not envisaged in the Directive, since its adoption predated the expansion of the Internet. The Court, however, ruled that the 'right to be forgotten' on the Internet can be directly inferred from Articles 7 and 8 of the Charter of Fundamental Rights and from the Directive. The Directive grants data subjects the right to demand erasure or blocking of data that is processed in breach of its provisions (Article 12(b)) and the right to object at any time, on compelling legitimate grounds relating to their particular situation, to the processing of their data (Article 14(a)).

According to the judgment in Case C-131/12, the search engine provider complies with these rights of the data subject if a search for information using the name of the data subject does not return links to web pages published by third parties, containing information relating to the data subject. An objection to processing of data by the search engine provider is complied with through erasure of the indicated information linked to the person's name, even if such information continues to be published on the source web page, regardless of whether the initial publication of the data was lawful.

The erasure of the links associated with the requesting person's name from the search results is therefore justified by the fact that the publication of such information in association with the requesting person's name is incompatible with the Directive at the time when the request is made. This does not imply that the original publication was a breach of the Directive. Its incompatibility with the Directive may result, as in the circumstances subject to the judgment in Case C-131/12, from the lapse of time, when the processing of data no longer serves any purpose (an announcement of a recovery of debt repaid 16 years prior) and presents the data subject in a negative light and compromises his or her reputation (points 91 and 93 of the judgment).

The 'right to be forgotten' as materialised in this way is an instrument for genuine enforcement of the right to privacy. Although the information in question may still be accessible on the source web page, its 'striking power' and destructive effect on the rights of the subject is severely limited if it is not visible in Web search engines; obtaining the information may thus require a more complicated search or knowledge of its prior publication location, and such a search may prove ineffective.

The Court, however, pointed out that the rights to object under Article 12(b) and Article 14(a) of the Directive are not absolute. The requesting person's right to have the information relating to him/her erased from the search results is subject to appraisal, whereby the person's right to privacy under the Charter of Fundamental Rights is weighed against the legitimate interest of the potential recipients of such information, for instance in the light of freedom of speech and media or the public function exercised by the requesting person (points 81 and 83 of the judgment). The breach of the requesting person's privacy, by keeping the links to pages associated with his/her name in the search results, may therefore be justified (subject to individual appraisal by a data protection authority and a court), if the public interest is seen in a particular case as overriding the right to privacy.

On the other hand, refusal to block search results may not be justified either by a conclusion that a publication of data through the search engine causes no harm to the complainant or by the economic interest of the search engine provider.

Following the judgment, Google emphasised that it considered it sufficient to remove the search results in question from its European search engines, e.g. google.de in Germany or google.fr in France (David Drummond, Google's Chief Legal Officer: 'It's our strong view that there needs to be some way of limiting the concept, because it is a European concept').[19] This practice is contrary to the recommendations of the Article 29 Working Party, which called for information to be removed globally, as users enjoy global access to any Google search engine they choose. Google's approach was clearly flawed and distorted the sense of the 'right to be forgotten'. The French data protection authority, CNIL (Commission nationale de l'informatique et des libertés), among others, ordered Google to change this approach and threatened it with sanctions in case of non-compliance.[20] Google rejected this demand and argued that the 'right to be forgotten' remained an EU requirement and did not extend to third countries (Peter Fleischer, Google's Global Privacy Counsel: 'While the right to be forgotten may now be the law in Europe, it is not the law globally').[21] Facebook also voiced its opinion in the dispute, arguing along the same lines as Google (Facebook's Global Deputy Chief Privacy Officer, Stephen Deadman: 'A number of authorities in Europe are using that

19. J. Fioretti, 'Google sticks to EU only application of 'right to be forgotten'', Reuters, 19 January 2015, http://www.reuters.com/article/2015/01/19/us-google-eu-privacy-idUSKBN0KS21E20150119.
20. J. Slegg, 'France Orders Google to Remove Right to Be Forgotten Results from All Google Sites', http://www.thesempost.com/france-orders-google-to-remove-right-to-be-forgotten-results-from-all-google-sites/, 12.06.2015.
21. J. Naughton, 'In the battle of free speech now it's France v Google', The Guardian, 9 August 2015, http://www.theguardian.com/commentisfree/2015/aug/09/battle-free-speech-france-google-right-to-be-forgotten.

judgment to challenge the status quo that's existed for many years. We think they're wrong. We think the model we have is right').[22]

CNIL rejected Google's informal appeal against the decision ordering it to apply the 'right to be forgotten' in search engines with all extensions, without using geographical criteria, including non-EU national extensions, such as google.com. The order results from the fact that each Internet user has access to the information regardless of the geographical extension. Disregarding this would mean that the 'right to be forgotten' on the Internet would be completely ineffective.[23]

Google complied with the CJEU judgment by making available a search removal request form (https://support.google.com/legal/contact/lr_eudpa?product= websearch), with which users may indicate their personal data and links to web pages they demand to be blocked in the search results, and to justify their demand. Within a year of the CJEU judgment, Google assessed 922,638 links and 254,271 requests for removal of links; 41.3% of requested links were removed. Within two year of the judgment, Google assessed 1,540,003 links and 440,620 requests for removal of links; 43% of requested links were removed.[24] By December 2017, the number of requests for the removal of URL addresses, received by Google, exceeded 2.3 million. Most of these were made by users from France, Germany, the UK, Spain and Italy and concerned search results redirecting to social networking services (Facebook, Google Plus, YouTube and Twitter). 51% of the requested links were removed.[25]

The CJEU's judgment related to Google, but the 'right to be forgotten' on the Internet is binding upon all Web search engines.

[F] Ensuring the Effectiveness of the 'Right to be Forgotten'

Ensuring the right to erasure of personal data from Internet circulation is certainly a just cause. However, implementing it may prove problematic, for the reasons presented below and illustrated with the example of social networking services.

The dramatic changes that have occurred in data processing technologies and environments, in particular the popularity and expanding functionalities of social media, have in practice called into question the significance of existing concepts relating to personal data protection, such as the concept of data controller.[26] The status of social networking services as personal data controllers has been confirmed by the

22. S. Gibbs, 'Facebook questions use of 'right to be forgotten' ruling', The Guardian, 7 July 2015, http://www.theguardian.com/technology/2015/jul/07/facebook-questions-use-of-right-to-be-forgotten-ruling.
23. http://www.cnil.fr/english/news-and-events/news/article/right-to-delisting-google-informal-appeal-rejected/.
24. Google Transparency Report, situation as of 13 June 2016, https://www.google.com/transparencyreport/removals/europeprivacy/?hl=en.
25. https://drive.google.com/file/d/1H4MKNwf5MgeztG7OnJRnl3ym3gIT3HUK/view.
26. This is also pointed out by D. Głowacka, 'Uwagi do strategii poprawy skuteczności unijnych przepisów dotyczących ochrony danych osobowych, przedstawionej przez Komisję Europejską', Stowarzyszenie 'Naukowe Centrum Prawno-Informatyczne', Warszawa, January 2011, p. 11, http://ec.europa.eu/justice/news/consulting_public/0006/contributions/not_registered/ncpi_pl.pdf (in Polish).

Article 29 Working Party.[27] Although run by companies, social networking services contain personal data that are added and modified online by users (which is known as Web 2.0). It is therefore necessary to consider that a social networking service provider receiving requests for erasure of data may in practice not have the technical capability to supervise data being added and modified by millions of users (not to mention possible accusations of censorship).[28] The right to demand data erasure from a social networking service provider must remain purely theoretical, since data are added to the service from multiple sources, other than the data subject, and become accessible on the Internet to an unlimited, unspecified pool of users, who can store the data obtained from the web, duplicate them and make them available to further users, even after the service provider has erased the data from the service.

Erasing data from a social networking service in a way precluding their re-publication within the service is impossible. To do that, the service provider would have to monitor the content of the service constantly and without a time limit. This would not only constitute a preventive breach of privacy of other service users (whose profiles would be subject to such surveillance) and raise fundamental questions as to whether such a measure is adequate for its purpose, but would also require that the service providers use instruments which they already have at their disposal and which

27. Opinion 5/2009 on online social networking of 12 June 2009, WP 163, http://ec.europa.eu/justice/policies/privacy/docs/wpdocs/2009/wp163_en.pdf. In Point 3.1 of its Opinion, the Article 29 Working Party states: 'SNS providers are data controllers under the Data Protection Directive. They provide the means for the processing of user data and provide all the 'basic' services related to user management (e.g. registration and deletion of accounts). SNS providers also determine the use that may be made of user data for advertising and marketing purposes – including advertising provided by third parties.' According to the Article 29 Working Party, social networking service users are not data controllers but data subjects, because the processing of data 'by a natural person in the course of a purely personal or household activity' constitutes a 'household exemption'. However, a reservation is made that, despite this general exemption, in some circumstances users might assume some of the responsibilities of a data controller. In Point 3.9 of its Opinion 5/2009, the Article 29 Working Party emphasised that social networking services have to respect the rights of data subjects laid down in Articles 12 and 14 of Directive 95/46/EC (the right of access to data and correction and restriction rights), as well as the SNS's obligation to create means of handling data protection complaints and to inform the users of the existence of such means. There were also other documents dealing with processing of personal data in social networking services, and the Article 29 Working Party included their conclusions in its Opinion 5/2009. These documents include the 'Rome Memorandum' of the Berlin International Working Group on Data Protection in Telecommunications, adopted in 2008: http://www.datenschutz-berlin.de/attachments/461/WP_social_network_services.pdf; Resolution on Privacy Protection in Social Network Services, adopted on 17 October 2008 at the 30th International Conference of Data Protection and Privacy Commissioners in Strasbourg, http://www.privacyconference2008.org/adopted_resolutions/STRASBOURG2008/resolution_social_networks_en.pdf; 'Security Issues and Recommendations for Online Social Networks' by the European Network and Information Security Agency (ENISA), https://www.enisa.europa.eu/publications/archive/security-issues-and-recommendations-for-online-social-networks/at_download/fullReport.

28. The risk of resorting to preventive censorship by social networking service providers has also been identified in: K. Szymielewicz, A. Mazga, Internet a prawa podstawowe. Ekspresowy przegląd problemów regulacyjnych, p. 18, Fundacja Panoptykon, August 2011, http://wolnyinternet.panoptykon.org/sites/default/files/raport_na_www.pdf (in Polish); F. La Rue, Report of the Special Rapporteur on the promotion and protection of the right to freedom of opinion and expression, 20 April 2010, United Nations, A/HRC/14/23.

cause protests – such as applications recognising faces on photographs and matching them with the relevant persons' identities. To monitor the effectiveness of the 'right to be forgotten', it would be necessary to use web tracking tools and tracking cookies with the pictures objected to.[29] Thus, efforts to ensure a full exercise of the 'right to be forgotten' would entail a disproportionate interference with the privacy of third persons, which would be fundamentally incompatible with European values.[30]

Furthermore, data added to a social networking service by its users are not limited to basic identity data or pictures. They also include comments and reports that could be biased or even defamatory (stalking), but could constitute opinions rather than personal data, and erasing the data from the service could require a civil lawsuit.

§9.06 RIGHT TO RESTRICTION OF PROCESSING

An alternative solution to erasure of data is a restriction of processing of data by the controller. The definition of 'restriction of processing' (Article 4(3) of the GDPR) implies that the data are not erased but remain in the system and are marked in order to modify the scope and form of their processing.

The definition may be interpreted in the light of the legislator's apparent intention: if data erasure is full and irreversible, as opposed to the restriction of processing, then the latter means a suspension of active operations listed in Article 4(2) of the GDPR, i.e., for instance, the use and in particular the disclosure of data, but the storage of data is continued.

The term 'restriction of processing' in the GDPR corresponds to the term 'blocking of data' in Article 12(b) of Directive 95/46/EC.

Where processing of data has been restricted, any active processing of such data (i.e. any operations except for storage) is only allowed with the data subject's consent or for the establishment, exercise or defence of legal claims, or for the protection of the rights of another natural or legal person, or for reasons of important public interest of the EU or of a Member State (Article 18(2) of the GDPR). However, invoking these circumstances requires application of the proportionality principle, and the right of the data subject to the restriction of processing must be weighed against the rights of another natural or legal person. A decision must therefore be made on which of these rights deserves to be protected in this particular situation at the expense of the other.

One possible method of restricting the processing of personal data (recital 67 of the preamble to the GDPR) is temporarily moving the selected data to another processing system, i.e. outside the system being currently used for customer service. Another method is making the selected personal data unavailable to users (thus the

29. The instruments and aspects of network monitoring in the context of privacy protection are discussed in the working document on Web Tracking, issued by the International Working Group on Privacy in Telecommunications (Prague, 15–16 April 2013), and the Resolution on web tracking and privacy, adopted at the 35th International Conference of Data Protection and Privacy Commissioners (Warsaw, 23–26 June 2013).

30. J. Rosen, 'The Right to Be Forgotten', in: The Privacy Paradox. Privacy and Its Conflicting Values, Stanford Law Review, 2 February – 12 April 2012, http://www.stanfordlawreview.org/online/privacy-paradox/right-to-be-forgotten.

data, while being processed by the controller, are only visible to selected employees), or temporarily removing published data from a website. This is practised, for example, in public loan registers, where there is no basis for making the data of former debtors available, or on public information bulletin websites, once the recruitment for official posts has been completed. Technical means should also be used to prevent any modification of data in those applications. Data whose processing has been restricted must be clearly marked in the system.

The data subject is entitled to demand restriction of processing from the controller in the following cases (Article 18(1) of the GDPR):

a) The accuracy of the personal data is contested by the data subject. The processing may be restricted for a period enabling the controller to verify the compatibility of the data with reality. According to the accuracy principle, the personal data being processed must be accurate and, where necessary, kept up to date. The data controller must therefore ensure that data are correct, factually accurate, complete, and up to date. Article 5(1)(d) of the GDPR requires every reasonable step to be taken to ensure that personal data which are inaccurate or incomplete are erased or rectified without delay. It is necessary to take into account the purposes for which the data are processed. One example of the restriction of data processing for a period enabling the controller to verify the challenged data is the suspension of selected processing operations on the data of a debtor who claims not to have incurred the debt, but to have been a victim of identity theft. The accuracy of data may also be contested, for example, if a request for erasure of a customer's mailing address is made not by the customer but by a person who demonstrates having purchased that customer's house. Certainly, such a third person may not give the customer's address and subsequently receive his/her mail. However, in this example, the third person is not giving the customer's new address but only notifying the service provider that an obsolete address of the customer is being kept in the service provider's database and that, consequently, the third person is receiving the customer's mail while not being entitled to receive it, or obliged to preserve it.
b) The processing is unlawful but the data subject opposes the erasure of the personal data and requests the restriction of their use instead. The obligation for data to be processed lawfully means the requirement to comply with statutory laws and regulations issued on the basis of such laws, substantive and procedural law, and case law. Unlawful processing is that which disregards obligations or prohibitions laid down by law; this includes in particular processing of data without legal basis or for unlawful purposes. This should lead to erasure of data, also in view of the financial sanctions which may be applicable to the controller, or possible criminal liability of its employees. However, the data subject may consider that leaving the data in the system, unavailable to third parties, may be necessary to demonstrate the unlawfulness of the processing.

c) The controller no longer needs the personal data for the purposes of the processing, but they are required by the data subject for the establishment, exercise or defence of legal claims. According to the purpose limitation principle, data may only be collected for specified purposes and must not be further processed in a manner that is incompatible with those purposes. The storage limitation principle prohibits the storage of data, in a form permitting identification of data subjects, for longer than is necessary for the purposes for which the data are processed. The purpose of the processing includes not only the performance of the contract to which the data subject is party, but also, for example, archiving data required by accountancy or tax regulations. Once the data are no longer necessary for the controller to meet the purpose of the processing, they must be erased or anonymised, even if their prior processing was justified and lawful.

One example of this type of situation is the case resolved by the CJEU in the judgment of 13 May 2014 in Case C-131/12 *Google Spain SL and Google Inc. v Agencia Española de Protección de Datos (AEPD) and Mario Costeja González*. In this case, despite the fact that the announcement of the real property being put up for auction had been published lawfully in the first place, the corresponding data had to be erased from the search results in the Web search engine since, given the lapse of time, the processing of data no longer served any purpose.

d) The data subject has objected to processing pursuant to Article 21(1) of the GDPR. In such a case, the processing is to be restricted pending verification of whether the legitimate grounds of the controller override the grounds of the data subject's objection. The objection may be on grounds relating to the data subject's particular situation, in particular where the data are processed for the purposes of the legitimate interests of the controller or a third party, including profiling. The obligation to comply with the objection and to erase the data depends on whether the data subject is indeed found to be in a situation different from others and whether there are legitimate grounds for processing of his/her data which prevail over the data subject's right to object or his/her interests.

The controller must inform the data subject of its intention to lift the restriction of processing, i.e. to return to the full scope of processing, particularly when it is to involve the publication of the data.

Notification Obligation Regarding Rectification or Erasure of Personal Data or Restriction of Processing: upon the rectification, completion, erasure, or restriction of the processing of data, the controller must communicate it to each recipient to whom the personal data have been disclosed, and consequently must also document having made such communication (Article 19 of the GDPR, Article 12(c) of Directive 95/46/EC). This obligation does not apply where the communication proves impossible or involves disproportionate effort. The provision thus takes into consideration justified limitations on the part of data controllers, such as a large number of recipients. At the same time, it attempts to compensate their consequences for the data subjects by requiring the controller to inform the data subject about those recipients if the data subject so requests. The obligation to specify data recipients may also prove impossible to meet, e.g. if the data have been published on the Internet. However, if the recipients are specified, e.g. loan registers receiving information on the customers' debts, the controller must register having made the communication and the request for correction to them. For processors who are data recipients, a convenient manner of communicating the correction or erasure of data may be part of the technical communication arrangements agreed upon between the controller and the processor. It may, for instance, be achieved through an update of the database content by exporting files.

§9.07 RIGHT TO DATA PORTABILITY

Another new right available to data subjects, not provided for in Directive 95/46/EC, is the right to data portability (Article 20 of the GDPR). It is one of the arrangements introduced to respond to the challenges resulting from new technologies of data processing, including online, not envisaged in the Directive. The data subject has the right to receive his/her data from the controller in a structured, commonly used and machine-readable format and to transmit those data to another controller without hindrance from the previous controller. The data subject also has the right to have his/her personal data transmitted directly from one controller to another, where technically feasible. However, if the amount of data is too large to be sent over the Internet, alternative means should be considered, e.g. streaming or using physical carriers, such as CDs or DVDs. To respond to data portability requests, a data controller may, for example, provide an appropriately safeguarded Application Programming Interface (API). This is a practical arrangement whereby personal data requests are made to a controller through dedicated software, either by the data subject or an authorised third party.[31]

The right to data portability increases the data subject's control over the processing of his/her data in automated systems. It should facilitate the migration of customers, e.g. between social networking services and service providers in different sectors, especially with the use of 'the cloud', eliminating the possibility of the existing controllers invoking spurious arguments and creating obstacles.

Thus, the right to data portability is an expansion of the right of access to data. The latter includes the right of the data subject to be provided with an electronic copy of his/her personal data being processed. However, the right to data portability also requires a structured, commonly used and machine-readable format to be used and the data to be transferred directly from the controller to another controller.

Data portability will enhance competition on the market by enabling data subjects to change their service suppliers more easily, including in the context of the single digital market. Similar obligations have already been binding upon, and carried out by, data controllers in specific contexts, such as the transfer of bank accounts

31. The Article 29 Working Party, Guidelines on the right to data portability, adopted on 13 December 2016, as last revised and adopted on 5 April 2017 (WP 242 rev. 01), pp. 15 and 18.

between banks, or mobile telephone numbers between telecom operators, at the request of customers. In such cases, where sectoral EU or Member State law provides for a form of data portability, it should be ascertained whether the data subject's intention is to exercise his/her law under such sectoral law or under the GDPR. In the former case, GDPR data portability provisions will not apply.[32]

The right to data portability is limited to automated processing. As such, it does not extend to data in paper-based filing systems. Still, it should be borne in mind that data from paper-based filing systems are often duplicated in electronic forms; e.g. data from loan applications received on paper are recorded in an IT system.

A genuine and effective operation of the right to data portability depends on whether a large proportion of the data controllers use IT systems generating data in formats which are machine-readable by other controllers. These must be interoperable formats, and the GDPR does encourage data controllers to develop such formats; this does not, however, mean that controllers are required to implement technically compatible processing systems (recital 68 of the preamble and the Article 29 Working Party Guidelines on the right to data portability.[33] Controllers and data subjects may differ in their assessment as to whether the format used by a controller to process data electronically is 'commonly used'; however, the burden of proof rests with the controller. Still, as data processing technologies and IT systems are becoming increasingly universal, their number currently in use is decreasing and the communication possibilities between them are growing. However, if a format is not commonly used in a sector, the data controller should use commonly used formats, such as XML, JSON or CSV.

The terms 'structured, commonly used and machine-readable format' relate to the means, whereas the interoperability is the expected result. Article 2(6) of Directive 2003/98/EC, as amended by Directive 2013/37/EU, defines 'machine readable format' as 'a file format structured so that software applications can easily identify, recognize and extract specific data, including individual statements of fact, and their internal structure.' The GDPR does not impose specific recommendations on the format of the personal data to be provided. The most appropriate format will differ across sectors, but sectoral differences should not be invoked to limit the universality of solutions and, therefore, 'formats that are subject to costly licensing constraints would not be considered an adequate approach'.[34]

The right to data portability only includes the data which the data subject him/herself has provided to the controller; it does not include data obtained by the controller from a different source. As such, the right to data portability covers 'data actively and knowingly provided by the data subject', such as in loan application or insurance forms. On the other hand, it does not cover data which have only been

32. The Article 29 Working Party, Guidelines on the right to data portability, adopted on 13 December 2016, as last revised and adopted on 5 April 2017 (WP 242 rev. 01), pp. 7–8.
33. The Article 29 Working Party, Guidelines on the right to data portability, adopted on 13 December 2016, as last revised and adopted on 5 April 2017 (WP 242 rev. 01), p. 5).
34. The Article 29 Working Party, Guidelines on the right to data portability, adopted on 13 December 2016, as last revised and adopted on 5 April 2017 (WP 242 rev. 01), p. 17.

generated by the controller, such as data on the bank customer's creditworthiness, or an insurance company's customer's risk profile, developed through profiling.

However, the scope of data covered by the data portability right is broader, as it covers data which result from the observation of the data subject's activity, such as raw data processed by a smart meter or other types of connected objects, activity logs, history of website usage or search activities. Still, 'this latter category of data does not include data that are created by the data controller (...) such as a user profile created by analysis of the raw smart metering data collected.'.[35]

The right to data portability applies to data being processed on the basis of the data subject's consent or a contract entered into by the data subject with the controller. Data covered by the portability right, on account of being processed under a contract, include the titles of books purchased by an individual from an online bookstore, or the songs listened to via a music streaming service.[36]

It does not apply where the data are processed for compliance with a legal obligation to which the controller is subject, or for the performance of a task carried out in the public interest or in the exercise of official authority vested in the controller, such as where the data are processed by financial institutions under their anti-money-laundering obligations.

Where the data subject has exercised his/her right to data portability, he/she may still demand erasure of the data by the previous controller, unless the data have been provided by the data subject for the purpose of concluding a contract and are still needed for the performance of that contract. The transmission of data under the right to portability does not automatically result in the erasure of such data from the controller's system and does not affect the original retention period of the transmitted data.

If the request to transmit data relates to a set of personal data which also includes, besides the requesting person's data, the personal data of other persons, the requesting person's right to obtain the data must not adversely affect the rights and freedoms of other data subjects. For instance, a data subject's bank account can contain personal data not just of the account holder, but also those of other individuals he/she entered into transactions with; similarly, telephone call registers may include the data of other persons contacted. The Article 29 Working Party has realised that the rights and freedoms of third parties may be adversely affected, e.g. upon the transmission of data from a bank account, if the subsequent data controller receiving the data uses them for other purposes, such as marketing.[37]

35. The Article 29 Working Party, Guidelines on the right to data portability, adopted on 13 December 2016, as last revised and adopted on 5 April 2017 (WP 242 rev. 01), pp. 9–10.
36. The Article 29 Working Party, Guidelines on the right to data portability, adopted on 13 December 2016, as last revised and adopted on 5 April 2017 (WP 242 rev. 01), p. 8.
37. The Article 29 Working Party, Guidelines on the right to data portability, adopted on 13 December 2016, as last revised and adopted on 5 April 2017 (WP 242 rev. 01), pp. 11–12.

§9.08 RIGHT TO OBJECT TO DATA PROCESSING ON GROUNDS RELATING TO THE PARTICULAR SITUATION OF THE DATA SUBJECT OR TO OBJECT TO DATA PROCESSING FOR THE PURPOSES OF DIRECT MARKETING, INCLUDING PROFILING

The term 'right to object to data processing' in the GDPR corresponds to the right based on the grounds relating to the particular situation of the data subject and the right relating to the cases of processing data for the purposes of direct marketing, including profiling (Article 21 of the GDPR). An objection to the processing of data, or the withdrawal of consent for processing, results in either the erasure of data (Article 17(1)(b) and (c) of the GDPR) or the restriction of processing (Article 18(1)(d) of the GDPR). The objection to data processing is one of the grounds for the erasure of data or, where erasure is not justified, the restriction of processing for a period of time (e.g. if the data subject questions the data accuracy, the processing may be restricted for the time necessary for the controller to verify the accuracy).

The data subject has the right to object to processing of personal data relating to him or her for grounds relating to his/her particular situation (Article 21(1)). This right is exercisable at any time, i.e. at any stage of processing, from collection to erasure. However, this right is not absolute, but is contingent on the conditions listed below.

The first one is the condition of the data subject being in a particular situation, to be assessed by the data controller. The obligation to comply with the objection depends on whether the data subject is indeed found to be in a situation different from others. The data subject should therefore present grounds for his/her objection. Whether the objection is indeed justified is to be assessed by the controller. If the data controller rejects the objection, the data subject is entitled to seek the enforcement of his/her right in proceedings before a data protection authority or a court.

The second condition is the restriction of the right to object to cases where data are processed for the performance of a task carried out in the public interest or in the exercise of official authority vested in the controller, or for pursuing the legitimate interests of the controller or a third party. Therefore, objection is not possible where the processing serves the purpose of performing a binding contract between the controller and the data subject. In such a case, the latter's objection would be virtually equivalent to terminating the contract. The admissibility thereof would have to be verified under laws governing contractual obligations, rather than data protection laws. The same applies when the data are processed by the controller for the purpose of performing its legal obligation, for example, for making data available in public loan registers, for tax reporting purposes or communicating data to a court under pending proceedings.

According to the third condition, the controller may reject the objection if it demonstrates compelling legitimate grounds for the processing which override the interests, rights and freedoms of the data subject or for the establishment, exercise or defence of legal claims. The criterion of overriding grounds for the processing necessitates an individual appraisal of how significant the interests, rights and freedoms of the data subject are and to what extent they would be violated if data continued to be processed by the controller, despite the data subject's objection. Thus, a decision must be made as to which of the two values deserves to be protected at the expense of the other one. If the data subject's interests are found to prevail, the controller may no longer process the data covered by the objection.

The right to object to data processing is similarly exempt if the processing is necessary for the performance of a task carried out by the controller in the public interest, where the objection refers to the particular situation of the data subject and the data are processed for scientific or historical research purposes or for statistical purposes.

Another situation where the data subject may object to the processing of his/her data is direct marketing including profiling **to the extent that it is related to direct marketing** (Article 21(2) of the GDPR). In this case too the data subject may object at any time.

As opposed to the data subject's right to object on the grounds of his/her particular situation, the right to object against processing of data for direct marketing and marketing profiling is unconditional. The subject does not have to present grounds for his or her request, and the request is not subject to assessment by the controller. Following the objection, the data may no longer be processed for direct marketing. The objection must be registered in the IT system to make sure that the requesting data subject is not targeted with direct marketing communications or subject to profiling as a means of direct marketing.

In practice, the right to object to the use of data for direct marketing is one of the most relevant. It includes all channels of direct marketing, i.e. paper advertisements, such as those distributed through leaflets or printed on the customers' bank account statements, as well as electronic marketing via telephone, text messages and email. If, as is usually the case, the objection to direct marketing is general and not expressly limited to a selected channel of marketing, it must be related to direct marketing in all its forms, despite consent being required separately for each form of direct marketing. Direct marketing through email and text messages or in the communication module of online banking may be subject to separate consent declarations, but a general objection towards direct marketing covers all these forms. As such, it should cover all the separate consent fields for individual types of marketing in the controller's IT system. The general objection covers paper-based marketing, such as advertisements printed on the customers' bank account statements or distributed through leaflets, as well as electronic marketing via telephone, text messages and email. It also requires the discontinuation of any activities which are not advertising in the strict sense but constitute direct marketing in a broad sense, such as customer satisfaction surveys, in relation to the data subject in question.

The data subject's refusal to give consent to direct marketing when prompted during the collection of data (such as on a form including 'consent' and 'no consent' options) is equivalent to an objection, since it is a direct reaction to a request for consent.

A withdrawal by the data subject of his/her prior consent has the same effect as an objection to the processing of data for direct marketing or profiling. Article 7(3) of the GDPR explicitly grants the data subject the right to withdraw his/her consent to data processing at any time.

The practice of creating artificial unjustified obstacles to data subjects objecting, or withdrawing consent, to data processing, such as accepting such statements only on the controller's forms, is unacceptable.

A solution tested in many countries and worthy of recommendation is the Mail Preference Service list, also known as the Robinson list. This is a public database of people who have objected to receiving direct marketing information in different forms, e.g. electronic (email or telephone spam), particularly widespread and bothersome for the consumers, or as paper leaflets. The database is made available to companies conducting direct marketing, who should then erase the contact details of objecting people from their mailing lists.

A person or entity using information society services, i.e. online services such as banking or retailing, may object through automated means using technical specifications, such as websites, email addresses for registering such objections, or the user's account in the controller's system. Such technical means facilitate the exercise of a data subject's right to object, as required by Article 12(2) of the GDPR. It is a facilitation for the controller as well: if the customer, having logged in to the system, can edit his/her own data, this limits the number of requests for the controller to process.

An objection may also be made via a telephone call, including to an automated call centre, provided that the requesting data subject's identity is verified.

The controller is obliged to inform the data subject of his or her right to object to the processing of data, whether on the grounds of the data subject's particular situation or in the context of direct marketing or profiling. This obligation is part of the requirement to provide the data subject with extensive information on the processing of data in the scope provided for in Articles 13 and 14 of the GDPR. However there is a particular emphasis on the requirement to make the data subject aware of his or her right to object (Article 21(4) of the GDPR); the information must be presented clearly and separately from any other information. This requirement cannot be met by using a clause formulated in obscure language, using jargon, or hidden in a long and complex policy statement. Where the data are obtained from a source other than the data subject, the information obligation takes into account the cost and organisational limitations of the controller as it is exercisable not upon the collection of data but, at the latest, upon the first communication with the data subject. Therefore it does not require a separate communication for the sole purpose of providing the data subject with the information on the right to object. However, the period between the collection of data and informing the data subject of his/her rights must not be excessive. It must be reasonable in the specific circumstances and must not exceed one month (Article 14(3) of the GDPR).

§9.09 PROFILING FOR MARKETING OR RISK ASSESSMENT AND OTHER AUTOMATED DECISIONS

One of the threats for the privacy and protection of personal data is the scale of automated decision making concerning individuals, including profiling, and those persons' unawareness of being subject to such operations which may have important consequences for them. The GDPR stipulates the right of data subjects not to be subject to decisions based solely on automated processing, including profiling, which produce legal effects concerning them or affect them in similarly significant ways (Article 22 of the GDPR).

This right is not new, as it was provided for already in Directive 95/46/EC (Article 15). However, since the entry into force of the Directive, the relevance of this right for data protection has increased dramatically due to the development and ubiquity of information technologies, the growing performance of computers, the advent of big data, the scale of data redundancy in systems, and access to external data sources such as social networking services.

Profiling is automated processing which uses personal data to evaluate certain personal aspects relating to a natural person, in particular to analyse or predict aspects concerning that natural person's performance at work, economic situation, health, personal preferences, interests, reliability, behaviour, location or movements (Article 4(4) of the GDPR). However, the right not to be subject to profiling does not include all cases of profiling. It only applies if the profiling meets the conditions of Article 22(1) of the GDPR, i.e. if it provides input to a decision which is based solely on automated processing and produces legal effects concerning the data subject or similarly significantly affects him or her, or the profiling includes the processing of sensitive data.

The criterion of legal effects produced by an automated decision is not defined in the GDPR. It has only been clarified, in recital 71 of the preamble to the GDPR, to also include other significant effects, also mentioned in Article 22 of the GDPR. Clarifying examples include the automatic refusal of an online loan application or e-recruiting practices without any human intervention. Legal effects obviously include decisions on the conclusion, amendment or termination of a contract. This happens when profiling determines a decision to grant or refuse an employment, loan or insurance contract, or the amount of the insurance premium.

The Article 29 Working Party has added further examples, such as denying a person the right to vote in an election or a social benefit, refusal of entry at a border, subjecting a person to increased security measures or surveillance by the competent authorities.[38]

The Article 29 Working Party also gives an example of a person being automatically disconnected from their mobile phone service for breach of contract because they forgot to pay their bill before going on holiday. I believe this to be an unjustified extension of the definition of profiling. Profiling is automated processing which uses personal data to evaluate certain personal aspects relating to a natural person. On the other hand, if automated processing leads to the simple finding that a payment has not been credited to a bank account, this implies no conclusions as to the customer's credibility. No personal aspects are thus evaluated. Consequently, in my opinion, this is not profiling.

38. Guidelines on Automated individual decision-making and Profiling for the purposes of Regulation 2016/679, adopted on 3 October 2017, as last revised and adopted on 6 February 2018, WP 251 rev.01, http://ec.europa.eu/newsroom/article29/item-detail.cfm?item_id=612053, p. 21.

On the other hand, no legal effects or other significant effects are involved when profiling is used to select persons to be targeted by direct marketing, i.e. when a data subject is included in a list of persons having certain features defined by the controller, to whom a personalised advertisement of tailored services is to be directed. Therefore, as it does not meet the conditions of legal effects or other significant effects, in my view, it is not covered by the prohibition of Article 22 of the GDPR. (Admittedly though, even profiling for direct marketing may, in some cases, significantly affect the person targeted with the advertisement. This might happen, for instance, if, based on the person's place of residence and his/her inferred financial standing, the algorithm will decide not to send the person information on high-level education opportunities available, despite the person's significant intellectual potential.)

One notorious case illustrating the significant effect profiling may have on individuals, and even on society at large, is Cambridge Analytica. Having obtained the data of 50 million users from Facebook, it created their profiles with these data, in clear conflict with the fundamental principles of personal data protection, unbeknown to the data subjects and in a way incompatible with the declared purpose. The profiles were created to maximise the impact of manipulated political marketing communications directed to the data subjects, largely based on false statements and fake news, designed to significantly bias the result of the 2017 US presidential election and the UK Brexit referendum.[39]

As mentioned above, examples of profiling, involving automated decision-making, may include the automatic rejection of an electronic loan application through automated creditworthiness assessment, or of an insurance application through automated risk assessment, or of a job application in an electronic recruitment process, solely by using an algorithm with predefined criteria, without any intervention of an employee of the institution receiving any such applications. By contrast, operations which do involve human intervention in the decision-making process are not automated processing within the meaning of Article 22 of the GDPR and, consequently, they do not constitute profiling. They do rely heavily on an IT input, but the decision involves a human intervention rather than being made solely by the IT system. Such processing is therefore not prohibited. The human intervention, though, must be genuine and not limited to entering data or rubber-stamping results generated by the IT system[40] (a disproportionately high number of decisions in relation to the number of analysts may indicate that this is the case). In practice, the officially declared human intervention, e.g. in the automated creditworthiness assessment procedure, is often fictitious, being limited to approving the automated decision rather than contributing meaningfully to the decision-making process.

39. Cambridge Analytica execs boast of role in getting Donald Trump elected, The Guardian, 21 March 2018, https://www.theguardian.com/uk-news/2018/mar/20/cambridge-analytica-execs-boast-of-role-in-getting-trump-elected.

40. Guidelines on Automated individual decision-making and Profiling for the purposes of Regulation 2016/679, adopted on 3 October 2017, last revised and adopted on 6 February 2018, WP 251rev.01, http://ec.europa.eu/newsroom/article29/item-detail.cfm?item_id=612053, p. 8 and 30.

Automated decision making, including profiling which meets the criteria of Article 22(1) of the GDPR, is still permitted if it meets one of the conditions below.

The first is profiling being necessary for entering into, or performance of, a contract between the data subject and data controller. The term 'necessary' must, however, not be interpreted broadly and equated with optimisation of the controller's processes. 'Necessary' means that the conclusion or exercise of the contract is impossible without fully automated decision-making. This should be indicated in the controller's information clause (privacy policy).

The second condition allowing profiling is the existence of a legal basis for it in the EU or Member State law to which the controller is subject, provided that it lays down suitable measures to safeguard the data subject's rights and freedoms and legitimate interests. One example is automated monitoring to prevent tax fraud and evasion, carried out according to the regulations and instructions of supervisory authorities (recital 71 of the preamble to the GDPR). A Member State law may, for instance, allow profiling for the assessment of a customer's creditworthiness by a bank, or for the assessment of the customer's insurance risk by an insurance company.

Importantly, such profiling, although being carried out by public trust institutions for their own risk assessment purposes, is not entirely risk-free for the customer: his/her history of card payments for hotel stays or purchases of jewellery or flowers may be interpreted as indicative of a divorce risk, which is taken into account in the assessment of married couples' creditworthiness. Even though the customer must be informed of the rules of profiling, he/she may hardly expect to obtain full information about such controversial criteria used to judge him or her.

The third condition is explicit consent of the data subject. In the cases of automated decision making or profiling based on a contract or consent, the controller is required to demonstrate that it has implemented suitable measures to safeguard the data subject's rights and freedoms and legitimate interests. Since automated decisions significantly affect the data subject and might be based on an overly schematic analysis, then any electronic process of, for example, creditworthiness or insurance risk assessment should include, as its last stage, a verification by a human being. In practice, the officially declared human intervention, e.g. in the automated creditworthiness assessment procedure, is often fictitious, being limited to approving the automated decision rather than contributing meaningfully to the decision-making process.

The minimum safeguard for the person subjected to profiling and other automated decisions where they are not taken on the basis of a contract or the person's consent is human intervention on the part of the controller and the possibility to challenge the automated decision by the person affected by it. An appeal against a fully automated decision should, therefore, be analysed and decided upon by a human being. This need not mean that the final decision made upon appeal against the automated decision must be different from the latter.

It should, however, be considered justified to provide for exemptions from the prohibition of automated decision making in individual cases, where such decisions relate, for instance, to granting low-value consumer loans as part of an offer targeted at a large group of customers, provided that the customer has given consent or the decision is made on the customer's request or in performance of a contract concluded with him/her. It is, moreover, advantageous for customers, who benefit from competition between banks and their flexibility allowing them to take lending decisions very quickly, precisely thanks to automatic data processing.

Still, any exemptions from the general ban on automated decisions significantly affecting the persons they relate to must never allow decisions based on sensitive data (as defined in Article 9(1) of the GDPR). The provision discussed here also prevents discrimination which could result from analysis of sensitive data, such as relating to racial or ethnic origin, health status, or genetic and biometric data (this threat is emphasised in recital 71 of the preamble to the GDPR). Sensitive data may be used for an automated decision only under the explicit consent of the data subject or if the processing is necessary for reasons of substantial public interest, proportionate to the purpose.

The risk of profiling and other automated decision making for the privacy and data protection results from the fact that the findings based on an analysis of personal features significantly affect the person subject to such operations. Consider an automatic rejection of an electronic loan application through automated creditworthiness assessment, or of an insurance application through automated risk assessment, or of a job application in an electronic recruitment process, solely by using an algorithm with predefined criteria, without any intervention of an employee of the institution receiving any of such applications.

The GDPR (Article 13(1)–(2) and Article 14(1)–(2)) requires the controller to provide the data subject, upon obtaining his/her data, with information on any automated decision making, including profiling, and other meaningful information about the logic involved, as well as the significance and the envisaged consequences of such processing for the data subject. The data subject must also be informed of his/her right to object to profiling (Article 21(4) of the GDPR).[41] This enables the data subject to verify, and consequently to challenge, the controller's practices. This is particularly important given that profiling may be used not only for creating customised offers for customers, targeted at their individual needs, as product and service suppliers declare. Profiling may also compromise privacy without compensation in the form of an attractive offer. Specifically, profiling may result in a given customer being offered a higher price than would normally be available, as the supplier may infer from the customer's past purchases that the customer is likely to accept such a price.

Sources of personal data used for such analyses and forecasts may include: locations where mobile phones, laptops and tablets log in to the networks, social networking services, online purchases, transactions, Internet users' queries on online forums, working time recording devices etc. Combining such traces in the IT systems with unique identifiers of natural persons, such as IP addresses, cookies, RFID tags and other information collected by servers, allows specific persons to be identified and their profiles to be created (recital 30 of the preamble to the GDPR). Some of those data are

41. M.J. Culnan, R.J. Bies, 'Managing Privacy Concerns Strategically: The Implications of Fair Information Practices in Marketing in the Twenty-First Century', in: Visions of Privacy: Policy Choices for the Digital Age, ed. by C.J. Bennett, R. Grant, Toronto 1999, pp. 149 et seq.

often made public by the data subjects themselves, for example on social networking services. A more serious threat to privacy is that other data are left as 'traces' by customers or Internet users who are unaware (much less consenting) that their data might be used in the future for other purposes. This also includes data which relate to the persons subject to profiling but are not necessarily obtained from them.

Automated decision making and profiling often leads to conclusions which are statistically probable but erroneous in the specific case.[42] This risk is inherent to the mechanism of profiling. Profiling may be based on information made available to the controller directly by the data subject; in such case, if the information is confirmed and relates directly to the data subject, the risk of error is relatively small. On the other hand, the risk of erroneous conclusions and a violation of the data subject's rights is much higher when profiling is based on data which are unconfirmed, incomplete, out of context or provided anonymously by third parties, and when persons are classified on that basis with negative consequences for their interests, unbeknown to them and beyond their control. This happens when results based on data relating to a specific person are supplemented with other data, obtained from external sources (such as social networking services) and the person is classified in a specific category, with statistical conclusions being drawn from this classification. This mechanism is based on an assumption that if the data subject has certain characteristics, it is statistically justified to presume that he/she also has other features shared by most people with a similar profile.

Projecting the characteristics and behaviours of a person on the basis of uncertain information, obtained from sources such as social networking services, processed through oversimplified algorithms defined by various institutions, may lead to discrimination and stigmatisation.

Drawing conclusions from data which are unconfirmed and taken out of context, and structuring these conclusions only on the assumption that they correspond to statistical behaviours and features, is statistically justified, but such conclusions might be completely untrue in relation to a specific person. This risk is emphasised in recital 71 of the preamble to the GDPR, which requires controllers to use appropriate mathematical or statistical procedures for the profiling, including measures to correct errors and minimise the risk of their occurrence.

Under this mechanism, if a given data subject has been found to have certain characteristics, e.g. to be a man aged between 35 and 50, living in a big city, working freelance etc., it is statistically justified to presume that he also has other features shared by most people with a similar profile.[43]

42. Recommendation CM/Rec(2010)13, adopted by the Committee of Ministers of the Council of Europe on 23 November 2010, on the protection of individuals with regard to automatic processing of personal data in the context of profiling, https://www.coe.int/t/dghl/standardsetting/cdcj/CDCJ%20Recommendations/CMRec(2010)13E_Profiling.pdf.
43. M. Hildebrandt, 'Defining Profiling: A New Type of Knowledge?', in: *Profiling the European Citizen. Cross-Disciplinary Perspectives*, ed. by M. Hildebrandt, S. Gutwirth, New York 2008, pp. 20 et seq.; D. Kreiss, 'Yes We Can (Profile You). A Brief Primer on Campaigns and Political Data', in: 'The Privacy Paradox. Privacy and Its Conflicting Values', *Stanford Law Review*, 2 February – 12 April 2012, http://www.stanfordlawreview.org/online/privacy-paradox/political-data.

Automated analysis may, for instance, result in an increased insurance premium based on information that the person in question regularly buys unhealthy foods or large-sized garments. It might also wrongly attribute an alcohol or gambling problem to a person who does not suffer from any such problems but deals with them professionally, e.g. as a therapist or journalist. Therefore a system should be put in place to limit the risk of wrong inferences and allow the data subject to correct the automatic conclusions.

§9.10 RESTRICTIONS OF DATA SUBJECTS' RIGHTS FOR PUBLIC INTEREST

The GDPR allows, in Article 23 (just as the Directive did in its Article 13(1)), EU or Member State law to restrict the scope of the obligations and rights such as the obligation to provide the data subject with information on his/her data having been collected by the controller, the right of access, the right to erasure (the 'right to be forgotten'), the right to object to data processing, and the obligation to communicate a personal data breach to the data subject (i.e. rights and obligations provided for in Articles 12–22 and 34, and Article 5 in the scope corresponding to the rights and obligations provided for in Articles 12 to 22). Any such restriction must, however, be a necessary and proportionate measure in a democratic society to safeguard public interests (specified in Article 23(1)(a)–(h) of the GDPR) and to protect the data subject or the rights and freedoms of others or to enforce civil law claims (Article 23(1)(i–(j) of the GDPR). In case of such a conflict between the rights provided for by the GDPR and the public or private interest, these values must be weighed against each other.

As a basic condition, the restriction of data subjects' rights under the GDPR, rendering the right to privacy in specific terms, must not infringe upon the essence of fundamental rights and freedoms, and specifically the rights provided for by the EU Charter of Fundamental Rights: the right to the protection of personal data (Article 8), the right to respect for private and family life (Article 7), the freedom of thought, conscience and religion (Article 10), the freedom of expression and information (Article 11), the freedom of assembly and of association (Article 12) and the freedom of the arts and sciences (Article 13).

The public interests which may justify a restriction of the controller's obligations and the data subject's rights include national and public security and the prevention and prosecution of crime. These considerations are particularly relevant in the context of the threat of terrorism in the EU, which has grown in recent years. However, any such restriction must respect the essence of the fundamental rights and freedoms, and must be necessary and proportionate for its purpose. Legislators must respect this principle in 'surveillance' laws. Otherwise the measures provided for in these laws might compromise the privacy of law-abiding citizens, while possibly being ineffective against terrorists and criminals, who are capable of evading them.

The right to privacy is subject to protection according to similar principles under the Convention for the Protection of Human Rights and Fundamental Freedoms. In its Article 8.2, the Convention prohibits any interference by a public authority with the exercise of the right to privacy except for cases provided for in law and necessary in a democratic society in view of national security, public safety or the economic well-being of the country, the prevention of disorder or crime, the protection of health or morals, or the protection of the rights and freedoms of others.

An analogous solution has been adopted, for example, in the Polish Constitution. It stipulates that the right to privacy (based on Article 47 of the Constitution) is not absolute. Article 31(3) of the Constitution, however, provides for weighing of the constitutional rights and freedoms by allowing them to be limited only in cases provided for in law and only where such limitations are necessary in a democratic state for the protection of its security or public order, or to protect the natural environment, health or public morals, or the freedoms and rights of other persons. The safeguard provided for in Article 31(3) of the Constitution of Poland is reinforced by a prohibition to violate the essence of freedoms and rights by means of such limitations.

Derogations from the right of access, rectification, restriction of processing and objection to processing may also be introduced in EU or Member State law in the context of processing of personal data for scientific or historical research purposes or statistical purposes (Article 89(2) of the GDPR). Where personal data are processed for archiving purposes in the public interest, the obligation to notify data recipients of the rectification or erasure of personal data or restriction of processing and the right to data portability may also be derogated from (Article 89(3) of the GDPR). Such derogations are permissible where those rights are likely to prevent or seriously impair the achievement of the specific purposes. However, in the event of derogations provided for in Article 89(2) of the GDPR, data minimisation or, where possible, data pseudonymisation is required.

In its judgment of 20 May 2003,[44] the CJEU emphasised the requirement to demonstrate that data disclosure is necessary for the aim pursued by the legislator – in the case in question, the appropriate management of public funds. Therefore, the CJEU allows the right to personal data protection to be limited by the Member States, but only if such limitations are provided for in statutory regulations or regulations issued on the basis of a statute, and only to the extent necessary to achieve the purposes specified in Article 13(1) of Directive 95/46/EC (Article 23 of the GDPR), such as public security.

Under Article 23(1)(e) of the GDPR, important economic or financial interests of a Member State may be invoked, for instance, to reduce (but not to exclude completely) the application of the information obligation to micro-, small- and medium-sized enterprises (SMEs) employing fewer than 250 persons, unless they process sensitive data. The assessment of whether an important economic interest of a Member State is at stake must be individualised and relate to the specific circumstances. The reference in the GDPR to enterprises employing fewer than 250 persons may justify an exemption from regulatory burdens which are disproportionate to the scale of activity of SMEs, which are the mainstay of a Member State's economy.

---

44. The joined cases of *Rechnungshof* (C-465/00) *v Österreichischer Rundfunk et al.* and *Christa Neukomm* (C-138/01), *Joseph Lauermann* (C-139/01) *v Österreichischer Rundfunk*, http://eur-lex.europa.eu/legal-content/EN/TXT/HTML/?uri=CELEX:62000CJ0465.

While Article 23 of the GDPR allows the scope of obligations and laws provided for in Articles 12 to 22 and Article 34 to be restricted in EU or Member State law, there are two reservations to be made. First, a restriction must not mean a complete exclusion (e.g. of information obligations or the right of access). Second, according to Article 23 of the GDPR, any such restriction must respect the essence of the fundamental rights and freedoms and be a necessary and proportionate measure in a democratic society for the purposes enumerated in Article 23 of the GDPR. I find it unacceptable to argue that a complete exclusion of an important data subject's right, such as a complete exemption of the information obligation towards small-and medium-sized enterprises (SMEs), meets these conditions.

National laws which liberalise the GDPR provisions in relation to SMEs are in place in the UK, France and Poland.

The justification for limiting the information obligation is noteworthy: it is the difficulty of providing the extensive information required by the GDPR during a telephone conversation or in the mobile-optimised version of a web page. This difficulty is indisputable but hardly limited to SMEs: big companies are confronted with the same challenge. Banks, insurance companies or large companies operating in other sectors experience the very same limitations as SMEs in terms of the reasonable duration of a telephone conversation and the customer's patience, or the size of a mobile phone screen used by customers to view web pages. These challenges are unrelated to the number of employees.

At the same time, the risk of a personal data breach is largely dependent on the sector which the controller operates in. Indeed, the below-250 employment threshold exempts online retailers, for example, from some obligations provided for in the GDPR. Moreover, it encourages business operators to spin off parts of their business into smaller companies employing fewer than 250 persons each as a purely formal measure, only to make them exempt from certain GDPR obligations.

CHAPTER 10

Data Controller and Joint Controllers; Data Processor; Processor Selection Criteria and Contractual Terms

§10.01 GENERAL REMARKS

Chapter IV of the GDPR lays down the respective scopes of responsibility and relations of the controller, joint controllers and processor (Articles 26 and 28 in connection with Article 4(7) and (8) of the GDPR). It formulates the obligations binding upon the controller, taking into account the nature, scope, context and purposes of processing as well as the likelihood of a possible breach and its severity for the rights and freedoms of natural persons. The controller's obligations must be interpreted in the context of the GDPR in its entirety, as their scope is defined, among others, by: the legal bases of lawful data processing (Article 6 of the GDPR), the key principles of personal data protection (Article 5 of the GDPR), such as the purpose limitation principle (definition and restriction of purpose), the data minimisation (proportionality) principle, the storage limitation principle, the obligation to provide information on data processing (Articles 13 and 14 of the GDPR), respect for data subjects' rights including rights of access, rectification and objection (Articles 15 to 22 of the GDPR), and the obligation for data transfers to non-EU countries to be based on appropriate grounds (Articles 44 to 49 of the GDPR).

The controller must be able to demonstrate having taken measures to ensure lawful and correct processing. Such measures may include the implementation of appropriate data protection policies, if this is proportionate to the data processing operations being carried out.

Measures applied by the controller must be reviewed and updated where justified. The GDPR does not specify the time intervals for such reviews. Consequently, the formulation 'where necessary' should be taken to mean necessity due to evolving legal or technological environment, the growth of certain threats and emergence of new threats (i.e. external factors), as well as a change in the controller's scope of activities or risk level ascertained through internal risk assessment (i.e. internal factors) (Article 24 of the GDPR). Examples of how the controller may demonstrate the lawfulness and correctness of its data processing operations are: by implementing a regulator-approved code of conduct, applicable in the sector in which the controller operates, or obtaining a certificate confirming the compliance of data processing operations with the GDPR, under an approved certification mechanism. This, obviously, is without prejudice to the supervisory authority's power to declare non-compliance with rules laid down in a code of conduct or a certification (Article 42 of the GDPR).

The controller's and processor's key obligations for the prevention of breaches of natural persons' rights and freedoms include the requirement to process personal data in a way ensuring an adequate level of protection, by implementing appropriate technical or organisational measures.

Actions to ensure the security, integrity and confidentiality of data and their processing include: the implementation of technical and organisational measures to ensure a level of security commensurate to the risk (Article 32 of the GDPR) and notification of any personal data breach to the supervisory authority and communication of such a breach to the data subject (Articles 33 and 34 of the GDPR).

The requirement to *implement* measures means that, where such measures include policies regulating specific aspects of data protection, they must be rendered in specific terms through procedures describing the roles and responsibilities of specified persons or teams in the organisation, as well as individual steps from the identification of an incident or registering a data subject's complaint, through the collection of information, case analysis, measures to prevent further deterioration, securing evidence and mitigation measures. Action must be taken (and documented) to make sure that employees know and understand the procedures, rather than merely sign a formal statement to that effect.

The other requirements specified in the remaining sections of Chapter IV of the GDPR also serve the purpose of data security, as they ensure the effectiveness of processing principles in the context of the GDPR as a whole. These include in particular the key principles of personal data protection, e.g. the purpose limitation principle, the data minimisation principle and the storage limitation principle. These requirements are presented below.

- Data protection by design and by default, i.e. the obligation to implement privacy safeguards already at the stage of designing services, systems or applications (Article 25 of the GDPR).
- Maintaining a record of personal data processing activities, documenting the key aspects of processing (Article 30 of the GDPR).
- Designation of a data protection officer, occupying an appropriate position in the controller's structure (Articles 37 to 39 of the GDPR).
- Analysis of the risk and potential impact of the intended data processing on the rights and freedoms of the data subjects (data protection impact assessment), where the rights and freedoms of natural persons may be compromised (Articles 35 to 36 of the GDPR).

As an optional measure to ensure the security of data and to comply with other processing principles in the context of the data protection system, a controller may also implement an approved code of conduct, applicable in the sector in which it operates, or obtain a certificate confirming the compliance of data processing operations with the GDPR, under an approved certification mechanism (Articles 40 to 43 of the GDPR).

§10.02 DATA CONTROLLER

The process of data processing involves the data controller, fully responsible for the correctness of the data processing, and the processor, which processes personal data on behalf of the controller, usually as an outsourced activity. Personal data may be processed jointly by several controllers, referred to as joint controllers. The data processor may also, subject to the controller's authorisation, subcontract the processing of data to a sub-processor, who then performs selected tasks of the processor.

The data processing process also involves other persons authorised by the controller or the processor, i.e. usually employed by them, and the data protection officer. However, these act only on behalf of the controller or the processor, rather than being separate entities authorised to process data. Other participants in the process are the data recipients to whom data have been disclosed. They are not a separate category of entities authorised to process data, but become data controllers or processors, depending on the purpose for which data have been provided to them. Neither the processor nor any person acting on behalf of the controller or a processor may access and process personal data without the controller's authorisation, unless the EU or Member State law so requires (Article 29 of the GDPR). The scope of responsibilities of persons authorised by the controller or the processor to process data, the data protection officer and data recipients are not discussed in this chapter, but in other chapters of this book.

An entity does not qualify as a data controller based solely on the criterion of having access to data, but also on determining, alone or jointly with others, the purposes and means of processing (Article 4(7) of the GDPR). The purposes of data processing are discussed in the comments on the purpose limitation principle (purpose definition and restriction, Article 5 of the GDPR) and on the legal bases of data processing (Article 6 of the GDPR). Determination of the means of processing is to be understood as selection of technical and organisational measures corresponding to the processing purposes and the characteristics of the controller (e.g. the sector it operates in, its budget, the identified threats to data security).

The key difference between the controller and the processor is that the processor's scope of responsibility does not include making decisions concurrently both on the purposes and on the means of data processing. The concurrent decision making is the key. A processor with a large market share in its sector indeed decides on the technical means of data processing. The fact that it has those means at its disposal is the reason why the controller outsources the processing to it. However, it is up to the controller, rather than the processor, to indicate the purposes of the processing. Thus, the processor does not concurrently decide on the purposes and the means. The processor processes data on instructions from the controller, on its behalf, within the scope and the purposes defined by the controller, which are binding to the processor.

Therefore, the status of controller is defined by the criterion of deciding concurrently on the purposes and the means of processing. For this reason, even if a contract specifies the respective statuses of the controller and the processor otherwise than implied by the definitions of the two terms (and contrary to the facts), this does not change their real status.

The data controller may operate in any legal form which enables it to acquire rights and enter into obligations, i.e. to specify the purposes and means of personal data processing, as part of its business, professional or statutory activities. A data controller may be a private or public sector entity, a natural person or a legal person (company, cooperative, association, foundation), a public entity (a central or local government authority or other state or municipal organisational unit), a non-incorporated organisational unit (e.g. a partnership under commercial law), or another entity.

Separate companies belonging to the same corporate group are separate data controllers. On the contrary, organisational units of the controller which process data as part of the scope of their tasks, defined in the corporate structure, are not separate data controllers, since they do not define the purposes and means of data processing but act within the purposes and means pre-determined within the subordination relationship.

For the same reasons, a branch of a company is also not usually a data controller, although, in selected areas of activity, it may be one because of its organisational autonomy. For instance, a branch of a company which does not enter into contracts with customers on its own behalf but serves the controller's customers within its structure is not a controller of the customers' personal data. However, if it enters into employment contracts with its own employees (which is often the case in EU-based financial institutions opening their branches in other EU Member States), it is the controller of its employees' personal data, in its capacity as employer.

Public authorities and bodies are also data controllers, although, importantly, they may not define the purposes and means of personal data processing beyond what is defined by laws laying out their respective scopes of responsibility. What is more, the status of certain public bodies as controllers of specific data is conferred upon them directly by law. For example, in certain countries the minister of justice and presidents of the competent courts are the controllers of data processed by courts in their adjudication capacity (this possibility is expressly provided for in the definition of data controller in Article 4(7) of the GDPR). In certain cases, laws may also specify means of data processing, e.g. the IT system to be provided by the competent minister and made available to be used, on a compulsory basis, by public institutions reporting to that minister for public registration purposes.

The Court of Justice of the EU, in the judgment of 13 May 2014 in Case C-131/12,[1] pointed out that the activity of search engines, consisting in finding information placed

1. Case C-131/12 for a preliminary ruling under Article 267 TFEU upon request made by Audiencia Nacional (Spain) by decision of 27 February 2012, received at the Court on 9 March 2012, in the

on the Internet by third parties, indexing it automatically, storing it temporarily and making it available to Web users according to criteria they specify, constitutes processing of personal data when this information contains personal data. A search engine provider is the controller of these personal data and is responsible for their processing.

The Court pointed out that, although web search engines direct to information made public by third parties, e.g. media, these operations too should be classified as processing of personal data, since exempting them, widespread as they are, from the scope of the Directive (and, consequently, the GDPR as well) would render its data protection provisions largely ineffective.

In the judgment of 5 June 2018 in the case of *Unabhängiges Landeszentrum für Datenschutz Schleswig-Holstein v Wirtschaftsakademie Schleswig-Holstein GmbH* (intervener: Facebook Ireland Ltd),[2] the CJEU ruled that 'the concept of 'controller' (...) encompasses the administrator of a fan page hosted on a social network'. The administrator of a fan page on Facebook is jointly responsible with Facebook for the processing of data of visitors to the page. The Court confirmed (point 35 of the judgment) that 'while the mere fact of making use of a social network such as Facebook does not make a Facebook user a controller jointly responsible for the processing of personal data by that network, it must be stated, on the other hand, that the administrator of a fan page hosted on Facebook, by creating such a page, gives Facebook the opportunity to place cookies on the computer or other device of a person visiting its fan page, whether or not that person has a Facebook account'.

In the judgment of 10 July 2018 in the case of *Tietosuojavaltuutettu v Jehovan todistajat — uskonnollinen yhdyskunta*,[3] the CJEU ruled that 'a religious community is a controller, jointly with its members who engage in preaching, for the processing of personal data carried out by the latter in the context of door-to-door preaching. The processing of personal data carried out in the context of such activity must respect the rules of EU law on the protection of personal data'.

§10.03 JOINT CONTROLLERS

Personal data may be processed jointly by several controllers, referred to as joint controllers. The GDPR does not preclude a situation where two independent controllers handle the same data (such as a bank and an insurance company, controlling data of the same customers who use bundled products). In such a case, the controllers process data for different purposes that they define themselves. On the other hand, Article 26 of the GDPR also introduces the possibility of two or more controllers jointly determining the purposes and means of processing. The respective controllers' scopes of responsibility for compliance with the obligations provided for in the GDPR, in

proceedings *Google Spain SL, Google Inc. v Agencia Española de Protección de Datos (AEPD), Mario Costeja González*, http://eur-lex.europa.eu/legal-content/EN/TXT/?uri=CELEX:62012CJ0131.

2. Case C-210/16, https://eur-lex.europa.eu/legal-content/EN/TXT/?uri=CELEX:62016CJ0210.
3. Case C-25/17, https://eur-lex.europa.eu/legal-content/EN/TXT/?uri=CELEX:62017CJ0025.

particular as regards the exercising of the rights of the data subject and compliance with the information obligations upon collection of data, is determined by means of an arrangement between the joint controllers (unless their respective responsibilities are determined by EU law or the Member State law to which the controllers are subject). Article 26 of the GDPR does not require a written contract between the joint controllers.

The essence of such an arrangement must be communicated to the data subjects. This formulation, in the context of Article 26 of the GDPR, implies that the data subjects must obtain information sufficient to enable them to exercise their rights. The form of such communication is not defined. In practice, it may prove optimal to include it in the privacy policy. Such arrangements between the joint controllers, including the designation of a contact point, are not binding for the data subject, though: he/she may make requests under his/her rights to any of the joint controllers. Importantly for the relations between the joint controllers, each of them is liable for the entire damage caused to data subjects.

A data processor who has exceeded the scope or purpose of processing specified by the controller may also be considered a joint controller.[4] Insofar as such a processor processes data in non-compliance with the authorisation provided for in the contract entered into with the controller, it becomes a controller itself. At the same time, it acts unlawfully, as it cannot demonstrate any basis for lawful data processing.

§10.04 DATA PROCESSOR. PROCESSOR SELECTION CONDITIONS AND CONTRACTUAL TERMS

The data processor processes personal data on behalf of the controller (Article 4(8) of the GDPR), usually under an outsourcing contract.

The key difference between the controller and the processor is that the processor's scope of responsibility does not include making decisions concurrently both on the purposes and on the means of data processing. The concurrent decision making is the key. A processor with a large market share in its sector indeed decides on the technical means of data processing. The fact that it has those means at its disposal is the reason why the controller outsources the processing to it. However, it is up to the controller, rather than the processor, to indicate the purposes of the processing. Thus, the processor does not concurrently decide on the purposes and the means. Moreover, the controller may interfere with the processor's decisions concerning the means of processing. The processor processes data on instructions from the controller, on its behalf, within the scope and the purposes defined by the controller, which are binding to the processor.

Therefore, the status of controller is defined by the criterion of deciding concurrently on the purposes and the means of processing. For this reason, even if a contract specifies the respective statuses of the controller and the processor otherwise than

4. Article 29 Working Party, Opinion 1/2010 on the concepts of 'controller' and 'processor', 16 February 2010, WP 169, and Opinion 10/2006 on the processing of personal data by the Society for Worldwide Interbank Financial Telecommunication (SWIFT), 22 November 2006, WP 128.

implied by the definitions of the two terms (and contrary to the facts), this does not change their real status.

A data processor may operate in any legal form, i.e. it can be a natural person or a legal person (company, cooperative, association, foundation), a public entity (a central or local government authority or other state or municipal organisational unit), a non-incorporated organisational unit (e.g. a partnership under commercial law) or another entity.

Outsourcing of activities such as generating bank account statements, distribution of insurance contracts by an agent, operation of a call centre, or HR services, necessarily includes entrusting the contractor with processing of personal data. Thus, the outsourcing contract should include provisions regulating the relations between the controller and the processor, including the subject matter and duration of the processing, its nature and scope, the type of personal data and the categories of data subjects, the processor's specific tasks and obligations, the obligation to implement data safeguards, and the obligation to erase or return data upon expiration of the processing purpose, unless the EU or Member State law applicable upon the processor requires it to archive the personal data.

A processing contract must require the processor to notify the controller of any personal data breach occurring on the processor's side. Given that the controller must notify any breach to the supervisory authority within 72 hours of becoming aware of it, the notification time for the processor must be adequately shorter.

The compulsory cooperation between the processor and the controller should also include handling customers' requests, such as complaints, data access or correction requests, or objections to processing. The processor's role in this respect may vary from very limited to significant, depending on the tasks entrusted to it. As a minimum, the processor must ensure that the controller will be notified of such requests having been made directly to the processor by the controller's customers. This is because the time limits defined in the GDPR for replying and processing the request must be complied with.

The contract should also require the processor to provide the controller with all the information the controller needs to demonstrate having met its obligations resulting from the processing contract. The processor should further be obliged under the contract to allow audits and inspections to be carried out by the controller or an auditor under the controller's authorisation. This obligation was included in the past in many outsourcing contracts, but occasionally met with processors' objections.

The processor's obligation must also include maintaining a record of processing activities, as this is not solely the controller's obligation. Micro-, small- and medium-sized enterprises (with fewer than 250 employees) are exempt from this obligation, but only provided that the processing they carry out does not result in a risk to the rights and freedoms of data subjects, the processing is occasional and does not include sensitive data or personal data relating to criminal convictions and offences.

Pursuant to Article 28(6) of the GDPR and recital 81 of its preamble, the controller may entrust the processing of data to a processor under an individual contract (subject to cases where contractual clauses are to safeguard the adequate level of data protection following a transfer to a third country under Article 46(2)(c) and (d) of the

GDPR; this issue is elaborated in the commentary to Article 46 of the GDPR). The parties may also resort completely or partly to the use of standard contractual clauses adopted directly by the European Commission in accordance with the examination procedure referred to in Article 93(2) of the GDPR or by a supervisory authority in accordance with the consistency mechanism referred to in Article 63 of the GDPR and subsequently adopted by the Commission.

The controller on whose behalf the data are to be processed must select a processor which provides sufficient guarantees (in particular in terms of expert knowledge, reliability, resources, technical and organisational measures) ensuring compliance with the GDPR and the protection of data subjects' rights (Article 28 of the GDPR, recital 81 of the preamble to the GDPR). This is one of the key data protection principles, as outsourcing data processing activities increases the risk to the controller's smooth and uninterrupted operation and to the data confidentiality. This includes basic risks, such as the inability to offer reasonable assurance that the data entrusted to the processor are erased after the cooperation is terminated.

The controller may demonstrate having met this requirement, for example, by the fact that the processor applies a regulator-approved code of conduct applicable in the processor's sector or holds a certificate (Articles 40 to 43 of the GDPR). An adequate level of data protection may also be ensured through other certificates relating to specific processes, such as the Payment Card Industry Data Security Standard (PCI DSS), which confirms the adequate security level of payment card holders' data. Any certificate's reliability as a guarantee measure results from its credibility, which corresponds to the credibility of the certifying body.

The implementation of a business continuity plan (BCP) is also important, at least for particularly significant outsourced processes.

The data processor may also, subject to the controller's authorisation, subcontract the processing of data to a sub-processor, who then performs selected tasks of the processor. The terms governing the cooperation with the processor must regulate and limit the use of such sub-outsourcing arrangements. In practice, IT processes (including cloud services), part of the key outsourced services, are often sub-outsourced to third countries in order to reduce their cost. This must not take place without the knowledge of the data controller, beyond its control and without its written authorisation. The data protection level ensured by the sub-processor must not be inferior to the level binding on the controller and required from the processor.

For controllers who outsource processing services on a large scale, it is impracticable to give separate authorisations to the sub-outsourcing of services to each sub-processor. However, Article 28(2) of the GDPR also allows a general authorisation. Under this arrangement, the processor must inform the controller of any intended changes on the sub-processors list and give the controller the possibility to object to such changes.

The processor may not process data beyond the purpose and scope specified in the processing contract. Such a contract is also a document confirming the controller's instruction to process data on its behalf; it may serve such a purpose indirectly, as the basis for further instructions. A processor using the entrusted data for its own purposes would be in breach of the processing contract. One example is when a controller outsources direct marketing to a call centre and provides the contractor with its database of customers but the call centre operator includes it in its own database, used for serving its other customers. The processor would thus unlawfully assume the position of a controller, i.e. it would decide upon the purposes and means of processing; it would also process data without a legal basis. A processor may become a data controller, but only upon meeting one of the alternative bases of lawful data processing provided for in Article 6 or Article 9 of the GDPR.

A processor who has exceeded the scope or purpose of processing specified by the controller may also become a joint controller.[5] Insofar as such a processor processes data in non-compliance with the authorisation provided for in the contract entered into with the controller, it becomes a controller itself. At the same time, it acts unlawfully, as it cannot demonstrate any basis for lawful data processing.

Importantly, the very essence of outsourcing implies that a controller may not entrust the processing of data which the controller itself is not authorised to process. Nor may it entrust the processing of data for purposes for which the controller itself is not authorised to process the data. One example is the cooperation between a bank and an insurance company. When a bank offers the insurance of a loan, this cannot be seen as the outsourcing of insurance activities by the bank, as the bank's statutory business scope does not include providing insurance services.

Article 28 of the GDPR does not require a written form of a contract with the processor: the data processing contract may be concluded in an electronic form, which means that cloud computing contracts may be concluded online. In practice, a provider of such services usually provides a model agreement on its website. The controller, as a customer, fills in its details and information on the envisaged processing and accepts the text generated as a result. This amounts to the conclusion of a contract (such a possibility is provided for in many national legislations, as an acceptance of a contractual model laid down in civil law).

It would not be practicable for a controller to impose its own model contract in relation with such a processor, especially a cloud provider which is a dominant market player. It is, therefore, important that the controller should assess whether the model agreement provided by the processor meets the GDPR requirements.

5. Article 29 Working Party, Opinion 1/2010 on the concepts of 'controller' and 'processor', 16 February 2010, WP 169, and Opinion 10/2006 on the processing of personal data by the Society for Worldwide Interbank Financial Telecommunication (SWIFT), 22 November 2006, WP 128.

CHAPTER 11

Data Protection by Design and by Default; Appropriateness of Data Security Measures in the Context of Risk-Based Approach; Records of Personal Data Processing Activities; Authority to Process Data; Notification of a Personal Data Breach to the Supervisory Authority and Communication to the Data Subject; Data Protection Impact Assessment; Consultation of Effects on Data Protection with a Supervisory Authority; Codes of Conduct and Certification

§11.01 DATA PROTECTION BY DESIGN AND BY DEFAULT

The GDPR introduces the principles of data protection by design and by default (Article 25). These principles have not to date been formulated in EU law or local laws implementing Directive 95/46/EC, although they are also implied by the data minimisation principle, requiring that the scope of data being processed is limited (in terms of the quantity and content of data) to what is necessary to satisfy the purposes of the processing (Article 5(1)(c) of the GDPR), as well as by the purpose limitation and storage limitation principles (Article 5(1)(b) and (e) of the GDPR). I perceive the data protection by design and by default principles to be the technological operationalisation of the above principles, which has been necessary due to data redundancy resulting from the growing performance of computers and decreasing data storage costs.

The principle of data protection by design requires implementation of privacy safeguards even at the stage of designing services, systems or applications, and throughout their development. The very assumptions underlying such instruments, and their structure, should thus provide for protection of data.[1] The principle of data protection by default requires a systemic approach to constructing services, systems or applications, allowing the data subject to configure privacy settings, with high privacy protection being the default option.

Data protection by design (privacy by design) requires the use of technical and organisational means designed for effective compliance with the data protection principles indicated above, including the minimisation of processed data to the necessary scope, and for integrating the necessary safeguards into the processing. One such technical and organisational means, given expressly as an example in Article 25 of the GDPR, is pseudonymisation; additionally, recital 78 of the preamble to the GDPR recommends that the controller adopts internal policies.

Privacy by default (data protection by default) consists in essence of limiting, by default, the scope of data processed (i.e. the amount of data collected, the period of storage and their availability) to the minimum required to meet the specific processing purpose, without the user's interference being necessary. The technical and organisational measures implemented by the controller must, in particular, ensure that the personal data will not be made available, without the data subject's intervention, to an unspecified number of natural persons. This, obviously, does not include cases where the personal data are published under a law, such as the publication of names and contact data of officials in a public information bulletin. Therefore, the extension of the scope of processed data, e.g. available to other users of a social networking service, must never result from the controller's settings, but only from changes introduced by the user him/herself. Experience shows that default settings introduced by the controller largely determine most users' subsequent privacy settings. One negative example is when a social networking service informs all the members of a user's network about the user's visit to a travel destination, merely because the user has activated the location function. In response to a complaint from the Federation of German Consumer Organisations (VZVB), a Berlin regional court ruled Facebook's default data sharing settings to be illegal. Facebook declared it would appeal.[2]

Accordingly, 'data protection by default' is an aspect of the broader 'data protection by design' concept.

1. A. Cavoukian, 'Privacy by Design: Leadership, Methods, and Results', pp. 175 et seq., R. De Wolf, R. Heyman, J. Pierson, 'Privacy by Design Through a Social Requirements Analysis of Social Network Sites form a User Perspective', pp. 241 et seq., in: *European Data Protection: Coming of Age*, ed. S. Gutwirth, R. Leenes, P. de Hert, Y. Poullet, Springer Dordrecht 2013.
2. H.-E. Busemann, N. Schimroszik, German court rules Facebook use of personal data illegal, Reuters, 12 February 2018, https://www.reuters.com/article/us-germany-facebook/german-court-rules-facebook-use-of-personal-data-illegal-idUSKBN1FW1FI [retrieved on 10 March 2018].

The 'privacy by design' concept is based on the demands made in the Resolution on Privacy by Design, adopted at the 32nd International Conference of Data Protection and Privacy Commissioners in Jerusalem, on 27–29 October 2010. Its key demands were 'Proactive not Reactive; Preventative not Remedial'.

The selection of technical and organisational measures ensuring data protection by design and by default should result from the nature, scope, context, and purposes of processing and the likelihood of a breach and its severity. The state of the art should be taken into account: the design should respond to the technology evolution, but with due consideration to the cost of implementing solutions and their market availability. These provisions take into account the practical limitations on the part of both the data controllers and the data processors, although they should not be assumed to relieve the controller of its obligation to apply specific measures where they are indispensable for ensuring a level of security commensurate to the risk.

While selecting and purchasing applications or services (whether ready-made or tailor-made), the controller should require the supplier to design such applications or services in compliance with the GDPR. A non-compliance would be, for example, the lack of a functionality for erasing data in an application for processing data which may be covered by an erasure obligation.

The 'privacy by design' principle should not be seen narrowly as imposing obligations only on controllers which design or modify data processing schemes in ICT systems. It should be viewed more broadly, as also applicable, for example, in public procurement specifications or law-making. One example is IT systems used in courts or public institutions, which generate printouts from the electronic population register to be included in the files for the identification of a person involved in the proceedings. The only purpose is to eliminate possible identification mistakes, for example when different people have certain identical personal data. However, where such printouts include extensive data exceeding this purpose, such as the history of a person's marital status, this is a breach of the 'privacy by design' principle. It is also in conflict with the data minimisation principle, requiring that data be limited to the purpose of the processing. This breach is even more serious given that the printouts are included in court case files.

The controller or processor may demonstrate having ensured data protection by design and by default, for example, by obtaining a certificate confirming the compliance of data processing operations with the GDPR, under an approved certification mechanism referred to in Article 42 of the GDPR.

However, unlike with the controller's obligation to implement appropriate technical and organisational measures under Article 24 of the GDPR, or to provide appropriate safeguards of data protection following their transfer to a third country under Article 46(2)(e) of the GDPR, compliance with data protection by design and by default principles may not be demonstrated through the use of approved codes of conduct, as referred to in Article 40 of the GDPR.

Data protection by design and by default principles must be implemented irrespective of when the data were collected. The controller must not argue that data collected prior to the GDPR becoming effective are not covered by these principles.

§11.02 APPROPRIATENESS OF DATA SECURITY MEASURES IN THE CONTEXT OF RISK-BASED APPROACH

The key obligations of the controller and processor include implementing appropriate technical and organisational measures for the security of data. 'Appropriate' means that they should be adequate to the nature, scope, context and purposes of processing as well as the likelihood and severity of a possible breach for the rights and freedoms of the data subject (Article 32 of the GDPR). The threats that the security measures should prevent, thus ensuring the integrity and confidentiality of data, include in particular unauthorised or unlawful processing and accidental loss, destruction or damage of data (Article 5(1)(f) of the GDPR). This means that protecting data against unauthorised disclosure is only one aspect of security of processing. This is to be borne in mind when the scope of the technical and organisational measures is defined. While this is not expressly stated in the GDPR, it should be inferred that security measures should be implemented before the controller or processor begins the processing of data. This is clear from the goal of introducing these measures and from the *ratio legis* of the GDPR.

The obligation to implement technical and organisational security measures is directly binding on the processor as well as the controller (Article 32(1) of the GDPR). Furthermore, the controller on whose behalf the data are to be processed must select a processor which provides sufficient guarantees (Article 28 of the GDPR, recital 81 of the preamble to the GDPR).

Data controllers and processors include entities from different sectors, of different nature and financial capacities, engaged in activities of varying scales, processing data for various purposes and in various scopes. For this reason, any attempts to compile a comprehensive list of recommended measures would be impracticable and pointless, also because rapid changes to data processing technologies would quickly make any such list outdated. Measures applied must be regularly tested and assessed for their effectiveness and should be updated where justified, e.g. by the evolving legal or technological environment or the controller's scope of activities.

The choice of appropriate measures is determined by the risk level entailed by the processing of data by the specific controller or processor. Thus, full assessment may in practice require, on top of an analysis by the data protection officer, further analyses by cyber-security teams, such as in the context of cloud processing, pseudonymisation and the encryption of personal data, transmission security measures, the capability to constantly ensure the confidentiality, integrity, accessibility and resilience of processing systems and services (particularly their resistance to external attacks), and the capability of quickly restoring the availability of personal data in the event of a physical or technical incident.

Given that, it was justified to lay down a general requirement to ensure that the security measures should be 'appropriate'. Their selection is determined in particular by the degree of risk associated with the processing, in particular the risk of accidental or unlawful destruction, loss, alteration, unauthorised disclosure of, or access to, the personal data.

Importantly, the GDPR is technologically neutral: it does not specifically impose pseudonymisation or the encryption of data but only indicates these measures as possible in cases where they are appropriate in specific circumstances according to the controller's or processor's analysis.

However, the Directive on security of network and information systems (the NIS Directive),[3] the EU's legislation on cybersecurity in the EU, adopted on 6 July 2016 and required to be transposed by Member States into their laws by 9 May 2018, applies to ICT infrastructures in sectors which are critical for the EU's economy and society, such as energy, transport, banking, financial market infrastructures, healthcare, water and digital infrastructure. Businesses in these sectors that are operators of essential services (to be identified by the Member States by 9 November 2018) have to take appropriate security measures and to notify serious incidents to the competent national authority. Each Member State has to designate one, or more, computer security incident response team(s) (CSIRT).

Technical and organisational measures used in practice may include the following:

- Safeguarding the area where personal data are processed against unauthorised access (physical safeguards, including the design and construction of buildings, magnetic access cards and ID badges, physical security, biometric identification, supervision of the keys to the rooms, CCTV, alarm systems, 24-hour monitoring of the alarm signal, ensuring that only selected employees have access to the alarm-disabling codes, servers, and key elements of the network infrastructure, locking documents in appropriate cabinets, use of paper shredders, enforcing a 'clean desk' policy).
- Access control mechanisms in IT systems (separate IDs for each user in the IT system; access to data only possible upon entering an ID and authorisation; unique and strong user passwords with forced regular password change; user access limited to specific resources, according to the authorisation; monitoring of and sanctions against employees who access and use information on customers for private purposes; securing the internal computer network by separating it from the public network by a firewall, DNS or other software; anti-virus software and scanners; cryptographic safeguards in portable computers; screen savers with a password required for resumption; screen settings preventing third-party observation.

  One more optional way of safeguarding data and ensuring lawful processing is implementing an approved code of conduct, applicable in the sector in which the controller operates, or obtaining a certificate confirming the compliance of data processing operations with the GDPR, under an approved certification mechanism.

3. Directive (EU) 2016/1148 of the European Parliament and of the Council of 6 July 2016 concerning measures for a high common level of security of network and information systems across the Union, OJ EU L 194, 19.7.2016, p. 1.

The selection of technical and organisational measures should take into account the state of the art: the design should respond to the technology evolution, e.g. the effects of online data processing, but with due consideration to the cost of implementing solutions and their market availability. These provisions take into account the practical budgetary and organisational limitations on the part of controllers and processors, although they should not be assumed to relieve the controller of its obligation to apply specific measures where they are indispensable for ensuring a level of security commensurate to the risk.[4]

The GDPR annuls the low-level checklists provided for to date in statutory laws or implementing regulations. On the other hand, it requires security measures to be analysed for their appropriateness.

Technological aspects of personal data protection are as important as the fundamental processing principles protecting the rights and freedoms of data subjects. The security level may, however, be significantly enhanced even with little cost. For instance, password strength needs to be reviewed given the growing password-cracking capabilities. An eight-character password can be cracked in one day, but a ten-character one takes 19 and a half months to crack using the same technologies.[5]

This approach is known as the risk-based approach.[6] It essentially consists in taking action to safeguard the data under processing in line with the priorities and timeframe resulting from the findings of the risk analysis. It prevents making investments without regard to the degree of risk, e.g. the type of risk and the nature of the data. On the contrary, it is based on mapping the key areas that require security reinforcements and prioritising them for increased expenditure.

The risk-based approach was already manifest in Directive 95/46/EC, particularly in the context of data processing security measures (Article 17) and the higher protection level applicable to sensitive data in comparison to ordinary data (Article 8). However, the Article 29 Working Party[7] emphasised that the risk-based approach has gained much more attention in the context of the GDPR, having been introduced as a core element of the accountability principle (Article 5(2)), as well as in the context of the requirement of ensuring appropriate data processing security measures (Article 32 of the GDPR), the obligation to carry out a data protection impact assessment (Article 35 of the GDPR), and the data protection by design and by default principles (Article 25).

4. An interpretation shared by the Polish Supreme Administrative Court in its judgment of 4 March 2002, II SA 3144/01, stating that no organisational or financial considerations can justify unlawful processing of personal data.
5. 2015 Trustwave Global Security Report, https://www2.trustwave.com/rs/815-RFM-693/images/2015_TrustwaveGlobalSecurityReport.pdf, p. 104.
6. Article 29 Working Party, Statement on the role of a risk-based approach in data protection legal frameworks, 30 May 2014, WP 218, http://ec.europa.eu/justice/article-29/documentation/opinion-recommendation/files/2014/wp218_en.pdf.
7. Statement on the role of a risk-based approach in data protection legal frameworks, 30 May 2014, WP 218, http://ec.europa.eu/justice/article-29/documentation/opinion-recommendation/files/2014/wp218_en.pdf [retrieved on 17 June 2018], p. 2.

In the same document (point 11, p. 4), the Article 29 Working Party defined the scope of the risk-based approach, indicating that it goes beyond a narrow 'harm-based-approach' but instead should take into consideration every potential as well as actual adverse effect, ranging from an impact on the person concerned to a general societal impact (e.g. loss of social trust).

The European Network and Information Security Agency (ENISA),[8] charged with increasing network and information security in the EU and the Member States and among European businesses, has pointed out that the deployment of hardware and software necessary for ensuring data security must be coupled with introducing internal regulations, which should include the following:

- ensuring sufficient employees' awareness of data security principles and of their obligations under data protection regulations through training courses and other forms of education
- clear division of competences relating to data protection management in the organisation's structure
- monitoring of the use of personal data under an authorisation or assigned tasks
- restriction of access to the area where data are processed and to the controller's and processor's hardware and software, including through verification of access rights
- documenting the disclosure of data to prevent their disclosure to an unauthorised person
- verification, through internal or external audits or penetration tests, of the practical application of measures specified in internal procedures.

One example of an action resulting from the risk-based approach is increasing staff's awareness. Such education activities may take various forms depending on the staff numbers, the budget or the organisation's communication channels. Crucially, the scope and presentation of the information should be adapted to the target audience's profile. Presenting excessive and specialised information is not only ill-adapted to the staff's needs, but causes the information with the practical risk-limiting potential to be lost in the overabundance of irrelevant information. Another good practice is including personal data confidentiality obligations in staff employment contracts.

§11.03 RECORDS OF PERSONAL DATA PROCESSING ACTIVITIES

Control over the correctness of processing is also ensured by the controller's and processor's obligation to maintain a record of personal data processing activities, which is a new type of documenting basic aspects of data processing. It introduces unified processing documentation by replacing various records used before the GDPR,

8. Regulation (EC) No 460/2004 of the European Parliament and of the Council of 10 March 2004 establishing the European Network and Information Security Agency, OJ EU L 77, 13.3.2004, p. 43.

such as records of personal data filing systems maintained by data protection authorities or internal filing system records maintained by the controller and made available to an authority on request. The record of processing activities is an internal record maintained by the controller and also, in a limited scope, by the processor (Article 30(1) and (2) of the GDPR).

The scope of information required to be included in the record is listed separately for the controller and the processor (Article 30(1) and (2), respectively, of the GDPR).

The controller maintains a record of processing activities relating to the personal data being processed 'under its responsibility'. This seems to stand for the personal data of which it is the controller, since the record maintained by the processor covers 'all categories of processing activities carried out on behalf of a controller' and it would not be correct to assume that the processor has no responsibility over the processing of data on behalf of the controller.

Article 30 offers no clarification of whether the processing activities entrusted to the processor should be included only in the processor's record or in the controller's record as well, since records are kept by both the controller and the processor. My interpretation is that such activities should also be included in the controller's record as, although the activities have been entrusted to the processor, the controller still remains responsible for them. At the same time, the controller's record also includes categories of recipients, which includes processors, in line with the definition of recipient in Article 4(9) of the GDPR.

It should be mentioned as an aside that, as opposed to information to be provided where personal data are collected from the data subject or obtained from another source (Article 13(1)(e) and Article 14(1)(e), respectively, of the GDPR), the controller's record of processing activities only includes categories of recipients, rather than detailed information on the recipients of personal data.

The record maintained by the controller, much broader than the record maintained by the processor, must include all of the following information (its scope is partly identical with information clauses under Articles 13 and 14 of the GDPR and is therefore discussed more broadly in the chapter on privacy notices):

- The identification and contact details of the controller and, where applicable, the joint controller, the controller's representative and the data protection officer (where the latter has been designated under the controller's obligations).
- The purposes of the processing.
- A description of the categories of data subjects and of the categories of personal data.
- The categories of recipients to whom the personal data have been or will be disclosed, including recipients in third countries or international organisations.
- Information on data transfers to third countries or international organisations, including their identification.

- Documentation of suitable safeguards, where the transfer could not be based on Article 45 of the GDPR (a European Commission decision declaring an adequate level of data protection in a third country) or Article 46 of the GDPR (appropriate safeguards introduced by the data controller, such as BCRs or standard contractual clauses), or any of the derogations under Article 49(1) of the GDPR (e.g. the data subject's informed consent). This applies where the transfer is not repetitive, concerns only a limited number of data subjects, is necessary for the purposes of compelling legitimate interests pursued by the controller which are not overridden by the interests or the rights and freedoms of the data subject, and the controller has assessed all the circumstances surrounding the data transfer and has, on the basis of that assessment, provided suitable safeguards with regard to the protection of personal data.
- Where possible, the envisaged time limits for erasure of the different categories of data, or at least the criteria used to determine such time limits.
- A general description of the technical and organisational security measures implemented under Article 32(1) of the GDPR, 'where possible'. The latter proviso is not clear to me. Admittedly, when processing activities are outsourced, the security measures are implemented by the processor, but the controller cannot be deemed to be unaware of them. Indeed, Article 28 of the GDPR requires that the processor selected must have provided guarantees to implement appropriate technical and organisational measures, including those required under Article 32 of the GDPR, and must also provide the controller with all the information necessary to demonstrate compliance with the obligations laid down in Article 28 of the GDPR.

The record is to include personal data processing activities. As a starting point, therefore, a list of the controller's business processes must be established. The scope of processing purposes includes numerous and diverse operations, including: marketing, answering contact requests, risk assessment, concluding contracts, entering payments, the distribution of products or services, processing complaints, the enforcement of payments and claims, the payment and reporting of salaries, taxes and social security contributions, archiving, the recruitment of staff and keeping of staff files etc. This is only a selection of the purposes of activities carried out by the data controller.

The list of information required to be included in the processor's record is shorter than the controller's list, as it does not include the processing purposes, categories of data subjects, categories of personal data, categories of recipients and retention periods. On the other hand, besides including all other information also required in the controller's record, it also includes information specific to the processor: the categories of processing carried out on behalf of each controller. The processor's record is also less detailed than the controller's record in that it includes categories of processing, while the controller's record includes processing activities.

The records are required to be maintained in writing, including in electronic form (Article 30(3) of the GDPR). The form, however, has purely technical significance, resulting from the need to ensure data integrity (data must not be modified or erased in an unauthorised way). No binding model of a record is provided. If the wording 'shall be in writing, including in electronic form' were to be construed as a requirement to maintain a record in both these forms, including on paper (as required e.g. by the Belgian data protection authority, Commission de la protection de la vie privée, in its recommendation no. 06/2017 of 14 June 2017),[9] it would amount to an overly strict obligation, neglecting the functionality of IT tools which ensure data integrity as well as efficient handling of the record, such as its updates by designated persons. However, depending on the definitions of written or electronic forms in national law and the approach of the national supervisory authority, these two forms may be viewed as alternative. All of the above relates to the form of current record maintenance.

The record must also be made available at the request of (and, presumably, within the time limit required by) the supervisory authority (Article 30(4) of the GDPR). Thus, the record must be kept in such a form as to allow complete information to be presented to the supervisory authority, in a way that is comprehensible also to people who have not been involved in preparing the records of a specific controller or processor.

An obligation to update the record regularly is not expressly laid down. However, in practice, in order for the record to be accurate and compatible with reality, it must be periodically reviewed according to the categories included in it. A procedure should also be implemented whereby the person or team maintaining the record are notified of any changes, such as the addition of a new processing purpose or a new category of recipients in the controller's scope of activity.

Given the complexity of recording data processing, micro, small and medium-sized enterprises (with fewer than 250 employees, presumably including persons working other than under an employment contract) are exempt from the obligation to maintain a record of processing activities, as long as the processing they carry out does not result in a risk to the rights and freedoms of data subjects, the processing is occasional, and it does not include sensitive data or personal data relating to criminal convictions and offences.

§11.04 AUTHORITY TO PROCESS DATA

Neither the processor nor any person acting on behalf of the controller or a processor may access and process personal data without the authorisation, unless EU or Member State law so requires (Article 29 and Article 32(4) of the GDPR).

This does not mean that the authorisation should be a separate statement by the controller or the processor, nor that its scope or content must not be inferred from an employment contract or an employee's job description or documents attached thereto, presented to the employee.

I believe that a statement by the controller or the processor, authorising a person to process data, may be construed as 'a clear affirmative action' and that the written

9. Recommandation n° 06/2017 du 14 juin 2017, Objet: Recommandation relative au Registre des activités de traitements (article 30 du RGPD) (CO-AR-2017-011), https://www.privacycommission.be/sites/privacycommission/files/documents/recommandation_06_2017_0.pdf [retrieved on 3 February 2018].

form is not required. Thus, the authorisation to process data may also be given through a factual and documented (under the procedure) granting of access to IT systems to the employee. Similarly, the authorisation may be withdrawn through the termination of the employment contract, but also by factually depriving the employee of access to data, particularly to IT systems, through disabling his/her account in the system.

The GDPR provides for an authorisation granted by the controller or the processor. Therefore, persons employed by the processor do not process data under direct authorisation from the controller, but from the processor who employs those persons, whereas the processor processes data under a processing contract with the controller.

An irregularity frequently occurs in practice when an authorisation to access data, issued to former employees, is still kept in the company's IT system, or no authorisations are present for temporary employees or contractors who may consult personal data as part of their duties.

§11.05 NOTIFICATION OF A PERSONAL DATA BREACH TO THE SUPERVISORY AUTHORITY AND COMMUNICATION TO THE DATA SUBJECT

A personal data breach, and a failure to address it in an appropriate and timely manner, may result in financial losses or non-material damage due e.g. to identity theft or fraud, committed, for example, in order to take a loan in the data subject's name or to obtain unauthorised access to his/her employer's IT system. It may also expose the data subject to discrimination in lending, insurance or employment decisions, or to an infringement of his/her personal rights (recital 85 of the preamble to the GDPR).

For these reasons, the controller must notify any personal data breach to the supervisory authority without undue delay, where possible, within 72 hours of becoming aware of it. The processor must, similarly, notify any such breach to the controller without undue delay, although no specific time is specified in the GDPR.

The starting point of the time limit is becoming aware of the breach, rather than its occurrence. Still, recital 87 of the preamble to the GDPR requires that the time between the breach and becoming aware of it must not be too long: all appropriate technological and organisational measures must be implemented to ensure that a breach is detected immediately. If the notification is made later, it must be accompanied by the reasons for the delay (Article 33(1) of the GDPR).

The same recital indicates the criteria for assessing whether the notification was made without undue delay: the nature and gravity of the personal data breach and its consequences and adverse effects for the data subject.

In order to limit the risk of a delay, if it is not possible to provide the information at the same time, the information may be provided in phases (Article 33(4) of the GDPR and recital 85 of the preamble to the GDPR).

If a personal data breach occurs on the processor's side, the processor must also notify it to the controller without undue delay after becoming aware of it (Article 33(2) of the GDPR). This can also be inferred from Article 28(3)(f) of the GDPR, stating that a contract whereby data processing is entrusted to a processor should require the processor to assist the controller in ensuring compliance with the obligation to ensure data security.

No time limit is specified, as is the case for the controller. However, given the requirement that the breach detection time is not excessive, the processing contract must require the processor to notify the controller of any personal data breach occurring on the processor's side. Given that the controller must notify any breach to the supervisory authority within 72 hours of becoming aware of it, the notification time for the processor must be adequately shorter.

The controller may be exempt from the obligation notification of a personal data breach to the supervisory authority if the breach is unlikely to result in a risk to the rights and freedoms of natural persons, but the controller must be able to demonstrate that this is the case, in line with the accountability principle.

This exemption, under Article 33(1) of the GDPR, is related to the controller's obligation; no exemption is expressly laid down in relation to the processor's obligation to notify a breach to the controller. Thus, the assessment of the risk to the rights and freedoms of natural persons is at the responsibility of the controller, not the processor.

The interpretation of the unlikelihood of the breach to result in a risk to the rights and freedoms of natural persons is key, as it determines the obligation to notify the breach. It implies that some personal data breaches do not result in violating natural persons' rights or freedoms. For instance: if an unauthorised person is admitted to an office building without being prompted to show their badge, contrary to the procedures, or if a USB flash drive found lying in a corridor is inserted to a computer, this is a personal data breach, which, however, need not result in a violation of natural persons' rights or freedoms, if safeguards implemented by the data controller prevent the building intruder from accessing data, or prevent the installation of a virus from the flash drive. In such an incident, therefore, the controller must take corrective action but need not notify the incident to a supervisory authority.

The GDPR lists the elements which must be included in a notification of a breach to the supervisory authority. They include information on the nature of the breach, the categories and approximate number of data subjects concerned, the likely consequences of the breach, and the measures taken or proposed to be taken by the controller to address the breach or mitigate its effects.

The elements required to be notified by a processor to a controller are not listed but should be assumed to be such as to allow the controller to assess the nature of the breach and to notify it to the supervisory authority where necessary.

However, the content of the notification to the competent national authority, and to the subscriber or individual, of personal data breaches by providers of publicly available electronic communications services is specified in Commission Regulation (EU) No 611/2013 of 24 June 2013 on the measures applicable to the notification of personal data breaches under Directive 2002/58/EC of the European Parliament and of the Council on privacy and electronic communications.[10]

10. OJ EU L 173, 26.6.2013, p. 2–8.

The controller must also communicate the personal data breach (and, in particular, describe its nature, consequences and measures taken to mitigate them) to the data subject without undue delay (Article 34 of the GDPR). This formulation is less stringent than the one applicable to the obligation to notify a breach to the supervisory authority. The latter applies as a rule, whenever there is a risk (not necessarily a high risk) to the rights and freedoms of data subjects, except where the risk is unlikely. On the other hand, the obligation to notify the data subject only applies where the breach is likely to result in a risk to the rights and freedoms of natural persons *and* this risk is high (i.e. the rights and freedoms may be significantly endangered).

A breach must be communicated to the data subject without undue delay, a concept already discussed above. In such a case, the communication must be made in such a time as to allow the data subject to take precautions to minimise the direct risk of damage (such as an identity theft). On the other hand, the need to implement appropriate measures against continuing or similar personal data breaches may justify more time for communication (recital 86 of the preamble to the GDPR).

The obligation to communicate the breach to the data subject does not apply when the controller has applied appropriate technical and organisational protection measures to the personal data affected by the personal data breach, rendering the personal data unintelligible to unauthorised persons (e.g. through encryption), or has taken subsequent measures to eliminate the high risk to the rights and freedoms of data subjects. The supervisory authority may, however, still require the controller to communicate the breach to the data subject.

Rules and procedures regulating exemptions from the notification obligation should take into account the legitimate interests of law-enforcement authorities, where early disclosure could unnecessarily hamper the investigation into the circumstances of a personal data breach (recital 88 of the preamble to the GDPR).

The obligation may also be exempted where a direct communication to the data subject (as is required) would involve disproportionate effort, e.g. where the breach has affected a substantial number of the controller's customers. For such cases, the GDPR allows the controller to make a public communication or a similar measure ensuring that the communication reaches the affected data subjects effectively.

A public communication (such as a media announcement), reaching an unlimited number of users, is detrimental to the controller's reputation and, as such, is unlikely to be used in practice, except where absolutely necessary. Sending paper letters to each data subject in the event of a mass breach would involve disproportionate effort, but many controllers may resort to electronic communication (email or an e-banking communications module), which is uncomplicated and effective.

A 'personal data breach' is defined in Article 4(12) of the GDPR as 'a breach of security leading to the accidental or unlawful destruction, loss, alteration, unauthorised disclosure of, or access to, personal data transmitted, stored or otherwise processed'. A breach may result from an (inadvertent or illegal) action or a failure to take action and can occur at any stage of data processing, e.g. during the archiving or transfer of data.[11]

The nature of a personal data breach that is required to be notified is not specified precisely in the GDPR. The Article 29 Working Party developed guidelines for controllers, for the purposes of Directive 2002/58/EC, on the criteria for making a decision to communicate breaches to data subjects.[12] Similar guidelines relating specifically to Articles 33 and 34 of the GDPR were subsequently developed and published as 'Guidelines on Personal data breach notification under Regulation 2016/679' of 3 October 2017, last revised and adopted on 6 February 2018, WP 250 rev.01.[13]

The Article 29 Working Party, in its opinion WP 250 rev.01 (p. 7), characterises a personal data breach by reference to its consequences, i.e. the controller being unable to ensure compliance with the principles relating to the processing of personal data, as outlined in Article 5 of the GDPR. The Article 29 Working Party therefore distinguishes between a security incident and a personal data breach: every personal data breach is a security incident, but a security incident need not be a personal data breach.

In its earlier opinion no. 3/2014 (WP 213), the Article 29 Working Party indicated types of personal data breaches, which may occur separately or concurrently: (a) confidentiality breach – an unauthorized or accidental disclosure of, or access to, personal data; (b) availability breach – an accidental or unlawful destruction or loss of personal data; (c) integrity breach – an unauthorised or accidental alteration of personal data.

The European Data Protection Board may also issue guidelines, recommendations and best practices e.g. on circumstances in which the personal data breach is required to be notified and on processing operations that are considered to be unlikely to result in a high risk to the rights and freedoms of natural persons (Article 70(1) (g) and (h) of the GDPR).

The obligation to notify a breach to the supervisory authority and to communicate it to the data subject covers not only serious data leaks or cyber-attacks affecting substantial numbers of customers[14] but also incidental breaches, not caused by systemic shortcomings in the controller's activities.

Personal data breaches may also result from human mistakes, including those resulting from employees' lack of professional experience or hardware or software

---

11. P. Fajgielski, 'Informowanie o naruszeniu ochrony danych osobowych w świetle przepisów ogólnego rozporządzenia o ochronie danych', *Monitor Prawniczy* 2016, no. 20, p. 45.
12. Opinion 03/2014 on Personal Data Breach Notification, 25 March 2014, WP 213, http://ec.europa.eu/justice/article-29/documentation/opinion-recommendation/files/2014/wp213_en.pdf.

    Directive 2002/58/EC (Article 4(2)) previously imposed an analogous obligation upon telecom operators ('providers of publicly available electronic communications services'), requiring them to notify a risk of a breach of data protection ('a particular risk to the security of the network') to the supervisory authority and to communicate it to the person affected.
13. http://ec.europa.eu/newsroom/article29/item-detail.cfm?item_id=612052.
14. One of the most serious incidents of this type to date was an attack of a Russian hacker group targeting 1.2 billion user names and passwords (N. Perlroth, D. Gelles, 'Russian Hackers Amass Over a Billion Internet Passwords', The New York Times, 5 August 2014, http://www.nytimes.com/2014/08/06/technology/russian-gang-said-to-amass-more-than-a-billion-stolen-internet-credentials.html).

errors. Some such incidents, even if occasioned by a single mistake appearing to be of little significance, may adversely affect data protection on a mass scale. An example of such seemingly minor mistakes of serious consequences is sending an email to a large group of recipients with the full list of recipients visible to all of them. Another example is where a bank account statement, instead of being sent to the account owner, is sent to the next person on the list and, consequently, all the further statements printed in the batch are also sent to the wrong people.

The obligation to notify breaches will be extremely difficult to comply with, given that at present, companies need an average of 86 days to detect personal data breaches.[15] The controller must document any personal data breaches, including the facts relating to the breach, its effects and the remedial action taken (Article 33(5) of the GDPR). Under this provision, the documentation requirement is not limited to breaches notified to the supervisory authority but covers 'any' personal data breaches. The purpose is to allow the supervisory authority to verify compliance with Article 33 of the GDPR. Therefore, in my view, any such documentation must also cover breaches deemed by the controller to be low-risk, and this judgment will be subsequently subject to an assessment by the supervisory authority.

In order to comply with the obligation, controllers will also have to develop procedures and information flow schemes, ensuring that information on breaches, appearing in various units of the organisation, are collected in the central database and constitute a record serving as the basis for the reporting. The information flow schemes must also ensure the reporting of a breach within the 72-hour time limit upon detecting it. This means that the time to transmit the information within the organisation (or, even more so, by the processor) must be shorter. The risk of delays may be limited e.g. by using an email address or an application for managing reports within the controller's organisation and a division of tasks between teams.

The existing records of personal data breaches are maintained on different legal bases by different controllers and serve other direct functions, namely the prevention of fraud by identity thieves. Such records include the *Dokumenty Zastrzeżone* system run by the Polish Bank Association or the ITRC Breach Database maintained by the US-based Identity Theft Research Center (ITRC).

During the first month of the GDPR applicability, the President of the UODO, the Polish data protection authority, received reports of more than 320 personal data breaches, i.e. an average of 10 breaches per day. Most of them related to unauthorised or accidental disclosure or availability of data.[16]

15. 2015 Trustwave Global Security Report, https://www2.trustwave.com/rs/815-RFM-693/images/2015_TrustwaveGlobalSecurityReport.pdf, pp. 23-26.
16. M. Maj, *Zgadnijcie ile naruszeń ochrony danych Polaków zgłoszono do UODO w związku z RODO?*, https://niebezpiecznik.pl/post/zgadnij-ile-naruszen-ochrony-danych-juz-zgloszono-w-zwiazku-z-rodo/ Source: UODO press office (retrieved on 5 July 2018).

§11.06 DATA PROTECTION IMPACT ASSESSMENT

One of the specific forms of the 'risk-based approach' discussed in this chapter is the data protection impact assessment (DPIA, Article 35 of the GDPR).[17] The Article 29 Working Party[18] defines the data protection impact assessment as 'a process designed to describe the processing, assess its necessity and proportionality and help manage the risks to the rights and freedoms of natural persons resulting from the processing of personal data by assessing them and determining the measures to address them'. The GDPR provides no definition but specifies, in particular, indications establishing the obligation and the scope of assessment.

The term used in the GDPR is, in practice, often interchangeable with 'privacy impact assessment' (PIA), as used e.g. in the Privacy Impact Assessment Handbook published by the Information Commissioner's Office (British data protection authority), while the Guidance on Data Protection Impact Assessments of the Belgian Commission for the Protection of Privacy uses the term 'data protection impact assessment'. This suggests that, as the protection of personal data is not the only aspect of the right to privacy (this topic is discussed in more detail in Chapter 2: *Definitions of the Right to Privacy; Protection of Personal Data as One Aspect of This Right*...), the scope of the assessment required by the GDPR is narrower than that of a privacy impact assessment.

However, some reservation is warranted to the extent that a data protection impact assessment must not be limited to a simple analysis of compatibility with the GDPR, but must relate more broadly to effects of the processing on the risk to the rights and freedoms of natural persons. Therefore, the scope of assessment should not be treated minimalistically: it must go beyond the compatibility with the GDPR, i.e. data protection, to cover the right to privacy in its entirety. However, 'rights and freedoms' do not only include the right to privacy (the right to respect for private and family life under Article 7 of the EU Charter of Fundamental Rights and the right to the protection of personal data under Article 8 of the Charter), although it is of the utmost importance for the assessment. Other rights and freedoms specified in the Charter, such as freedom of thought, conscience and religion (Article 10), freedom of expression and information (Article 11), freedom of assembly and of association (Article 12) and freedom of the arts and sciences (Article 13), should also be taken into account.[19] The subject of the assessment is the impact of the implementation of, among others, new technologies, such as apps, services or business practices, particularly on the privacy of data

17. L. Hempel, L. Lammerant, 'Impact Assessment as Negotiated Knowledge', in: *Reforming European Data Protection Law*, (ed.) S. Gutwirth, R. Leenes, P. de Hert, Dordrecht 2015, pp. 125-126.
18. The Article 29 Working Party, Guidelines on Data Protection Impact Assessment (DPIA) and determining whether processing is 'likely to result in a high risk' for the purposes of Regulation 2016/679, WP 248 rev.01, adopted on 4 April 2017, as last revised and adopted on 4 October 2017, http://ec.europa.eu/newsroom/document.cfm?doc_id=47711, p. 4.
19. The Article 29 Working Party, Guidelines on Data Protection Impact Assessment (DPIA) and determining whether processing is 'likely to result in a high risk' for the purposes of Regulation 2016/679, WP 248 rev.01, p. 7.

subjects, as well as the measures limiting or excluding the possibility of violation of the right to privacy during the implementation.

The assessment referred to in Article 35 of the GDPR should primarily focus on the impact of the envisaged processing operations on the rights or freedoms of data subjects, rather than, for example, on the threat of fines or civil liability for the controller. However, including the latter aspect in the assessment may be considered a good practice of the controller.

The obligation to carry out the data protection impact assessment arises when a type of processing is likely to result in a risk to the rights and freedoms of natural persons, due to its nature, scope, context and purposes, but only if, firstly, there is a substantial likelihood of such an impact and, secondly, the assumed risk is high. These vague terms show that a data protection impact assessment is not required if, according to the analysis of the controller in a specific processing situation, the impact of the processing on the rights or freedoms of data subjects, or the likelihood of a high risk, is low or only insignificantly increased.

Article 35(1) of the GDPR emphasises that the risk of a breach of the rights or freedoms of natural persons may result, in particular, from the use of new technologies. However, the provision does not specify if it refers to technologies which are new on the market or to those which have been available on the market but are new to the controller. In my opinion, the second option should also be taken into consideration because the impacts of using technologies are individual, they may differ between different controllers, depending on the nature, scope and context of the processing and, furthermore, using the same technology may be assessed as proportionate or as excessive interference with privacy, depending on the purpose of the processing.

However, even in cases where there is no obligation to carry out a DPIA pursuant to Article 35 of the GDPR, a risk related to the processing is often subject to assessment in practice, and the result of such an assessment is the identification of a risk level – whether the risk is high and likely, and consequently, whether a full data protection impact assessment fulfilling the criteria specified in Article 35 of the GDPR is needed.[20]

The controller is obliged to carry out the impact assessment of the envisaged operations prior to the processing (Article 35(1) of the GDPR imposes this obligation directly, also by using the term 'envisaged'). In addition, further reviews to assessments which have been carried out are obligatory (Article 35(11) of the GDPR), at least when there is a change in the risk represented by processing operations (e.g. if the scope of the processing purposes has been extended), because a previous assessment may require adaptation to new circumstances, but also for the purpose of verification if the processing is carried out in accordance with the data protection impact assessment. Good practices should include carrying out regular reviews.

It is obligatory to carry out DPIAs for data processing operations fulfilling criteria specified in Article 35 of the GDPR which have started after 25 May 2018, i.e. after the

20. The Article 29 Working Party, Guidelines on Data Protection Impact Assessment (DPIA) and determining whether processing is 'likely to result in a high risk' for the purposes of Regulation 2016/679, WP 248 rev.01, p. 7.

GDPR became applicable. However, the Article 29 Working Party specifies[21] that operations which did not require an impact assessment on 25 May 2018 according to the controller should also be subject to such an assessment at the appropriate time, during a periodic review or as a result of new circumstances, as part of general accountability obligations.

It is permitted to carry out a single assessment for a set of similar (not necessarily identical) data processing operations that present similar high risks (Article 35(1) of the GDPR). The Article 29 Working Party[22] defines the similarity of operations undergoing a collective assessment as using similar technology to collect the same sort of data for the same purposes, e.g. using similar CCTV systems by separate controllers under a local government.

Article 35(3) of the GDPR provides the following non-exhaustive list of cases where a DPIA is required:

- A systematic (i.e. not incidental or occasional) and extensive[23] (i.e. not limited to one feature) evaluation of personal aspects relating to natural persons which is based on automated processing, including profiling, and on which decisions are based that produce legal effects concerning the natural person or similarly significantly affect the natural person. Processing data on a large scale does not include, for example, processing the personal data of patients by a single medical clinic or of clients by a single law firm, so a DPIA is not required in such cases.
- The processing of sensitive data (special categories of data referred to in Article 9(1)), or of personal data relating to criminal convictions and offences (referred to in Article 10 of the GDPR), if the processing is carried out on a large scale.
- a systematic (not occasional) large-scale monitoring of a publicly accessible area.

In practice, due to technological evolution, a case subject to the assessment may fulfil the criteria of more than one point at the same time. For example, the systematic monitoring of public areas with the use of cameras with a face and voice recognition system and a number-plate recognition system fulfils the criteria of all the cases listed in Article 35(3) of the GDPR.

National supervisory authorities must establish and publish a list of the types of processing operations which require a DPIA, i.e. they must indicate operations which they consider likely to result in a high risk to the rights and freedoms of natural persons (Article 35(4) of the GDPR). An opposite list, i.e. of the types of processing operations

21. Guidelines on Data Protection Impact Assessment (DPIA) and determining whether processing is 'likely to result in a high risk' for the purposes of Regulation 2016/679, WP 248 rev.01, p. 17.
22. Guidelines on Data Protection Impact Assessment (DPIA) and determining whether processing is 'likely to result in a high risk' for the purposes of Regulation 2016/679, WP 248 rev.01, p. 8.
23. A 'systematic' evaluation has been defined by the Article 29 Working Party in the Guidelines on Data Protection Officers, adopted on 13 December 2016, as last revised and adopted on 5 April 2017 (WP 243 rev.01) – this topic is discussed in more detail in the comments on the data protection officer in this chapter.

for which no data protection impact assessment is required, may be useful in practice, but the supervisory authority is not obliged to establish and publish such a list (Article 35(5) of the GDPR).

A data protection impact assessment is carried out by the controller but it is obliged to seek the advice of the data protection officer, where designated (regarding the initial assessment and during a review) (Article 35(2) of the GDPR). The results of such consultations and decisions made should be documented.

The GDPR (Article 35(7)) provides for the minimum scope of a DPIA:

- a systematic description of the envisaged processing operations and the purposes of the processing;
- the legitimate interest pursued by the controller, provided it is a basis for the processing (e.g. an indication that the purpose of the implementation of a new information system and procedure is to counter abuse); however, although it is only required to indicate that basis for processing, it should be assumed that if the processing is carried out on other grounds, they should also be indicated in justified cases; otherwise, the lawfulness of the processing will not be proven;
- an assessment of the necessity and proportionality of the processing operations in relation to the purposes (i.e. if the achievement of the pursued purpose is possible without the operations subject to the assessment);
- an assessment of the risks to the rights and freedoms of data subjects (i.e. if the assessed operations carried out for a specific purpose do not interfere excessively with, in particular, the right to privacy);
- the measures envisaged to prevent the risks, including safeguards, security measures and mechanisms to ensure the protection of personal data and to demonstrate compliance with the GDPR, taking into account the rights and legitimate interests of data subjects.

The applied assessment scheme should include a standardised risk level and its likehood (e.g. high, medium or low) and the measures envisaged to prevent the risk should result from that level (e.g. no necessity to implement such measures in the case of negligible risk, the pseudonymisation of data or even renouncing the implementation of the assessed operation).

Consulting the Supervisory Authority regarding Data Protection Impacts

The controller is obliged to consult the supervisory authority regarding the operations in question where a data protection impact assessment carried out under Article 35 of the GDPR indicates that the envisaged processing would result in a high risk and the controller has not taken any measures to mitigate the risk, or it can be assumed that the measures taken are insufficient (Article 36(1) of the GDPR). In practice, the consultation obligation is also likely to arise in cases where, according to the controller's assessment, the implemented measures will not lead to the reduction of a high risk level, e.g. due to the unavailability of effective technologies on the market or due to cost inadequacy. It could hardly be expected that a reason for the consultation declared by the controller would be admitting that it has not implemented risk reduction measures.

The scope of information to be contained in a request for consultation (Article 36(3) of the GDPR) should include, among others, the purposes and means of the intended processing, the measures to protect the right to privacy and the result of the data protection impact assessment.

The request for consultation must be submitted by the controller prior to the processing. Responding to the request, the supervisory authority may provide written recommendations addressed to the controller or the processor, if it considers that the intended processing would be in breach of the GDPR, in particular where the controller has insufficiently identified or mitigated the risk. This means that the supervisory authority may not only assess negatively the effectiveness of risk reduction measures, but also increase the risk level in comparison to that resulting from the controller's assessment, although it must have been already high as it was the subject of consultation.

Business processes of the controller are affected by deadlines for submitting recommendations (Article 36(2) of the GDPR) – up to eight weeks of receipt of the request for consultation, which may be extended by six weeks, taking into account the complexity of the intended processing (those periods may be suspended until the supervisory authority has obtained the information it has requested during the procedure). This provision sets deadlines to submit recommendations by the authority in case of a negative assessment of the risk or risk reduction measures. It seems, therefore, that the lack of recommendations of the supervisory authority within the standard or extended period authorises the controller to launch processes which have been the subject of consultation. However, the absence of a reaction of the supervisory authority within that period should be without prejudice to any intervention of the supervisory authority, in accordance with its supervisory powers laid down in Article 58 of the GDPR (recital 94 of the preamble to the GDPR), including a temporary or definitive limitation including a ban on processing.

§11.07 CODES OF CONDUCT AND CERTIFICATION

The implementation of a code of conduct approved by a supervisory authority, applicable in the sector in which the controller or the processor operate, or obtaining a certificate confirming the compliance of data processing operations with the GDPR, under an approved certification mechanism, is (depending on the circumstances) one way of demonstrating the lawfulness and correctness of data processing, a basis for transferring personal data to a third country, or means of avoiding a fine imposed by a supervisory authority or reducing its amount.

A controller or a processor who has implemented a code of conduct or obtained a certificate confirms, in this way, that it has high data protection standards in place in its structure and operating practice. It may be used as one of the elements by which to demonstrate that the controller or the processor comply with their obligations under the GDPR (in the context of its entirety), i.e. process data on one of the lawfulness bases, comply with the key personal data protection principles, and respect the data subjects' rights of access to data, the rectification of data, objection to the processing of data and other rights (Article 24(3) of the GDPR).

In addition to demonstrating lawfulness of data processing in these general terms, individual provisions of the GDPR formulate selected aspects in which the implementation of a code of conduct or obtaining a certificate is a means to comply with a legal obligation:

- Data protection by design and by default, i.e. the obligation to implement privacy safeguards already at the stage of designing services, systems or applications (Article 25 of the GDPR).
- Entrusting the processing of data on behalf of a controller to a processor only upon the condition of providing guarantees to implement appropriate technical and organisational measures so that the processing meets the requirements of the GDPR and the rights of the data subject are protected (code of conduct or certification on the part of the processor, Article 28 of the GDPR).
- Implementation of appropriate technical and organisational measures to ensure data processing security adequate to the risk, including the ability to ensure the ongoing confidentiality and resilience of processing systems and services (Article 32 of the GDPR).
- Covering data transferred to a third country with appropriate safeguards, as an alternative to, for example, binding corporate rules or standard data protection clauses (Article 46 of the GDPR).

The implementation of an approved code of conduct or obtaining a certificate is also a means of influencing the decision of a supervisory authority to impose a fine, and the amount of the fine (Article 83 of the GDPR).

Codes of Conduct

The GDPR allows associations and other bodies representing specific sectors in which data controllers or processors operate (and supervisory authorities and the European Data Protection Board encourage them) to develop codes of conduct laying down precise rules of application of the GDPR, taking into account specific characteristics of the respective sectors (Article 40 of the GDPR). The codes of conduct may regulate issues which require different approaches depending on the sector, such as the determination of legitimate interests applicable to the sector, methods of data pseudonymisation, the exercise of data subjects' rights, e.g. the 'right to be forgotten' or to data portability, data protection by design and by default, notification of personal data breaches to the supervisory authority, and transfers of personal data to third countries. Thus, sectoral codes of conduct should specify best practices, resulting from the experience of organisations representing the sector and recommended by them as the ways of choice for ensuring compliance with data protection requirements in the context of the specific sector. If the practical aspects of operation in a given sector, or applicable to micro-, small and medium-sized enterprises, are taken into account, this ensures genuine compliance with the principles formulated in the code of conduct.

Importantly (as ensured by the requirement for a code of conduct to be approved by a supervisory authority), the reference to specific features of a sector is intended to ensure that effective means of complying with GDPR requirements are defined, rather than such specific features being invoked as a justification for circumventing those requirements in a given sector. For instance, a sectoral code of conduct may define the procedure of resolving disputes between controllers and data subjects, but must not restrict the data subjects' rights under Articles 77 and 79 of the GDPR, e.g. it must not set a maximum compensation for a personal data breach. Indeed, as the protection under GDPR covers natural persons, including consumers, such practices would also be unacceptable as abusive clauses.

One example is the European code of conduct developed by the Federation of European Direct and Interactive Marketing (FEDMA), regulating the use of personal data in direct marketing, including electronic marketing communications.[24] Other codes of conduct have been developed by associations of banks or insurance companies in order to bring their activities in line with the GDPR also in the context of sectoral legislation, such as on banking or insurance secrecy, or reconciling the application of the GDPR and of the Payment Services Directive 2 (PSD 2).

Where the territorial scope of a code of conduct does not exceed one Member State, the draft code of conduct (and drafts of any amendments, including extensions) is assessed and approved by the competent supervisory authority (Article 40(5), in conjunction with Article 55, of the GDPR). Where the territorial scope is broader and covers more than one Member State, the competent supervisory authority consults the European Data Protection Board prior to approving the draft code of conduct or an amendment thereof (Article 40(7), in conjunction with Article 63, of the GDPR). If the Board issues a favourable opinion, the European Commission may decide that the approved code of conduct or amendment of the extension thereof have general validity within the EU (Article 93(2) of the GDPR).

A draft amendment or extension of a code of conduct adopted prior to the application date of the GDPR should be treated as a draft of a new code of conduct, where the purpose of the amendment is to bring the code of conduct in compliance with the GDPR.

The monitoring of compliance with approved codes of conduct is within the remit of the competent supervisory authority (Article 57(1)(a) and Article 58(1) and (2) of the GDPR), but it may also be carried out by an external body accredited for that purpose by the competent supervisory authority (Article 41(1) of the GDPR). The terms and modalities of the accreditation of an entity monitoring the code of conduct, and the arrangements for approval of a code of conduct, may be regulated by Member State national laws. Entrusting an external body with the monitoring of the compliance of the controller's or the processor's activities with the code of conduct is without prejudice to the powers of the supervisory authorities under Articles 57 and 58 of the GDPR

24. The code of conduct was approved by the Article 29 Working Party in 2010: Opinion 4/2010 on the European code of conduct of FEDMA for the use of personal data in direct marketing, WP 174, 13 July 2010, http://ec.europa.eu/justice/article-29/documentation/opinion-recommendation/files/2010/wp174_en.pdf.

towards the body bound by the code of conduct. The supervisory authority may still monitor the compliance of such a body's activities with the GDPR and exercise its corrective powers, such as the power to order the controller or processor to bring the processing activities in line with the GDPR and the code of conduct, or even imposing a processing ban. An accredited body authorised to monitor the compliance of a controller's or processor's practices with a code of conduct must have an appropriate level of expertise in relation to the subject-matter of the code. Such expertise must therefore not be limited to the GDPR itself, but also cover specific features of data processing in the particular sector, given the rationale of resorting to codes of conduct. This must include the knowledge of processes used e.g. in banking, telecoms or direct marketing.

Approved codes of conduct, including any amendments and extensions thereof, are public information made available by the European Data Protection Board (Article 40(11) of the GDPR).

Certification

The GDPR (Article 42(1)) obliges the Member States, the supervisory authorities, the European Data Protection Board and the European Commission to promote certification mechanisms and quality seals and marks, which have the purpose of assuring data subjects of the compliance with the GDPR of processing operations carried out by controllers and processors, when offering and providing products and services. The purpose is also to take account of the specific features of micro-, small and medium-sized enterprises because, in their case, it is necessary to explore ways of ensuring the compliance with the GDPR, considering the scale of their activities and their importance for the economies of the Member States.

Certification introduced by the GDPR is a new solution. So far, there have been (and there still are) other kinds of certificates demonstrating compliance with the information security principles, related to certain processes, e.g. the Payment Card Industry Data Security Standard (PCI DSS), confirming an adequate level of protection of payment card holders' data. However, these are not certificates awarded pursuant to the certification provisions of the GDPR, and the subject matter of the certification is not directly the compliance with the GDPR, but other important information security aspects which may also result from the GDPR, but so far it has not been their direct legal basis.

The GDPR introduces certification and data protection seals and marks, and it seems that seals and marks are supposed to be graphic labels which clearly show that a certificate of compliance with the GDPR has been awarded. Due to the function of such seals and marks, their main feature should be common recognition, not among entrepreneurs who are active in a certain industry (though, among them as well, if the certificate is a criterion for the selection of a processor by the controller), but mainly among consumers who entrust their data to the entrepreneur and for whom data security is of the utmost importance, particularly in such industries as information society services, and for whom it is hardly possible to verify data protection standards on their own. Such labels as 'GDPR seal', 'GDPR certified' or 'GDPR compliant' may be suggested if consumer awareness surveys show that they are widely recognisable. It is also advisable to launch information campaigns by the supervisory authorities or the European Commission prior to using such labels.

Obtaining by the controller of a certificate confirming the compliance of data processing operations with the GDPR, under an approved certification mechanism, is (depending on the circumstances) one way of demonstrating the lawfulness and correctness of data processing, a basis for transferring personal data to a third country, or means of avoiding a fine imposed by a supervisory authority or reducing its amount. This certainly does not mean that voluntary certification relieves the controller or processor of the obligation to comply with the GDPR or that it limits the powers of a supervisory authority in relation to a controller or processor who have thus demonstrated the lawfulness of their operation (Article 42(4) of the GDPR). The fact that a controller or a processor holds a certificate does not deprive the supervisory authority of powers to demonstrate the non-compliance of processing with the GDPR and of corrective powers to order the controller or processor to bring the processing activities in line with the GDPR and the certification rules, or even to impose a processing ban (Article 58(2) of the GDPR).

Certification may be carried out by the competent supervisory authority, but the introduction of certification also opens the market of certifying bodies. Certification criteria are subject to approval by a supervisory authority or the European Data Protection Board. The latter may result in a Europe-wide certification, the European Data Protection Seal. Certification is issued for a specified period. It may be renewed voluntarily after a maximum period of three years, provided that the certifying body finds that the controller or processor continues to meet its conditions.

A controller or processor applying for a certificate of compliance with the GDPR must provide the certification body with all information and access to its processing activities to the extent necessary to conduct the certification procedure (Article 42(6) of the GDPR). The wording of this provision is typical for analogous provisions on auditing procedures. Nevertheless, it may potentially lead to disputes in individual cases where the certifying body and the certified body disagree on whether specific information is required for the verification of compliance. Certifying bodies must be required to respect the data minimisation principle, e.g. to comply with the requirement to pseudonymise the data of a bank's or an insurance company's customers, since their data are covered by banking or insurance secrecy, and the assessment of the compliance of processing operations is possible without disclosing the customers' identity.

One already existing trans-European privacy protection certificate is EuroPriSe, applicable to IT products and services, particularly software, certified for compliance with EU personal data protection rules. A certificate developed under an EU project carried out as part of Trans-European Telecommunications Networks (eTEN) was awarded, among others, to Microsoft and SAP products.[25]

25. https://www.european-privacy-seal.eu/EPS-en/Home.

Certification bodies are subject to accreditation (Article 43(1) of the GDPR) by the supervisory authority competent for the Member State or by the leading supervisory authority, i.e. one selected, in case of trans-border data processing, from a number of competent supervisory authorities in different Member States, corresponding to the location of the controller's or the processor's main organisational unit. Certification bodies may also be accredited by a national accreditation body named pursuant to Regulation (EC) No 765/2008 of the European Parliament and of the Council[26] in accordance with EN-ISO/IEC 17065/2012 and with the additional requirements established by the supervisory authority.

A certification should be notified to the supervisory authority to enable it to exercise its power to withdraw a certification or to oblige the certification body to withdraw or refuse it where the certification requirements are not, or are no longer, met. The supervisory authority is also empowered, on its territory of competence, to review the certifications issued (Article 43(1) of the GDPR).

Accreditation is issued for a maximum period of five years, renewable provided that the certification body still meets the following requirements:

- It has demonstrated its independence (e.g. resulting from its shareholding structure or composition of its governing bodies) and expertise in relation to the subject-matter of the certification to the satisfaction of the competent supervisory authority (crucially, it must present its experts' team).
- It has undertaken to respect the criteria serving as the basis for certification, approved by the supervisory authority or by the European Data Protection Board.
- It has established procedures for the issuing, periodic review and withdrawal of data protection certification, seals and marks.
- It has established procedures and structures to handle complaints about infringements of the certification or the manner in which the certification has been, or is being, implemented by the controller or processor.
- It has demonstrated, to the satisfaction of the competent supervisory authority, that the tasks and duties of the certification body do not result in a conflict of interests. This means that the activities of the certifying body need not be limited to certification, but its other activities must not be in conflict with the certification activities.

The supervisory authority must publish, in an easily accessible form, the requirements serving as the basis for the accreditation of the certifying bodies, as well as the criteria of certification carried out by the certifying bodies. These requirements and criteria must also be transmitted to the European Data Protection Board which maintains a public register of certificates and data protection seals (Article 43(6) of the GDPR).

26. Regulation (EC) No 765/2008 of the European Parliament and of the Council of 9 July 2008 setting out the requirements for accreditation and market surveillance relating to the marketing of products and repealing Regulation (EEC) No 339/93 (OJ EU L 218, 13.8.2008, p. 30).

During the development of Member State national laws, there has been an observable trend of entrusting the certifying powers to bodies accredited by the supervisory authority. The terms and modalities of the accreditation of the certifying body may be regulated by Member State national laws. I believe this to be not only a good solution but the only viable one. If the supervisory authority, already burdened with numerous statutory obligations, were to be the only certifying body, waiting times for obtaining a certificate would be very long. As a practical result, very few bodies would obtain certification. This would affect not only the personal data protection level but also the market competitiveness of companies, where certification would be required by large controllers as a method of demonstrating an appropriate protection standard, e.g. by IT companies bidding in a tender procedure for a service contract.

Companies could also be legitimately reluctant to apply for a certificate to a supervisory authority due to a concern about such an authority's dual role: besides controlling powers, a supervisory authority may also impose fines and, presumably, could not disregard breaches found during a certification exercise.

CHAPTER 12

Data Protection Officer (DPO)

§12.01 CRITERIA FOR THE OBLIGATION TO DESIGNATE A DPO. CORE ACTIVITIES OF THE CONTROLLER OR THE PROCESSOR. LARGE SCALE OF PROCESSING

The GDPR significantly increases the role of the data protection officer (DPO) in the controller's or processor's data protection system and his/her position in the organisational structure; it provides for independence safeguards and specifies his/her tasks. The conditions governing the designation of a data protection officer and the performance of this function, formulated in the GDPR in Articles 37-39, have been specified in the Guidelines of the Article 29 Working Party.[1]

The DPO has become a key element of ensuring the compliance of data processing with the GDPR. The obligation to designate the officer, his/her status and scope of responsibilities should be considered in the context of a new approach to the data protection system in institutions. Pursuant to the GDPR, the DPO is subject to the risk-based approach – adequacy of the applied measures to the nature, scope, context and purposes of the processing and to the likelihood of a breach and its severity for the rights and freedoms of data subjects, as well as priorities resulting from the findings of the risk analysis.

The duties of the data protection officer are also implied by the accountability principle (Article 5(2) of the GDPR), requiring data controllers to implement arrangements to ensure the lawfulness of data processing, i.e., in particular, its compliance with the key principles of data protection. This constitutes an obligation of proactive behaviour, to act on their own initiative rather than wait for complaints and requests from customers or critical remarks and recommendations of supervisory authorities.

1. Guidelines on Data Protection Officers ('DPOs'), adopted on 13 December 2016, as last revised and adopted on 5 April 2017, WP 243 rev.01, http://ec.europa.eu/newsroom/document.cfm?doc_id=44100.

The GDPR (Article 37(1)) specifies criteria determining the obligation to designate a DPO by the controller or the processor. These criteria specify the data processing entities (public authorities and bodies) and data processing contexts (the core activities and large-scale processing involving certain processing operations or data categories) to which the obligation applies.

Designation of the DPO is compulsory for:

(a) public authorities and bodies, except for courts acting in their judicial capacity,
(b) data controllers and processors whose core activities require regular and systematic monitoring of data subjects on a large scale,
(c) controllers and processors whose core activities consist of the processing on a large scale of sensitive data and personal data relating to criminal convictions and offences.

Ad (a): The only public authorities or bodies exempt from the obligation to designate a DPO are therefore courts in their adjudication capacity. The GDPR does not define public authorities or bodies. They are defined under national laws and are usually classified as 'the State, regional or local authorities' but the concept, under the applicable national laws, typically also includes a range of other bodies governed by public law (definitions of a 'public sector body' and a 'body governed by public law' are provided in Article 2(1) and (2) of Directive 2003/98/EC.[2,3]

Thus, the designation of a DPO is mandatory for the State authorities, local government bodies and other State and local organisational units. Although this obligation does not apply directly (Article 37(1)(a) of the GDPR) to non-public entities carrying out public tasks in the public interest or in the exercise of official authority, the Article 29 Working Party recommends that as a good practice. Therefore, the recommendation is addressed to non-public entities processing personal data in the performance of their tasks, carried out according to the national regulations of Member States, e.g. public transport services, water and energy supply, road infrastructure and regulated professions etc.[4]

Ad (b) and (c): The circumstances entailing the obligation to designate a DPO include carrying out specified processing operations, i.e. the monitoring of data subjects and processing certain categories of data (sensitive data and data relating to criminal convictions and offences, listed in Article 37(1)(b) and (c) of the GDPR), but also two other joint conditions: the core activities of the controller or the processor and a large scale of processing.

2. Directive 2003/98/EC of the European Parliament and of the Council of 17 November 2003 on the re-use of public sector information (OJ L 345, 31.12.2003, p. 90).
3. The Article 29 Working Party, Guidelines on Data Protection Officers ('DPOs'), WP 243 rev.01, p. 6.
4. The Article 29 Working Party, Guidelines on Data Protection Officers ('DPOs'), WP 243 rev.01, p. 6.

The criteria of the core activities and a large scale of processing are cumulative, which means that, for example, the processing of sensitive data and data relating to criminal convictions in the case of necessary debt enforcement operations does not imply the obligation to designate a DPO, as those operations are occasional and carried out on a small scale.

'The core activities of a controller or a processor' are 'its primary activities and do not relate to (...) ancillary activities' (recital 97 of the preamble to the GDPR). The Article 29 Working Party[5] defines that as key operations necessary to achieve the controller's or processor's goals. This includes, in particular, operations constituting legal or statutory tasks or activities indicated in a public register as the company's business. The obligation to designate a DPO results from the processing of data, which is an inextricable part of the controller's or processor's core activity, defined as above. Examples include the processing of data in order to assess creditworthiness by banks, to analyse insurance risks by insurance companies or to provide health care by a hospital. These tasks, which constitute the core activities of the above-mentioned institutions, cannot be performed without the processing of data.

In the case of the entities mentioned in this example – banks, insurance companies or hospitals – their core activities do not include such operations as the administration of salaries and human resources, IT support or physical protection. Such activities are necessary to carry out the core activities, but they are not a part of them, they are only ancillary activities. However, such activities may constitute the core activities, e.g. of the processors providing services supporting the core activities of the controllers under an outsourcing contract, for example, the administration of human resources or the provision of IT services for a bank or a hospital. In these examples, both the controllers and the processors are obliged to designate a DPO due to their core activities, yet carried out in different sectors.

A large scale of processing, which is the second cumulative object-based criterion for the designation of a DPO, is difficult to be assessed in individual cases. It is not defined by the GDPR. Interpretation difficulties may result, for example, from a comparison of entities operating in the same sector but on very different scales. For example, one of the biggest banks in the country, keeping millions of bank accounts, and a regional cooperative bank whose purposes and processing operations are similar but the number of customers is significantly lower. Such concerns are also expressed by professional associations. In my opinion, it should be assumed that a relatively significantly lower scale of processing does not mean the scale is not large if it fulfils the conditions referred to in recital 91 of the preamble to the GDPR, i.e. if it includes 'a considerable amount of personal data at regional, national or supranational level and which could affect a large number of data subjects and which are likely to result in a high risk, for example, on account of their sensitivity, where in accordance with the achieved state of technological knowledge a new technology is used on a large scale as well as to other processing operations which result in a high risk to the rights and

5. The Article 29 Working Party, Guidelines on Data Protection Officers ('DPOs'), WP 243 rev.01, p. 7.

freedoms of data subjects, in particular where those operations render it more difficult for data subjects to exercise their rights'.

Factors determining that the processing is carried out on a large scale are, among others:[6]

- a significant number of data subjects concerned, either as an absolute value (a specific number) or a relative value (a proportion of the relevant population);
- the volume of data items being processed and the range of their different categories;
- the duration of the data processing activity;
- the geographical extent of the processing activity.

However, even the above-mentioned criteria, thus defined, e.g. excluding a local scale of activity (lower than a regional one), do not give an answer to a practical question, be it, for example, if the institutions operating only in one city are active on a local scale or a regional scale if it is a big city.

Examples of cases where the processing is carried out on a large scale include the processing of data of, among others:[7]

- customers in the regular course of business by a bank or an insurance company;
- patients in the regular course of business of a hospital;
- passengers using a city's public transport system (e.g. via magnetic travel cards);
- real time geo-location data of customers of an international fast food chain for statistical purposes by a processor specialised in providing these services;
- for behavioural advertising by a search engine;
- by telephone or internet service providers (content, traffic and location).

Examples that are not related to the large-scale processing of data include activities of individual physicians or lawyers.

The Article 29 Working Party has also defined 'regular and systematic monitoring of data subjects' (Article 37(1)(b) of the GDPR), which is another criterion for the obligation to designate a data protection officer. The monitoring of data subjects is observing their online activities and choices and profiling on the basis of conclusions from these observations, i.e. making use of the results in order to analyse and forecast the future decisions, preferences and behaviours of data subjects, including for the purpose of behavioural advertising. However, monitoring need not be limited to online activities.

The Article 29 Working Party understands 'regular' monitoring as carrying out such activities on an ongoing or recurring basis, or at particular intervals for a certain period, or at fixed times.

6. The Article 29 Working Party, Guidelines on Data Protection Officers ('DPOs'), WP 243 rev.01, p. 8.
7. The Article 29 Working Party, Guidelines on Data Protection Officers ('DPOs'), WP 243 rev.01, p. 8.

'Systematic' monitoring is carried out according to a system, organised or methodical, as part of a general plan for data collection, as part of a strategy.

The Article 29 Working Party gives several examples from a number of sectors, or common to many sectors, in which monitoring activities are carried out, including:

- profiling and scoring for purposes of risk assessment (e.g. for purposes of credit or insurance scoring, fraud and money-laundering prevention);
- providing telecommunications services;
- location tracking, for example, by mobile apps;
- loyalty programs;
- behavioural advertising;
- monitoring of fitness and health data via devices worn by a data subject;
- CCTV surveillance;
- smart meters, e.g. for electricity;
- smart cars;
- smart homes.

§12.02 DPO FOR A CORPORATE GROUP

The GDPR (Article 37(2) and (3)) allows for the appointment of a single data protection officer by controllers or processors if they operate within a group of undertakings or if they are public authorities or bodies. An officer may be appointed for a number of entities by each such entity or authority separately, but, in practice, in the case of international corporate groups a DPO is considered a joint officer for a group, and is not appointed separately by each member of a group. The main information systems in such a group are centralised and made available for the use of the entities belonging to the group, and members of the group are subject to joint policies and procedures ensuring business process coherence. This approach may be illustrated e.g. by approving BCRs by the supervisory authority.

In my opinion, it is also justified to consider a DPO as a joint officer for a corporate group because Article 37(2) of the GDPR directly allows for the appointment of a single DPO by 'a group of undertakings', which means a controlling undertaking and its controlled undertakings (Article 4(19) of the GDPR), but that does not exclude the possibility of the appointment of one person as a DPO by unrelated entities. The explicit indication of a group of undertakings allows the assumption that a DPO, if he/she has been designated pursuant to the conditions specified in Articles 37-39 of the GDPR, performs his/her tasks within a group, and not separately for each entity belonging to the group.

In my view, it is also allowed to treat a DPO as performing his/her duties at a corporate group level because of the condition that a joint DPO is easily accessible from each establishment. In the practice of corporate groups, easy accessibility results from a joint email service and a joint address book with contact details of all persons employed by particular entities belonging to the group as separate employers.

Returning to the aspect indirectly mentioned above, doubts are expressed in the literature if allowing for the appointment of a single DPO by a 'group of undertakings' in Article 37(2) of the GDPR excludes the possibility of the appointment of the same person as a DPO by entities which do not form such a group. So far, numerous national laws have not excluded such a possibility; we know a number of cases where a single person has provided the services of a data protection officer for tens of unrelated entities (however, this should be assumed contrary to the rules). In my opinion, Article 37(2) of the GDPR allows for the appointment of a DPO for a group of undertakings, but it does not forbid his/her appointment by an entity from outside the group at the same time. However, this shall not mean it is allowed to 'break records' in terms of numbers of data controllers and processors served by a single DPO. The assessment criterion should be that a DPO is easily accessible by each entity served and is able to perform his/her duties in a real and not illusory manner.

A condition for the appointment of a single officer for a group of undertakings is that he/she is easily accessible for each establishment, and for public institutions – taking account of their organisational structure and size. These criteria should be seen as compatible because conferring responsibilities to someone within a large and complex organisational structure would not ensure the real availability of a DPO.

The notion of availability refers to the function of the officer as a contact point with respect to data subjects and the supervisory authority, but also internally within the organisation. In particular, it is the real availability of the officer, i.e. physical availability in the premises of the institution or via email or other communication means. This also includes the technical possibility of communication, for example, providing the contact details of the officer – the GDPR requires such information to be provided in information clauses for the clients (Article 13(1)(b) and Article 14(1)(b)) and in a notification to the supervisory authority (Article 37(7)). Effective communication also requires the ability to speak the language used by the data subjects and the supervisory authority.

Therefore, it should be emphasised that the appointment of a joint DPO is fully allowed, but only provided that the officer has a real possibility to perform his/her statutory responsibilities effectively for the controllers covered by the joint function. Thus, the number of such institutions may not be too high, which would call into question the DPO's genuine ability to perform his/her responsibilities.

§12.03 PROFESSIONAL QUALITIES OF A DPO

One criterion for the designation of a data protection officer is his/her professional qualities and, in particular, expert knowledge of data protection law and practices and the ability to fulfil the statutory tasks (Article 37(5) of the GDPR). The GDPR does not specify the professional qualities required from a DPO as prerequisites for the designation of a specific person for that function. The Article 29 Working Party finds that the professional qualities and expertise of the officer shall include:[8]

- expertise in national and European data protection laws and practices and an in-depth understanding of the GDPR;
- a good understanding of the processing operations carried out, information technologies and data security;
- knowledge of the organisation and the business sector in which the officer is active;
- ability to promote a data protection culture within the organisation.

Considering the complexity of the tasks of a DPO and the importance of the proportionality of risk assessments and recommendations prepared by him/her, it is required that a DPO has not only acquired formal data protection qualifications, which is a crucial condition, but also that he/she has knowledge of the organisation and of the business sector in which he/she is active, which is emphasised by the Article 29 Working Party, as well as having professional experience, including the ability to cooperate effectively within the organisation. Such qualities and features cannot be realistically expected from early-stage employees; they require years of professional experience.

Outlining the criterion of professional qualities, the Article 29 Working Party underlines that an adequately higher qualification level of the officer's qualities should be expected in the case of controllers and processors which process data on a large scale and carry out complex processing operations, or which process sensitive data, or are under additional protection resulting from a specific sector, e.g. bank or insurance secrecy. Professional Standards for Data Protection Officers of the EU institutions and bodies working under Regulation (EC) 45/2001) may also be useful.[9]

§12.04 STATUS OF THE DPO; POSITION IN THE STRUCTURE AND AUTONOMY

The data protection officer does not have to be a staff member of the controller or processor (depending on the national laws, it should be understood as a form of employment); it is also allowed to outsource this function to an external expert or a company (Article 37(6) of the GDPR). All the requirements listed in Articles 37-39 of the GDPR shall fully apply both to the internal and the external officer, which should be taken into account, e.g. in the case of termination of an outsourcing contract, also with an external enterprise, the reason of which may not be an attempt to ignore recommendations or risk assessments formulated by the DPO.

8. The Article 29 Working Party, Guidelines on Data Protection Officers ('DPOs'), WP 243 rev.01, p. 11.
9. Professional Standards for Data Protection Officers of the EU institutions and bodies working under Regulation (EC) 45/2001 adopted by the Network of Data Protection Officers of the EU institutions and bodies on 14 October 2010, http://ec.europa.eu/dataprotectionofficer/docs/dpo_standards_en.pdf.

The function of the officer may be outsourced to a team, but it should be supervised by a leader indicated in the contract on the delegation of duties of the officer, or in an internal document appointing the DPO, including the allocation of tasks in that team, with safeguards preventing conflicts of interest.

The GDPR introduces the function of a DPO, but does not provide any direct grounds to, for example, appoint his/her deputies in the entities belonging to a corporate group. This shall not mean that it is not allowed or purposeful. What is more, cooperation within an interdisciplinary team of lawyers (in my view, a DPO should be a lawyer with a field of expertise in data protection), IT specialists, cyber security specialists and HR analysts is necessary and highly recommended. Bringing these specialisations together is necessary so that, for example, the assessment of risk resulting from the envisaged data processing or the verification of the processor are comprehensive.

Cooperation of the DPO with the interdisciplinary team, or the subordination of such a team to him/her, may be considered as providing resources necessary to carry out his/her tasks, i.e. the fulfilment of a condition specified in Article 38(2) of the GDPR, which may be purposeful or even necessary due to the scope of tasks of an officer, resulting from, e.g. the size of the organisation, the amount of data processed, the complexity of systems, the number of data transfers, complaints and requests.

The GDPR (Article 38(2)) obliges the controller and processor to support the data protection officer in performing the tasks referred to in Article 39 of the GDPR. Such support may be given by providing him/her with necessary resources. In organisations where it is justified by the scale of processing, such resources include the above-mentioned subordination of a team to the officer which supports him/her in the performance of the selected tasks, e.g. with respect to contacting data subjects filing complaints and requests regarding their rights. It is also recommended that the controller or the processor ensure systematic cooperation of the DPO within an interdisciplinary team, bringing together professionals with different qualifications (e.g. cyber security) who are not subordinated to the DPO but cooperate with him/her, e.g. as part of the comprehensive assessment of risk resulting from the processing.

Another prerequisite for the performance of the tasks of the DPO is providing him/her with the access to personal data and processing operations. Isolating the DPO from the information and systems naturally prevents him/her from the performance of any tasks requiring the preparation of assessments based on the knowledge of internal processes, including such basic tasks as responding to the requests of data subjects or the preparation of risk assessments.

The GDPR also requires the DPO to be provided with resources necessary to maintain his/her expert knowledge. Although the candidate's expert knowledge of data protection law and practices is a prerequisite to be appointed a DPO, this field is subject to many changes resulting from, among others, the evolution of technologies, so the knowledge needs to be updated, e.g. through training courses, attending conferences and membership in associations, which enables the exchange of experiences.

Supporting the data protection officer in the performance of his/her tasks also includes the following aspects recommended by the Article 29 Working Party:[10]

- active support of the DPO by management;
- ensuring sufficient time to fulfil his/her duties, particularly if the DPO also carries out tasks in another field;
- adequate support in terms of financial resources and infrastructure (e.g. by ensuring premises and facilities);
- official communication of the designation of the DPO to all staff.

The GDPR requires that the data protection officer is independent within the data controller's and processor's structures (Article 38(3)). It forbids to give him/her instructions regarding the exercise of this function and subordinates him/her directly to the highest management level of the controller or the processor. He/she may not be dismissed or penalised for performing his/her statutory tasks either. If such independence safeguards were not provided for, he/she could be under informal pressure from the data controller, the processor or a superior in the event that the officer's conclusions were to result in substantial costs to be borne by those bodies or the liability of specific persons. The prohibited penalties for the performance of tasks should also include informal retaliation or harassment, which have not been documented but result from a given situation context, e.g. the change of treatment, delay of promotion and prevention from career advancement.

The autonomy of the DPO in the performance of his/her tasks referred to in Article 39 of the GDPR means that he/she must not be instructed how to deal with a matter or which measures should be taken, and must not be instructed to take a certain view of an issue related to data protection law, for example, a particular interpretation of the law. However, the decision-making powers of the DPO do not extend beyond his/her tasks pursuant to Article 39 of the GDPR.[11]

The management board of the controller or the processor is not obliged to apply the recommendations of the DPO, being free to make a different decision. However, the Article 29 Working Party recommends giving the DPO a possibility to make his/her dissenting opinion clear to the highest management level.

Furthermore, independence safeguards include entrusting the officer with other tasks and duties, only if they do not result in a conflict of interests (Article 38(6)). The appointment of a person defining the purposes and methods of the personal data processing in the organisation as the DPO would constitute a breach of the prohibition of a conflict of interests. Therefore, the function of the DPO should not be combined with such functions as a board member, operating officer, financial director, chief marketing officer, HR or IT officer.

10. The Article 29 Working Party, Guidelines on Data Protection Officers ('DPOs'), WP 243 rev.01, p. 14.
11. The Article 29 Working Party, Guidelines on Data Protection Officers ('DPOs'), WP 243 rev.01, p. 15.

However, the Article 29 Working Party makes a reservation that the appointment of a data protection officer does not mean delegating to him/her full responsibility for breaches and non-compliance of the organisation's activities with the GDPR. The responsibility to ensure compliance rests with the controller or the processor (Article 24 of the GDPR), although the DPO has a crucial role in that process. Also paramount are the importance of ensuring the above-mentioned independence safeguards by the controller or the processor as well as the genuine possibility to perform tasks by the officer.

§12.05 TASKS OF THE DPO

The non-exhaustive list of the DPO's tasks under Article 39(1) of the GDPR includes activities in external relations (with the supervisory authority and data subjects) and in internal relations (with the controller or the processor and their employees).

Tasks regarding external relations are:

- cooperation with the supervisory authority (in the proceedings where the controller or the processor are applicants as well as on request pursuant to Article 31 of the GDPR, i.e. in the scope and within the deadline specified by that authority);
- acting as the contact point for the supervisory authority on issues relating to processing, including the prior consultation resulting from a negative risk assessment (Article 36 of the GDPR) and holding consultations with regard to any other matter.

It should be noted that the list of tasks of the DPO does not include responding to data subjects' requests, e.g. regarding the access to data, although information clauses used during the collection of data contain the DPO's contact details (Article 13(1)(b) and Article 14(1)(b) of the GDPR).

Tasks of the DPO regarding internal relations are:

- Informing and advising the controller, the processor and the employees who carry out processing of their obligations under the GDPR and other Union or Member State data protection laws. Although the order of specifying these tasks should not be seen as implying their relative importance, it is noteworthy that the expert advisory function has been emphasised, which corresponds to the obligation of including the DPO in all matters regarding personal data protection (Article 38(1) of the GDPR), including issuing opinions on new processes, procedures and apps before their implementation.
- Awareness-raising activities, including training staff involved in processing operations. Such activities may take various forms, depending on the scope of operations of the institutions, communication channels and budget etc.
- Monitoring (including audits) of compliance with the GDPR, other EU or Member State data protection laws and the controller's or processor's data protection policies, including the assignment of responsibilities.

- Providing advice where requested as regards the data protection impact assessment and monitoring its implementation pursuant to Article 35 of the GDPR.

CHAPTER 13

Transferring Personal Data to Non-EU/EEA Countries

§13.01 LEGAL BASIS AND RULES GOVERNING TRANSFERS OF PERSONAL DATA FROM THE EU TO THIRD COUNTRIES

[A] Definition of Third Countries

The EU and other EEA countries have introduced a unique stringent standard of personal data protection. Data protection regimes equivalent to the European model have also been adopted in some non-EU countries, such as Argentina, Israel, Canada, New Zealand, Switzerland and Uruguay, and the European Commission has found these countries to ensure a level of protection adequate to the EU level (Article 45(1) of the GDPR, Article 25(6) of Directive 95/46/EC). Regulations with largely analogous solutions are also in place e.g. in Japan,[1] South Korea,[2] Singapore, United Arab Emirates and South Africa. This model, however, is not shared by all the major global players. On the contrary: diverging scopes and methods of personal data protection regulation between the EU and such key economies as the US or China and the lack of adequate data protection safeguards in some countries may lead to conflicts concerning

1. Joint statement by Commissioner Věra Jourová and Haruhi Kumazawa, Commissioner of the Personal Information Protection Commission of Japan on the state of play of the dialogue on data protection, 4.7.2017, http://europa.eu/rapid/press-release_STATEMENT-17-1880_en.htm. The EU Commission and the Japanese data protection authority have agreed to mutually recognize their data protection systems as 'equivalent'. (Tokyo, 17 July 2018, http://europa.eu/rapid/press-release_IP-18-4501_en.htm).
2. Press statement by Commissioner Věra Jourová, Mr. Lee Hyo-seong, Chairman of the Korea Communications Commission and Mr. Jeong Hyun-cheol, Vice President of the Korea Internet & Security Agency, 20.11.2017, http://europa.eu/rapid/press-release_STATEMENT-17-4739_en.htm.

protection safeguards applicable to European citizens' personal data in cases where such data are transferred to those countries (however California passed the California Consumer Privacy Act of 2018 and in China the Cybersecurity Law was passed in 2016 and non-binding rules were introduced in September 2018; they have some similarities to the GDPR). One example of such discrepancies is the fact that the EU has established general data processing rules which apply irrespective of the data controller's sector, whereas the US uses a sectoral approach which combines regulation and self-regulation in different areas of the economy and social life, deemed particularly important. Another significant difference is that US law only protects the privacy of US citizens, whereas the privacy protection provisions under EU law are not limited to European citizens but extend to third-country nationals' data when such data are processed within the EU.

It is therefore essential to implement arrangements which guarantee the protection – at a level equivalent to the European standards – of personal data transferred to non-EU countries but at the same time do not create any unnecessary obstacles to EU Member States' exports or their international cooperation in other areas.

The Council of Europe had this in mind when adopting its Convention No. 108 for the Protection of Individuals with regard to Automatic Processing of Personal Data of 28 January 1981,[3] as it pointed out in the preamble to the Convention that 'it is desirable to extend the safeguards for everyone's rights and fundamental freedoms, and in particular the right to the respect for privacy, taking account of the increasing flow across frontiers of personal data undergoing automatic processing', and declared 'at the same time [its] commitment to freedom of information regardless of frontiers'. As a way of preventing any conflict between these two values, it declared that 'it is necessary to reconcile the fundamental values of the respect for privacy and the free flow of information between peoples'. The need to harmonise personal data protection regulations between Member countries of the Organisation for Economic Co-operation and Development (OECD), i.e. in relations between the EU/EEA Member States and third countries, including the US, is reflected in the OECD Recommendation of 11 July 2013, 'The OECD Privacy Framework'.[4]

The preconditions that must be met when personal data is to be transferred to third countries[5] are laid down in Articles 44 to 49 of the GDPR (Articles 25 and 26 of Directive 95/46/EC).

In order to specify the scope of those provisions, we must first define 'third countries' and the 'transfer of personal data' as an aspect of data processing.

Unrestricted exchange of personal data between EU Member States is one of the key principles.

3. Convention No. 108 has been modernised: on 18 May 2018, in Elsinore, Denmark, the 128th Ministerial Session of the Council of Europe's Committee of Ministers adopted the Protocol (CETS No. 223) amending the Convention and endorsed its Explanatory Report (https://search.coe.int/cm/Pages/result_details.aspx?ObjectId=09000016807c65bf).
4. Recommendation of the Council Concerning Guidelines Governing the Protection of Privacy and Transborder Flows of Personal Data, http://oecd.org/sti/ieconomy/oecd_privacy_framework.pdf.
5. These provisions also apply to international organisations. For ease of reference, I use the term 'third countries' herein to refer jointly to third countries and international organisations.

This principle is inferred from the four fundamental freedoms of movement which define the EU, i.e. free movement of persons, goods, services, and capital, introduced by the 1957 Rome Treaty establishing the European Economic Community, which continues to be a foundation of the EU. It is also expressly provided for in Article 1(3) of the GDPR (Article 1(2) of Directive 95/46/EC), which precludes any restriction or prohibition of free movement of personal data within the EU.

Along with the formulation of the principle of free exchange of personal data within the EU, a uniform data protection standard is established. It prevents the creation of barriers to international economic cooperation within the EU which could result from restriction of data transfer between Member States. At the same time, it ensures that the right of the citizens of the Member States to protection of their personal data is respected.[6]

The need for legal provisions governing personal data transfer within the EU was made evident in 1989, when the French personal data protection authority, Commission Nationale de l'Informatique et des Libertés (CNIL), objected to personal data being transferred from the French branch of Fiat to its Italian branch, on the grounds that Italy had no law on personal data protection at that time. CNIL made the transfer contingent on a contractual obligation by the Italian branch to cover the transferred data with protection equivalent to that applicable in France.[7]

As pointed out above, freedom of exchange of personal data within the EU and restriction of transfer of data to third countries is the general rule. Third countries are not defined in the GDPR. The free transfer applies not only to the EU but is also implied by the Agreement on the European Economic Area (EEA), signed[8] on 2 May 1992 in Porto and effective since 1 January 1994, which is the legal basis for the free trade area that includes all the EU Member States and three of the four member states of the European Free Trade Association (EFTA): Iceland, Liechtenstein and Norway. These countries are therefore not third countries within the meaning of Articles 44 et seq. of the GDPR. On the other hand, Switzerland, also an EFTA member state, is a third country, as it is not a member of the EEA, unlike the three other EFTA members. Transfer of data to Switzerland as a third country is allowed under Commission Decision 2000/518/EC of 26 July 2000 on the adequate protection of personal data provided in Switzerland.[9]

6. Attempts made in the directives to reconcile privacy protection with free flow of data are presented in: B. Martenczuk, S. van Thiel, *Justice, Liberty, Security: New Challenges for EU External Relations*, Brussels 2008, pp. 304 et seq.
7. M. Jagielski, *Prawo do ochrony danych osobowych. Standardy europejskie*, Warszawa 2010, p. 29; C. Kuner, *European Data Protection Law. Corporate Compliance and Regulation*, Oxford–New York 2007, p. 89.
8. Pursuant to Article 310 of the Treaty establishing the European Economic Community (the Rome Treaty of 1957), currently Article 217 of the TFEU.
9. 2000/518/EC, OJ EU L 215, 25.8.2000, p. 1.

[B] Definition of Transfer of Personal Data

No legal definition of transfer of data is provided for in the GDPR. The particularity of data transfer within the meaning of Articles 44–49 of the GDPR is that the mere movement of data outside the EEA is sufficient to be deemed data transfer to third countries. Furthermore, the GDPR does not differentiate the requirements applicable to transfer of data according to the intended scope of their processing in the third country after the transfer.

The rules of permissibility of data transfer outside the EEA therefore apply irrespective of whether the data are to be actively used or only stored.

Transfer of data to third countries includes making data available as provided for in Article 4(2) of the GDPR (Article 2(b) of Directive 95/46/EC) as well as processing of data other than making them available, including on servers belonging to the data controller, located in a third country. Therefore transfer of data also includes their transmission within an IT system belonging to the data controller, between the controller's units (departments, branches, joint service centres), even if the transfer does not involve any entities other than the controller.[10] Obviously, therefore, data transfer to third countries is also deemed to occur when data are being transferred between separate data controllers, even where they are part of the same corporate group, as well as when data are transmitted to a processor in order to be processed on behalf of the controller, and in cases where data are made available to public authorities in third countries.

The rules for transferring data apply to all forms of transfer, including sending personal data by e-mail, allowing someone access to a customer database, exchange of data through a dedicated application, communicating data in a telephone conversation or handing them over in paper documents etc.

[C] Definition of Data Recipient

Transfers of data are not limited to 'data recipients' as defined in Article 4(9) of the GDPR. The importer of data transferred under Articles 44 et seq. of the GDPR is not synonymous with the recipient of data as defined in Article 4(9) of the GDPR.

The scope of the definition of recipient excludes 'authorities which may receive data in the framework of a particular inquiry'; there are no grounds to infer that a transfer of data to such public authorities in third countries in exercise of a legal provision is not transfer of data within the meaning of Articles 44–49 of the GDPR. The status of the data recipient as defined in Article 4(9) of the GDPR is not a defining criterion of data transfer. A data transfer is deemed to occur through the mere movement of data to a location outside the EEA, or even the processing of data on the controller's servers located in a third country, even an operation not intended to provide access to the data to any entity other than the controller.

10. A. Drozd, *Ustawa o ochronie danych osobowych. Komentarz*, Warszawa 2004, p. 287.

[D] Exclusion of the Applicability of EU Law to a Return of Data to Their Controller in a Third Country

It seems uncertain whether, in the event that data have been conferred by a controller from a third country to an EU-based processor for processing, or to an EU-located branch of the controller for specific operations, Member State law provisions apply to the return of such data to their controller. If this were the case, it would mean that a return transfer of data to their controller is only allowed if adequate protection of such data is ensured in the relevant third country; moreover, European law would be the applicable law even after the return of data to their controller.

Such an interpretation is unlikely in view of a teleological interpretation and an analysis of the possible effects of applying such a rule to a return transfer of data. The provisions on transfer of data to third countries aim at requiring European data controllers to ensure that data being transferred to a third country will be adequately protected even after the transfer. It would be a distortion of provisions on personal data transfer to third countries if they were to apply not only to transfers made by European data controllers but also to return transfers of data from the EU to data controllers in third countries, i.e. if such a return were to be made contingent on the controller complying with requirements of the GDPR and to be refused in case of lack of data protection equivalent to that in the EU.[11]

One should also bear in mind that such a pattern of data processing is commonplace, especially in corporate groups which include entities based in EU Member States as well as those based in third countries and which use global IT systems and databases. It is common practice in such groups to share data within the group, e.g. by placing it in a common database accessible by other entities of the group. This is done for the purposes of risk assessment of relations with partners and customers of the group entities, assigning customers with sequence codes which are uniform throughout the group, entrusting one entity with specific operations for the rest of the group, use of global recruitment and employee evaluation systems, etc.

If – as a literal interpretation would imply – after a transmission of data to an EU-based processor or a branch of the data controller for specific operations, the return of such data were to be covered by EU Member State law and that law continued to be binding after the return, this would in practice halt all international cooperation with EU entities as described above, as it would expose third-country controllers to significant legal, economic and reputational risk.

Therefore, in my view, a return of data to their controller in a third country may not be denied on the basis of an assessment of data protection standards in such a third country, but only in an extraordinary situation, implying a significant risk of a material breach of the data subjects' fundamental rights and freedoms, e.g. resulting from the political system in place.

11. X. Konarski, G. Sibiga, 'Zasady przekazywania danych osobowych do państwa trzeciego w prawie polskim i Unii Europejskiej', in: *Ochrona danych osobowych. Aktualne problemy i nowe wyzwania*, ed. X. Konarski, G. Sibiga, Warszawa–Kraków 2007, pp. 90–91.

[E] Putting Personal Data on a Website as an Exception to the Rules on Transfer of Data to Third Countries

It should also be determined whether putting personal data on a website is also to be deemed a transfer of data to third countries. It would seem so, as any personal data put on such a website becomes accessible to an unlimited and uncontrolled pool of Internet users in third countries, including those where the data protection level is drastically lower than in the EU. Diversifying the accessibility of websites and blocking their availability to users from third countries which do not ensure adequate data protection is technically impossible; any attempt at its partial practicability would require use of methods that are incompatible not only with EU law, but also with the fundamental values of the European Union.

Since data transfer is only allowed to third countries ensuring adequate protection and this condition is only met in some countries, a conclusion that putting data on a website is equivalent to their transfer outside the EEA would have the disastrous consequence of banning users altogether from putting personal data on the Internet. Such a ban would only cover EEA member states. It would be a serious obstacle for the business of European entrepreneurs and would give a competitive advantage to third-country companies. The ban would also have to cover the publication of data in online media (Internet press and television).

However, in the CJEU's judgment of 6 November 2003 in the Case *Bodil Lindqvist v Aklagarkammaren i Jönköping*,[12] it ruled that putting personal data on a website hosted on a server in an EEA member state, thus making such data accessible to users in third countries where data protection level is not adequate, does not constitute transfer of data to third countries within the meaning of Articles 25 and 26 of Directive 95/46/EC (consequently, at present also Articles 44 et seq. of the GDPR). Transfer of data outside the EEA would only be deemed to occur if the website had a function of sending data automatically from the server to users. On the other hand, according to the CJEU, no transfer of data to third countries takes place where data put on the website are not addressed and sent directly to specific Internet users but could only reach those users if found among different web pages and copied by the website visitors.

If a company established in an EEA member state makes data available to other companies of the same corporate group over the intranet, this constitutes transfer of data to a non-EEA country. Putting personal data on an intranet site is a form of direct communication between companies; the data are addressed to other employees of those companies. In such a case, intranet is an alternative to other forms of making data available.

12. C-101/01, OJ EU C 7, 10.1.2004, p. 3; G.J.H. Smith, Internet Law And Regulation, London 2007, p. 691.

§13.02 ADEQUATE LEVEL OF PROTECTION AS A REQUIREMENT FOR TRANSFER OF PERSONAL DATA FROM THE EU

[A] Definition of an Adequate Level of Protection of Personal Data

Any transfer of personal data from the EU to a third country is subject to the fundamental requirement (Articles 44 and 45 of the GDPR, Article 25(1) of Directive 95/46/EC) that protection of data subjects' rights at a level equivalent to that guaranteed by the GDPR is maintained following the transfer. However, transfer of data to countries which do not ensure such adequate level of protection is not absolutely prohibited. Exceptions from this prohibition are laid down in Articles 46–49 of the GDPR (Article 26(1) and (2) of Directive 95/46/EC) and discussed later in this chapter.

The criteria of assessment of an 'adequate level of protection' afforded by a third country are laid down in Article 45(2) of the GDPR (Article 25(2) of Directive 95/46/EC).[13] Such an assessment must take into account the following aspects:

- The rule of law, respect for human rights and fundamental freedoms, relevant legislation, both general and sectoral, including concerning public and national security, criminal law and the access of public authorities to personal data, data protection rules, security measures, including rules for the onward transfer of personal data to another third country, case-law, and effective and enforceable data subject rights.
- The existence and effective functioning of one or more independent supervisory authorities in the third country, with responsibility for ensuring and enforcing compliance with the data protection rules.
- The international commitments the third country has entered into, or other obligations arising from legally binding conventions or instruments as well as from its participation in multilateral or regional systems, in particular in relation to the protection of personal data.

Analogous criteria for assessing the protection level afforded by a third country were laid down in Directive 95/46/EC (Article 25(2)). They included all the circumstances surrounding a data transfer operation, with particular consideration to the nature of the data, the purpose and the duration of the proposed data processing operations, the country of final destination of the transferred data, the general and sectoral rules of law applicable in the third country and the security measures used.

The institution authorised to decide, according to these criteria, that an adequate level of protection is afforded by a third country is the European Commission (Article 45(1) of the GDPR, Article 25(6) of Directive 95/46/EC). To date, the European

13. A. Zinser, 'European Data Protection Directive: the Determination of the Adequacy Requirement in International Data Transfers', *Tulane Journal of Technology & Intellectual Property* 2004, No. 16, p. 176; C.J. Bennett, 'International Privacy Standards: A Continuing Convergence?', *Privacy Laws and Business International* 2010, Vol. 105, pp. 13 et seq.

Commission has found[14] that adequate level of protection is ensured by the following third countries:[15]

- Argentina: Commission Decision 2003/490/EC of 30 June 2003 on the adequate protection of personal data in Argentina, OJ EC L 168, 5.7.2003, p. 19
- Israel: Commission Decision 2011/61/EU of 31 January 2011 on the adequate protection of personal data by the State of Israel with regard to automated processing of personal data, OJ EU L 27, 1.2.2011, p. 39
- Canada: Commission Decision 2002/2/EU of 20 December 2001 on the adequate protection of personal data provided by the Canadian Personal Information Protection and Electronic Documents Act, OJ EC L 2, 4.1.2002, p. 13
- New Zealand: Commission Implementing Decision 2013/65/EU of 19 December 2012 on the adequate protection of personal data by New Zealand, OJ EU L 28, 30.1.2013, p. 12
- Switzerland: Commission Decision 2000/518/EC of 26 July 2000 on the adequate protection of personal data provided in Switzerland, OJ EC L 215, 25.8.2000, p. 1
- Uruguay: Commission Implementing Decision 2012/484/EU of 21 January 2012 on the adequate protection of personal data by the Eastern Republic of Uruguay with regard to automated processing of personal data, OJ EC L 227, 23.8.2012, p. 11.

The European Commission has also confirmed that adequate data protection is ensured by:

- Andorra: Commission Decision 2010/625/EU of 19 October 2010 on the adequate protection of personal data in Andorra, OJ EU L 277, 21.10.2010, p. 27
- Guernsey: Commission Decision 2003/821/EC of 21 November 2003 on the adequate protection of personal data in Guernsey, OJ EC L 308, 25.11.2003, p. 27
- Jersey: Commission Decision 2008/393/EC of 8 May 2008 on the adequate protection of personal data in Jersey, OJ EC L 138, 28.5.2008, p. 21

14. The Article 29 Working Party also expressed a positive assessment of the level of data protection in Monaco (Opinion 7/2012 on the level of protection of personal data in the Principality of Monaco, adopted on 19 July 2012, WP 198, http://ec.europa.eu/justice/article-29/documentation/opinion-recommendation/files/2012/wp198_en.pdf). Therefore the list of third countries considered by the European Commission to ensure adequate data protection is likely to be expanded. The Article 29 Working Party has also evaluated the adequacy of data protection level in Quebec (press release of the Article 29 Working Party of 3 October 2012; Opinion of Article 29 Working Party No. 7/2014 of 4 June 2014 on the protection of personal data in Quebec, WP 219, http://ec.europa.eu/justice/article-29/documentation/opinion-recommendation/files/2014/wp219_en.pdf).
15. Pursuant to Article 45(9) of the GDPR, decisions adopted by the European Commission concerning the adequate level of personal data protection are to remain in force until amended, replaced or repealed by a European Commission decision.

- The Isle of Man: Commission Decision 2004/411/EU of 28 April 2004 on the adequate protection of personal data in the Isle of Man, OJ EU L 151, 30.4.2004, p. 50
- The Faroe Islands: Commission Decision 2010/146/EC of 5 March 2010 on the adequate protection provided by the Faeroese Act on processing of personal data, OJ EU L 58, 9.3.2010, p. 17.

In the context of trans-Atlantic trade, Commission Decision 2000/520/EC of 26 July 2000 on 'Safe Harbour'[16] was crucially important. It constituted one possible legal basis for lawful transfer of personal data from the EU to the US (it was not the sole legal basis, though, as data exporters could, and still can, use BCRs, standard contractual clauses and other instruments). For entities which submitted a declaration of adherence to Safe Harbour and complied with its principles, the Commission Decision removed the barrier resulting from the US's status as a third country. This applied to specified US importers rather than to the United States as a country.

However the CJEU invalidated Commission Decision 2000/520/EC (the 'Safe Harbour decision') in its ground-breaking judgment of 6 October 2015 in Case C-362/14 *Maximilian Schrems v Data Protection Commissioner*. The new legal act which has replaced the invalidated Safe Harbour scheme as the legal basis for trans-Atlantic data transfers is the European Commission decision of 12 July 2016 declaring an adequate level of data protection within the 'EU-US Privacy Shield' scheme. The Safe Harbour scheme, the CJEU judgment invalidating it, and the Privacy Shield are discussed later in this chapter.

The European Commission has to date not issued any decision declaring the lack of adequate data protection in any country, taking into consideration the potential adverse political consequences on the part of third countries possibly included on such a 'black list' by the Commission.[17] The Article 29 Working Party in its Document No. WP 4 of 26 June 1997 on first orientations on transfers of personal data to third countries[18] pointed out that a third country not being included on a list of countries found by the European Commission to ensure adequate level of protection does not imply that such protection is not ensured in the country; rather, that the scope of protection in that country has not yet been assessed by the Commission.

16. Commission Decision 2000/520/EC of 26 July 2000 pursuant to Directive 95/46/EC of the European Parliament and of the Council on the adequacy of the protection provided by the safe harbour privacy principles and related frequently asked questions issued by the US Department of Commerce ('Safe Harbour'), OJ EC L 215 of 25.08.2000, p. 7.
17. The same was also pointed out by the Article 29 Working Party in its Document No. WP 4 of 26 June 1997 on first orientations on transfers of personal data to third countries (page 4): 'The establishment of an explicit black-list of countries, even if for the purposes of guidance, would be politically very sensitive'.
18. The Article 29 Data Protection Working Party, First Orientations on Transfers of Personal Data to Third Countries – Possible Ways Forward in Assessing Adequacy, WP 4, XV D/5020/97-EN, http://ec.europa.eu/justice/policies/privacy/docs/wpdocs/1997/wp4_en.pdf.

[B] Brexit

A new challenge for the transfer of data to non-EU countries is now being posed by Brexit. In the absence of a European Commission decision declaring an adequate level of personal data protection in the United Kingdom following its withdrawal from the EU, it will subsequently be deemed a third country. (This problem remained unsolved during the preparation of this book.)

Until the withdrawal date, the GDPR remains part of the UK's legal system. However, the duration and course of negotiations between the European Commission and the UK (assuming their positive outcome) may result in a period of uncertainty between the withdrawal and the adoption by the European Commission of an adequacy decision concerning data protection in the UK. The moment in time when the European Commission will be able to initiate its work on an adequacy decision is bound to be affected by the fact that such a decision can only relate to a third country, which the UK will become only after its withdrawal from the EU.

Public declarations of the UK Government thus far have indicated that it will seek an adequacy decision. Prime Minister Theresa May declared in her speech during the Munich Security Conference on 17 February 2018 that the new UK data protection act will ensure consistency with the framework EU data protection legislation and a high protection standard.[19] The UK also intends to maintain its data protection authority, the Information Commissioner's Office. One year prior, the British Minister for Digital and Culture, Matt Hancock, also declared that a European Commission decision on the adequate level of data protection in the UK will be the most likely basis of data transfers following Brexit.[20]

[C] Criteria of Assessment of the Level of Protection Afforded by a Third Country

Pursuant to the GDPR (Article 45(1)), data may be transferred to a non-EEA country provided that the data protection level is 'adequate'. Adequate level of data protection does not mean that the protection must be exactly as provided for in the GDPR. That would prevent any transfer of data from the EU to non-EEA countries (with few exceptions), as the EU model and scope of personal data protection is unique.

Therefore, the 'adequate' level of data protection provided for in the GDPR is to be understood as 'essentially equivalent' to the European level. The protection must not be at a lower level, as the protection of natural persons guaranteed in the GDPR, as interpreted in the context of the Charter of Fundamental Rights, must not be compromised (Article 44).

---

19. The British Data Protection Act 2018,http://www.legislation.gov.uk/ukpga/2018/12/pdfs/ukpga_20180012_en.pdf.
20. Prime Minister stresses the importance of data protection, Privacy Laws&Business, 19 February 2018, https://www.privacylaws.com/Publications/enews/UK-E-news/Dates/2018/2/Prime-Minister-stresses-the-importance-of-data-protection/.

The criteria, laid down in Article 45(2) of the GDPR (Article 25(2) of Directive 95/46/EC), for assessing the level of protection ensured by third countries were explained in specific terms by the Article 29 Working Party in its working documents: No. WP 4 of 26 June 1997 on first orientations on the transfers of personal data to third countries and No. WP 12 of 24 June 1997 on the transfers of personal data to third countries under Articles 25 and 26 of Directive 95/46/EC,[21] subsequently updated in the Adequacy Referential (update) document of 28 November 2017, WP 254[22] and WP 254 rev.01 of 6 February 2018,[23] in its part relating to the criteria of adequate protection in a third country in the context of the GDPR and the CJEU judgment of 6 October 2015 in Case C-362/14 *Maximilian Schrems v Data Protection Commissioner*.

In these documents, Article 29 Working Party refers to the EU principles of personal data protection (discussed in detail in other chapters of this book) as the key conditions of adequate protection:

- The purpose limitation principle, whereby data may only be processed for specified purposes and must not be further processed in a manner that is incompatible with those purposes.[24]
- The data quality and data minimisation (data proportionality) principle, whereby data should be accurate, kept up to date where necessary, and not excessive to the purposes of the transfer.
- The transparency principle, whereby data subjects should be provided with information relating to the aspects of the processing of their personal data, in particular to the purpose of the processing and the identity of the data controller in the third country.
- The security principle, whereby technical and organisational measures of data security should be taken that are appropriate to the risks presented by the processing; any processing of data on instructions from the controller must be within the scope of authorisation granted to the processor.
- The rights of access, rectification and opposition (right to object), whereby the data subject should have a right to obtain information on his/her data being processed, including a copy of the data, a right to have those data rectified where they are inaccurate, and, in certain situations, the right to object to the processing of the data.
- Restrictions on onward transfers, whereby further transfers of the personal data by an entity in a third country should only be allowed if the further entity is also bound by rules ensuring an adequate level of protection.

---

21. Working Party on the Protection of Individuals with regard to the Processing of Personal Data, Transfers of personal data to third countries: Applying Articles 25 and 26 of the EU data protection directive, WP 12, DG XV D/5025/98, http://ec.europa.eu/justice/policies/privacy/docs/wpdocs/1998/wp12_en.pdf.
22. http://ec.europa.eu/newsroom/just/document.cfm?doc_id = 48827.
23. http://ec.europa.eu/newsroom/article29/item-detail.cfm?item_id = 614108.
24. Opinion of Article 29 Working Party No. 3/2013 of 2 April 2013 on purpose limitation, WP 203, http://ec.europa.eu/justice/article-29/documentation/opinion-recommendation/files/2013/wp203_en.pdf, pp. 15–19.

- The principle of ensuring the availability of procedural and enforcement mechanisms to data subjects, allowing them to have their complaints examined independently and to enforce an appropriate compensation in cases of a breach of the principles of personal data processing; also required is the existence of an independent supervisory authority responsible for ensuring compliance with data protection laws, and the existence of effective judicial and administrative procedures for the enforcement of data subjects' rights.

  The Article 29 Working Party also specified the following additional principles in the two working documents:
- More stringent safeguards must be applied to sensitive data, in order to ensure lawful processing and the data subjects' rights. The data subject's explicit consent is given as an example of such a safeguard.
- The data subject must have a right to opt out from having his/her data transferred and subsequently processed for direct marketing.
- The data subject must have the right to be informed on aspects taken into account in the process of taking of automated individual decisions; measures should be taken to safeguard the data subject's legitimate interest.

The guidelines contained in the Article 29 Working Party's working documents no. WP 4 and no. WP 12 help ascertain whether the data protection system in a third country ensures an adequate level of compatibility with personal data processing principles. Although the guidelines were issued before the GDPR became effective, they are based on the key data processing principles, i.e. lawfulness and accuracy, which remain relevant in the GDPR context.

The criteria for that assessment include (besides an analysis of whether and to what extent the third country has implemented data processing principles in its legislation) data controllers' awareness of their obligations. It should also be assessed whether sanctions provided for in the third country are effective and whether its supervisory authorities are independent and effective.[25] Working documents no. WP 4 and no. WP 12 also recommend that the assessment of data subjects' ability to enforce their rights also includes the rapidity and effectiveness of such an enforcement, as well as its costs, which should not be prohibitive.

25. The importance of the independence of data protection authorities in EU Member States, made compulsory under Article 28(1) of the Directive, was emphasised by the Court of Justice of the European Union in its judgment of 16 October 2012 in Case C-614/10 *European Commission v Republic of Austria* (http://eur-lex.europa.eu/legal-content/EN/TXT/?uri=CELEX:62010CJ0614). The European Commission's complaints, which the Court found justified, related to the status of a managing member of the Austrian Data Protection Commission, who was also a federal official, lack of an organisational separation between the Data Protection Commission and the Federal Chancellery (Bundeskanzleramt), and the Austrian Federal Chancellor's right to obtain information on all management aspects of the Data Protection Commission. The Court found in particular that there was a service-related link between the managing member of the Data Protection Commission and a federal authority, whereby the managing member could be supervised in his/her function. According to the Court, there was a risk of a 'prior compliance' on the part of the managing member of the Data Protection Commission towards his/her superior.

An adequate level of data protection may also be found in a third country if it has ratified Convention No. 108 of the Council of Europe for the Protection of Individuals with regard to Automatic Processing of Personal Data, done in Strasbourg on 28 January 1981. However, the fact that a third country has ratified the Convention should not imply that an assessment of the adequacy of data protection in that country is redundant. As the Article 29 Working Party has emphasised, the Council of Europe Convention No. 108 does not oblige its contracting parties to establish institutional mechanisms allowing the independent investigation of complaints (although in practice ratifying countries have generally done so). Therefore, ratification of the Convention does not automatically mean that the protection level in the signatory country concerned can be found adequate, but it can be legitimately considered to be an important element in the assessment of the adequacy of protection.

Among factors ensuring an adequate level of protection of personal data in a third country, Article 45(2)(a) of the GDPR (and Article 25(2) of Directive 95/46/EC) lists not only the generally applicable legislation but also regulations applicable in the industry, sector or profession in which the importer of the data transferred by a European controller operates (working document no. WP 12, Chapter 3 'Applying the approach to industry self-regulation').[26]

In this document, self-regulation was defined as a set of data protection rules applying to a plurality of data controllers from the same profession or industry sector, the content of which has been determined primarily by members of the industry or profession concerned. According to this definition, measures that may be considered to ensure an adequate level of data protection include both internal regulations of industry associations grouping only a few members, and sectoral regulations, such as professional ethic codes, applicable to entire professions, such as doctors or bankers, and the institutions employing them, operating in these industries, as well as, for example, associations of companies in the direct marketing sector. Importantly, the self-regulation instruments should be unambiguous and transparent for the data subjects: they should be drafted in plain language and offer practical examples to illustrate the provisions. It is important that data subjects are aware of their rights provided for in the sectoral regulations and know how complaints should be lodged, how they are investigated, and what the costs of rights enforcement are. Prohibitive costs which compel data subjects to abandon attempts to enforce their legitimate rights are serious grounds for criticism. However, as has been pointed out, the use of ethical codes carries a risk. From the data subject's standpoint, the multitude of associations representing the same industry and governed by separate internal regulations may make it challenging to assess the real level of data protection, especially in sectors such as direct marketing, where personal data are normally exchanged between numerous businesses subject to different sectoral regulations.

---

26. The Article 29 Working Party previously formulated its comments on self-regulation, including its definition and criteria for assessing its effectiveness, in working document no. WP 7 of 14 January 1998 'Judging industry self-regulation: when does it make a meaningful contribution to the level of data protection in a third country?', http://ec.europa.eu/justice/policies/privacy/docs/wpdocs/1998/wp7_en.pdf.

§13.03 EXCLUSIONS FROM THE PROHIBITION TO TRANSFER PERSONAL DATA TO THIRD COUNTRIES WHICH DO NOT ENSURE AN ADEQUATE LEVEL OF PROTECTION

The transfer of data to countries which do not ensure an adequate level of data protection, as declared in a European Commission decision under Article 45(3) of the GDPR (Article 25(2) of Directive 95/46/EC), is not absolutely prohibited. There are two categories of situations where the requirement of adequate protection of data to be ensured by the third country is not a precondition of data transfer (Articles 46 to 49 of the GDPR, Article 26(1) and (2) of Directive 95/46/EC).

The first of these categories of situations (Articles 46 and 47 of the GDPR) is when the controller or processor guarantees that the recipient or other importer of data will introduce appropriate safeguards and ensure the enforceability of data subjects' rights thanks to effective legal remedies. Such appropriate safeguards include a legally binding and enforceable instrument between public authorities or bodies: (i) binding corporate rules (BCRs), (ii) standard data protection clauses (or standard contractual clauses, SCCs) adopted by the European Commission or adopted by a supervisory authority and approved by the Commission, (iii) an approved code of conduct regulating data protection in the sector in which the data importer operates, (iv) obtaining a certificate through an approved certification mechanism confirming an adequate data protection standard implemented by the data importer.

These instruments, through their legally binding character, ensure adequate protection of data subsequent to the transfer, irrespective of the third country's legal status concerning data protection.

The other category of exclusions is derogations from the prohibition to transfer personal data to third countries which do not ensure adequate protection. Such derogations apply in specific cases (Article 49 of the GDPR, Article 26(1) of Directive 95/46/EC). They include, but are not limited to: (i) the data subject's explicit consent to the transfer (the consent must be explicit and the data subject must have been informed of the risk resulting from the lack of adequate protection), (ii) the transfer being necessary for the performance of a contract between the data subject and the controller, (iii) the transfer being necessary for the conclusion or performance of a contract concluded in the interest of the data subject between the controller and another person.

Data transfer to a third country which does not ensure an adequate level of data protection is also allowed when a supervisory authority gives its authorisation (Article 46(3) of the GDPR) for other data protection safeguards being provided for after the transfer, such as contractual clauses between the exporter and the importer or administrative arrangements between public authorities or bodies.

The GDPR provides for one more derogation as a 'safety valve' for specific situations. This derogation allows data to be transferred to a non-EEA country even where the European Commission has not issued a decision declaring adequate protection of data in such a country, the data exporter has not provided for safeguards such as BCRs or SCCs, and no derogation on grounds such as the data subject's consent can be invoked. Where the above conditions have not been met, a transfer to a third country may take place only if the transfer is not repetitive, concerns only a limited number of data subjects, and is necessary for the purposes of compelling legitimate interests pursued by the controller which are not overridden by the interests or rights and freedoms of the data subject, and the controller has assessed all the circumstances surrounding the data transfer and has, on the basis of that assessment, provided suitable personal data protection safeguards and informed the supervisory authority and the data subject of the transfer (second subparagraph of Article 49(1) of the GDPR).

The provisions on data transfer establish a hierarchy of exclusions from the prohibition to transfer personal data to third countries which do not ensure an adequate level of protection. The system of data transfer to third countries must be based on appropriate safeguards ensured by the data exporter, such as BCRs, approved SCCs, sectoral regulations or certification, referred to in Article 46(2) of the GDPR, whereupon an authorisation from a supervisory authority is not required. Where no such safeguards are in place, transfer may be made under authorisation by a supervisory authority (Article 46(3) of the GDPR) for other safeguards to be implemented. Derogations on grounds such as data subject's consent for the transfer or the transfer being necessary for important public interest may be invoked as the last resort, where all possibilities of ensuring protection through appropriate safeguards have been exhausted. A further emergency arrangement, foregoing all the above legal bases, is an incidental transfer of data relating to a limited number of people, subject to other conditions specified in Article 49(1) of the GDPR, which include informing the supervisory authority and the data subject of the transfer.

There is a fundamental difference between transfers made with safeguards ensured by the data exporter and transfers made under a derogation from the prohibition on transfer. BCRs, standard data protection clauses (standard contractual clauses, SCCs), sectoral regulations or certification all allow data to be transferred to a third country which does not ensure an adequate level of data protection, but are themselves designed to ensure an adequate level of protection of the transferred personal data. Despite the fact that the third country to which data are to be transferred does not ensure an adequate level of data protection, the data to be transferred are still protected through appropriate safeguards under these instruments.

On the other hand, derogations from the prohibition of transfer on grounds such as the data subject's consent for the transfer or the transfer being necessary for important public interest are not designed to compensate for the lack of appropriate protection in the third country in question. On the contrary: they allow a transfer to be made to those countries despite the fact that no adequate protection is ensured under either legal provisions, sectoral regulations in the country, or safeguards provided for by the controller. Thus, consent of the data subject or other alternative grounds for derogations legalise the transfers of data whereupon the data will not be protected as required in the GDPR.

Such a significant deviation from the principle that personal data transferred outside the EU must be adequately protected also subsequent to the transfer is justified by the assumption that the derogations are only to be applied in rare cases posing a negligible risk; the derogations, constituting exceptions from the general rule of an adequate protection of data to be transferred, must be interpreted strictly. Controllers must, as a matter of priority, ensure the adequate protection of personal data also subsequent to the transfer, e.g. by applying BCRs or SCCs; they may only resort to the derogations once it proves impossible or excessively difficult to ensure protection of the data, and the risk of a breach of data subjects' rights is small.[27] This recommendation of the Article 29 Working Party is addressed in particular to international corporations which have organisational and financial means to ensure adequate protection of data. The Article 29 Working Party considers it particularly inappropriate for such controllers to transfer data on a mass scale or systematically without using safeguards such as BCRs or standard data protection clauses. If transfers are made on inappropriate grounds, this means that data are provided to unauthorised persons, data subjects are deprived of the protection which they are entitled to, and data are processed unlawfully.

[A] Binding Corporate Rules (BCRs)

As a key principle, transfer of personal data to third countries which have not been found, by a European Commission decision, to ensure an adequate standard of data protection is only allowed if the data exporter ensures that the data will be covered with appropriate safeguards after the transfer. One category of such safeguards is binding corporate rules (Article 46(2)(b) and Article 47 of the GDPR). They are the instruments of choice for intra-group transfers, i.e. transfers within multinational corporations and corporate groups.

BCRs are defined in the GDPR (Article 4(20) as personal data protection policies which are adhered to by a controller or processor, established on the territory of a Member State, for transfers or a set of transfers of personal data to a controller or processor in one or more third countries within a group of undertakings (i.e. a controlling undertaking and its controlled undertakings – Article 4(19) of the GDPR), or group of enterprises engaged in a joint economic activity.

BCRs are used within corporate groups, unlike standard data protection clauses (standard contractual clauses, SCCs), which apply to transferring data outside corporate groups, towards entities which are not part of the corporation in question, including those to which data processing is outsourced. BCRs may also be the preferred solution for cloud computing providers whose structures include centres and servers located in third countries.

BCRs are intended to enable entities within a corporate group to exchange personal data freely between them on a global scale, without requiring them to enter into separate contractual arrangements. At the same time, their purpose is to ensure adequate protection of personal data subsequent to a transfer to entities which belong to the same corporate group and are located in third countries which do not ensure adequate protection.

27. Article 29 Working Party, Chapter V of working document no. WP 12 of 24 July 1998 and Section 1.2 of working document no. WP 114 of 25 November 2005 on a common interpretation of Article 26(1) of Directive 95/46/EC, http://ec.europa.eu/justice/policies/privacy/docs/wpdocs/2005/wp114_en.pdf.

Transfers of data under BCRs may be made within corporations grouping entities and organisational units which are located both within and outside the EU (EEA) and which exchange data systematically on a large scale as an inherent part of their cooperation, within a corporate group using joint global IT systems and databases. In such circumstances, transferring data under, for instance, consent of the data subject would be incompatible with the GDPR, namely with the principle whereby data may only be transferred if adequate protection thereof is ensured. It would also be impractical and irrational as a systemic arrangement, given that consent is voluntary and can be withdrawn.

Implementing BCRs and using them as the basis for transferring data does not require a separate authorisation from a supervisory authority, provided that the BCRs have been approved by the competent supervisory authority and meet other conditions indicated in Article 47 of the GDPR (the conditions of their approval by the supervisory authority), including being legally binding upon all the group entities and their employees and expressly conferring enforceable rights upon data subjects in regard to the processing of their personal data.

The rules and requirements concerning the application of BCRs were laid down by the Article 29 Working Party in its working document no. WP 74 of 3 June 2003: 'Transfers of personal data to third countries: Applying Article 26(2) of the EU Data Protection Directive to Binding Corporate Rules for International Data Transfers'.[28] This was the first of several documents formulating precise rules on BCRs.

The Article 29 Working Party defined BCRs by specifying their characteristics. These include the scope of entities bound by the rules. BCRs apply within a corporate group, which in this context means any group of undertakings effectively subjected to the rules defined in Section 3.3 of working document no. WP 74. Among these rules are: the binding nature of corporate rules within a group, their legal enforceability by the data subjects and by the data protection authorities, and the requirement to promptly inform the headquarters or another group member based in an EU Member State with delegated personal data protection responsibilities on cases where local laws applicable to a group member are in conflict with its obligations under the corporate rules.

The Article 29 Working Party allows the term 'corporate group' to be defined flexibly in each country for the purposes of the application of BCRs.[29] Groups which regulate international transfers of data through BCRs may vary, depending on their business environment, from those grouping close-knit entities in a hierarchical structure, in particular companies and organisational units, to groups where entities are loosely bound through a cooperation, not necessarily in the same sector. However, the Article 29 Working Party emphasises a point which must be taken into account when submitting and considering a request: in loose conglomerates, enforceability of corporate rules is likely to be less effective. This may be prevented by differentiating subgroups within such groups, considering their similar nature and the practicability of ensuring effective enforcement of corporate rules.

28. http://ec.europa.eu/justice/policies/privacy/docs/wpdocs/2003/wp74_en.pdf.
29. *Ibidem.*

The key feature of BCRs, allowing them to be considered a safeguard and a basis for transferring data to a third country, is the fact that they are legally binding and legally enforceable in both internal and external relations and apply to each entity within the group of companies or entrepreneurs (including external subcontractors) and all their employees.

Means of ensuring practical effectiveness of BCRs include: setting them up as a comprehensive system; adopting them by the board of directors of the group's parent entity (and imposing them by the parent as binding on each entity of the group), ensuring employees' and subcontractors' awareness of the rules by providing comprehensible and accessible education programmes for them, e.g. on the corporate intranet; obliging the employees of the group companies to comply with the rules (with due consideration to forms of imposing obligations, which may be regulated in different ways in the local labour laws, e.g. by introducing internal policies for employees and granting them authorisations to process personal data); appointing supervisors of correctness of data processing; introducing disciplinary sanctions. Another means of ensuring effectiveness of corporate rules could be introducing a general standard in information security management.

The legal enforceability of BCRs by data subjects and supervisory authorities means that a data subject should be entitled under the BCRs to make claims directly against the entities of the group bound by the BCRs. Granting enforceable rights expressly to data subjects in relation to their personal data is also a precondition of approving BCRs by the supervisory authority. Legal enforceability of BCRs by the data subject also includes the data subject's right to lodge a complaint with a competent data protection authority or a competent court within the EU.

[1] Ensuring the Effectiveness of BCRs

Section 5 of working document no. WP 74 sets out the following requirements, which (in addition to other conditions of lawful data processing, indicated in the document) ensure the effectiveness of BCRs:

- Audits. BCRs should provide for, and lay down the rules of, regular internal and external audits. The audit findings should be notified to the parent entity of the corporate group and the data protection supervisory authority. The rules should also make it obligatory to undergo audits carried out by inspectors of the supervisory authority or independent auditors on behalf of the supervisory authority, where the audit has not been carried out on the initiative of the entity in question, the quality of the audit was insufficient, or the circumstances require an urgent direct participation of the supervisory authority. The Article 29 Working Party expects each group member bound by the corporate rules, and the group in its entirety, to undertake to respect the audit findings. However, it takes into consideration that trade secrets of the group entities must be respected; therefore, the scope of the audit is to be narrowly limited to ascertaining compliance with the binding corporate rules.

- Complaint handling. BCRs should define a clear system of handling complaints lodged by the data subjects, and in particular indicate the organisational units empowered to handle complaints within the group or one of its entities.
- The obligation to cooperate with data protection authorities. The level of institutional support available to individual data subjects is an important element for assessing the adequacy of a self-regulatory system. BCRs should therefore introduce the obligation, and define the modality, of cooperation with data protection authorities, and should oblige the corporate group and each of its entities to respect the guidelines and interpretations of the competent regulator, concerning the application of BCRs.
- The rules on liability and the right to obtain compensation. BCRs should indicate the legal redress and liability rights available to the data subject, in the same scope and extent as would be applicable if the data had never left EU territory. In order to guarantee the enforcement of the liability towards the data subject, the group is required to provide evidence that the EU headquarters or an EU-based member of the group has sufficient assets in the EU to cover the payment of a possible compensation or that it has taken measures to ensure that it would be able to meet such claims (for example through insurance coverage for liability).
- Enforceability of data subjects' claims through court litigation, i.e. the possibility to enforce such claims not only through administrative proceedings before data protection authorities but also in court. This is because, although data protection authorities are empowered to impose sanctions, they have no powers to decide on claims for compensation for damages due to personal data breach.
- Transparency. The corporate group must be in a position to demonstrate that data subjects have been informed that their data are being transferred to other group members outside the EU under BCRs implemented with the authorisation of a competent data protection authority. The content of the BCRs should be readily accessible for the data subjects. The group is also required to demonstrate that it has made the data subjects aware of its personal data protection obligations and the means available to data subjects in order to enforce compliance by the group members with the data protection rules.

[2] The Procedure for Approval of BCRs by Data Protection Authorities

Once BCRs are approved by the competent supervisory authority, they become a safeguard of protection of data transferred to a third country. They are thus the legal basis for the transfer, and no separate authorisation from a supervisory authority is required for it. A corporate group may have its draft BCRs approved provided that the BCRs are legally binding and applicable to each member of the group and its employees and they formulate enforceable rights to which data subjects are entitled. The assessment covers the content of the BCRs, which must include at least the aspects listed in Article 47(2) of the GDPR, including the structure of the corporate group, the tasks of the data protection officer, and the complaint procedures.

BCRs are approved in accordance with the consistency mechanism (Article 63 of the GDPR) designed to ensure the consistent application of the GDPR throughout the EU through cooperation of supervisory authorities. The lead authority circulates the request with the supporting documents to other data protection authorities which must take part in the assessment of the draft BCR due to the territorial scope of operation of the requesting corporate group; this includes data protection authorities in countries from which data are to be transferred to third countries. Another means to ensure consistency is the obligation (Article 64(1)(f) of the GDPR) of the competent supervisory authority to consult the draft decision on the approval of BCRs with the European Data Protection Board (which has replaced the Article 29 Working Party).

The Article 29 Working Party's working documents no. WP 107 of 14 April 2005,[30] no. WP 263 rev.01 (discussed below) and no. WP 108 of 14 April 2005[31] (and recital 124 of the preamble to the GDPR) formulate the criteria that a corporate group should use to select a national data protection authority as the lead authority for the procedure of approval of BCRs within the cooperation between national data protection authorities (mutual recognition procedure).[32] This procedure is intended to accelerate and simplify the process and to avoid discrepancies and duplication of administrative procedures involving the competence of several supervisory authorities in different Member States. Measures to accelerate and simplify the procedure include appointing (based on the requesting group's scale of operation, i.e. the number of the respective countries) one or two supervisory authorities acting, along with the lead authority, as co-reviewers of the BCR approval request. The lead authority ('BCR Lead') starts the discussions with the applicant and reviews the draft BCR documents. It sends a first revised draft of the BCRs and the related documents to one or two concerned supervisory authorities (depending on the number of Member States from whose territories the transfers will take place), which will act as co-reviewers and support the lead authority in the assessment. As a rule, the BCR Lead consults two co-reviewers whenever 14 Member States or more are concerned by transfers. Under this threshold, it is possible to have one or two co-reviewers depending on the specific case and the availability of supervisory authorities.[33]

30. Working Document Setting Forth a Co-Operation Procedure for Issuing Common Opinions on Adequate Safeguards Resulting From 'Binding Corporate Rules', http://ec.europa.eu/justice/article-29/documentation/opinion-recommendation/files/2005/wp107_en.pdf.
31. Working Document Establishing a Model Checklist Application for Approval of Binding Corporate Rules, http:ec.europa.eu/justice/article-29/documentation/opinion-recommendation/files/2005/wp108_en.pdf.
32. The Article 29 Working Party's guidelines on the selection of the lead authority are also included in: Guidelines for identifying a controller or processor's lead supervisory authority, 13.12.2016, last revised and adopted 5.4.2017, WP 244 rev.01, http://ec.europa.eu/newsroom/document.cfm?doc_id=44102.
33. The Article 29 Working Party's Working Document Setting Forth a Co-Operation Procedure for the approval of 'Binding Corporate Rules' for controllers and processors under the GDPR no. WP 263 rev.01 of 11 April 2018 (point 2.2), updating the WP 107.

The criteria to be used by the applicant to select one data protection authority as the lead authority in the mutual recognition procedure include in particular the location of the group's European headquarters. This is the priority criterion, but the applicant may also indicate alternative criteria, such as the place where most decisions are taken on the purposes and the means of data processing or the EU Member State from which most transfers to non-EEA countries will take place.

The corporate group submits its request for approval of BCRs, which must meet the criteria described below.

The Article 29 Working Party has compiled the requirements specified in its documents no. WP 74 of 3 June 2003 and no. WP 108 of 14 April 2005 a in a table showing respective elements which should be included in the BCR and in a request for authorisation for the transfer of personal data to third countries under a BCR.

Standard forms of requests for the approval of BCRs have been provided – separately for requests relating to transfers made by controllers and to transfers made by processors – in the Article 29 Working Party's documents no. WP 133 of 10 January 2007[34] and no. WP 195a of 17 September 2012,[35] respectively.

The Article 29 Working Party specified the 'checklist' of necessary elements of a request for approval of BCRs in working document no. WP 108. The checklist also includes the requirements specified by the Article 29 Working Party in working document no. WP 74. The list may be supplemented by corporations to comply with specific local laws. The checklist set out in document no. WP 108 includes the following elements which must be included in a request for approval of BCRs:

- The contact details of the person responsible in the corporate group for replying to queries of the data subjects.
- The criteria justifying the selection of the lead data protection authority, including the group structure and the nature of data processing within the EEA, with particular reference to the place where decisions are made concerning the processing of data within the group, the locations where the group members are based within the EU, the purposes of data processing, the locations from which transfers are to be made, and the receiving third countries.
- A description of how the BCRs will satisfy the requirements of document no. WP 74, including an indication of documents comprised in the BCR in the given group (a declaration on the principles of data processing in the group, the internal policy, procedures, contracts, internal notices).
- Evidence of the binding character of the corporate rules, both in internal relations within the corporate group and in external relations towards the data

34. Working Document WP 133: Recommendation 1/2007 on the Standard Application for Approval of Binding Corporate Rules for the Transfer of Personal Data, http://ec.europa.eu/justice/article-29/documentation/opinion-recommendation/files/2007/wp133_en.doc [retrieved on 1 July 2017].
35. Recommendation 1/2012 on the Standard Application form for Approval of Binding Corporate Rules for the Transfer of Personal Data for Processing Activities, WP 195a, http://ec.europa.eu/justice/article-29/documentation/opinion-recommendation/files/2012/wp195a_application_form_en.doc [retrieved on 1 July 2017].

subjects. The enforceability of the binding rules towards the members of the corporate group is particularly important in structures with no head office or with one located outside the EEA. The means of ensuring enforceability, specified in the checklist, include internal regulations, audits, training programmes, and sanctions which may be imposed on the employees of the group entities, defined in the employment contracts and disciplinary procedures. The checklist also includes the requirement of indicating clauses used in the subcontracting agreements, and sanctions or other consequences of non-compliance with the BCRs, defined therein.

- Verification of the compliance of the corporate group members' operation with the BCRs through internal and external audits. The data protection audit plan should be laid down precisely in the group's internal documents and made available at the request of the data protection authority in order to enable it to verify the completeness of the plan and to ensure that the necessary correction measures are taken.
- Description of the processing and flows of data, including the nature of the data: whether the data processing rules laid down in the BCRs relate to uniform data or various categories of data. Data security safeguards should be described in a way allowing an assessment of their relevance to the needs. The purposes of data processing should be indicated, along with the extent to which transfers of data in the group are subject to BCRs. There should be an indication of group entities based in the EU which can be data exporters and group entities based outside the EEA which can be data importers.
- Indication of whether BCRs cover only the transfers of data from the EU to a destination outside it or also onward transfers made by non-EEA-based data importers belonging to the group.
- A description of ways of ensuring compatibility of the BCRs with the fundamental principles of personal data processing, including the principles of: fairness and lawfulness, purpose limitation, data quality and data minimisation, security, access, rectification, objection, and restrictions on onward transfers.
- A description of the compulsory mechanism of monitoring of changes of purposes and other aspects of processing, the group's structure, its members' scope of operation, and legal changes significantly affecting the compliance with the binding corporate rules compared with the situation when the data protection authority approved the BCRs. The checklist includes a description of the way that these changes should be notified to the group entities and the data protection authority.

The mandatory elements required in the BCRs are listed in Article 47(2) of the GDPR and quoted below. This list is partly identical to the checklist of elements required in the request for approval of BCRs, provided in working document no. 108, but also includes new requirements, not formulated in previous legal acts but introduced by the GDPR.

- The structure and contact details of the corporate group and each of its members.
- The data transfers or set of transfers, including the categories of personal data, the type of processing and its purposes, the categories of data subjects affected and the identification of the receiving third countries.
- The internally and externally legally binding nature of the BCRs.
- The application of the general data protection principles, in particular purpose limitation, data minimisation, storage limitation, data quality, data protection by design and by default, legal basis for processing, including of sensitive data, measures to ensure data security, and restrictions on onward transfers of data to bodies not bound by the BCRs.
- The rights of data subjects in regard to processing and the means to exercise those rights, including the right not to be subject to profiling and other decisions based solely on automated processing, the right to lodge a complaint with the competent supervisory authority and before the competent courts of the Member States and to obtain redress or compensation for a breach of the binding corporate rules.
- The acceptance by the controller or processor established on the territory of a Member State of liability for any breaches of the BCRs by any entity of the group not established in the EU; the controller or the processor is exempt from this liability, in whole or in part, only if it proves that that entity of the group is not responsible for the event which gave rise to the damage.
- The way data subjects are provided with information on the BCRs (other than information provided to them obligatorily upon data collection).
- The tasks of a data protection officer or any other person or entity in charge of the monitoring compliance with the BCRs within the corporate group and monitoring training and complaint-handling.
- Complaint procedures.
- The mechanisms used within the corporate group for ensuring the verification of compliance with the BCRs, including data protection audits and corrective actions. Results of such verification should be communicated, among others, to the board of the parent entity of the group and to the competent supervisory authority, upon its request.
- The mechanisms for recording changes to the rules and reporting them to the supervisory authority.
- The cooperation mechanism with the supervisory authority to ensure compliance by any member of the corporate group.
- The mechanisms for reporting to the competent supervisory authority any legal requirements to which a member of the group is subject in a third country which are likely to have a substantial adverse effect on the guarantees provided by the BCRs.
- Appropriate data protection training to personnel who have permanent or regular access to personal data.

The requirements specified in documents no. WP 74 and no. WP 108 were compiled by the Article 29 Working Party in tables indicating which of those requirements must be included in either the BCRs or the application for authorisation for transferring personal data to third countries under the BCRs. These requirements have been formulated separately specifically in relation to data transfers:

- made by the data controllers, e.g. transfers of data of the controller's customers or employees ('BCR for your own data') – in document no. WP 153 of 24 June 2008;[36] subsequently, after Article 27(2) of the GDPR expanded the list of aspects required to be included in BCRs and modified the terminology, an updated list of requirements was provided in document no. WP 256 of 29 November 2017[37] and in document no. WP 256 rev.01 last revised and adopted on 6 February 2018;[38] the Article 29 Working Party's Recommendation on the Standard Application for Approval of Controller Binding Corporate Rules for the Transfer of Personal Data (document no. WP 264 of 11 April 2018) has provided the form based on the document no. WP 133, Article 47 of the GDPR and the document no. WP 256;
- made by data processors on instructions from the data controllers, e.g. as part of outsourcing ('BCRs for third party data') – in document no. WP 195 of 6 June 2012[39] updated by the Working Document no. WP 257 setting up a table with the elements and principles to be found in Processor Binding Corporate Rules (updated) of 29 November 2017[40] and in document no. WP 257 rev.01 last revised and adopted on 6 February 2018;[41] the Article 29 Working Party's Recommendation on the Standard Application form for Approval of Processor Binding Corporate Rules for the Transfer of Personal Data no. WP 265 of 11 April 2018 has provided the form based on WP 257; further explanations and instructions on BCRs applicable to processors are provided in the Article 29 Working Party's Explanatory Document on the Processor Binding Corporate Rules of 19 April 2013, revised on 22 May 2015.[42]

These documents indicate in particular the following elements which must be included either in the corporate rules or in the approval applications:

- A description of the binding character of corporate rules in internal relations (upon the group members and employees) and external relations, i.e. the data

36. Working Document setting up a table with the elements and principles to be found in Binding Corporate Rules, http://ec.europa.eu/justice/article-29/documentation/opinion-recommendation/files/2008/wp153_en.pdf.
37. Working Document setting up a table with the elements and principles to be found in Binding Corporate Rules (updated), http://ec.europa.eu/newsroom/just/document.cfm?doc_id=48798, [retrieved on 24 February 2018].
38. http://ec.europa.eu/newsroom/article29/item-detail.cfm?item_id=614109.
39. Working Document 02/2012 setting up a table with the elements and principles to be found in Processor Binding Corporate Rules, http://ec.europa.eu/justice/article-29/documentation/opinion-recommendation/files/2012/wp195_en.pdf.
40. http://ec.europa.eu/newsroom/just/document.cfm?doc_id=48799.
41. http://ec.europa.eu/newsroom/article29/item-detail.cfm?item_id=614110.
42. WP 204 rev.01, http://ec.europa.eu/justice/article-29/documentation/opinion-recommendation/files/2015/wp204.rev_en.pdf.

subject's right to enforce BCRs by lodging a complaint with a data protection authority or a court, and liability for compensation for a breach of the corporate rules.
- Effectiveness ensured by education programmes, complaint handling mechanisms, and audits.
- Obligation to cooperate within the group and with data protection authorities.
- Description of data processing and transfers, including categories of data and data subjects and the countries of origin and destination of the data.
- The mechanism of introducing and notifying updates and other revisions of the corporate rules.
- Means of complying with the fundamental principles of personal data protection.
- A list of entities bound by the corporate rules.

The Article 29 Working Party also defined the structural framework of the BCRs in its working document no. WP 154 of 24 June 2008.[43] It pointed out that this document should not be seen as the standard model of corporate rules, but only as a suggestion and assistance for corporate groups for developing customised corporate rules adjusted to the specific setting and compliant with the requirements of working documents no. WP 74 and no. WP 108.

The elements specified in document no. WP 154, required to be included in the corporate rules, include: the territorial scope and the scope of entities and transfers that the BCRs should cover, and the fundamental data processing principles, in particular the principles of purpose limitation, data quality, data minimisation, security, rights of access, right to rectification, right to object, restrictions of transfers of data outside the group, complaint handling mechanism, liability for breach of corporate rules, and rules for the update of corporate rules.

Standard forms of requests for the approval of BCRs have been provided – separately for requests relating to transfers made by controllers as provided for in document no. WP 256[44] and WP 256rev.01[45] (which replaced document no. WP 153) and to transfers made by processors as provided for in document WP 195 (updated by document no. WP 257[46] and WP 257rev.01[47]) – in the Article 29 Working Party's

43. Working Document Setting up a framework for the structure of Binding Corporate Rules, http://ec.europa.eu/justice/policies/privacy/docs/wpdocs/2008/wp154_en.pdf.
44. The Article 29 Working Party's Recommendation on the Standard Application for Approval of Controller Binding Corporate Rules for the Transfer of Personal Data no. WP264 of 11 April 2018 has provided the form based on the document no. WP 133, Article 47 of the GDPR and the document no. WP 256.
45. http://ec.europa.eu/newsroom/article29/item-detail.cfm?item_id=614109.
46. The Article 29 Working Party's Recommendation on the Standard Application form for Approval of Processor Binding Corporate Rules for the Transfer of Personal Data no. WP 265 of 11 April 2018 has provided the form based on the document no. WP 257.
47. http://ec.europa.eu/newsroom/article29/item-detail.cfm?item_id=614110.

documents no. WP 133 of 10 January 2007[48] and no. WP 195a of 17 September 2012,[49] respectively.

The use of binding corporate rules has not yet become commonplace. As of 24 May 2018, just 130 global corporations had had their BCR mutual recognition procedure completed.[50] In most of the cases (two thirds in total), the lead authority was either the French data protection authority, the Commission nationale de l'informatique et des libertés (CNIL) (34 cases), the British data protection authority, the Information Commissioner's Office (ICO) (27 cases), or the Dutch data protection authority, the Autoriteit Persoonsgegevens (22 cases).

The share of these three institutions in the total number of approved BCRs has decreased slightly as more BCRs have been approved by several other data protection authorities, which had not previously acted as lead authorities or had done so in fewer cases. These include the Belgian, Danish, Irish, Luxembourgish, Maltese, Norwegian and Swedish data protection authorities, as well as some in German Länder, such as Bavaria.

I would like to use this opportunity to extend my very special thanks to the Information Commissioner's Office (ICO, UK), the Commission nationale de l'informatique et des libertés (CNIL, France), the Commission Nationale pour la Protection des Données (CNPD, Luxembourg) and the Urząd Ochrony Danych Osobowych (UODO, Poland) for their professional and friendly attitude I experienced in my work contacts with them.

The Article 29 Working Party, together with the Asia-Pacific Economic Cooperation (APEC), agreed the rules of data transfers between multinational corporations operating in Europe and in the Asia-Pacific region. The Cross Border Privacy Rules (CBPR) developed by APEC in 2012 became the instrument of ensuring an adequate level of data protection in the Asia-Pacific region, analogous to the binding corporate rules adopted in the EU. The Article 29 Working Party developed an unofficial practical checklist for organisations applying for approval of binding corporate rules (BCRs) or for certification of cross-border privacy rules (CBPR). The checklist is not intended to lead to mutual recognition of the two systems, but may be a tool enabling data processors to meet the requirements of data protection authorities both in the EU and in the Asia-Pacific region.

[B] Standard Data Protection Clauses (Standard Contractual Clauses)

As a key principle, transfer of personal data to third countries which have not been found, by European Commission decision, to ensure an adequate standard of data

48. Working Document WP 133: Recommendation 1/2007 on the Standard Application for Approval of Binding Corporate Rules for the Transfer of Personal Data, http://ec.europa.eu/justice/article-29/documentation/opinion-recommendation/files/2007/wp133_en.doc.
49. Recommendation 1/2012 on the Standard Application form for Approval of Binding Corporate Rules for the Transfer of Personal Data for Processing Activities, http://ec.europa.eu/justice/article-29/documentation/opinion-recommendation/files/2012/wp195a_application_form_en.doc.
50. http://ec.europa.eu/newsroom/article29/item-detail.cfm?item_id=613841.

protection, is only allowed if the data exporter ensures that the data will be covered with appropriate safeguards after the transfer. One category of such safeguards is standard data protection clauses (standard contractual clauses (SCCs)) adopted by the European Commission or adopted by a supervisory authority and approved by the European Commission (Article 46(2)(c) and (d) of the GDPR).

An adequate level of protection, i.e. one equivalent to the EU level, includes the prohibition on collecting data, or processing data collected, in an unlawful manner. For instance, where data are to be processed under the consent of the data subject, such consent must be unambiguous and freely given, with a refusal having no potential adverse consequences. The obligations also include the requirement to specify the purpose of data processing and the data recipients, to ensure access to the data, to implement measures to ensure the security of processing at an adequate level, as well as to process data for specified and lawful purposes which are compatible with the purposes for which the data were collected, ensuring that the scope of data is not excessive in relation to those purposes, and erasing data which enable identification of persons once the purpose of the processing has expired.

Standard clauses serve as a basis for transferring data out of a corporate group (i.e. to entities which are not part of the group but cooperate with the group members; this includes entities to which data processing is outsourced), unlike BCRs which are used within corporate groups.

By their legally binding character, they ensure adequate protection of data subsequent to the transfer, equivalent to the EU standard, irrespective of the third country's legal status concerning data protection, even where the third country has no general or sectoral laws in place, adequate to the standard laid down in the GDPR.

Standard clauses are used as the basis of systemic transfers of large volumes of data. In such circumstances, transferring data under, for instance, consent of the data subject would be incompatible with the GDPR, namely with the principle whereby data may only be transferred if adequate protection thereof is ensured. It would also be impractical and irrational as a systemic arrangement, given that consent is voluntary and can be withdrawn.

The use of this instrument by such institutions which necessarily transfer personal data on a mass scale and in a systematic way as part of their business is recommended by the Article 29 Working Party in its working document no. WP 114 of 25 November 2005.

According to the GDPR, standard data protection clauses, as a package of clauses adopted by the European Commission or adopted by a supervisory authority and approved by the Commission, are the legal basis for transferring data to a third country without the need to obtain a separate authorisation from a supervisory authority. In contrast, under Directive 95/46/EC the requirement to obtain an authorisation for a transfer was not exempted from even if the controller used standard clauses. However, in most Member States a transfer of data under SCCs did not require an authorisation from a data protection authority. Still, Member States whose laws did require it were obliged to use a simplified transfer approval procedure, taking into account the fact that the controller used standard clauses adopted by the European Commission. In Member States, European Commission's decisions are binding, so including standard contractual clauses in a contract precluded national authorities from refusing authorisation for a transfer on the grounds that standard clauses do not ensure sufficient protection.[51]

The idea of using standard clauses as an instrument of ensuring adequate protection of data after transfer stems[52] from the common document issued on 2 November 1992 by the Council of Europe, the International Chamber of Commerce and the European Commission, entitled 'Model contract to ensure equivalent data protection in the context of transborder data flows with explanatory memorandum'. Appendix I to that document contains recommended model contractual clauses. Contractual clauses had already been in use in Europe since the late 1980s, though, particularly in France.[53] One of their earliest uses, setting a precedent, was when the data protection authority of Berlin-Brandenburg obliged Deutsche Bahn (the German railway operator) and Citibank to regulate the protection of personal data being transferred between the two as part of their cooperation on the 'Bahncard'.[54]

Under the delegation in Article 26(4) of the Directive, the European Commission issued three decisions on the adoption of standard contractual clauses:[55]

(1) Commission Decision 2001/497/EC of 15 June 2001 on standard contractual clauses for the transfer of personal data to third countries, under Directive 95/46/EC.[56]

51. Article 29 Working Party, Working Document Setting Forth a Co-Operation Procedure for Issuing Common Opinions on 'Contractual clauses' Considered as compliant with the EC Model Clauses, 26 November 2014, WP 226, http://ec.europa.eu/justice/article-29/documentation/opinion-recommendation/files/2014/wp226_en.pdf.
52. As indicated by the Article 29 Working Party in its document 'Preliminary views on the use of contractual provisions in the context of transfers of personal data to third countries', WP 9 of 22.4.1998, http://ec.europa.eu/justice/policies/privacy/docs/wpdocs/1998/wp9_en.pdf, p. 2.
53. L. Kong, 'Data Protection and Transborder Data Flow in the European and Global Context', European Journal of International Law *2010*, Vol. 21, No. 2, pp. 446 et seq., http://www.ejil.org/pdfs/21/2/2007.pdf; working document WP 12 of the Article 29 Working Party of 24 June 1998, p. 15.
54. A. Dix, Berliner Datenschutzbeauftragter, 'The German Railway Card – A Model Contractual Solution of the Adequate Level of Protection Issue?', 18th Annual International Privacy and Data Protection Conference, Ottawa, Canada, September 1996; J.R. Reidenberg, 'Resolving Conflicting International Data Privacy Rules in Cyberspace', *Stanford Law Review* 2000, Vol. 52, p. 1375, http://reidenberg.home.sprynet.com/international_rules.pdf; C.H. Manny, 'Personal privacy – transatlantic perspectives, European and American privacy: commerce, rights and justice – part 1', *Computer Law and Security Report* 2003, Vol. 19, No. 1, p. 5, http://www.its.ohiou.edu/bernt/ITS351/transatlantic1.pdf.
55. Detailed guidelines on how to correctly formulate standard contractual clauses under Decision 2001/497/EC and Decision 2002/16/EC of 27 December 2001 (superseded by Decision 2010/87/EU) are provided in the document 'Guide to the preparation of contractual clauses governing data protection during the transfer of personal data to third parties not bound by an adequate level of data protection' of 2002, developed by the Consultative Committee of the Convention for the Protection of Individuals with regard to Automatic Processing of Personal Data (T-PD); http://www.coe.int/t/dghl/standardsetting/dataprotection/Reports/Guide_contractual_clauses_2002.pdf.
56. OJ EU L 181, 4.7.2001, p. 19.

(2) Commission Decision 2004/915/EC of 27 December 2004 amending Decision 2001/497/EC as regards the introduction of an alternative set of standard contractual clauses for the transfer of personal data to third countries.[57]

(3) Commission Decision 2010/87/EU of 5 February 2010 on standard contractual clauses for the transfer of personal data to processors established in third countries under Directive 95/46/EC of the European Parliament and of the Council.[58]

The first two of these decisions lay down alternative sets of standard contractual clauses to be used where both the data exporter and the data importer are controllers (controller-to-controller data transfer). The third decision formulates standard contractual clauses to be used in contracts whereby processing of personal data is contracted by a controller established in the EU to a processor in a third country (controller-to-processor data transfer).

On 21 March 2014, having realised that these scenarios lacked an important aspect, the Article 29 Working Party adopted a draft of contractual clauses to be used in contracts whereby an EU-based processor subcontracts processing of personal data to a subcontractor outside the EU.[59] To date, however, these clauses have not been adopted by the European Commission and therefore are not binding law ensuring adequate protection of data subsequent to transfer.

Article 1 of Decision 2001/497/EC, recitals 1 and 9 of the preamble to Decision 2004/915/EC and Article 1 of Decision 2010/87/EU emphasise that the standard contractual clauses included in these decisions lay down appropriate safeguards of the privacy and fundamental rights and freedoms of data subjects and of the exercise of data subjects' rights, and as such they meet the precondition, set forth in Articles 44 and 45(1) of the GDPR (Article 26(2) of Directive 95/46/EC), for allowing data to be transferred to third countries.[60]

The sets of model clauses formulate the obligations of data exporters and importers, including their obligation to introduce data protection safeguards and to provide data subjects with information on the aspects of processing of their data and the consequences of the transfers of their data to a third country, including possible access by the third country's public authorities to such data, and of the data subjects' rights, including the rights of access, rectification or erasure. Standard clauses also formulate the rules for obtaining compensation by data subjects for damages resulting

57. OJ EU L 385, 29.12.2004, p. 74.
58. OJ EU L 39, 12.2.2010, p. 5. The Article 29 Working Party referred to the draft of that Decision in its Opinion no. 3/2009 of 5 March 2009, WP 161, http://ec.europa.eu/justice/policies/privacy/docs/wpdocs/2009/wp161_en.pdf.
59. Working document 01/2014 on Draft Ad hoc contractual clauses 'EU data processor to non-EU sub-processor', WP 214, http://ec.europa.eu/justice/article-29/documentation/opinion-recommendation/files/2014/wp214_en.pdf.
60. The European Commission took into consideration the recommendations of the Article 29 Working Party on the security level ensured by standard contractual clauses, included in Opinion 8/2003 on the draft standard contractual clauses submitted by a group of business associations ('the alternative model contract') (document no. WP 84 of 17 December 2003, http://ec.europa.eu/justice/policies/privacy/docs/wpdocs/2003/wp84_en.pdf).

from non-compliance with the contractual clauses by any party to the transfer, and the data subjects' right to seek redress before a data protection authority or a court of a Member State.

The rationale for establishing different clauses for controller-to-controller transfers and controller-to-processor transfers is that, unlike a data importer which is a subsequent controller of the data, the processor may only process data on instructions from the controller and is thus bound by the scope and purpose of processing defined in the processing contract. It should therefore be assumed that a transfer of data under a processing contract entails a smaller risk than a transfer of data between separate controllers (the same argument is included in recital 8 to the preamble of Decision 2001/497/EC). It is more likely that adequate protection will be ensured subsequent to transfer to a third country by using standard contractual clauses in a processing contract; accordingly, standard contractual clauses between controllers should introduce safeguards that are proportionately more stringent than the ones in processing contracts.

Decisions 2001/497/EC and 2004/915/EC, being in force simultaneously, enable controllers, in line with Article 1 of Decision 2001/497/EC as amended by Article 1(1) of Decision 2004/915/EC, to choose one of two alternative sets of clauses: Set I annexed to Decision 2001/497/EC or Set II annexed to Decision 2004/915/EC, in accordance with the character of a specific transfer. However, as pointed out in Decision 2004/915/EC, namely in recital 3 of its preamble, its Article 1(1) amending Article 1 of Decision 2001/497/EC, and in its Clause VII, the two sets of clauses are invariable models that controllers can choose between, but they cannot amend the sets or combine clauses from the two sets.

The GDPR allow additions to be made by the controller to the standard data protection clauses to reflect the nature of the data transfer and of the controller's activities. Standard clauses may be incorporated in a broader contract; they can also provide for additional safeguards. Such supplementary provisions, however, may not be in conflict with the standard clauses or render them less strict (recital 109 of the GDPR, recital 5 and Clause 11 of Decision 2001/497/EC, Clause VII of Set II of Decision 2004/915/EC, recital 4 and Clause 10 of Decision 2010/87/EU).

The Irish High Court referred a question (Decision 2016 No. 4809 P. of 3 October 2017) to the Court of Justice of the European Union (CJEU) for a preliminary ruling, concerning the compatibility of transfers of Facebook users' personal data by Facebook's Ireland-based subsidiary to the US headquarters, based on Standard Contractual Clauses (SCC). The Irish High Court refused on 2 May 2018 a request by Facebook to delay the referral to CJEU. It is a continuation ('Schrems 2.0') of Case C-362/14 *Maximilian Schrems v Data Protection Commissioner*, whereby the CJEU invalidated Commission Decision 2000/520/EC (the 'Safe Harbour decision') in its judgment of 6 October 2015 ('Schrems 1.0'). The High Court's concerns resulted from an analysis of US laws (particularly Section 702 of the Foreign Intelligence Surveillance Act) which allow US intelligence agencies to access the personal data of Europeans. Standard contractual clauses do not prevent this. The CJEU's decision will be paramount for future models of legal bases for trans-Atlantic data transfers, as now 89% of EU-based companies make such transfers under SCCs.[61] Any decision must take into account that a hasty and far-reaching invalidation of legal bases for data transfers, which are now invoked by the vast majority of market players, would have serious consequences for the economy as well as cooperation in other areas.

§13.04 DEROGATIONS FROM THE PROHIBITION TO TRANSFER PERSONAL DATA TO THIRD COUNTRIES WHICH DO NOT ENSURE ADEQUATE PROTECTION

[A] Definition of Derogations

There is a fundamental difference between transferring data with safeguards ensured by the data exporter and transferring data under a derogation from the prohibition on transfer. Safeguards ensured by the data exporter, such as BCRs, standard data protection clauses, sectoral regulations or certification all allow personal data to be transferred to a third country which does not ensure an adequate level of data protection, but are themselves designed to ensure an adequate level of protection of the transferred data. Despite the fact that the third country to which data are to be transferred does not ensure an adequate level of data protection, the transferred data are still protected through appropriate safeguards under these instruments.

On the other hand, derogations from the prohibition of transfer (Article 49 of the GDPR, Article 26(1) of Directive 95/46/EC) on grounds such as a data subject's consent for the transfer or the transfer being necessary for important public interest are not designed to compensate for the lack of appropriate protection in the third country in question. On the contrary: they allow a transfer to be made to those countries despite the fact that no adequate protection is ensured under either legal provisions, sectoral regulations in the country, or safeguards provided for by the controller. Thus, the consent of the data subject or other alternative grounds for derogations legalise the transfers of data whereupon the data will not be protected in accordance with the GDPR standard.

Such a significant deviation from the principle that personal data transferred outside the EU must be adequately protected also subsequent to the transfer is justified by the assumption that the derogations are only to be applied in rare cases posing a negligible risk; the derogations, constituting exceptions from the general rule of an adequate protection of data to be transferred, must be interpreted strictly. Under Article 49 of the GDPR, derogations may only apply in 'specific situations'. Controllers must, as a matter of priority, ensure adequate protection of personal data also subsequent to the transfer, e.g. by applying BCRs or standard data protection clauses; they may only resort to the derogations once it proves impossible or excessively difficult to ensure

61. IAPP-EY Annual Privacy Governance Report 2016, https://iapp.org/media/pdf/resource_center/IAPP%202016%20GOVERNANCE%20SURVEY-FINAL3.pdf.

protection of the data, and the risk of a breach of data subjects' rights is small.[62] This recommendation of the Article 29 Working Party is addressed in particular to international corporations which have organisational and financial means to ensure adequate protection of data. The Article 29 Working Party considers it particularly inappropriate for such controllers to transfer data on a mass scale or systematically without using safeguards such as BCRs or standard data protection clauses. If transfers are made on inappropriate grounds, this means that data are provided to unauthorised persons, data subjects are deprived of the protection to which they are entitled, and data are processed without a legal basis.

Derogations which may serve as grounds for a transfer in specific situations despite the lack of a European Commission decision declaring an adequate level of data protection in a third country or sector and despite the lack of safeguards ensured by the data exporter, such as BCRs or standard clauses, may only be applied on the following conditions:

- The data subject has consented to the transfer having been informed of the risks due to the absence of appropriate data protection safeguards.
- The transfer is necessary for the conclusion of a contract at the data subject's request or the performance of a contract between the data subject and the controller.
- The transfer is necessary for the conclusion or performance of a contract concluded in the interest of the data subject between the controller and a third party.
- The transfer is necessary for important reasons of public interest.
- The transfer is necessary for the establishment, exercise or defence of legal claims.
- The transfer is necessary in order to protect the vital interests of the data subject or of other persons, where the data subject is incapable of giving consent.
- The transfer is made from a public register.

[B] Data Subject's Consent

The data subject's consent to a transfer of data to a third country must be explicit. If the statement of consent also concerns other matters, the request for consent must be presented in a manner which is clearly distinguishable from the other matters and must be worded in an intelligible form, using clear and plain language (Article 7(2) of the GDPR). This condition is not met if the data subject is referred to general contractual terms or regulations where the transfer of data is indicated as one of data processing

62. Article 29 Working Party, Chapter V of working document no. WP 12 of 24 July 1998 and Section 1.2 of working document no. WP 114 of 25 November 2005 on a common interpretation of Article 26(1) of Directive 95/46/EC, http://ec.europa.eu/justice/policies/privacy/docs/wpdocs/2005/wp114_en.pdf.

operations. Any blank consent would also be void, as consent must not relate to an unspecified scope of data and purpose of transfer.

If a data controller uses pre-ticked boxes on its website to obtain data subject's consent online, such consent is not a specific indication and thus cannot serve as a basis for a transfer of data.[63]

The burden of proving that the data subject has consented to the transfer of data to a third country rests with the controller (Article 7(1) of the GDPR). The controller must also demonstrate that the consent was given freely (the employee might indeed feel informally pressured to give his/her consent when requested by the employer, which means that the voluntary nature of the employees' consent might be called into question).[64] Thus, it is unacceptable for the performance of the contract (including the provision of a service) to be made conditional upon giving consent to transfer of data where, in reality, the transfer is not necessary for this purpose (Article 7(4) of the GDPR).

The data subject's consent relates to 'the proposed transfer' of data, which implies that the transfer to a third country must not be made prior to the controller obtaining the data subject's consent, if consent is to be the basis for the transfer.

Another precondition for the consent to be valid is providing the data subject with information on the possible risk of data transfer due to the lack of an adequate level of data protection in the third country in question and the lack of appropriate safeguards ensured by the controller. Furthermore, consent is only valid if information has been provided in accordance with Articles 13 and 14 of the GDPR, including information on the purpose of the transfer, the identity of the data importer, and the categories of data to be transferred. In Section 2.1 of its working document no. WP 114 of 25 November 2005 on a common interpretation of Article 26(1) of Directive 95/46/EC, the Article 29 Working Party points out that the data controller must be in a position to demonstrate that the data subject's consent was given on the basis of sufficiently precise information, including an indication that the data will not be subject to adequate protection in the third country of destination.

It should also be verified whether the circumstances of the transfer consented to by the data subject changed after the consent was granted. Whenever the purpose of the transfer, the destination country, or the categories of data to be transferred change, the controller is obliged to provide the required information again and to obtain consent in relation to the changed circumstances.

In cases where the data subject's consent is required for a lawful processing of data, i.e. where the transfer is not made on other grounds specified in legal provisions

---

63. The Article 29 Working Party, opinion no. WP 90 of 27 February 2004 concerning the interpretation of Article 13 of Directive 2002/58/EC of the European Parliament and of the Council of 12 July 2002 concerning the processing of personal data and the protection of privacy in the electronic communications sector (Directive on privacy and electronic communications), Section 3.2.
64. Opinion 2/2017 adopted on 8 June 2017 on data processing at work, WP 249, pp. 3–4: 'Consent is highly unlikely to be a legal basis for data processing at work, unless employees can refuse without adverse consequence', 'It is important to state that employees are seldom in a position to freely give, refuse or revoke consent, given the dependency that results from the employer/employee relationship.'

governing data transfers to third countries, the transfer becomes unlawful if the information obligation is not complied with or there is a change in the circumstances to which the data subject's consent related.

Consent may be withdrawn at any time, but the withdrawal does not affect the lawfulness of processing of data based on consent prior to its withdrawal (Article 7(3) of the GDPR). The data subject's right to withdraw consent makes it risky to resort to consent as the basis for systematic or structural transfers of data, e.g. within corporate groups using common global databases. Even more importantly, it would be incompatible with the principle whereby data may only be transferred if adequate protection thereof is ensured.

The data subject may also avoid the legal effects of his or her consent expressed in the conditions of a material error. Such an error may result from misleading or insufficient information provided to the data subject by the controller on the purpose or scope of the planned transfer, the destination countries or entities, or the risk due to the lack of insufficient data protection after the transfer.

[C] Performance of a Contract or Pre-Contractual Measures

One derogation from the prohibition of transferring data to a third country where adequate protection is lacking applies when the data transfer is necessary for the performance of a contract between the data subject and the controller or the implementation of pre-contractual measures taken at the data subject's request. It also applies where the transfer is necessary for the conclusion or performance of a contract concluded between the controller and a third party, not by the data subject but in his or her interest.

In both these cases, the derogation only applies if the transfer is considered 'necessary'. Derogations, as exceptions from the rule, may not be applied under a broad interpretation whereby 'necessary' could be considered synonymous with, for example, 'useful', 'justified', 'facilitating' or 'economical'. The assumption that the transfer of personal data is necessary should be defined to mean that the purpose cannot possibly be achieved without the transfer. The Article 29 Working Party stresses, on page 13 of its working document no. WP 114, that the ''necessity test' here requires a close and substantial connection between the data subject and the purposes of the contract'.

The Article 29 Working Party has criticised the commonplace practice whereby multinational corporate groups process employees' data in the group's joint IT system provided by the parent company, claiming that this is necessary for the performance of the employment contract. Such systems are often used for centralised handling of information on employees' absences or for periodic evaluation of employees. According to the Working Party, presenting such transfers as necessary for the performance of an employment contract between the data subject and the controller is a misinterpretation. The Working Party has argued that transferring data to a joint IT system accessible to the parent company and, in many cases, also other companies of the group is not directly and objectively linked to performance of an employment contract.

On the other hand, a transfer of data by a tour operator to hotels and other commercial partners organising the tourists' stay is one which can be justified; so is the transfer of payment information to a third country for the execution of a bank transfer. However, such a transfer may not go beyond what is necessary; it may not, for instance, include data to facilitate direct marketing in the future.

The data minimisation (data proportionality) principle is also applicable: not only must the transfer itself be necessary but the scope of data must be adequate to the purpose of the transfer. The controller must specify the scope of data without which the scope of the transfer cannot be achieved.

The precontractual measures invoked as the justification of the transfer may not be taken at the controller's initiative, but only at the data subject's request.

One example of invoking, wrongly, the necessity of a transfer for the performance of a contract concluded in the data subject's interest is the practice of multinational corporations which outsource their corporate payroll management to providers outside the EEA, and consequently transfer the data of their employees to those providers. The Article 29 Working Party disagreed with the argument that the transfer of employees' data is necessary for the performance of the outsourcing contract, which has ostensibly been entered into in the interest of the data subjects (the controller's employees), as it concerns payroll management. There is no close link between the purpose of the outsourcing agreement and the transfer of data, on the one hand, and the data subjects' interest on the other. Indeed, payroll management is, by law, the data controller's responsibility; if the controller outsources it in order to optimise its administration costs, this is in the interest of the controller rather than the data subject.

[D] Important Reasons of Public Interest

A derogation from the prohibition of transferring data to a third country where adequate protection is lacking is also possible where the transfer is necessary for important reasons of public interest. According to the provision, the public interest (i.e. that held valuable by the society, such as public security and order), may only be invoked if it is important, which means that its importance is above average and justifies a higher degree of protection than the privacy of an individual.

The public interest justifying a transfer of data despite the lack of adequate protection must be one which is recognised in the EU or Member State law applicable to the controller (Article 49(4) of the GDPR and working document no. WP 114 of the Article 29 Working Party). It might be, for example, international data exchange between competition authorities, tax or customs administrations, between financial supervisory authorities, between services competent for social security matters, or for public health, for example in the case of contact tracing for contagious diseases or in order to reduce and/or eliminate doping in sport (recital 112 of the preamble to the GDPR).

However, the Article 29 Working Party argued in its working document no. WP 114 that transfers of data in such cases must not be on a mass scale but must relate to legal proceedings in particular cases, and must not be justified by the interest of public authorities in a third country but only by the interest of authorities of an EU Member State. Furthermore, as expressed in document no. WP 114 and in Opinion 6/2002 of 24 October 2002 (document no. WP 66),[65] the Article 29 Working Party rejected the possibility of invoking important public interest as the grounds for transferring data by European data controllers to the US authorities. It is argued that routine and wholesale transfer of personal data is not acceptable where it is justified by a unilateral decision taken by a third country for reasons of its own public interest.

As in other cases where necessity is the grounds for the derogation, necessity is to be interpreted strictly. Consequently, data may not be transferred in order to support public interest goals, but only if the achievement of these goals is not possible unless data is transferred in the scope specified.

[E] Establishment, Exercise or Defence of Legal Claims

Data may be transferred to a third country on the grounds of being necessary for the establishment, exercise or defence or legal claims in the context of a specific judicial or administrative procedure or other out-of-court procedure, in relation to a specific data subject. A transfer must not be made on a contingency basis, in contemplation of a possible future occurrence of legal claims, or on a mass scale. One example is the transfer of a specific customer's data as evidence in a lawsuit brought by this customer against a data controller.

[F] Protection of Vital Interests in the Event of Incapability to Give Consent

Data may be transferred to a third country even in the lack of an adequate data protection standard in order to protect the vital interest of a person (whether the data subject or another person). A 'vital interest' is a critical one, essential for a person's physical integrity, life or health. Only in exceptional circumstances may this include economic interests. Examples include transfer being necessary for humanitarian purposes, including for monitoring epidemics and their spread or in situations of humanitarian emergencies, in particular in situations of natural and man-made disasters (recital 46 of the preamble to the GDPR).

The derogation for the protection of vital interests applies in cases where the data subject is physically or legally incapable of giving consent and the transfer of data is necessary. One example is when the immediate transfer of medical data, without waiting for consent, is essential for saving the life or health or a person or for making a quick diagnosis (document no. WP 114 of the Article 29 Working Party). Such protection of vital interests may benefit not only the data subject but also other persons whose life or health may be in danger due to a lack of information on the data subject.

65. Opinion 6/2002 on transmission of Passenger Manifest Information and other data from Airlines to the United States, http://ec.europa.eu/justice/policies/privacy/docs/wpdocs/2002/wp66_en.pdf.

On the other hand, the provision does not refer to transferring data as a contribution to medical research; such a transfer requires a different legal basis.

[G] Public Registers

The prohibition of transferring data to a third country which does not ensure an adequate level of protection may also be derogated from if the transfer is made from a public register, i.e. a register which, according to EU or Member State law, is intended to provide information to the public and which is open to consultation by the public in general or by any person who can demonstrate a legitimate interest. Public registers, i.e. registers maintained by public entities under law and serving public purposes, include business registers, national criminal records, land and mortgage registers, population registers, or tax identification systems.

A transfer of data available to the general public may not include the totality, or an entire category, of personal data from the register. Where the register is intended for consultation by persons with a legitimate interest, the transfer can only be made at the request of those persons or if they are to be the recipients. The access to data from such registers is conditional upon fulfilment of requirements specified in EU or Member State law.

[H] Transfer of Data to a Third Country Despite Non-Compliance with the Conditions. Legitimate Interest

The GDPR provides for one more derogations as a 'safety valve' for specific situations. It allows data to be transferred to a non-EEA country even where the European Commission has not issued a decision declaring an adequate protection of data in such a country, the data exporter has not provided for safeguards such as BCRs or SCCs, and no derogation on grounds such as the data subject's consent can be invoked. Where the above conditions have not been met, a transfer to a third country may take place under Article 49(1) of the GDPR only if:

- the transfer is not repetitive;
- it concerns only a limited number of data subjects;
- it is necessary for the purposes of compelling legitimate interests pursued by the controller which are not overridden by the interests or rights and freedoms of the data subject;
- the controller has assessed all the circumstances surrounding the data transfer and has on the basis of that assessment provided suitable personal data protection safeguards;
- and has informed the supervisory authority and the data subject of the transfer.

This implies that the legitimate interest pursued by the controller (Article 6(1)(f) of the GDPR) allows this derogation from the prohibition of transferring data to a third country in the absence of adequate protection subsequent to the transfer.

This derogation, as well as derogations based on the data subject's consent or the transfer being necessary for the performance of a contract concluded with the data subject or in the data subject's interest, do not apply to activities carried out by public authorities in the exercise of their public powers.

§13.05 AUTHORISATION BY A SUPERVISORY AUTHORITY FOR A TRANSFER OF PERSONAL DATA TO THIRD COUNTRIES WHICH DO NOT ENSURE ADEQUATE PROTECTION

A data exporter may lawfully transfer data to non-EU/EEA countries, without obtaining a specific authorisation from a supervisory authority, by resorting to legal grounds which constitute systemic instruments approved by public authorities.

One of these legal grounds is the adequate level of data protection ensured subsequent to the transfer in the third country or sector of destination, as declared by a European Commission decision (Article 45(1) of the GDPR).

Where a third country has not been declared by a European Commission decision to ensure an adequate protection under law or sectoral regulations, data may be transferred to such a country provided that appropriate data safeguards are ensured by the data exporter (Article 46(2) of the GDPR). Such appropriate safeguards include: (i) BCRs, (ii) standard data protection clauses, (iii) an approved code of conduct regulating data protection in the sector in which the data importer operates, (iv) a certification mechanism confirming an adequate data protection standard implemented by the data importer. These instruments, through their legally binding character, ensure adequate protection of data subsequent to the transfer, irrespective of the third country's legal status concerning data protection.

Transfers of data to a third country based on such safeguards do not require a separate authorisation from a supervisory authority, as they are institutional arrangements approved by public authorities and meeting specific conditions. For example, implementing BCRs and using them as the basis for transferring data does not require a separate authorisation from a supervisory authority provided that the BCRs have been approved by the competent supervisory authority. Similarly, standard data protection clauses (SCCs) are a legal basis for transferring data to a third country without the need to obtain a separate authorisation from a supervisory authority, being a package of clauses adopted by the European Commission or adopted by a supervisory authority and approved by the Commission.

On the other hand, where the European Commission has not confirmed any adequate standard of data protection to have been ensured in the third country, or sector of destination, and no systemic safeguards have been implemented by the data controller and approved by the competent authority, data may be transferred under other safeguards (compensating for a lack of adequate protection in the third country, as mentioned in recital 108 of the preamble to the GDPR), which must, however, be authorised by a supervisory authority (Article 46(3) of the GDPR). Such safeguards may include in particular contractual clauses between the controller or processor and the controller, processor or recipient of the personal data in the third country or administrative arrangements between public authorities or bodies.

Thus, an individual authorisation from a supervisory authority is not required to data transfers under standard clauses adopted by a supervisory authority and approved by the European Commission, but is required for clauses formulated and negotiated on an ad hoc basis by the parties to the transfer.

I believe that a processor (as opposed to a controller) may only request a supervisory authority for an authorisation to the use of such clauses if entitled to do so by the controller.

Where data protection in the given third country of destination has been found by a European Commission decision to meet the adequate level or where appropriate safeguards have been adduced, such as BCRs or standard data protection clauses, the administrative procedure for issuing authorisation for data transfer is pointless and should be closed.[66] Consequently, any proceedings for issuing an authorisation, carried out by a supervisory authority, should include a verification of whether these grounds for a data transfer are met.

The authorisation by a supervisory authority produces legal effects upon the issuance of the decision. Where the authorisation by a supervisory authority is the sole grounds for the transfer of data (i.e. there are no other circumstances allowing data to be transferred), it should be considered unlawful to start a transfer before the authorisation is obtained.

The assessment by a supervisory authority should determine whether the safeguards adduced by the controller with respect to the protection of data subsequent to the transfer are 'adequate'. An adequate level of protection of European data subjects' data does not mean that the protection must be exactly as provided for in the GDPR (i.e. identical). This would prevent any transfer of data from the EU to non-EEA countries (with few exceptions), as the EU model and scope of personal data protection is unique. Therefore, the 'adequate' level of data protection is described in the GDPR as 'essentially equivalent' to the European level. The protection must not be at a lower level, as the protection of natural persons guaranteed in the GDPR, as interpreted in the context of the Charter of Fundamental Rights, must not be compromised (Article 44(1)).

The supervisory authority, in its proceedings for an authorisation of a transfer of data, should ascertain whether the measures taken ensure protection of the processed data at a level equivalent to the EU standard. In its evaluation, the authority should not disregard technical measures to be used for the transfer and the subsequent processing of data because, in practice, IT safeguards are crucial for protecting data against unauthorised access, loss, or damage.[67]

The assessment made by the supervisory authority should also take into account any onward transfers of the data by the importer in the third country. Any onward transfer of data is only permitted if the subsequent recipient is also subjected to rules

66. G. Sibiga, *Postępowanie w sprawach ochrony danych osobowych*, Warszawa 2003, p. 205.
67. Polish Supreme Administrative Court in its judgment of 16 April 2003, II SA 3878/02, ONSA 2004, no. 1, p. 41.

ensuring an adequate level of personal data protection. Any contracts entered into by the processor with subsequent recipients in the third country should be based on instructions from the controller and include safeguards such as contractual clauses, analogous to those included in the contract of the initial data transfer. Thus, they should also regulate issues such as information technologies used for the transfer and subsequent processing of data or information obligations towards data subjects.

§13.06 TRANSFERRING PERSONAL DATA FROM THE EU TO THE UNITED STATES

My reason for this chapter's particular focus on data transfers to the United States is not my critical assessment of the personal data protection situation in that country. On the contrary: the respect for privacy, including the protection of personal data, has long been a well-established value in the US in historical, cultural and legal terms. Allegations of Internet sector giants' and US intelligence services' interference with the privacy of Americans and Europeans, concerning though they certainly are, should not lead to the generalised and unjust conclusion that the US, or its citizens, do not respect the right to privacy. Rather, the detailed account and discussion of transfers to the United States in this chapter is motivated by the close cultural and historical ties, and the scale of cooperation, between Europe and the US in many areas.

[A] European Commission Decisions on Adequate Level of Protection as the Legal Basis for EU-US Data Transfers

The United States is a third country. Its legislation does not ensure a personal data protection level adequate to the EU requirements. The US personal data protection regime is fundamentally different from the one in place in the EU. The EU has established general rules of data processing, which are applicable to every type of data controller or processor; these rules were formulated in Directive 95/46/EC and subsequently in the GDPR. On the other hand, the US only regulates personal data protection in selected sectors and areas identified as exposed to the risk of data protection breaches.[68]

The flow of data between the EU and the US is of particular economic significance. The US is the European Union's largest trade partner. The value of EU-US trade in goods and services accounts for a third of the global cash flow. The EU and the US jointly generate half of the global GDP. The total value of US investment in the EU is

68. C.J. Bennett, *Regulating Privacy: Data Protection and Public Policy in Europe and the United States*, New York 1992, pp. 45 et seq.; C.J. Bennett, C.D. Raab, 'The Adequacy of Privacy: The European Union Data Protection Directive and the North American Response', *The Information Society* 1997, Vol. 13, No. 3; C.D. Raab, 'Regulating the Computer: comparing policy instruments in Europe and the United States', *European Journal of Political Research* 1988, Vol. 16, No. 5; idem, 'Different Processes, One Result: The Convergence of Data Protection Policy in Europe and the United States', *Governance* 1988, Vol. 1, No. 4.

three times higher than its investment in Asia; the value of European investment in the US is eight times the value of European investment in China and India combined.[69]

Commission Decision 2000/520/EC of 26 July 2000 on 'Safe Harbour'[70] was crucially important as a legal basis for lawful transfers of personal data from the EU to the US (it was not the sole legal basis, though, as data exporters could, and still can, use BCRs, standard clauses and other instruments).[71] For entities which submitted a declaration of adherence to Safe Harbour and complied with its principles, the Commission Decision removed the barrier resulting from the US's status as a third country. This applied to specified US importers rather than the United States as a country.

However, the CJEU invalidated the European Commission Decision 2000/520/EC (the 'Safe Harbour decision') in its ground-breaking judgment of 6 October 2015 in Case C-362/14 *Maximilian Schrems v Data Protection Commissioner*. The new legal act which has replaced the invalidated Safe Harbour scheme as the legal basis for trans-Atlantic data transfers is the European Commission decision of 12 July 2016 declaring an adequate level of data protection within the 'EU-US Privacy Shield' scheme. Criticism of the Safe Harbour scheme, the CJEU judgment in Case C-362/14, and the Privacy Shield scheme are discussed later in this chapter.

Safe Harbour was based on a compromise which, while allowing for differences in EU and US privacy protection regimes, recognised the need to overcome those differences pragmatically so that they did not become a barrier to free trans-Atlantic trade. The compromise, reflecting the particular nature of EU-US relations, enabled US data importers to adjust to European privacy protection principles by using the self-regulation and self-certification mechanism, typical of this legal domain in the US.

Annex I to the Decision provided that an organisation qualified as a 'Safe Harbour' if it adhered to the programme and complied with its principles. An organisation could adhere to Safe Harbour through self-certification, by submitting to the US Department of Commerce a written declaration including: a description of its activities with respect to personal data received from the EU; a description of the organisation's privacy policy; the location where the privacy policy was available for viewing by the public; the procedure of handling complaints and requests arising from a Safe Harbour adherent's obligations; the methods of verification used by the organisation. The US Department of Commerce was obliged to maintain a public list of Safe Harbour adherents.

---

69. Source of data: http://ec.europa.eu/trade/policy/countries-and-regions/countries/united-states.
70. Commission Decision 2000/520/EC of 26 July 2000 pursuant to Directive 95/46/EC of the European Parliament and of the Council on the adequacy of the protection provided by the safe harbour privacy principles and related frequently asked questions issued by the US Department of Commerce ('Safe Harbour'), OJ EC L 215 of 25.08.2000, p. 7.
71. Communication from the Commission to the European Parliament and the Council on the Transfer of Personal Data from the EU to the United States of America under Directive 95/46/EC following the Judgment by the Court of Justice in Case C-362/14 (Schrems), 6.11.2015, COM(2015) 566 final, http://ec.europa.eu/justice/data-protection/international-transfers/adequacy/files/eu-us_data_flows_communication_final.pdf.

An adequate level of protection of data transferred from the EU to US organisations was to be ensured through: compliance with the Safe Harbour principles and the frequently asked questions (FAQs); publishing privacy policies by the adherents; submitting the adherents to the jurisdiction of the US Federal Trade Commission or another authority supervising compliance with the Safe Harbour principles; periodic updates of the list of adherents based on annual re-certification requests sent to the US Department of Commerce; and a procedure for removing organisations from the Safe Harbour adherents list and stripping them of the associated privileges.

Safe Harbour was not equivalent to a declaration that an adequate level of personal data protection was ensured in the US as a whole, but only that it was ensured by those US organisations which adhered to Safe Harbour and met the conditions laid down in the Decision.[72]

[B] CJEU Judgment of 6 October 2015 in Case C-362/14 *Maximilian Schrems v Data Protection Commissioner*, Invalidating Safe Harbour; Other Criticism of Safe Harbour

In its ground-breaking judgment of 6 October 2015 in Case C-362/14 *Maximilian Schrems v Data Protection Commissioner*,[73] the CJEU declared the European Commission Decision 2000/520/EC on 'Safe Harbour' to be invalid.

The proceedings which led to the judgment were initiated by a complaint made by Mr Maximilian Schrems, an Austrian national, against the refusal by the Irish data protection authority, Data Protection Commissioner, to examine his objection to the transferring of personal data of Facebook users by Facebook Ireland Ltd. to the US and storing such data on servers in the US. The complainant pointed to the fact that the law and practice in the US do not ensure a sufficient protection of personal data from surveillance by US public authorities. These concerns resulted from information on the practices of the US National Security Agency, revealed by Edward Snowden.[74] (It is worth mentioning that such practices are against the Fourth Amendment to the US Constitution, which prohibits a search when not justified by probable cause. However, only US citizens are entitled to protection under the US Constitution; nationals of other countries may be subject to surveillance by US authorities.[75]) The Data Protection

72. An example of a decision confirming an adequate level of protection of personal data having been ensured by a third country as a whole rather than only specific entities established in that country is Commission Decision 2002/2/EU of 20 December 2001 on the adequate protection of personal data provided by the Canadian Personal Information Protection and Electronic Documents Act. Pursuant to Article 1 of that decision, Canada is considered a country providing an adequate level of protection for personal data transferred from the EU to recipients subject to the Canadian act.
73. http://eur-lex.europa.eu/legal-content/EN/TXT/?uri=CELEX:62014CJ0362.
74. Edward Snowden, a former employee of the US intelligence agencies CIA and NSA, revealed the practice to the media in, for example: E. MacAskill, 'Edward Snowden: how the spy story of the age leaked out', The Guardian, 12 June 2013, http://www.theguardian.com/world/2013/jun/11/edward-snowden-nsa-whistleblower-profile/print.
75. Judgment of the United States Supreme Court in case *US v Verdugo-Urquidez* – 494 U.S. 259 (1990), p. 494 U.S. 264–266. This results also from the Foreign Intelligence Surveillance Act of

Commissioner rejected Mr Schrems's complaint, arguing that the issue of the level of protection of personal data subsequent to a transfer from the EU to the US was regulated by European Commission decision 2000/520/EC on Safe Harbour and that this decision found the data protection standard to be adequate and the decision was consequently the legal basis of transfers of personal data from the EU to the US.

Mr Schrems challenged this decision before the High Court of Ireland. The High Court found that, although the electronic surveillance and interception of personal data transferred from the EU to the US served the public interest, the actions by the NSA and other US federal agencies were a 'significant over-reach'. Data monitoring was carried out on a mass scale rather than being focused on individuals for justifiable reasons. Therefore, the interference with privacy was disproportionate to the justified and lawful purposes, did not pursue the public interest and was a breach of the constitutional principles and the EU citizens' fundamental rights. Moreover, EU citizens had no means to exercise their rights effectively and the oversight of the intelligence services' actions was carried out within an ex parte and secret procedure. Thus, personal data were being transferred to the US in breach of the principle of adequate level of protection of data in the destination country subsequent to the transfer.

The High Court stayed the proceedings and referred a question to the CJEU for a preliminary ruling.

The CJEU observed that European Commission Decision 2000/520/EC on Safe Harbour was presumed to be lawful and accordingly produced legal effects and constituted the legal basis of data transfers from the EU to the US until being withdrawn or declared invalid. In effect, the Decision prevented persons whose personal data had been or could have been transferred to the US from lodging with the national supervisory authorities claims concerning the protection of their privacy and personal data. However, a European Commission decision could not eliminate or reduce the powers expressly accorded to the national supervisory authorities under Directive 95/46/EC, including the right to control the transfer of personal data to third countries subject to such a decision.

The CJEU also emphasised that the Safe Harbour system of declaring a data protection level to be adequate was not reliable, as it did not provide for effective mechanism for detecting infringements and verifying the protection standard implemented by the importer. US organisations could adhere to Safe Harbour through self-certification which resulted in a presumption of an adequate level of protection.

Indeed, the CJEU had good reasons to declare the European Commission's Safe Harbour decision invalid. Further points of criticism, besides those formulated in the judgment, could be made. The experience from the practical application of Safe

1978 ('FISA', Pub.L. 95-511, 92 Stat. 1783, 50 U.S.C. ch. 36), a US act regulating physical and electronic surveillance. Following the 11 September 2001 terrorist attacks in New York City and Washington, D.C., the scope of the Act was extended under the FISA Amendments Act of 10 July 2008 (the Foreign Intelligence Surveillance Act of 1978 Amendments Act of 2008, H.R. 6304), initially to remain in force until 31 December 2012, but later extended by Congress to the beginning of 2018, then finally for another 6 years, on the grounds of the increased threat of terrorist attacks. The act entitles the US authorities to monitor various forms of electronic communications of foreigners.

Harbour suggests that, contrary to the programme's assumptions, instead of being an instrument ensuring an appropriate standard of data protection following a transfer to importers in the US, the programme was in many cases used as an unacceptable exemption from that requirement. The decision did include formal safeguards to ensure its effectiveness, but they did not function in practice. Although the Safe Harbour decision was a binding legal basis for transferring data from the EU to the US, European data exporters ought not to have merely relied on the statement of the data importer claiming that it had a Safe Harbour certification, but should have sought evidence that the importer participated in the programme and met its obligations thereunder.[76]

Declarations made by US importers that they adhered to Safe Harbour while in fact they did not meet its requirements, or violations of fundamental principles of personal data protection specified therein, corrupted the compromise and deprived EU citizens of the protection that they were entitled to. Moreover, these irregularities resulted in data being in fact transferred from the EU without a legal basis.

A study conducted in 2008 by the Australian company Galexia showed that, out of 1,597 organisations appearing on the Safe Harbour list on the study day, only 1,109 were in fact Safe Harbour adherents. Many of the remaining ones had not renewed their certification or even were no longer in existence. There were also double entries. Only 348 of the Safe Harbour-listed organisations met the basic requirements of participation. This implied that, although European data controllers consulting the list could have inferred that 1,597 US importers ensured adequate protection of data after transfer, that inference would have been false for all but 21.8% of those importers.[77] In the remaining cases, even though transfers of data to the US would have been lawful under Commission Decision 2000/520/EC, the data would not in fact have been protected after the transfer.

Galexia's report also pointed out that US data importers declaring participation in Safe Harbour hampered the exercise of rights by data subjects whose data were processed in breach of the fundamental principles. As many as 209 Safe Harbour-listed organisations had selected a dispute resolution provider whose arbitration was not affordable in practice due to prohibitive costs. These costs were undoubtedly a barrier for rights enforcement, amounting to between USD 120 and 1,200 per hour, with a four-hour minimum charge, plus a USD 950 administration fee (the American Arbitration Association, AAA), or between USD 350 and 800 per hour plus a USD 275 administration fee (the Judicial Arbitration Mediation Service, JAMS).

This diagnosis was even more alarming given that serious concerns about Safe Harbour and the effectiveness of the protection it afforded had already been voiced in the European Commission's review reports in 2002 and 2004. Among the findings of the 2002 review was that a substantial number of US organisations which had

76. Article 29 Working Party, Opinion 5/2012 of 1 July 2012 on Cloud Computing, WP 196, point 3.5.1; http://ec.europa.eu/justice/article-29/documentation/opinion-recommendation/files/2012/wp196_en.pdf.

77. C. Connolly, 'New Galexia Study: The US Safe Harbor – Fact or Fiction?', Privacy Laws and Business International 2008, no. 96 of 2 December 2008, p. 4, http://www.galexia.com/public/research/assets/safe_harbor_fact_or_fiction_2008/safe_harbor_fact_or_fiction.pdf.

self-certified adherence to Safe Harbour did not have sufficiently transparent privacy policies or dispute resolution procedures in place.[78] In 2004, the review report included the finding that fewer than half of Safe Harbour adherents reflected all the programme principles in their privacy policies.[79]

On 27 November 2013, the European Commission issued a Communication to the European Parliament and the Council, entitled 'Rebuilding Trust in EU-US Data Flows'.[80] In this document, the Commission formulated its reservations to the level of protection of EU citizens' personal data transferred to the US under Safe Harbour. Those reservations related, for example, to the scheme being based on declarations of its adherents and not ensuring transparency and enforceability of its principles. In its subsequent Communication to the European Parliament and the Council of 27 November 2013 on the Functioning of Safe Harbour from the Perspective of EU Citizens and Companies Established in the EU,[81] the European Commission pointed out that a large proportion of organisations which formally adhered to Safe Harbour did not fully comply with its principles. In this document, the Commission formulated 13 recommendations aiming at an improvement of the functioning of Safe Harbour. The recommended measures included the following: the adherent organisations should publish their privacy policies, essentially on their websites; they should publicly disclose the terms of agreements they concluded with subcontractors, e.g. cloud providers; the US Department of Commerce should clearly flag on its website all companies which no longer met the scheme requirements; organisations which misinform consumers with their false claims on Safe Harbour adherence should be prosecuted. The EU and the US made a joint statement declaring their intention to strengthen Safe Harbour in a comprehensive manner by summer 2014.[82] The scheme was not revised, though. Its irregularities led to the invalidation of the European Commission decision 2000/520/EC by the CJEU judgment in Case C-362/14.

[C] Change of Legal Basis for EU-US Data Transfers: Invalidation of Safe Harbour, Adoption of EU-US Privacy Shield

European Commission Decision 2000/520/EC on Safe Harbour was a key legal basis for transferring data from the EU to the US (though not the only one, as data exporters

78. European Commission, The application of Commission Decision on the adequate protection of personal data provided by the Safe Harbour Privacy Principles, 13 February 2002, p. 2, http://web.archive.org/web/20060724174359/http://www.ec.europa.eu/justice_home/fsj/privacy/docs/adequacy/sec-2002-196/sec-2002-196_en.pdf.
79. European Commission, The implementation of Commission Decision on the adequate protection of personal data provided by the Safe Harbour Privacy Principles, 20 October 2004, http://web.archive.org/web/20060724173657/http://www.ec.europa.eu/justice_home/fsj/privacy/docs/adequacy/sec-2004-1323_en.pdf.
80. COM(2013) 846 final, 27.11.2013, https://eur-lex.europa.eu/legal-content/EN/TXT/?uri=CELEX:52013DC0846.
81. COM(2013) 847, 27.11.2013, https://eur-lex.europa.eu/legal-content/EN/TXT/?uri=CELEX:52013DC0847.
82. EU-US Summit – Joint Statement, Brussels, 26 March 2014, http://europa.eu/rapid/press-release_STATEMENT-14-84_en.htm, point 14.

could, and still can, make transfers based on BCRs, SCCs and other instruments). Once this decision was invalidated by the CJEU through its judgment in Case C-362/14, it urgently had to be replaced with another arrangement. Providing an optimal basis for trans-Atlantic data transfers is essential for trade, as virtually all forms of cooperation involve, even indirectly, making personal data available. However, given the very critical findings formulated, among others, by the European Commission and the CJEU concerning the compliance of Safe Harbour with EU law (discussed earlier in this chapter), it was clear that any new arrangement ought not to be an ad hoc one but ought to guarantee a data protection standard compliant with the requirements of EU law interpreted in the context of the Charter of Fundamental Rights.

The new legal act which has replaced the invalidated Safe Harbour scheme as the legal basis for EU-US data transfers is the European Commission Implementing Decision (EU) 2016/1250 of 12 July 2016 declaring an adequate level of data protection within the 'EU-US Privacy Shield' scheme.[83]

In recitals 136 to 141 (Section 4) of the preamble to this Decision and in its Article 1, the European Commission declared that the United States ensures an adequate level of protection of personal data transferred from the European Union to self-certified organisations under the EU-US Privacy Shield. The European Commission declared that the principles of the Privacy Shield scheme, formulated by the US Department of Commerce, ensure protection of personal data at a level equivalent to the basic principles laid down in Directive 95/46/EC, also interpreted in the light of the Charter of Fundamental Rights of the EU, and comply with the conclusions of the CJEU judgment in Case C-362/14 *Maximilian Schrems v Data Protection Commissioner*.

However, an important point is that the Privacy Shield decision does not amount to a declaration that an adequate level of personal data protection is ensured in the US as a whole, but only that it is ensured by those US organisations which participate in the scheme and meet the conditions laid down in the decision.

The Privacy Shield is based on the following foundations, which are intended to remove the shortcomings of its predecessor, Safe Harbour:

[1] Verification of Whether an Organisation's Inclusion on the List Was Justified and Whether the Organisation Complies with the Principles of the Scheme; Procedure for Removal of an Organisation from the List

The Privacy Shield is based on the same premises as Safe Harbour. It is likewise based on self-certification of the adherents, i.e. an organisation's declaration before a public authority that it complies with the principles formulated in the decision. A transfer of data by an EU-based exporter (controller or processor) to a US-based importer included in the publicly available list kept by the Department of Commerce is lawful.

83. Commission Implementing Decision (EU) 2016/1250 of 12 July 2016 pursuant to Directive 95/46/EC of the European Parliament and of the Council on the adequacy of the protection provided by the EU-U.S. Privacy Shield, OJ EU L 207, 1.8.2016, p. 1, https://eur-lex.europa.eu/legal-content/EN/TXT/?uri=CELEX:32016D1250.

However, based on an analysis, the European Commission declared in the decision that US law now provides for a number of limitations of access to, and use of, personal data transferred from the EU to the US as well as mechanisms of supervision and enforcement of claims, which provide a sufficient safeguard against unlawful breaches. The European Commission observed that these measures have been significantly reinforced since its critical communications and demands relating to the functioning of Safe Harbour (COM(2013) 846 final and COM(2013) 847 final of 27.11.2013). These measures are indicated in sections 3.1.1 and 3.2 of the preamble to the Privacy Shield decision.

The decision provides for periodic reviews, to be carried out jointly by the European Commission and the US Department of Commerce with the support of experts and European data protection authorities, of whether the finding of an adequate level of data protection under the Privacy Shield is still factually and legally justified (Section 6 of the decision: 'Periodic review of adequacy finding'). If it is found that the scheme no longer ensures a data protection standard adequate to the one in the EU or there are clear indications that the US public authorities abuse the data transferred from the EU, the decision provides for its partial or complete suspension or repeal by the EU (Section 7 of the preamble to the decision, 'Suspension of the adequacy decision', and Article 4 of the decision).

The first annual review of the Privacy Shield, involving eight representatives of the Article 29 Working Party, was completed in December 2017.[84] The Article 29 Working Party noted that the data protection standard under the Privacy Shield had improved in comparison with the invalidated Safe Harbour scheme. However, a key demand was made for an appointment, by 25 May 2018 at the latest, of an independent Privacy Shield Ombudsperson who would supervise the flow of data between the EU and the US, investigate data subjects' complaints, and be empowered to enforce his/her decisions, such as orders to erase, or cease the processing of, personal data.

Nevertheless, the European Parliament voted in a non-binding resolution to suspend the Privacy Shield 'unless the U.S. is fully compliant' by 1 September 2018, as 'the current Privacy Shield arrangement does not provide the adequate level of protection required by Union data protection law and the EU Charter as interpreted by the CJEU'.[85]

At the same time, the US Department of Commerce is obliged to update the list of adherents based on their annual re-certification requests and on verification of whether the applicants' privacy policies are compatible with the principles of the scheme, and whether their practice complies with those policies. Any cases of a withdrawal or removal of an adherent from the list must also be taken into account.

Self-certified organisations within the Privacy Shield are also subject to supervision by the US Federal Trade Commission, and any breach of the scheme principles

84. EU–U.S. Privacy Shield – First annual Joint Review, document no. WP 255 of 28 November 2017, http://ec.europa.eu/newsroom/just/document.cfm?doc_id = 48782 [retrieved on 20 February 2018].
85. European Parliament resolution of 5 July 2018 on the adequacy of the protection afforded by the EU-US Privacy Shield (2018/2645(RSP), http://www.europarl.europa.eu/sides/getDoc.do?pubRef = -//EP//TEXT + TA + P8-TA-2018-0315 + 0 + DOC + XML + V0//EN.

could be deemed a violation of Section 5 of the Federal Trade Commission Act, prohibiting unfair or deceptive acts or practices in commerce.

Whenever an organisation leaves the scheme, it must remove all public statements which imply, even indirectly, that it meets the requirements of adequate data protection under the Privacy Shield. The Department of Commerce tracks all misrepresentations on adherence to the scheme. Such misrepresentations are subject to administrative measures by the Federal Trade Commission or another competent authority and may be actionable under the False Statements Act (18 U.S.C. § 1001). Upon leaving the scheme, an organisation must return or delete the personal data it obtained as a result of being found to ensure adequate protection under the Privacy Shield. Compliance with this obligation is subject to oversight by the Department of Commerce.

The Privacy Shield also requires its adherents to carry out periodic compliance reviews through documented self-assessment, external audits, or random checks. They must also implement effective claim enforcement and complaint handling mechanisms.

[2] Legal Basis and Proportionality of Access by US Government Administration to Personal Data Transferred from the EU

One of the key criticisms of the practice of Safe Harbour was that data were monitored by the US National Security Agency on a mass scale rather than being focused on particular persons for justifiable reasons. Such an interference with the right to privacy was disproportionate in relation to legitimate and lawful goals. The Privacy Shield is intended to prevent such excessive access to data transferred from the EU: US public authorities may only access the data in such cases and in such scope as is necessary for the national security or other important public interest.

Within the Privacy Shield, the US Government, represented by the Office of the Director of National Intelligence (ODNI), the top layer of the US intelligence structure, provided the European Commission with detailed representations and commitments contained in Annex VI to the Privacy Shield decision, relating to access restrictions and safeguards and the use of personal data transferred from the EU to the US (recital 65 of the preamble to the Decision). Access restrictions and safeguards and the use of data by public authorities have also been described by the US Department of Justice and attached as Annex VII to the decision.

[3] Guarantees of Effective Enforceability of Rights by the Data Subjects; Redress

Safe Harbour was also deficient in that it did not provide for a dispute resolution mechanism and data subjects whose data were processed in breach of the fundamental principles were hampered in their attempts of exercising their rights. Many Safe Harbour-listed organisations selected a dispute resolution provider whose arbitration was not affordable in practice due to prohibitive costs. Moreover, the oversight of the intelligence services' actions was carried out within an ex parte and secret procedure.

By contrast, within the Privacy Shield a data subject may raise a complaint directly with the data importer, who must respond within 45 days. Privacy Shield adherents who process human resources data in the employment context must comply with advice from competent EU data protection authorities. Others are encouraged by the European Commission to use such advice as a support.

Complaints may also be made to an independent EU or US-based dispute resolution body to which the data importer has adhered and which provides an unpaid or affordable alternative dispute resolution procedure (ADR). The data importer must publish a link to the website of such a body.

A complaint may also be brought to the Federal Trade Commission or – an important new arrangement – to a national data protection authority in the EU. A competent national data protection authority is empowered to intervene with the US Department of Commerce or the Federal Trade Commission on the complaint of a European data subject.

Moreover, according to a letter from the US Secretary of State attached to the decision as Annex III, the US Government established a new position of Privacy Shield Ombudsperson, independent from the Intelligence Community, to represent data subjects in disputes with US intelligence services (this function is exercised by the Under Secretary of State for Economic Growth, Energy, and the Environment).

[4] Precise Formulation of Conditions of Onward Transfers

Onward transfers of data by a US-based importer adherent to the Privacy Shield to a further recipient in the US or another third country is also covered by the Privacy Shield principles. An onward transfer of personal data transferred from the EU may not result in protection of such data being reduced to a level below that defined by the Privacy Shield.

The Privacy Shield decision reiterates the key principles of data processing compliant with EU law (Section 2.1 of the Decision). The regularity of data processing by an adherent to the Privacy Shield is judged against these principles. They include providing data subjects with information on the key aspects of data processing, e.g. its purpose and the rights of the data subject. They also provide for a restriction of data processing to the scope necessary to achieve the purpose of the processing, and prohibit processing of data for a purpose incompatible with the initial one or one subsequently authorised by the data subject. The data subject may object to processing of his/her data for a purpose which is compatible with but different from the original purpose or processing data for direct marketing. Processing of sensitive data requires the data subject's consent. Processing of identifiable data is only allowed for as long as is necessary to achieve the purpose of the processing. Data safeguards adequate to the risk and the nature of the data must be implemented, including by a subprocessor, if any. Under the Privacy Shield, data subjects also have the right to obtain information on the processing of their data without excessive charges and without being obliged to justify their request. They may also demand rectification or erasure of data which are inaccurate or processed in breach of the principles. The decision also guarantees protection from negative results of profiling and other automated decisions which may influence positive or negative decisions in matters such as lending, insurance, or employment.

Once the Safe Harbour scheme, which served as a legal basis (though not the only one) for EU-US data transfers, was invalidated by the CJEU judgment in Case C-362/14, the scale of economic cooperation required the adoption of a similar instrument, the Privacy Shield scheme, to replace Safe Harbour. This was intended as a ground-breaking scheme in that, despite being based on similar foundations as Safe Harbour, including the self-certification system, it strengthened the means to enforce data subjects' rights and compliance of importers' actions. Whether the Privacy Shield avoids becoming the target of critical opinions such as were voiced by the European Commission and the CJEU concerning the compliance of Safe Harbour with the EU law depends on whether the oversight by public authorities is genuinely effective, whether entries on the list of scheme adherents are effectively verified in terms of being justified or up-to-date, whether it is practicable to remove a non-compliant adherent from the list, and whether cooperation procedures between the EU data protection authorities and the US authorities are in place.

[D] EU-US Agreement on the Transfer of Financial Messaging Data in the SWIFT System

An agreement[86] between the EU and the US provides the legal basis for the access by the US Treasury Department to financial messaging data of European financial institutions' customers in the SWIFT system for the purposes of the Terrorist Finance Tracking Program (the agreement is therefore referred to by the abbreviations SWIFT or TFTP). The Terrorist Finance Tracking Program (TFTP), whose implementation required the conclusion of the agreement, was implemented by the US Treasury Department, along with other measures, in the aftermath of the traumatic experience of the 11 September 2001 terrorist attacks.[87] However, the existence of the programme was made public by the US media only in 2006.

Before 2009, data on banking operations conducted in the EU were also processed on SWIFT servers which were located in the US, before being transferred to Europe. Such a location of the servers allowed the US Treasury Department to access European data as a result not of meeting any legal requirements but only of technical circumstances (i.e. data-processing servers being kept, for IT security reasons, in both the US and Europe, with identical contents), without the data subjects' awareness. Therefore,

86. The Agreement of 28.6.2010 between the European Union and the United States of America on the processing and transfer of Financial Messaging Data from the European Union to the United States for the purposes of the Terrorist Finance Tracking Program entered into force on 1 August 2010. OJ EU L 195 of 27.7.2010, p. 5.
87. The legal basis for the Terrorist Finance Tracking Program is Executive Order 13224 issued by US President George W. Bush on 23 September 2001 under the Emergency Economic Powers Act, 50 U.S.C., §§ 1701–1706.

the rules of processing financial messaging data originating from the EU, both covered by bank secrecy and constituting personal data, required a substantial change and reorganisation.

The SWIFT agreement was concluded in order to subject transfers of the customers of European financial institutions to the fundamental principles of data protection, such as necessity, data minimisation, and purpose limitation. Indeed, the full relevance of information subject to bank secrecy for the existence and scope of the right to privacy needs to be fully grasped. The ubiquity of cashless payments, made in forms such as bank transfers or with a payment card, means that information on a bank customer's account movements and liabilities may reveal the sources and recipients of monies transferred to and from the bank account, and consequently lead indirectly to the disclosure of the account owner's financial standing, lifestyle, behaviours, interests, creed, or health status.

The extent of data made available to the US Treasury Department under the TFTP agreement is enormous. The data are sourced from SWIFT, i.e. the Society for Worldwide Interbank Financial Telecommunication, based in La Hulpe, Belgium. SWIFT is the global operator acting as an intermediary in interbank information exchange. It brings together approx. 9,000 banks and other financial institutions in more than 200 countries and operates an estimated 80% of electronic financial transfers, which amounts to 9 million transfer orders totalling USD 6 trillion per day.[88]

Article 8 of the SWIFT agreement contains the key declaration that the US Treasury Department is deemed to ensure an adequate level of protection of the financial messaging data transferred from the EU to the US for the purposes of the agreement. This removes the barrier for the transfer of personal data from the EU to the US provided for today in Article 44 of the GDPR (and previously, when the SWIFT agreement entered into force, Article 25 of Directive 95/46/EC), resulting from the US's status as a third country which does not ensure an adequate level of personal data protection in its legislation.

The agreement provides that operations of searching data provided under the Terrorist Finance Tracking Program are limited to the needs resulting from a justified reason to believe that the subject of the search has a link to terrorism or the financing thereof. This provision therefore prohibits collection and analysis of data of an unlimited pool of users and attempts to justify such 'data mining' practice,[89] or other algorithmic or automated data profiling or filtering, with an effort to verify whether they include data of persons possibly linked with terrorism or terrorist financing. This restriction is rendered in specific terms by the requirement that any US Treasury Department request to a European entity for providing data should:

88. Situation as at September 2010, when the Agreement entered into force; http://www.swift.com.
89. For a comprehensive presentation of data mining methods, see: P. Giudici, S. Figini, Applied Data Mining for Business and Industry, Chichester 2009; J. Han, M. Kamber, Data Mining: Concepts and Techniques, San Diego 2001 (including a description of data mining [pp. 5 et seq.] and architecture of data mining systems [pp. 171 et seq.]); I.H. Witten, E. Frank, M.A. Hall, Data Mining: Practical Machine Learning Tools and Techniques, Burlington 2011, pp. 85 et seq. (a description of the use of algorithms in data mining).

- identify as clearly as possible the categories of data necessary for the purpose of the prevention, investigation, detection, or prosecution of terrorism or terrorist financing;
- specify the narrowest possible scope of data allowing an analysis of the terrorism threat;
- substantiate the necessity of obtaining data; such a substantiation must not be a repetitive formula but must refer to the specific case.

The fulfilment of these obligations is verified by Europol.

The agreement specifies the scope of information which may be provided to the US Treasury Department. It includes the identifying information about the originator or recipient of a transaction, including name, account number, address, and national identification number. This indication of categories of data specifies the maximum extent of data which can be provided to the US Treasury Department. The actual data scope should be specified in each individual case depending on what data are necessary in the specific situation.

Compliance by parties to the SWIFT agreement with its provisions is to be ensured through periodic checks carried out by Europol's Joint Supervisory Body (JSB) and periodic reviews carried out jointly by the European Commission and the US Treasury Department under Article 13 of the agreement.

According to the procedure specified in Article 4(3)–(5) of the Agreement, where the US Treasury Department seeks to obtain data from the SWIFT database, it must provide a copy of the request, with supplemental documents, to Europol, and Europol must verify whether the request complies with Article 4(2) of the Agreement. It is up to the JSB to verify the correctness of Europol's verification of whether the requests from the US Treasury Department meet the requirements of Article 4 of the Agreement, in particular whether the scope of data which the US seeks to obtain is adequate for the purposes of prevention of terrorism or terrorism financing in the particular case.

Past inspections showed breaches in the initial period after the conclusion of the agreement. Afterwards, there was some improvement in the way Europol performed its task of verifying the US Treasury Department's requests for information from the SWIFT database.

Initially, despite this improvement, the problem of unauthorised access by US authorities to data had not been fully resolved, as subsequent media reports demonstrated. (These allegations date several years back; on the other hand, in the European Commission's report to the European Parliament and the Council on the joint review of the SWIFT Agreement implementation,[90] no infringement was found.)

Evidence of US bodies obtaining direct and unrestricted access to European financial messages in the SWIFT system and obtaining such data for purposes other than terrorism prevention, in violation of the Agreement, was presented, among

90. Joint Review Report of 19 January 2017, Section 4. Recommendations and Conclusion, http://eur-lex.europa.eu/legal-content/EN/TXT/?uri=CELEX%3A52017SC0017).

others, by the Danish daily *Berlingske*.[91] It reported on the takeover of a USD 26,000 transfer from a Danish bank to a German bank in payment for a batch of Cuban cigars imported to Germany by a German supplier. This action by the US Treasury Department was being justified by a breach of the Danish purchaser of the US embargo on Cuba.

Der Spiegel also published information about SWIFT financial messages, including bank transfers and card transactions made by customers, having been monitored by the National Security Agency (NSA).[92] The magazine quoted Edward Snowden's claims that NSA had a branch named 'Follow the Money' separated in its structure for that purpose, and that information obtained by it was then put in a financial database known as Tracfin. According to *Der Spiegel*, in 2011 Tracfin had 180 million datasets, 84 percent of which related to customers using credit cards and credit transactions.

After the NSA was confirmed to have direct access to European citizens' personal and financial data in the SWIFT database, the European Parliament expressed concern about breaches of the TFTP and requested the European Commission to suspend the SWIFT agreement.[93] The resolution emphasised that such direct access was not only lacking legal grounds under the SWIFT agreement, but largely exceeded the data scope necessary for the purposes of fighting terrorism, diverged from those purposes, and violated the principles of necessity, data minimisation, and purpose limitation, formulated in the Agreement. The resolution was not binding, though. Earlier, the European Parliament's Committee on Civil Liberties, Justice and Home Affairs (LIBE) declared its understanding of the disastrous international and economic consequences that suspension of data exchange in SWIFT would entail, and emphasised that its recommendation should not be taken literally, but as a radical call for solving the issue of privacy violations.

Past inspections conducted by Europol's Joint Supervisory Body, as well as periodic joint reviews by the European Commission and the US Treasury Department, showed breaches in the initial period after the conclusion of the agreement. Afterwards, there was some improvement in the way Europol performed its task of verifying the US Treasury Department's requests for information from the SWIFT database.

In the European Commission's report to the European Parliament and the Council of 19 January 2017 on the fourth joint review of the SWIFT Agreement implementation[94] (Section 4 'Recommendations and conclusion'), the Commission declared that

91. S. Bendtsen, P. Suppli Benson, 'Dansk politimand fanget i amerikansk terrrornet', Berlingske, 26 February 2012, http://www.b.dk/nationalt/dansk-politimand-fanget-i-amerikansk-terrornet.
92. G.-P. Schmitz, 'SWIFT Suspension? EU Parliament Furious about NSA Bank Spying', Spiegel Online International, 18 September 2013, http://www.spiegel.de/international/europe/nsa-spying-european-parliamentarians-call-for-swift-suspension-a-922920.html.
93. European Parliament resolution of 23 October 2013 on the suspension of the TFTP agreement as a result of US National Security Agency surveillance (2013/2831(RSP)), http://www.europarl.europa.eu/sides/getDoc.do?pubRef=-//EP//TEXT+TA+P7-TA-2013-0449+0+DOC+XML+V0//EN.
94. Report from the Commission to the European Parliament and the Council on the joint review of the implementation of the Agreement between the European Union and the United States of America on the processing and transfer of Financial Messaging Data from the European Union

the SWIFT Agreement and its safeguards and controls were properly implemented and the findings of the third joint review had been followed up.[95]

[E] The US Foreign Account Tax Compliance Act (FATCA)

Transfer of personal data from the EU (and other countries) to the US also results indirectly from the US Foreign Account Tax Compliance Act (FATCA).[96] The link is indirect, as FATCA is part of US law and therefore may not directly serve as a basis for transferring data by European entities to the US without bilateral agreements between individual EU Member States and the US. Such agreements have indeed been concluded.

FATCA, implemented in EU countries under bilateral agreements, requires financial institutions (banks, investment funds, trust funds, insurance companies) to identify and report their customers who are US taxpayers to the US federal tax authority.[97] FATCA is designed to prevent the evasion by US taxpayers of their tax obligations towards the US Treasury by locating their funds in other countries via foreign financial institutions. The scope of persons covered by FATCA, i.e. whose data must be reported by European institutions, includes 'US persons'. This term as used in the act covers in particular US citizens, including those who are not US residents, as well as US residents including persons who spend a significant portion of the year on the US territory, and US corporations and companies.

FATCA only applies to US entities; as part of US legislation, it may not be a source of generally applicable law in EU Member States, or bind, or impose any obligations upon, European entities. Consequently, data can be transferred to the US under FATCA only by EU Member State-based data controllers who have concluded bilateral agreements with the United States, regulating the transfer of data according to specific rules.[98] The United States has concluded such bilateral agreements with all EU Member States and many major non-EU economies, such as Australia, Brazil, Canada, China, Hong Kong, India, Japan, Mexico, New Zealand, Singapore, South Africa, South Korea, Turkey, and the United Arab Emirates.

In countries where bank secrecy, insurance secrecy or other similar professional secrecy arrangements or local privacy laws prevent any direct transfer of information by financial institutions to US tax authorities, alternative arrangements to implement

to the United States for the purposes of the Terrorist Finance Tracking Program, http://eur-lex.europa.eu/legal-content/EN/TXT/?uri=CELEX%3A52017SC0017 [retrieved on 21 February 2018].

95. 'On the basis of the information and explanations received from the Treasury, Europol, the Designated Provider and the independent overseers, verification of relevant documents and of a representative sample of the searches run on the TFTP provided data, the Commission is satisfied that the Agreement and its safeguards and controls are properly implemented and that the findings of the third joint review have been followed up by the Treasury.'
96. The Foreign Account Tax Compliance Act (FATCA), 26 USC §§ 1471-1474, 26 USC § 6038D.
97. Internal Revenue Service (IRS).
98. As at 14 February 2018, the US has concluded 113 bilateral agreements on FATCA; http://www.treasury.gov/resource-center/tax-policy/treaties/Pages/FATCA.aspx.

FATCA have been put in place. They provide for transferring information on accounts kept for US taxpayers by financial institutions in those countries to the competent national tax authorities in those countries, who then forward that information to the US tax authorities.

The Article 29 Working Party has ruled out the possibility of invoking FATCA as the legal basis of transferring data to the US, because FATCA is not a source of European law. It has also pointed out that FATCA is incompatible with the fundamental principles of personal data protection specified in EU law.[99] It has observed the incompatibility of FATCA with the principle of proportionality of data to the purposes of processing thereof. It has declared the practice of providing the US tax authorities with bulk reports containing personal and financial data of European financial institutions' customers solely according to the criteria of those persons' US citizenship or residence to constitute 'fishing expeditions', which are incompatible with this principle. In contrast, the Article 29 Working Party has recommended selective measures which would make sure that only selected data, adequate to the purposes pursued by FATCA, are provided. The Working Party has also called for an analysis of whether the purposes of FATCA indeed require bulk transfers of personal and financial data and whether those purposes would be attainable without (or with less) interference with the privacy of European financial institutions' customers, e.g. by transferring anonymised data.

The Article 29 Working Party has also pointed out that transferring data to the US must be made dependent upon the data importer being bound by principles ensuring an adequate level of protection of the transferred personal data. For this purpose, data subjects must be able to enforce their rights also subsequent to the transfer.

Consequently, the application of bilateral agreements concluded by EU Member States with the US, implementing FATCA, should take into account the reservations made by the Article 29 Working Party. One current example is the letter of the Chairwoman of the Article 29 Working Party of 8 February 2018, relating to the application of FATCA to EU citizens who are either 'accidental Americans' or dual EU/US nationals. The Chairwoman remarked that the decision whether such people were covered by FATCA was beyond the competence of the Article 29 Working Party as it related to the interpretation of the notion of an 'American taxpayer', but complaints in this respect could still be investigated by national data protection authorities, courts and tax authorities.[100]

99. Opinion of Article 29 Working Party to the European Commission (Taxation and Customs Union DG), Ref. Ares(2012)746461 – 21/06/2012, http://ec.europa.eu/justice/data-protection/article-29/documentation/other-document/files/2012/20120621_letter_to_taxud_fatca_en.pdf. The opinion of the Article 29 Working Party is also contained in the study: E.-M. Poptcheva, A FATCA for the EU? Data protection aspects of automatic exchange of bank information, Library of the European Parliament, 27 May 2013, http://www.europarl.europa.eu/RegData/bibliotheque/briefing/2013/130530/LDM_BRI(2013)130530_REV1_EN.pdf.

100. Letter of the Chair of the Article 29 Working Party, Isabelle Falque-Pierrotin, to FATCA, 8 February 2018, http://ec.europa.eu/newsroom/article29/document.cfm?doc_id=49770, p. 2 [retrieved on 21 February 2018].

§13.07 PASSENGER NAME RECORD (PNR) DATA

International exchange of data for prevention of terrorism and other serious crime also includes Passenger Name Record (PNR) data relating to airline passengers. PNR data are collected upon flight reservation and check-in, and include: the passenger's name, the date of flight, the route, information on the ticket, contact data, the identity of the travel agency which made the reservation, the payment method, the seat number, and information on the luggage. They also include information on the passenger's membership in a frequent flyer scheme, information on one-way flights, and requests for special services, e.g. special meals on board, typical of certain religions.

Organised crime, e.g. smuggling, or terrorism are often associated with overseas travel of the people involved. Thus, analysing and exchanging PNR data may assist law enforcement authorities in identifying persons not previously suspected of links with organised crime or terrorism and find out about behaviours which may be indicative of unlawful practices.

PNR data are exchanged by the EU with Australia, Canada and the US under agreements concluded with these countries:[101]

- Agreement of 29 September 2011 between the European Union and Australia on the processing and transfer of Passenger Name Record (PNR) data by air carriers to the Australian Customs and Border Protection Service.[102]
- Agreement of 3 October 2005 between the European Community and the Government of Canada on the processing of Advance Passenger Information and Passenger Name Record data[103] (Agreement of 20 November 2013 between Canada and the European Union on the transfer and processing of passenger Name Record Data – did not enter into force until the publication of this book).
- Agreement of 14 December 2011 between the United States of America and the European Union on the use and transfer of passenger name records to the United States Department of Homeland Security.[104]

It should be borne in mind that the European Commission found the personal data protection level under the law of Australia and Canada to be adequate, i.e. substantially equivalent to the European level. On the other hand, in the data protection context, the United States is recognised as a third country which does not ensure a level of data protection adequate to the EU standard. The agreement with the US declares that for the application thereof, the US Department of Homeland Security (DHS) ensures an adequate level of protection of PNR data transferred from the EU.

---

101. In June 2015 the EU Council adopted a decision authorising the opening of negotiations for a similar agreement with Mexico.
102. OJ EU L 186 of 14.7.2012, p. 4.
103. OJ EU L 82 of 21.3.2006, p. 15.
104. OJ EU L 215 of 11.8.2012, p. 5.

Legal basis for the exchange of PNR data is also provided by Directive (EU) 2016/681 of the European Parliament and of the Council of 27 April 2016 on the use of passenger name record (PNR) data for the prevention, detection, investigation and prosecution of terrorist offences and serious crime[105] (which Member States are required to implement by 25 May 2018).

The Directive responds to the need for monitoring of crime and terrorism risk so that the benefits of removing border controls on the EU internal borders under the Schengen Agreement are not offset by reduced security. As such, it formulates the rules for providing the Member States by air carriers with PNR data on passengers of international flights from and to the EU and selected intra-EU flights. It also regulates the processing of such data by competent authorities and the exchange of information between law enforcement bodies of Member States.

The Directive recognises the purpose limitation and data minimisation principles: it lists the purposes which justify the processing of PNR data by law enforcement bodies. The list includes assessment of lists of passengers prior to their arrival using pre-established risk criteria, formulating further risk symptoms, identification of specific persons on that basis and using the data for investigation and prosecution. The Directive also recognises the storage limitation principle by setting the data retention period at five years. After the initial six months the data must be anonymised. The Directive prohibits making decisions producing adverse legal effect or significantly affecting a person only through automated processing, based solely on algorithms without a human verification.

§13.08 THE CALIFORNIA CONSUMER PRIVACY ACT OF 2018

Importantly for trans-Atlantic cooperation, new legislative initiatives consistent with the GDPR are being taken in the United States

California passed the California Consumer Privacy Act of 2018, to become effective on January 1, 2020.[106]

Although the Act does not cover all businesses, it applies to those which meet the following criteria (practically analogous to those specified in the GDPR, as they imply that the core activities of a business consist of the large-scale processing of personal data):

- the annual gross revenue of the business is in excess of $25 million, or
- the business annually buys, receives for its commercial purposes, sells, or shares for commercial purposes, alone or in combination, the personal information of 50,000 or more consumers, households, or devices, or
- the business derives 50 per cent or more of its annual revenues from selling consumers' personal information.

105. OJ EU L 119, 4.5.2016, p. 132.
106. Assembly Bill No. 375, Chapter 55, approved by Governor June 28, 2018, https://leginfo.legislature.ca.gov/faces/billTextClient.xhtml?bill_id=201720180AB375.

The Act shares, among others, the following similarities with the GDPR:

- The definition of 'personal information': information that identifies, relates to, describes, is capable of being associated with, or could reasonably be linked, directly or indirectly, with a particular consumer or household, such as identifiers (a real name, alias, postal address, unique personal identifier, online identifier Internet Protocol address, email address, account name, social security number, driver's license number, passport number, or other), commercial information, including records of personal property, products or services purchased, obtained, or considered, or other purchasing or consuming histories or tendencies, and biometric information.
- The definition of 'deidentified' personal information: information that cannot reasonably identify, relate to, describe, be capable of being associated with, or be linked, directly or indirectly, to a particular consumer, provided that a business that uses deidentified information inter alia has implemented technical safeguards that prohibit reidentification of the consumer to whom the information may pertain, and makes no attempt to reidentify the information.
- The definition of 'pseudonymise' or 'pseudonymisation': the processing of personal information in a manner that renders the personal information no longer attributable to a specific consumer without the use of additional information, provided that the additional information is kept separately and is subject to technical and organisational measures to ensure that the personal information is not attributed to an identified or identifiable consumer).

One significant difference is that 'personal information' under the Act does not include publicly available information, which means 'information that is lawfully made available from federal, state, or local government records, if any conditions are associated with such information'.

Another similarity to the GDPR is the consumer's right to request deletion of any personal information about him/her. This, however, does not apply to all information but only information which the business has collected from the consumer.

A business that receives a verifiable request from a consumer to delete the consumer's personal information must delete the consumer's personal information from its records and direct any service providers to delete the consumer's personal information from their records. However, a business is not required to delete the consumer's personal information if maintaining it is necessary for the business or service provider in order to, inter alia:

- complete the transaction for which the personal information was collected, provide a good or service requested by the consumer, or reasonably anticipated within the context of a business's ongoing business relationship with the consumer, or otherwise perform a contract between the business and the consumer;
- detect security incidents, protect against malicious, deceptive, fraudulent, or illegal activity; or prosecute those responsible for that activity.

CHAPTER 14
Privacy in the Internet Age; Technology and Threats to Privacy

§14.01 TECHNOLOGY CHALLENGES TO PRIVACY PROTECTION

The global scale and evolution of information technologies have changed the data processing environment and brought new challenges. These result in particular from the widespread online processing of data, the ubiquity of devices with access to the Internet, common use of social networking services,[1] online shopping and online banking, the exponential growth of personal data processing,[2] mass transfers of data within multinational corporations, and the growing capacity of data processing hardware and software.

The Internet and mobile telephony, along with other technologies, are indirectly used by third parties to obtain (predominantly, though not exclusively, for commercial purposes) data on their users' location at specific times, their interpersonal relations, professional activities, interests, health, or wealth. New categories of data emerge, such as geolocation data, IP addresses, or profiles of Internet users as consumers.[3] The

1. Online social networking services (SNS); M. Czerniawski, 'Portale społecznościowe a prawo do ochrony danych osobowych – zarys problemu', in: *Internet. Prawno-informatyczne problemy sieci, portali i e-usług*, ed. G. Szpor, W. Wiewiórowski (Assistant European Data Protection Supervisor), Warszawa 2012, p. 163.
2. P.M. Schwartz, Managing Global Data Privacy: Cross-Border Information Flows in a Networked Environment (A report from thePrivacyProjects.org), 2009, http://theprivacyprojects.org/wp-content/uploads/2009/08/The-Privacy-Projects-Paul-Schwartz-Global-Data-Flows-20093.pdf.
3. These arguments in favour of a reform of data protection law were also voiced by the European Data Protection Supervisor in his opinion of 14 January 2011 on the Communication from the Commission to the European Parliament, the Council, the Economic and Social Committee and the Committee of the Regions – 'A comprehensive approach on personal data protection in the European Union', Section A, point 2, OJ EU C 181, 22.6.2011, p. 1; M.-T. Tinnefeld, 'Jak Internet zmienia prawne ramy prywatności?', in: *Internet. Prawno-informatyczne problemy sieci, portali i e-usług*, ed. G. Szpor, W. Wiewiórowski (Assistant European Data Protection Supervisor), Warszawa 2012, p. 3.

impact of new technologies is increasing. Some have existed before, such as the Internet of Things or facial recognition systems, but are increasingly important as they become common. All these developments mean that the threat to the right to privacy grows in proportion to the scale of data redundancy and retention.

These challenges have made it necessary to update the existing data protection regulations to take into account the new conditions of data processing, radically different from those prevalent at the time when Directive 95/46/EC entered into force. The 21 years which have elapsed since its adoption is a very long time in the area of digital technology. The right to privacy, consumer rights, and the digital services market all need new foundations in new, updated personal data protection law, adapted to the current situation.

In order to respond to these challenges and bridge the technological gap between the legally prescribed level of personal data protection and the actual level, the General Data Protection Regulation has been adopted, the most significant reform of the data protection regime since Directive 95/46/EC was enacted 21 years ago.

Admittedly, the effectiveness of legal norms is universally dependent on the implementation of measures enforcing them, irrespective of the regulated area (e.g. the enforcement of the principle 'thou shalt not steal' requires technical, procedural or penitentiary measures as well). However, in the context of the right to privacy, technical and organisational measures are crucial. This relationship has been noticed, for instance, in the context of stalking, i.e. persistent harassment which significantly infringes upon a person's privacy or causes the person to feel under threat; or impersonation of a person by using his or her image or other personal data with the intention to cause loss or harm to the person affected. Persistent harassment has always been possible, but its scale has grown in recent years, and this is when the word 'stalking' entered into common usage. This is undoubtedly due to the availability of technologies allowing a person to contact their victim anonymously via email or text messages and to spread information very widely by posting anonymous opinions on Internet forums or social networking services. If these tools were not available, a stalker's 'striking power' would be much smaller and detection of the offence would be easier.

The list of challenges for privacy protection, resulting from the technical conditions of online data processing and new categories of data, is open-ended, as these challenges inherently entail mutations of the existing forms and emergence of new ones. Below, I present a selection of such considerations. Analysing the effect they have on privacy protection suggests that privacy has become the price to be paid for solutions facilitating the lives of individuals and societies. The growing technological sophistication of tools used (irrespective of their declared purpose) for controlling individuals by states and companies, and the rapidly growing amounts of data being collected, are all making the data subjects' right to control the modalities and purposes of the processing of their data largely theoretical.[4]

4. A. Kozinski, 'The Dead Past', in: The Privacy Paradox. Privacy and Its Conflicting Values, Stanford Law Review, 2 February – 12 April 2012, http://www.stanfordlawreview.org/online/privacy-paradox/dead-past.

In this context, the collection of geolocation profiles and profiling of Internet users are particularly important issues. Given the widespread use of the Internet and the ubiquity of smartphones or tablets and applications developed for them, the extent of threats to personal data protection is massive, and the data subjects' control over the processing of their data has become very limited. When a person uses, or merely possesses, a mobile phone, his or her location and movements are constantly monitored, the number and duration of his or her calls are recorded, and the people he or she connects with are identified. Moreover, the numerous applications used on smartphones or tablets require access to the user's data, such as his or her location or data stored in the device, which generates further privacy risk.[5] A study conducted by 26 data protection authorities (the Global Privacy Enforcement Network) and involving more than 1,200 mobile applications showed that one-third of them require access authorisation to an excessive amount of personal data; at the same time, 85% of applications do not provide sufficient information on data processing, in particular on making data available.[6]

Other issues not to be overlooked include the processing of the user's geolocation data, his or her preferred books, films, discussion forums, queries on medical sites, leisure activities, political opinions, financial standing, etc.[7] For instance, Google uses the AdSense algorithm to generate advertisements targeted at the specific user based on his/her search history (such as advertisements of airlines or hotels displayed when the user has searched for information on a specific travel destination). A similar mechanism is used in marketing automation, whereby the activity of visitors to a website is monitored to immediately offer them services corresponding, according to an analysis by the data controller, to their expectations, based not only on their profile but even on the specific moment in time. The model used by companies such as the US-based Cardlytics is similar: card transactions are analysed in cooperation with banks and serve for the identification of potential customers or business counterparties seeking marketing services for their products (e.g. targeting advertisements of a fuel company or restaurant chain to the customers of competing brands in the respective sectors).[8]

5. Article 29 Working Party, Opinion 02/2013 on apps on smart devices, 27 February 2013, WP 202, http://ec.europa.eu/justice/article-29/documentation/opinion-recommendation/files/2013/wp202_en.pdf, and Opinion 13/2011 on Geolocation services on smart mobile devices, 16 May 2011, WP 185, http://ec.europa.eu/justice/policies/privacy/docs/wpdocs/2011/wp185_en.pdf.
6. Results of the 2014 Global Privacy Enforcement Network Sweep, Office of the Privacy Commissioner of Canada, https://www.priv.gc.ca/media/nr-c/2014/bg_140910_e.asp, 10.09.2014.
7. International Working Group on Data Protection in Telecommunications (a.k.a. the Berlin Group), Working Paper of 15-16 April 2013: Web Tracking and Privacy: Respect for context, transparency and control remains essential, https://www.coe.int/t/dghl/standardsetting/dataprotection/News/Web%20tacking.pdf. The Article 29 Working Party has mentioned these privacy threats and emphasised the significance and binding character of the fundamental rights of Internet users; it has also pointed to the need to ensure transparency and monitoring of online activity as well as privacy by design.
8. Opinion 2/2010 of the Article 29 Working Party on online behavioural advertising of 22 June 2010, WP 171, http://ec.europa.eu/justice/policies/privacy/docs/wpdocs/2010/wp171_en.pdf; Opinion 16/2011 of the Article 29 Working Party on EASA/IAB Best Practice Recommendation on Online Behavioural Advertising of 8 December 2011, WP 188, http://ec.europa.eu/justice/article-29/documentation/opinion-recommendation/files/2011/wp188_en.pdf. Also the

The importance of geolocation data ought not to be underestimated. The belief that consent to the collection of such data does not lead to the identification of specific persons is misleading. While the entity collecting such data does not directly recognise the persons the information relates to, it may identify such persons by linking their location information to other data. Information on several locations visited by an unidentified person at specified times, obtained through geolocation or based on that person's entries on online forums, coupled with information on that person's card payment, allows him/her to be identified (as few as four such pieces of information enabled the identification of 90% of persons in an anonymised database in a study by Yves-Alexandre de Montjoye's team at Massachusetts Institute of Technology).[9]

A tool used for monitoring the activities, preferences and behaviours of Internet users, mostly those visiting online portals and retailers, is 'cookies', used very commonly for targeting advertisements and offers based on the user's characteristics derived from the previously collected data on him or her. Cookies are files generated by the server of the website's owner and saved to the hard disk of the visitor's computer. They contain information on the user and his/her previous visits on the website.[10] Although they do not contain the user's identification data, a collection of numerous cookies allow the user to be profiled concerning his/her gender, age, interests, purchased items, and amounts spent on purchases.

Indeed, online data processing technologies and the scale of information involved mean that scattered data (or metadata) can easily be linked with other data on the Web. Hopes that the disclosure of, for instance, a telephone number only does not compromise anonymity as no other data are involved were dashed by an experiment conducted by Jonathan Mayer and Patrick Mutchler of Stanford University. Their aim was to verify whether it was possible to identify the names of the owners of phone numbers based solely on the information these individuals themselves disclosed on the Internet. The researchers found the task 'trivially easy': using Google Places, Facebook, Yelp and Intelius alone they were able find out the names of 91 phone owners, from a random sample of 100 phone numbers.[11]

Alarming figures on the use of cookies were revealed by the Information Commissioner's Office (ICO), the British data protection authority, in the report on international research it coordinated:[12]

European Parliament, in its resolution of 6 July 2011 on a comprehensive approach to personal data protection in the European Union (2011/2025(INI), P7_TA-PROV(2011)0323), expressed its concern over abuses of online behavioural advertising.

9. de Montjoye Y.-A., Radaelli L., Singh V. K., Pentland A. S., 'Unique in the shopping mall: On the reidentifiability of credit card metadata', Science, 30 January 2015, Vol. 347 no. 6221 pp. 536-539.
10. For a definition of cookies, see RFC (Request for Comments) 6265 published by the Internet Engineering Task Force (IETF), http://tools.ietf.org/html/rfc6265.
11. R.J. Rosen, 'Stanford Researchers: It Is Trivially Easy to Match Metadata to Real People', The Atlantic, 24 December 2013, http://www.theatlantic.com/technology/archive/2013/12/stanford-researchers-it-is-trivially-easy-to-match-metadata-to-real-people/282642/.
12. Information Commissioner's Office (ICO), A cookie can last 7,984 years, according to new international privacy study, 17.02.2015, https://ico.org.uk/about-the-ico/news-and-events/news-and-blogs/2015/02/a-cookie-can-last-7984-years-according-to-new-study/.

- An average website placed 34 cookies on the visitor's device during the first visit.
- 70% of these were third-party cookies placed by websites other than the one being visited.
- As much as 86% of the cookies were persistent cookies which remain on the visitor's device after the session ends; only 14% were session cookies, removed after the end of the visit.
- While the average expiration period of a cookie was set at one or two years, cookies were also detected which were set to expire after 10, 100 or even close to 8,000 years.[13]

Mozilla, the owner of Firefox, one of the dominant Web browsers on the market, introduced the option of disabling third-party cookies by default, as it found through its own analyses that by using the Internet for two days with average intensity, approx. 100 cookies from websites the user had not visited were saved to his/her device.

A similar example of an interference with privacy is the software developed by companies (e.g. Alphonso) which uses a smartphone's microphone to identify audio signals in TV shows, films and advertisements being watched by the user.[14] The software, installed in more than 250 games, is used to verify which advertisements have been effective in encouraging the user to visit specific shops in his/her neighbourhood (which is identifiable to the company thanks to geo-location data from the user's smartphone). The software supplier has emphasised that the microphone and location module are only used by the app if the user has given their informed consent. However, the informed nature of the consent is very dubious: the user can hardly be deemed to be fully aware that, by expressing consent for the use of the microphone and location module, he/she is agreeing to be constantly supervised solely for the financial benefit of the software supplier and its customers.

Another risk for privacy and the protection of personal data results from the widespread use of profiling. Profiling is automated processing which uses personal data to evaluate certain personal aspects relating to a natural person, in particular to analyse or predict aspects concerning that natural person's performance at work, economic situation, health, personal preferences, interests, reliability, behaviour, location or movements.

The risk of profiling and other automated decision-making for the privacy and data protection results from the fact that the findings based on an analysis of personal features significantly affect the person subject to such operations. The findings of profiling may lead to stigmatisation and discrimination and may influence positive or negative decisions in matters such as lending, insurance, or employment.[15]

13. C. Castellucia, Behavioral tracking on the Internet, a technical perspective. In European Data Protection: In Good Health? Springer Netherlands, 2012, p. 25.
14. S. Maheshwari, 28.12.2017, That Game on Your Phone May Be Tracking What You're Watching on TV, https://www.nytimes.com/2017/12/28/business/media/alphonso-app-tracking.html.
15. For a discussion on the stigmatisation and discrimination risk resulting from profiling, see: C.J. Bennett, 'In Defence of Privacy: The Concept and the Regime', Surveillance and Society 2011, no. 4, p. 490; F. Bosco, N. Creemers, V. Ferraris, D. Guagnin, B.-J. Koops, Profiling Technologies

Examples include automatic rejection of an electronic loan application through an automated creditworthiness assessment, or of an insurance application through an automated risk assessment, or of a job application in an electronic recruitment process, solely by using an algorithm with predefined criteria.

Sources of personal data used for such analyses and forecasts may include: locations where mobile phones, laptops and tablets log in to the networks, social networking services, online purchases, transactions, Internet users' queries on online forums, working time recording devices etc. Combining such traces in the IT systems with unique identifiers of natural persons, such as IP addresses, cookies, RFID tags and other information collected by servers allows specific persons to be identified and their profiles to be created (recital 30 of the preamble to the GDPR). Some of these data are often made public by the data subjects themselves, for example on social networking services. A more serious threat to privacy is that other data are left as 'traces' by customers or Internet users who are unaware (much less consenting) that their data might be used in the future for other purposes. This also includes data which relate to the persons subject to profiling but are not necessarily obtained from them.

Automated decision making and profiling often leads to conclusions which are statistically probable but erroneous in the specific case. They arise from creating profiles based on data which are unconfirmed, inaccurate, incomplete, or provided anonymously by third parties, and classifying persons on that basis with negative consequences for their interests, unbeknown to them and beyond their control. Projecting the characteristics and behaviours of a person on the basis of uncertain information, obtained from sources such as social networking services, processed through oversimplified algorithms defined by various institutions, may lead to discrimination and stigmatisation.

Drawing conclusions from data which are unconfirmed and taken out of context, and structuring these conclusions only on the assumption that they correspond to statistical behaviours and features, is statistically justified, but such conclusions might be completely untrue in relation to a specific person. Under this mechanism, if a given data subject has been found to have certain characteristics, e.g. to be a man aged between 35 and 50, living in a big city, working freelance etc., it is statistically justified to presume that he also has other features shared by most people with a similar profile.[16]

---

and Fundamental Rights and Values: Regulatory Challenges and Perspectives From European Data Protection Authorities, in: Reforming European Data Protection Law, (ed.) S. Gutwirth, R. Leenes, P. de Hert, Springer 2015, p. 11-12; A. Canhoto and J. Blackhouse, General Description of Behavioural Profiling, in Profiling European Citizens. Cross-Disciplinary Perspectives, ed. M. Hildebrandt and S. Gutwirth (Springer, Dordrecht 2008), p. 47-63. Threats resulting from profiling were signalled by the Article 29 Working Party in its press release of 28 May 2013 and the attached advice paper (http://ec.europa.eu/justice/data-protection/article-29/press-material/press-release/art29_press_material/2013/20130528_pr_profiling_en.pdf).

16. M. Hildebrandt, 'Defining Profiling: A New Type of Knowledge?', in: Profiling the European Citizen. Cross-Disciplinary Perspectives, ed. by M. Hildebrandt, S. Gutwirth, New York 2008, pp. 20 et seq.; D. Kreiss, 'Yes We Can (Profile You). A Brief Primer on Campaigns and Political Data', in: The Privacy Paradox. Privacy and Its Conflicting Values, Stanford Law Review, 2 February – 12 April 2012, http://www.stanfordlawreview.org/online/privacy-paradox/political-data.

Automated analysis may, for instance, result in an increased insurance premium based on information that the person in question regularly buys unhealthy foods or large-sized garments. It might also wrongly attribute an alcohol or gambling problem to a person who does not suffer from any such problems but deals with them professionally, e.g. as a therapist or journalist. Therefore a system should be put in place to limit the risk of wrong inferences and allow the data subject to correct the automatic conclusions.

One notorious case illustrating the significant effect profiling may have on individuals, and even on society at large, is Cambridge Analytica. Having obtained the data of 50 million users from Facebook, it created their profiles with these data, in clear conflict with the fundamental principles of personal data protection, unbeknown to the data subjects and in a way incompatible with the declared purpose. The profiles were created to maximise the impact of manipulated political marketing communications directed to the data subjects, largely based on false statements and fake news, designed to significantly bias the result of the 2017 US presidential election and the UK Brexit referendum.[17] Paradoxically, even Brian Acton, the co-founder of the WhatsApp messaging service now owned by Facebook, has advised users to delete their Facebook accounts as he thought that their continued use was unsafe.[18] Even more telling is the deletion of Tesla and SpaceX pages from Facebook by Elon Musk, which can hardly be seen as the departure of just a single user.[19]

Importantly, this is another case where the introduction of necessary regulation and control measures is being triggered by whistleblowing, similarly to when Edward Snowden revealed the constant massive surveillance of electronic communications by the US National Security Agency. The common feature of these situations is the grave breach of personal data protection principles and the right to privacy. However, the Cambridge Analytica scandal has additionally shed light on the inconsistency concerning the sanctions applicable for publishing intentionally misleading or defamatory information via online media, such as on Facebook, YouTube or Twitter, as opposed to traditional media (e.g. press). The scale of fake news being published by online media is enormous and their liability is illusory, despite them enjoying increased profitability thanks to the high click-through rate of scandalising information. This is even more baffling given that traditional media have also shifted a large proportion of their activity to the Internet and continue to do so.

Another risk for data protection results from cloud computing. This is a form of outsourcing of data processing,[20] including to such strong market players as Google,

17. Cambridge Analytica execs boast of role in getting Donald Trump elected, The Guardian, 21 March 2018, https://www.theguardian.com/uk-news/2018/mar/20/cambridge-analytica-execs-boast-of-role-in-getting-trump-elected.
18. Delete facebook, says Whatsapp founder Brian Acton as data scandal continues, https://www.independent.co.uk/life-style/gadgets-and-tech/news/facebook-delete-whatsapp-cambridge-analytica-brian-acton-jan-koum-a8266116.html.
19. http://money.cnn.com/2018/03/23/technology/elon-musk-facebook/index.html.
20. X. Konarski, 'Przetwarzanie danych osobowych w chmurze obliczeniowej', Monitor Prawniczy 2013, no. 8 – special appendix 'Aktualne problemy prawnej ochrony danych osobowych 2013', pp. 39 et seq., confirming that cloud users are data controllers and the cloud providers are data processors. G. Szpor, 'Prawne aspekty dostępności chmur', in: *Internet. Cloud computing.*

Microsoft, or Amazon. Models of cloud services include: IaaS (infrastructure as a service, i.e. renting IT infrastructure, such as virtual servers or disk space, from the cloud provider), PaaS (platform as a service, whereby a provider provides an environment for creating, testing and managing applications), and SaaS (software as a service, the most comprehensive solution including providing applications as well as the infrastructure for its hosting and maintenance, including updates).

The US National Institute of Standards and Technology (NIST) defined cloud computing as 'a model for enabling ubiquitous, convenient, on-demand network access to a shared pool of configurable computing resources (e.g., networks, servers, storage, applications, and services) that can be rapidly provisioned and released with minimal management effort or service provider interaction'.[21] Other than trade secret classified data introduced by businesses, data of individuals, including sensitive data, in the form of, for example, emails or photographs, are also processed in the cloud on a mass scale.

Threats associated with this form of data processing were pointed out by the Article 29 Working Party in its Opinion 05/2012 of 1 July 2012 on Cloud Computing.[22] The identified risk factors were classified into two categories: lack of control of data committed to the cloud and lack of transparency of processing (lack of knowledge on the processors and the processing locations). Despite the importance of the data being processed, the data subjects have no insight to, or influence on, whether the safeguards are adequate or whether their data are made available under the contracts concluded by the provider or the legal regulations binding upon it. An example of the risk is where cloud solutions, including email services such as Gmail, are used by persons bound by professional secrecy obligations, such as law practitioners.

Similar conclusions were published by the International Working Group on Data Protection in Telecommunications, known as the Berlin Group, in its Working Paper of 24 April 2012 on Cloud Computing – Privacy and data protection issues (the 'Sopot Memorandum').[23] The risk factors listed therein included the inability to monitor the service provider or the processing of data in the cloud.

In its opinion 05/2012 of 1 July 2012, the Article 29 Working Party emphasised that the cloud client, as the person who determines the purpose of the processing and decides on the outsourcing that the cloud processing service consists in, is the data controller, while the cloud provider is the processor (however, the cloud provider might also become the data controller if it processes personal data on a separate legal basis and for the purposes it has defined itself). The Article 29 Working Party has pointed out that, while in the business practice cloud clients have very limited actual possibilities of influencing the modalities of cloud computing services, since cloud providers with a strong market position act under model contracts and technical

---

Przetwarzanie w chmurach, ed. G. Szpor, Warszawa 2013, p. 233; C. Osterwalder, 'Cloud computing. Przetwarzanie na dużą skalę i bezpieczeństwo danych', in: *Internet. Cloud computing. Przetwarzanie w chmurach*, ed. G. Szpor, Warszawa 2013, p. 13.

21. Special Publication 800-145, The NIST Definition of Cloud Computing, 2011, p. 3.
22. WP 196, http://ec.europa.eu/justice/article-29/documentation/opinion-recommendation/files/2012/wp196_en.pdf.
23. http://datenschutz-berlin.de/attachments/873/Sopot_Memorandum_Cloud_Computing.pdf.

standards, it is still the client who decides on the outsourcing of part or the totality of the processing and consequently has the status of data controller.

Thus, the scopes of the client's and the provider's responsibilities result from their respective roles.[24] The client's basic responsibility as the data controller is to analyse the risk and to choose the cloud provider that guarantees compliance with personal data protection legislation, which includes in particular technical and organisational safety measures, adequate protection of data processed outside the EEA, independent and reliable third-party audits, and service certification.

Another threat to the right to privacy is posed by the collection and further processing of data through CCTV cameras, which have become ubiquitous in public places and on private premises. There are an estimated 50 million CCTV cameras currently operating worldwide. The scale of the monitoring is illustrated by the fact that in the UK, on average cameras in public places record each person 300 times per day.[25]

The operation of closed-circuit television should be regulated by law. Demands should be made for such a law to specify locations where no cameras may be installed to prevent an unacceptable intrusion upon privacy and intimacy; and to require that recordings are stored only for as long as is necessary.

Privacy is also being threatened because of the growing popularity of drones. The Article 29 Working Party[26] pointed to this risk, resulting in particular from the possibility of making, storing and distributing video recordings of people in private locations without their knowledge. The Working Party emphasised that, irrespective of the lack of detailed regulations relating to drones, they should be covered by the general personal data processing regulations. It also pointed to the similarities to CCTV.

The possibility of collecting, in public places, information on people's behaviours and personal characteristics and analysing such information using automated means is limited only by the availability and cost of the technology. One illustration is INDECT, i.e. the 'Intelligent information system supporting observation, searching and detection for security of citizens in an urban environment', developed by AGH University of Science and Technology in Kraków, Poland, in cooperation with other centres, and AISight, developed by the US-based company BRS Labs. INDECT allows surveillance of public places (such as streets, public transport, or shopping centres) by cameras as well as detectors of motion, sound, temperature, or selected chemicals. The connected IT system analyses the data based on predefined algorithms; for instance, it signals specific movement patterns and speeds which might constitute potential acts of violence, or singles out specific words. AISight, which has been put in place in many airports and railway stations, detects suspicious or unconventional behaviours or

24. Opinion 1/2010 of the Article 29 Working Party on the concepts of 'controller' and 'processor' of 16 February 2010, WP 169, http://ec.europa.eu/justice/policies/privacy/docs/wpdocs/2010/wp169_en.pdf.
25. C. Behrens, 'Big Brother – Now with Added Intelligence', Süddeutsche Zeitung, 12 March 2013, http://www.worldcrunch.com/rss/tech-science/big-brother-now-with-added-intelligence/person-of-interest-cctv-pattern-recognition-aisight/c4s11156/.
26. Opinion 1/2015 on Privacy and Data Protection Issues relating to the Utilisation of Drones (WP 231) adopted on 16 June 2015, http://ec.europa.eu/justice/article-29/documentation/opinion-recommendation/files/2015/wp231_en.pdf.

occurrences, such as left luggage or a person jumping out of a car or over a fence. Such functionalities, which are in principle useful for protecting public security, might, however, also be used in a way which is contrary to, or incompatible with, their declared purpose, and lead to excessive surveillance.

The risk that privacy principles might lose their safeguarding power is further confirmed by existing systems which are not yet in common use. Examples include in particular: the Internet of Things (IoT, or Object Naming Service, ONS),[27] linking devices and appliances into a network enabling them to communicate (such as a refrigerator being connected with the supplying shop, the car and the motorway);[28] the RFID (radio-frequency identification) labels technology transmitting data over the radio to identify the labelled product (the technology is designed to manage stocks in shops but also allows the tracking of purchases made by identified customers);[29] the NFC (Near Field Communication) technology allowing wireless data exchange, used in contactless payment devices (the scale of its use is growing dynamically, as evidenced by Poland, the fastest growing market of contactless payments, where nearly 15 million contactless cards have been issued in three years);[30] or facial recognition systems allowing an automated identification of persons who have found themselves in an area covered by CCTV or whose photographs are stored in a database.[31]

One well-publicised example of new technologies is Google Glass, a computer device in the form of a pair of eyeglasses with a camera, microphone, GPS module and Internet access. European personal data protection supervisors were concerned with

27. The Article 29 Data Protection Working Party, Opinion 8/2014 on the on Recent Developments on the Internet of Things, No. WP 223 of 16 September 2014, http://ec.europa.eu/justice/article-29/documentation/opinion-recommendation/files/2014/wp223_en.pdf.
28. In selected US locations, the Safeway and Giant Eagle retail chains use sensors located on the shelves, which connect to the smartphones of passing customers. They display advertisements and offers but also analyse the customer's behaviour, his/her interest in a product, and the time the customer has spent near a shelf looking at a particular product; thus, the client is profiled.
29. The European Parliament, in its resolution of 6 July 2011 on a comprehensive approach on personal data protection in the European Union (2011/2025(INI), P7_TA-PROV(2011)0323), welcomed the agreement signed on 11 April 2011 between the European Commission, industry representatives, ENISA (the European Agency for Network and Information Security) and European data and privacy protection organisations, relating to protection of data in the context of the use of RFID, which seeks to resolve problems resulting from the use of RFID labels before they enter into mass use. M. Czerniawski, 'Prawne aspekty identyfikacji z użyciem fal radiowych (RFID)', *Kwartalnik Prawa Publicznego* 2010, no. 3, p. 95. The European Commission announced a technical standard for Radio Frequency Identification to comply with the requirements under the Data Protection Directive (95/46/EC) and the European Commission's 2009 Recommendation on RFID: 'Information technology – Notification of RFID – The information sign and additional information to be provided by operators of RFID application systems', The European Committee for Standardization, 16.07.2014, http://standards.cen.eu/dyn/www/f?p=204:110:0::::FSP_PROJECT,FSP_ORG_ID:38350,6206&cs=1BAE0547EB314F2AF0D24EF8AADCD6A0E.
30. See http://www.firstdata.pl/100196.xml, situation as of May 2013.
31. For a comprehensive presentation of technologies which have threats to privacy as a side effect, see: R. Vamosi, When Gadgets Betray Us: The Dark Side of Our Infatuation with New Technologies, New York 2011. Also see Opinion 02/2012 of the Article 29 Working Party on facial recognition in online and mobile services of 22 March 2012, WP 192, http://ec.europa.eu/justice/article-29/documentation/opinion-recommendation/files/2012/wp192_en.pdf.

Google's announcements and addressed Google with questions[32] on threats for privacy which may possibly arise from Google Glass's functionalities, its capability of recording and identifying random people without their knowing, and of disseminating the information thus recorded. Furthermore, certain restaurants, concerned with privacy infringements, have banned the use of Google Glass on their premises. Noticeably, however, such threats are associated with the use of smartphones as well.

The right to privacy may also be compromised by smart power grids and smart metering systems designed to increase energy efficiency and reduce energy consumption costs.[33] Although such systems have clear advantages in terms of their functionality, we should not overlook the fact that they collect personal data, e.g. the information on their users' daily schedule – when they are at home and when they use specific electric appliances.[34] Implementation of such solutions does therefore require that privacy safeguards be put in place.[35]

Even today, the Internet, mobile telephony and other technologies mentioned above constantly supervise the movements of their users, their family and social ties, their hobbies and professional activities, their health and wealth status; and the scope of this surveillance grows by the day to cover new areas. Call registers, thematic and trade websites, public transport timetables and booking systems, and social networking services are all an inexhaustible source of such information. Technologies of the future, such as the Internet of Things, are bound to make this supervision still far more

32. Letter of 18 June 2013, signed by the Article 29 Working Party and privacy or data protection commissioners of Australia, Canada (including the provinces of Alberta, British Columbia and Quebec), Israel, Mexico, New Zealand and Switzerland.
33. The implementation of such instruments is required under Directive 2006/32/EC of the European Parliament and of the Council of 5 April 2006 on energy end-use efficiency and energy services (OJ EU L 114, 27.4.2006, p. 64) and Directive 2009/72/EC of the European Parliament and of the Council of 13 July 2009 concerning common rules for the internal market in electricity (OJ EU L 211, 14.8.2009, p. 55).
34. For a discussion on the risk of profiling people based on data from smart metering devices, see: C. Cuijpers, B.-J. Koops, Smart Metering and Privacy in Europe: Lessons from the Dutch Case, in European Data Protection: Coming of Age, ed. S. Gutwirth, R. Leenes, P. de Hert, Y. Poullet, Springer Dordrecht 2013, pp. 269 et seq.; W.R. Wiewiórowski (Assistant European Data Protection Supervisor), 'Prawo do prywatności w systemie inteligentnych sieci', Monitor Prawniczy 2013, no. 8 – special appendix 'Aktualne problemy prawnej ochrony danych osobowych 2013', pp. 22 et seq. This risk is illustrated on page 31 with a humorous slogan used in an anti-smart-metering social campaign: 'My brother spends longer in the shower so the auditors think he has a girlfriend!'. Also see: R. Brownsword, M. Goodwin, Law and Technologies of Twenty-First Century. Text and Materials, Cambridge 2012, pp. 223, 224; R. Knyrim, G. Trieb, 'Smart metering under EU data protection law', International Data Privacy Law 2011, Vol. 1, No. 2, p. 121–128; letter of request from the Polish Inspector General for Personal Data Protection (GIODO) to the Minister for Economy of 24 August 2011, http://www.giodo.gov.pl/plik/id_p/2484/j/pl/ (in Polish); Opinion of Article 29 Working Party No. 12/2011 of 4 April 2011 on smart metering, WP 183, http://ec.europa.eu/justice/policies/privacy/docs/wpdocs/2011/wp183_en.pdf.
35. The Article 29 Working Party presented its recommended data protection impact assessment templates for smart grid and smart metering systems in its opinions no. 7/2013 of 4 December 2013, WP 209, http://ec.europa.eu/justice/article-29/documentation/opinion-recommendation/files/2013/wp209_en.pdf, and no. 4/2013 of 22 April 2013, WP 205, http://ec.europa.eu/justice/article-29/documentation/opinion-recommendation/files/2013/wp205_en.pdf.

intense and comprehensive. Some tools already available for implementation, designed to measure electronically the body temperature, heart rate, blood pressure, or to monitor the facial expressions or atypical frequency of eye squinting, can easily find new uses. Where such monitoring is to be used on car or train drivers or airline pilots to limit the risk of a crash due to the person falling asleep or having a health problem, it is most likely – rightly – to find public approval. However, those technologies may slowly and imperceptibly make their way into other areas of life. For instance, employers may use them for automated monitoring of their employees' activities or their behaviour towards customers, which is bound to provide them with the employees' private information as well.

A fascinating vision of a future world overwhelmed with ubiquitous IT surveillance of each individual's life is offered by Kazimierz Krzysztofek: 'The generation being born today will come of age in a reality where smart grids and networks will have covered the planet like live skin. Sensors placed everywhere will transmit all information directly to the network, which will be a self-monitoring global organism, much like nerves sending information directly to the brain'.[36]

Constant surveillance of the movements of people as Internet and mobile phone users only (which is but a small portion of the surveillance they are subject to) is reminiscent of the electronic bracelet used for the surveillance of convicts serving time outside of prison.

The scope of data already being processed in the systems described above is enormous and still systematically and rapidly growing. This only confirms David Lyon's assertion that what he calls a surveillance society has emerged.[37] He defines this as a society where individuals are subject to surveillance involving the access of public authorities and private sector entities to their personal data, including sensitive data, as well as analysis of their actions and behaviours through highly efficient IT systems and databases.[38] Importantly, this efficiency of IT systems is crucial for the scale of the

36. K. Krzysztofek, 'Big Data Society. Technologie samozapisu i samopokazu: ku humanistyce cyfrowej', Kultura i Historia, 3 March 2012, UMCS, Lublin, http://www.kulturaihistoria.umcs.lublin.pl/archives/3626.
37. The term 'surveillance society' was first coined by Gary T. Marx in 'The Surveillance Society: the threat of 1984-style techniques', The Futurist, June 1985, p. 21.
38. D. Lyon, A Report on the Surveillance Society for the Information Commissioners Office by the Surveillance Studies Network: Full Report, September 2006, http://www.ico.gov.uk/upload/documents/library/data_protection/practical_application/surveillance_society_full_report_2006.pdf. Surveillance society is also portrayed e.g. by Emrys Westacott, 'Does Surveillance Make Us Morally Better?', Philosophy Now, November–December 2010, http://www.philosophynow.org/issue79/Does_Surveillance_Make_Us_Morally_Better. Growing surveillance of individuals is analysed in its various aspects by C.J. Bennett, 'Cookies, web bugs, webcams and cue cats: Patterns of Surveillance on the world wide web', Ethics and Information Technology 2001, Vol. 3, No. 3, pp. 195 et seq. See also: C.J. Bennett, D. Lyon, Playing the Identity Card: Surveillance, Security and Identification in Global Perspective, London 2008, and C.J. Bennett, 'Storming the Barricades so we can all be Private Together: Everyday Surveillance and the Politics of Privacy Advocacy', Leviathan 2010, Vol. 25, p. 299. N.M. Richards, 'The Dangers of Surveillance', Harvard Law Review, 25 March 2013, http://papers.ssrn.com/sol3/papers.cfm?abstract_id=2239412, formulates principles he finds necessary to be complied with in the future evolution of laws regulating states' surveillance of their citizens to ensure a balance of costs and benefits of surveillance.

permanent intrusion of public authorities and private businesses upon the privacy of individuals. Examples include the development of Big Data[39] and Business Intelligence systems involving tools for creating customers' profiles in KYC (Know Your Customer) databases and projecting their future behaviours. Some of these tools are CRM (Customer Relation Management) or CEM (Customer Experience Management), an instrument to analyse the customers' experience and emotions while using certain products or services, or CIM (Customer Involvement Management), a tool to involve customers in the process of designing products.[40]

Furthermore, the analysis of digital traces left by Internet users allows models of their future behaviours and preferences to be made, using the Social Network Analysis method, developed, among others, by Albert-László Barabási.[41]

The Web retailer Amazon has patented a system, to be deployed in the future, analysing the customer's purchases to date, their search history, or even the movements of their mouse pointers on the website, in order to predict, with high probability, the products they are about to purchase. The products are then to be sent to a warehouse near where the customer lives to make sure they can be delivered to the customer almost immediately after the order is placed. Convenient though this may seem in many cases, it is surely disconcerting to realise that analysts and traders often know better than you do what you would like or what you are likely to do soon.

The assertion that privacy regulations need to be supplemented with necessary technical means is confirmed by the fact that privacy infringements on the Internet are effectively prevented by solutions or settings in applications. They make it possible, for example, to: encrypt email messages in Google (SSL) or send them anonymously (e.g. Send-Email, Anone-Mail); browse the Web anonymously using Google Chrome, Firefox and some other browsers; select content to be visible for others on a person's Facebook profile (Privacyfix.com); block the possibility of tracking Facebook accounts by ad providers (Abine, DisconnectMe or Ghostery); disable Google-generated advertisements attributed by AdSense to a specific user based on his/her Web activity to date (Google Ads Preferences Manager); or analyse cookies by the user on whose computer they are installed (Lightbeam, an application provided by Mozilla, in its web browser Firefox).

39. Big Data is described, and its benefits and threats are discussed, e.g. in: V. Mayer-Schönberger, K. Cukier, Big Data: A Revolution That Will Transform How We Live, Work, and Think, New York 2013; E. Siegel, Predictive Analytics: The Power to Predict Who Will Click, Buy, Lie, or Die, New Jersey 2013, O. Tene, J. Polonetsky, 'Privacy in the Age of Big Data. A Time for Big Decisions', in: The Privacy Paradox. Privacy and Its Conflicting Values, Stanford Law Review, 2 February – 12 April 2012, http://www.stanfordlawreview.org/online/privacy-paradox/big-data; T. Craig, M.E. Ludloff, Privacy and Big Data, Sebastopol, CA 2011.
40. For a broader description of Business Intelligence tools, see: K. Krzysztofek, 'Świat w wersji hiper: Od hipermedium do hiperspołeczeństwa', in: *Kulturowe kody technologii cyfrowych*, P. Celiński (ed.), Lublin 2011, and K. Krzysztofek, 'The @lgorithmic Society: Digitarians of the World Unite', in: P.T. Kidd (ed.) European Visions for the Knowledge Age. A Quest for New Horizons in the Information Society, Cheshire Henbury, UK 2006, p. 89.
41. A.-L. Barabási, *Bursts: The Hidden Pattern Behind Everything We Do, From Your Email to Bloody Crusades*, New York 2010.

As found in a Eurobarometer survey published by the European Commission on 16 June 2011,[42] 42% of Internet users in the EU use the available tools to limit the number of electronic messages and 23% modify security settings in their web browsers. This demonstrates that the actual protection of personal data processed on the Internet depends on the availability and ease of use of protection instruments by an average user.

§14.02 INTRUSION UPON PRIVACY AS THE PRICE TO BE PAID FOR SECURITY AND AVAILABILITY OF SERVICES

Intrusion on privacy by collecting data which allow a detailed profile of a person's characteristics to be developed seems a price to be paid for the associated benefits.[43] This motivates some people to give up a significant amount of their privacy. Thanks to profiling customers, the service providers may offer tailored services to them. Collection of geolocation data by mobile phone operators and profiling of Internet users serves the purpose of offering them services or functionalities such as displaying service providers in their vicinity or sending them prompts on preferential offers based on their purchase history (service-oriented architecture, or SOA). These data may even be used in an emergency for rescue services or the police to locate the user (as illustrated by the European Union's requirement for the EU Member States to introduce the obligation for new cars sold in the EU to be equipped with the eCall system sending an emergency call automatically in case of an accident). Cloud data processing gives the cloud provider access to trade secrets and sensitive data in text files, email messages or photos, but allows users to use applications or server space without purchasing them. The omnipresence of CCTV cameras in public places increases security, or at least the sense of security. A customer allowing retailers to access information on his/her purchases or card transactions may, in exchange, collect points in loyalty schemes and obtain discounts.

Companies using their customers' or prospective customers' personal data often justify it with the benefits that those customers may obtain by surrendering some of their privacy. Crucially though, such a renouncement of privacy should only result from the exclusive decision of the data subject, as he or she (rather than the service provider) is the sole person authorised to make the choice between his/her privacy and the benefits involved in the services.

Thus, any interference with a person's privacy should require the person's consent, enabling that person to object, and providing them with prior information

42. See http://europa.eu/rapid/press-release_IP-11-742_en.htm.
43. G. Valkenburg, Privacy Versus Security: Problems and Possibilities for the Trade-Off Model, pp. 252 et seq.; M. Leese, Privacy and Security – On the Evolution of a European Conflict, pp. 271 et seq., in: Reforming European Data Protection Law, (ed.) S. Gutwirth, R. Leenes, P. de Hert, Springer 2015.

necessary to make an informed decision.[44] One example is the use of cookies, as discussed earlier.

Providers might even collect personal data with adverse effect to the data subject's privacy but without any compensation in the form of an offer of useful services. As an example, a customer might be offered a higher price than he/she could obtain in other circumstances, as the supplier may adjust the price to the customer's financial standing as estimated from amounts paid by the customer in the past. In this way, the customer is not obtaining useful services in exchange for renouncing his/her personal data. On the contrary, his/her privacy is compromised solely for the profit of the service provider. Therefore, the use of such methods unbeknown to the users affected must be considered a breach of privacy.

The judgment must be different where a user accepts the intrusion upon his/her privacy because this is necessary for the provision of services to him/her. However, it would be overoptimistic to assume that anyone using email or social networking services is fully aware of the loss of privacy it entails and accepts it. Few users envisage such scarcely predictable purposes of the processing of their data as scanning and generation of personal profiles. An example of such unacceptable intrusion on privacy beyond what is justified by the nature of a service is when web search results include information which the user has not searched for but which correspond to his/her holiday plans mentioned in his/her emails or on a social networking service (such as offers of flights to, or hotels in, a destination which the user has, to his/her knowledge, only revealed to a closed circle of his family or friends).

As found by Stanford University researchers, only 9% of advertisements displayed on the 500 most popular websites featured information that the user was being tracked online.[45] The findings of a Eurobarometer survey published by the European Commission on 16 June 2011[46] show that, although 58% of Internet users read the privacy information on the web, some of them find it incomprehensible.

I pointed out above that the renouncement of a significant amount of one's privacy, or the acceptance of the risk of its infringement, e.g. by the collection of geolocation data or data relating to the characteristics of mobile phone or Internet users, may be seen as the price to be paid for the individual or collective benefits resulting from the processing of such data. A particularly important and controversial example of such benefits is public security.

A much publicised dispute was occasioned by the USA PATRIOT Act of 26 October 2001 – a US law enacted as a response to the 11 September 2001 terrorist attacks in New York City and Washington, DC.[47] Among other measures, not relevant to the subject matter of this book, the Patriot Act allowed mass collection of electronic communications data, not only of people suspected of posing a threat for national

44. M.J. Culnan, R.J. Bies, 'Managing Privacy Concerns Strategically: The Implications of Fair Information Practices in Marketing in the Twenty-First Century', in: Visions of Privacy: Policy Choices for the Digital Age, ed. by C.J. Bennett, R. Grant, Toronto 1999, pp. 149 et seq.
45. Gazeta Wyborcza, 19 August 2011.
46. http://europa.eu/rapid/press-release_IP-11-742_en.htm.
47. 'Uniting and Strengthening America by Providing Appropriate Tools Required to Intercept and Obstruct Terrorism Act of 2001', Public Law 107-56, 26 October 2001.

security. Arguments put forward at the opposite ends of the spectrum of the dispute included, on the one side, the constitutional rights and freedoms, which justified protests against excessive interference with those values;[48] on the other side, the necessity, made evident by terrorist attacks, of resorting to measures which, while interfering with civic rights and freedoms, were seen as effective in preventing future attacks. According to this point of view, the fundamental human freedoms include freedom from fear of a terrorist attack.

The applicability period of Section 215 of the Patriot Act has not been extended by US Congress. Thus, the legal basis for mass collection of electronic communications data, including on telephone conversations, expired on 1 June 2015. The scale of support in Congress for the abandonment of this controversial measure is worthy of notice: in the House of Representatives, as many as 338 voted in favour, with 88 votes against; in the Senate, the votes were 67 to 32.

The mass collection of all data on telecommunication connections was replaced with a measure respecting the right to privacy and the proportionality principle: data on the connections are stored in the telecom operators' databases, and the US National Security Agency may only access the data of specific persons who are under suspicion (the USA Freedom Act of 2 June 2015).

A similar debate was triggered by the terrorist attack on the Norwegian island of Utøya and in Oslo. In the discussion, the right to privacy was juxtaposed with public security, which, in the context of acts of terror featuring explosives, could be enhanced by the state services monitoring, for example, websites for explosives enthusiasts, online purchases of books or films on subjects of interest for extremist groups, card payments, or movements of people.

This debate has returned to the public forum both in Europe and in other continents as a result of the internal terrorist threat, much more difficult to control and prevent: numerous attacks or attempted attacks have been perpetrated by Islamic fanatics, many of whom are second- or even third-generation EU Member State nationals.

David Lyon expressed his view that privacy and security are not in contradiction, declaring that civic rights and freedoms must not be curtailed, regardless of the circumstances; and that practical experience of surveying the symptoms of potential public security threats by state services have brought no evidence that surveillance of citizens' privacy makes terrorism prevention more efficient.[49] Criminals may indeed conceal their actions successfully, e.g. by using applications or devices ensuring their anonymity online, or using a number of prepaid mobile phones. Solutions such as the requirement to register prepaid telephone cards, introduced in France, Germany, Italy, Poland, and Spain, have proven ineffective. Sweden, the UK, Mexico and South Korea, having analysed the effectiveness of this measure, have all decided against introducing

48. Report by the American Civil Liberties Union, Reclaiming Patriotism: A Call to Reconsider the Patriot Act, March 2009, New York, http://www.aclu.org/pdfs/safefree/patriot_report_20090310.pdf.
49. Interview by A. Leszczyński with D. Lyon, 'Statystycznie podobny do Breivika', Gazeta Wyborcza, 30–31 July 2011, http://wyborcza.pl/1,98077,10030938,Statystycznie_podobny_do_Breivika.html.

it. It proved to be no hindrance to criminals, who purchased cards registered in other persons' names, stole other people's identities, or used foreign numbers. Doubts as to the effectiveness of registering prepaid cards as a crime control measure were voiced by European Commissioner Cecilia Malmström.[50]

However, Lyon's conclusions may be challenged by intelligence and security agencies, which, as their representatives have asserted in the media, have at times been successful in identifying perpetrators of acts of terror and other crimes and in neutralising terrorist and criminal groups, thus preventing planned acts of terror, by analysing the available data.[51]

This claim, however, was challenged in the course of the work of a US Congress committee on the possible extension of the applicability period of Section 215 of the Patriot Act in 2015 (which allowed unrestricted surveillance on electronic communications and was eventually repealed). The committee found mass collection of telecommunications data to be an ineffective anti-terrorism instrument and an excessive intrusion upon privacy, in addition to being disproportionately expensive in relation to its effects. The committee failed to find any case of preventing an act of terror thanks to this measure. The only detected case was that of a San Diego taxi driver and his accomplices sending USD 8,500 to the Somali terrorist group Al-Shabaab.[52]

The assertion by Benjamin Franklin, one of the Founding Fathers of the United States, that society renouncing essential liberty to purchase temporary safety deserves neither,[53] is perhaps overly idealistic in the context of terrorist threat. It is, however, crucial to define the permissible and non-extendible limits of intrusion upon privacy justified by the necessity to guarantee public security, and thus to strike a reasonable balance between the two values.[54]

Such a reasonable balance is hardly to be found in the practice, revealed progressively since June 2013,[55] of constant surveillance of telephone calls, email messages (in Google and Yahoo!), Facebook messages, Skype conversations and bank

50. http://www.europarl.europa.eu/sides/getAllAnswers.do?reference=P-2012-006014&language=EN.
51. The Government of the United Kingdom, in its report Securing Britain in an Age of Uncertainty: The Strategic Defence and Security Review, informed that telecommunications data have been used in all significant antiterrorist operations and 95% of important investigations against organised crime; 21 October 2010, https://www.gov.uk/government/uploads/system/uploads/attachment_data/file/62482/strategic-defence-security-review.pdf.
52. M. Schwartz, 'The Whole Haystack', The New Yorker, 26 January 2015, http://www.newyorker.com/magazine/2015/01/26/whole-haystack.
53. 'Those who would give up essential Liberty, to purchase a little temporary Safety, deserve neither Liberty nor Safety'.
54. In the judgment of Polish Constitutional Tribunal of 3 October 2000 (K 33/99, OTK 2000, No. 6, item 188), this balance was defined as 'the use of measures which are necessary (essential) in that they will protect the values in question in the manner, or to the extent, which would not be achievable with the use of other measures; the burden of such measures for the individuals or entities whose rights or freedoms are curtailed should be as little as possible'.
55. The practice was revealed to the media by Edward Snowden, a former employee of the US intelligence agencies CIA and NSA. See, e.g.: G. Greenwald & E. MacAskill, 'NSA Prism program taps in to user data of Apple, Google and others', The Guardian, 7 June 2013, http://www.theguardian.com/world/2013/jun/06/us-tech-giants-nsa-data; E. MacAskill, 'Edward Snowden: how the spy story of the age leaked out', The Guardian, 12 June 2013, http://www.theguardian.com/world/2013/jun/11/edward-snowden-nsa-whistleblower-profile/print.

transfers as part of the US Government's PRISM scheme, implemented in 2007 by President George W. Bush's administration and continued and expanded by President Barack Obama's administration. The European Parliament declared that there exists evidence[56] of 'the existence of far-reaching, complex and highly technologically advanced systems designed by US and some Member States' intelligence services to collect, store and analyse communication data, including content data, location data and metadata of all citizens around the world, on an unprecedented scale and in an indiscriminate and non-suspicion-based manner'. It pointed, among others, to the mass surveillance of EU citizens under the PRISM programme, the analysis of content and metadata under the Xkeyscore system, decryption (BULLRUN, Edgehill), access to telecommunications networks and geolocation data in the Tempora programme.

Such actions, justified though they are for fighting terrorism provided that they target people selected under certain specific criteria, are inadequate where applied to everyone, whether targeted justifiably or not.

The Article 29 Working Party considered that 'the availability of strong and trusted encryption is a necessity in the modern digital world. Encryption must remain standardised, strong and efficient, which would no longer be the case if providers were compelled to include backdoors or provide master keys. Law enforcement agencies already have access to vast quantities of data via their existing powers. They should focus on improving their capabilities to interpret those data to investigate and prosecute criminals.'[57]

On 14 June 2014, the State Council of China announced the implementation of a Social Credit System. Under this scheme, the government will be legally authorised to access users' data collected on a mass scale by private providers. The wide range of sources, covering hundreds of millions of users, is to include Web search engines, social networking services, online retailers and transaction services, applications for monitoring users' health and physical activity, payments for purchases of goods and services etc. The data obtained by monitoring each user's purchases, travels, social relationships, health status, books read, films watched, games played and goods or services paid for, will feed into his/her individual social credit score, defining his/her value for the society as a citizen. This score will then determine the citizen's eligibility to access a variety of services, such as a mortgage, a particular job, or specific education opportunities for his/her children. The evaluation will be carried out with algorithms which are not to be revealed in detail to the people being evaluated. Participation in the system is voluntary until 2020; afterwards, it will become mandatory for all.[58]

---

56. Resolution of the European Parliament of 12 March 2014 on the US NSA surveillance programme, surveillance bodies in various Member States and their impact on EU citizens' fundamental rights and on transatlantic cooperation in Justice and Home Affairs (2013/2188(INI)), 12 March 2014, http://www.europarl.europa.eu/sides/getDoc.do?pubRef=-//EP//TEXT+TA+P7-TA-2014-0230+0+DOC+XML+V0//EN.
57. The Article 29 Working Party's Statement on encryption and their impact on the protection of individuals with regard to the processing of their personal data in the EU of 11 April 11 2018, http://ec.europa.eu/newsroom/article29/item-detail.cfm?item_id=622229.
58. R. Botsman, Big data meets Big Brother as China moves to rate its citizens, 21 October 2017, http://www.wired.co.uk/article/chinese-government-social-credit-score-privacy-invasion.

Also worth noting is the dispute on retention of telecommunications data under Directive 2006/24/EC of the European Parliament and of the Council of 15 March 2006 on the retention of data generated or processed in connection with the provision of publicly available electronic communications services or of public communications networks.[59]

The dispute concerned the circumstances authorising the collection by network operators and telecom providers of transmission data relating to telecom connections, in particular personal data and the time and location of the connection or attempted connection, and the retention of such data for a period of six months to two years from the connection date for the use by the competent public services and bodies, in order to ensure public security. The scope of such data collection and supervision thereof were also a subject of the discussion. The two-year retention period was criticised as excessive and unnecessary for investigating and combating crime. Very seldom do authorities make use of data which have been retained for longer than six months.

A ground-breaking approach to data retention was formulated by the Court of Justice of the EU in its judgment of 8 April 2014, declaring the 'Retention Directive' to be invalid.[60] The Court judgment was based directly on the incompatibility of the directive with the right to privacy enshrined in the Charter of Fundamental Rights, i.e. one of human rights. The Court did not call into question the purpose of the Directive but found the interference with privacy to be excessive in relation to that purpose, i.e. ensuring public security and preventing and combating crime. The Court also pointed to the lack of criteria relating to the established periods of data retention.[61]

The CJEU ruled to the same effect in its judgment of 21 December 2016 in the joined Cases C-203/15 and C-698/15,[62] arguing that EU law did not allow the mass retention of all network traffic and location data. Member State laws can lawfully provide for the retention of certain data for the purpose of fighting serious crime, but the scope of data, categories, data subjects and retention periods may not go beyond what is necessary for that purpose. The national law must also specify the conditions of public authorities' access to the data being retained, and provide for controls of the basis and scope of this access by an independent authority.

59. OJ EU L 105, 14.4.2006, p. 54.

60. Joined Cases C-293/12 and C-594/12, *Digital Rights Ireland Ltd* (C-293/12) *v Minister for Communications, Marine and Natural Resources and Others* and *Kärntner Landesregierung* (C-594/12), *Michael Seitlinger, Christof Tschohl and Others*, http://eur-lex.europa.eu/legal-content/EN/TXT/?uri=CELEX%3A62012CJ0293. For a discussion on the CJEU drawing a line between combating crime and the right to privacy by reference to the Charter of Fundamental Rights, and personal data protection in the context of retention of telecommunications data, see A. Grzelak, 'Granica między skuteczną walką z przestępczością a prawem do prywatności i do ochrony danych osobowych – glosa do wyroku TS z 8.04.2014 r. w sprawach połączonych: C-293/12 i C-594/12 Digital Rights Ireland', *Europejski Przegląd Sądowy*, no. 7/2014, p. 45.

61. The Article 29 Data Protection Working Party, Document No. WP 220 of 1 August 2014, Statement on the ruling of the Court of Justice of the European Union (CJEU) which invalidates the Data Retention Directive, http://ec.europa.eu/justice/article-29/documentation/opinion-recommendation/files/2014/wp220_en.pdf.

62. *Tele2 Sverige AB* (C-203/15) *v Post- och telestyrelsen*, and *Secretary of State for the Home Department* (C-698/15) *v Tom Watson, Peter Brice, Geoffrey Lewis*; https://eur-lex.europa.eu/legal-content/EN/TXT/?uri=CELEX:62015CJ0203.

Previously, in a judgment of 2 March 2010, the German Constitutional Court ruled the implementation of the directive on retention of telecommunications data to be incompatible with Article 10 of the German Constitution as constituting an infringement of postal secrecy and of the proportionality principle, as well as an intrusion on privacy of every citizen, unrelated to their actions.

Retention of data was also challenged by the Polish Constitutional Tribunal in its judgment of 12 December 2005 (K 32/04).[63] The Tribunal ruled that: 'In a democratic state ruled by law, it is not necessary to retain information on citizens, obtained during operational activities, on the grounds of potential usefulness of such information. Such a retention is only permissible in the context of specific proceedings conducted under a statute allowing a restriction of freedoms for reasons of State security and public order'.

§14.03 CONCLUSIONS

I have demonstrated that the development of technologies used for collecting and handling data, particularly for commercial purposes, and the emergence of new categories of data, such as geolocation data or profiles of Internet users as consumers, are important threats to the right to privacy. The privacy protection regulations applicable to date were developed in fundamentally different technological circumstances and therefore needed to be updated to restore their effectiveness. In order to respond to these challenges and bridge the technological gap between the legally prescribed level of personal data protection and the actual level, the General Data Protection Regulation has been adopted, the most significant reform of the data protection regime since Directive 95/46/EC was enacted 21 years ago.

It is important to use various means to strive for effective privacy protection. Legislative measures must be accompanied by adequate IT tools, education, and measures to raise awareness on the threats resulting from online data processing. The GDPR has introduced dissuasive fines against non-compliant data controllers. Still, we should realise that the development and ubiquity of information technologies make it extremely difficult to protect the privacy of Internet users, smartphone and tablet users, credit card owners, online shoppers, social networking service users and other people whose data make it onto the Internet.

I sincerely hope that Facebook founder Mark Zuckerberg is wrong in his assertion: 'Privacy is dead – deal with it'. The right to privacy is the prerequisite of freedom. This is why privacy must be saved. If through this book I can contribute to this, it will be my greatest reward.

63. Dziennik Ustaw (Polish Journal of Laws) of 2005, No. 250, item 2116.

Bibliography

Barabási A.L., *Bursts: The Hidden Pattern Behind Everything We Do, From Your Email to Bloody Crusades*, New York 2010

Barta J., Fajgielski P., Markiewicz R., *Ochrona danych osobowych. Komentarz*, Kraków 2004, 2007

Barta P., Litwiński P., *Ustawa o ochronie danych osobowych. Komentarz*, Warszawa 2009, 2016

Behrens Ch., 'Big Brother – Now With Added Intelligence', *Süddeutsche Zeitung*, 12.3.2013, http://www.worldcrunch.com/rss/tech-science/big-brother-now-with-added-intelligence/person-of-interest-cctv-pattern-recognition-aisight/c4s11156/

Bell G., Gemmell J., *Total Recall: How the E-Memory Revolution Will Change Everything*, New York 2009

Bendtsen S., Suppli Benson P., 'Dansk politimand fanget i amerikansk terrrornet', *Berlingske*, 26.2.2012, http://www.b.dk/nationalt/dansk-politimand-fanget-i-amerikansk-terrornet

Bennet C.J., 'Cookies, web bugs, webcams and cue cats: Patterns of Surveillance on the world wide web', *Ethics and Information Technology* 2001, Vol. 3, No. 3

Bennet C.J., 'In Defence of Privacy: The Concept and the Regime', *Surveillance and Society* 2011, No. 4

Bennet C.J., *International Privacy Standards: A Continuing Convergence?*, 'Privacy Laws and Business International' 2010, Vol. 105

Bennet C.J., *Regulating Privacy: Data Protection and Public Policy in Europe and the United States*, New York 1992

Bennet C.J., 'Storming the Barricades So We Can All Be Private Together: Everyday Surveillance and the Politics of Privacy Advocacy', *Leviathan* 2010, Vol. 25

Bennet C.J., Lyon D., *Playing the Identity Card: Surveillance, Security and Identification in Global Perspective*, London 2008

Bennet C.J., Raab Ch.D., 'The Adequacy of Privacy: The European Union Data Protection Directive and the North American Response', *The Information Society* 1997, Vol. 13, No. 3

Bennet C.J., Raab Ch.D., *The Governance of Privacy. Policy Instruments in Global Perspective*, London 2006

Blume P., 'Transborder Data Floin: Is There a Solution in Sight?', *International Journal of Law and Information Technology* 2000, No. 8

Botsman R., *Big Data Meets Big Brother as China Moves to Rate Its Citizens*, 21 October 2017, http://www.wired.co.uk/article/chinese-government-social-credit-score-privacy-invasion

Braciak J., *Prawo do prywatności*, Warszawa 2004

Brownsword R., 'Consent in Data Protection Lain: Privacy, Fair Processing and Confidentiality', in: *Reinventing Data Protection?*, ed. by S. Gutwirth, Y. Poulet, P. de Hert, S. Nouwt, C. de Terwangne, Dordrecht 2009

Browsword R., Goodwin M., *Law and Technologies of Twenty-First Century. Text and Materials*, Cambridge 2012

Busemann H.-E., Schimroszik N., *German Court Rules Facebook Use of Personal Data Illegal, Reuters*, 12 February 2018, https://www.reuters.com/article/us-germany-facebook/german-court-rules-facebook-use-of-personal-data-illegal-idUSKBN1FW1FI

Bygrave L.A., 'International Agreements to Protect Personal Data', in: *Global Privacy Protection. The First Generation*, ed. by J.B. Rule, G. Greenleaf, Cheltenham–Northampton 2007

Bygrave L.A., 'Privacy Protection in a Global Context – A Comparative Overview', *Scandinavian Studies in Law* 2004, Vol. 47

Carey P., *Data Protection*, Oxford 2004

Ciechomska M., *Zmiana Konwencji nr 108 Rady Europy o ochronie osób w związku z automatycznym przetwarzaniem danych osobowych szansą na powstanie globalnego instrumentu ochrony danych*, Monitor Prawniczy no. 16/2017, August 2017

Connolly Ch., 'New Galexia Study: The US Safe Harbor – Fact or Fiction?', *Privacy Laws and Business International* 2008, No. 96, 2.12.2008, http://www.galexia.com/public/research/assets/safe_harbor_fact_or_fiction_2008/safe_harbor_fact_or_fiction.pdf

Craig P., de Búrca G., *EU Lain: Text, Cases, and Materials*, Oxford 2008

Craig T., Ludloff M.E., *Privacy and Big Data*, Sebastopol, CA 2011

Crawford S., 'Keeping it to Themselves: Bank Privacy Towards 2000', *Ottawa Law Review* 1998, No. 29

Culnan M.J., Bies R.J., 'Managing Privacy Concerns Strategically: The Implications of Fair Information Practices in Marketing in the Twenty-First Century', in: *Visions of Privacy: Policy Choices for the Digital Age*, ed. by C.J. Bennet, R. Grant, Toronto 1999

Czerniawski M., *Zakres terytorialny a pojęcie 'jednostki organizacyjnej' w przepisach ogólnego rozporządzenia o ochronie danych – zarys problemu*, in: *Ogólne rozporządzenie o ochronie danych. Aktualne problemy prawnej ochrony danych osobowych 2016*, Monitor Prawniczy, ed. G. Sibiga

Czerniawski M., 'Portale społecznościowe a prawo do ochrony danych osobowych – zarys problemu', in: *Internet. Prawno-informatyczne problemy sieci, portali i e-usług*, ed. G. Szpor, W. Wiewiórowski (Assistant European Data Protection Supervisor), Warszawa 2012

Dix A., Berliner Datenschutzbeauftragter, 'The German Railway Card – A Model Contractual Solution of the Adequate Level of Protection Issue?', 18th Annual

International Privacy and Data Protection Conference, Ottawa, Canada, September 1996
Doyle C., Bagaric M., 'The Right to Privacy: Appealing but Flawed', *International Journal of Human Rights* 2005, Vol. 9, No. 1
Drozd A., *Ustawa o ochronie danych osobowych. Komentarz,* Warszawa 2004
Ehmann E. von, Helfrich M., *EG-Datenschutzrichtlinie: Kurzkommentar*, Köln 1999
Etzioni A., *The Limits of Privacy,* New York 1999
Fajgielski P., *Informowanie o naruszeniu ochrony danych osobowych w świetle przepisów ogólnego rozporządzenia o ochronie danych*, Monitor Prawniczy 2016, no. 20
Fajgielski P., 'Funkcjonowanie portali Internetowych – wybrane problemy prawne', in: *Internet. Prawno-informatyczne problemy sieci, portali i e-usług*, ed. by G. Szpor, W. Wiewiórowski, Warszawa 2012
Fischer Ph.E., *Will Privacy Law in the 21st Century be American, European or International?*, London 2010
Flaherty D.H., 'Visions of Privacy: Past, Present and Future', in: *Visions of Privacy: Policy Choices for the Digital Age*, ed. by C.J. Bennet, R. Grant, Toronto 1999
Giudici P., Figini S., Applied Data Mining for Business and Industry, Chichester 2009
Gorczyński G., 'Sąd cywilny a tajemnica bankowa – uwagi na tle uchwały Sądu Najwyższego z 7 grudnia 2006', *Prawo Bankowe* 2007, No. 12
Greenwald G., MacAskill E., 'NSA Prism program taps in to user data of Apple, Google and others', *The Guardian*, 7.6.2013, http://www.theguardian.com/world/2013/jun/06/us-tech--giants-nsa-data
Grzelak A., 'Granica między skuteczną walką z przestępczością a prawem do prywatności i do ochrony danych osobowych – glosa do wyroku TS z 8.4.2014 w sprawach połączonych: C-293/12 i C-594/12 Digital Rights Ireland', *Europejski Przegląd Sądowy* 2014, No. 7
Han J., Kamber M., *Data Mining: Concepts and Techniques*, San Diego 2001
Hempel L., Lammerant L., *Impact Assessment as Negotiated Knowledge*, in: *Reforming European Data Protection Law*, eds. S. Gutwirth, R. Leenes, P. de Hert, Dordrecht 2015
Hildebrandt M., 'Defining Profiling: A New Type of Knowledge?', in: *Profiling the European Citizen. Cross-Disciplinary Perspectives*, ed. by M. Hildebrandt, S. Gutwirth, New York
Jagielski M., *Prawo do ochrony danych osobowych. Standardy europejskie*, Warszawa 2010
Jay R., Hamilton A., *Data Protection Law and Practice*, London 2003
Jurkowska-Zeidler A., 'Tajemnica bankowa jako środek ochrony prawa do prywatności', in: *Prawa człowieka: wczoraj – dziś – jutro*, ed. by J. Zajadło, Gdańskie Studia Prawnicze 2005, Vol. 13
Karwala D., 'Nowe zasady przechowywania informacji w telekomunikacyjnych urządzeniach końcowych (uwagi na temat znowelizowanego art. 173 PrTelekom)', MoP 2013, No. 8 – dodatek specjalny Aktualne problemy prawnej ochrony danych osobowych 2013

Kawecki M., 'Wybór rozporządzenia jako instrumentu prawnego unijnej reformy prawa ochrony danych osobowych oraz konsekwencje takiego *rozwiązania*', in: *Ogólne rozporządzenie o ochronie danych osobowych. Wybrane zagadnienia*, ed. M. Kawecki, T. Osiej

Kirby M., 'The history, achievement and future of the 1980 OECD guidelines on privacy', *International Data Privacy Law* 2011, vol. 1, No. 1, http://idpl.oxfordjournals.org/content/1/1/6.full

Kierkegaard S., Waters N., Greenleaf G., Bygrave L.A., Lloyd I., Saxby S., '30 Years On – The Review of the Council of Europe Data Protection Convention 108', *Computer Law & Security Review* No. 27/2011

Klosek J., *Data Privacy in the Information Age*, Westport 2000

Knyrim R., Trieb G., 'Smart metering under EU data protection law', *International Data Privacy Law* 2011, vol. 1, No. 2

Konarski X., 'Przetwarzanie danych osobowych w chmurze obliczeniowej', *Monitor Prawniczy* 2013, No. 8 – dodatek specjalny Aktualne problemy prawnej ochrony danych osobowych 2013

Konarski X., Sibiga G., 'Zasady przekazywania danych osobowych do państwa trzeciego w prawie polskim i Unii Europejskiej', in: *Ochrona danych osobowych. Aktualne problemy i nowe wyzwania*, ed. by X. Konarski, G. Sibiga, Warszawa–Kraków 2007

Kong L., 'Data Protection and Transborder Data Flow in the European and Global Context', *European Journal of International Law* 2010, Vol. 21, No. 2, http://www.ejil.org/pdfs/21/2/2007.pdf

Kozinski A., 'The Dead Past', in: *The Privacy Paradox. Privacy and Its Conflicting Values, Stanford Law Review*, 2.2.–12.4.2012, http://www.stanfordlawreview.org/online/privacy-paradox/dead-past

Kreiss D., 'Yes We Can (Profile You). A Brief Primer on Campaigns and Political Data', in: *The Privacy Paradox. Privacy and Its Conflicting Values, Stanford Law Review*, 2.2–12.4.2012, http://www.stanfordlawreview.org/online/privacy-paradox/political-data

Krzysztofek K., 'Big Data Society. Technologie samozapisu i samopokazu: ku humanistyce cyfrowej', *Kultura i Historia*, 3.3.2012, http://www.kulturaihistoria.umcs.lublin.pl/archives/3626

Krzysztofek K., 'Świat w wersji hiper: Od hipermedium do hiperspołeczeństwa', in: *Kulturowe kody technologii cyfrowych*, ed. by P. Celiński, Lublin 2011

Krzysztofek K., 'The @lgorithmic Society: Digitarians of the World Unite', in: *European Visions for the Knowledge Age. A Quest for New Horizons in the Information Society*, ed. by P.T. Kidd, Cheshire Henbury 2006

Krzysztofek M., *Post-Reform Personal Data Protection in the European Union*, Kluwer Law International BV, The Netherlands 2017

Krzysztofek M., *Ochrona danych osobowych w Unii Europejskiej po reformie. Komentarz do rozporządzenia Parlamentu Europejskiego i Rady (UE) 2016/679*, Warszawa 2016

Krzysztofek M., *'The Right to be Forgotten' on a Swing'*, 27(6) European Business Law Review (2016)

Krzysztofek M., *Tajemnice zawodowe i ochrona danych osobowych w instytucjach finansowych*, Warszawa 2015

Krzysztofek M., *Zgoda pracownika jako podstawa przetwarzania danych biometrycznych w RODO i w projekcie Przepisów wprowadzających ustawę o ochronie danych osobowych*, Informacja w Administracji Publicznej No. 4/2017

Krzysztofek M., *Ograniczenie dostępu do danych osobowych członków organów spółek w rejestrach publicznych (glosa do wyroku Trybunału Sprawiedliwości EU z dnia 9 marca 2017 r. w sprawie Camera di Commercio, Industria, Artigianato e Agricoltura di Lecce przeciwko Salvatore Manniemu, C-398/15*, Informacja w Administracji Publicznej 3/2017

Krzysztofek M., *Konkretyzacja statusu inspektora ochrony danych z RODO w wytycznych Grupy Roboczej Art. 29, Informacja* w Administracji Publicznej 1/2017

Krzysztofek M., *Ochrona danych osobowych w Unii Europejskiej*, Warszawa 2014

Krzysztofek M., 'Prawo do bycia zapomnianym i inne aspekty prywatności w epoce Internetu w prawie UE', *Europejski Przegląd Sądowy* 2012, No. 8

Krzysztofek M., 'Prawo do bycia zapomnianym, Part 1 and 2', *Computerworld* 2012, No. 10 and 11

Krzysztofek M., 'Przetwarzanie danych biometrycznych w celu ewidencjonowania czasu pracy pracowników Urzędu Skarbowego – glosa do wyroku Naczelnego Sądu Administracyjnego, 6.9.2011, I OSK 1476/10', *Monitor Prawa Celnego i Podatkowego* 2012, No. 5

Krzysztofek M., *Transfer of Financial Messaging Data in the SWIFT System from the EU to the USA*, Państwo i Prawo 2011, Issue 7-8, p. 125

Krzysztofek M., *Tajemnica bankowa i ochrona danych osobowych w praktyce bankowej*, Warszawa 2010

Kulesza E., 'Przesłanki przetwarzania danych osobowych pracowników przez pracodawcę', *Monitor Prawniczy* 2012, No. 7 – special appendix Ochrona danych osobowych 2012

Kuner Ch., *European Data Privacy Law and Online Business*, Oxford–New York 2003

Kuner Ch., *European Data Protection Law. Corporate Compliance and Regulation*, Oxford–New York 2007

Kuner Ch., 'Regulation of Transborder Data Flows under Data Protection and Privacy Lain: Past, Present, and Future', Tilburg University, the Netherlands, TILT Law & Technology Working Paper 2010, No. 016, Version: 1.0, http://www.tilburguniversity.edu/research/institutes-and--research-groups/tilt/publications/workingpapers/ckuner16.pdf

Kuner Ch., Transborder Data Flows and Data Privacy Law, Oxford 2013

Kuner Ch., 'Reality and *Illusion* in EU Data Transfer Regulation Post Schrems', 18 German Law Journal 881 (2017)

Leopold N., Meints M., 'Profiling in Employment Situation (Fraud), podrozdział Legal Grounds with Respect to Data Protection in the Working Context', in: *Profiling the European Citizen. Cross-Disciplinary Perspectives*, ed. by M. Hildebrandt, S. Gutwirth, New York 2008

Lipowicz I., *Uwagi do strategii poprawy skuteczności unijnych przepisów dotyczących ochrony danych osobowych, przedstawionej przez Komisję Europejską, przygotowane przez Stowarzyszenie Naukowe Centrum Prawno-Informatyczne*, Warszawa 2011, http://ec.europa.eu/justice/news/consulting_public/0006/contributions/not_registered/ncpi_pl.pdf

Litwiński P., Barta P., Kawecki M., *Rozporządzenie UE w sprawie ochrony osób fizycznych w związku z przetwarzaniem danych osobowych i swobodnym przepływem takich danych. Komentarz*, Warszawa 2017

Litwiński P., "Pojęcie danych osobowych w ogólnym rozporządzeniu o ochronie danych osobowych – glosa do wyroku Trybunału Sprawiedliwości z 19.10.2016 r. w sprawie C-582/14 Patrick Breyer", *Europejski Przegląd Sądowy*, No. 5/2017 *Nowe prawo unijne o ochronie danych osobowych*

Litwiński P., 'Świadczenie usług drogą elektroniczną', in: *Prawo Internetu*, ed. by P. Podrecki, Warszawa 2007

Lyon D., *A Report on the Surveillance Society for the Information Commissioners Office by the Surveillance Studies Network: Full Report*, September 2006

MacAskill E., 'Edward Snowden: how the spy story of the age leaked out', *The Guardian*, 12.6.2013, http://www.theguardian.com/world/2013/jun/11/edward-snowden-nsa-whistleblower-profile/print

Manny C.H., 'Personal privacy – transatlantic perspectives, European and American privacy: commerce, rights and justice – Part 1', *Computer Law and Security Report* 2003, vol. 19, No. 1, http://www.its.ohiou.edu/bernt/ITS351/trans atlantic1.pdf

Martenczuk B., van Thiel S., *Justice, Liberty, Security: New Challenges for EU External Relations*, Brussels 2008

Mayer-Schoenberger V., Delete: *The Virtue of Forgetting in the Digital Age*, Princeton 2009

Mayer-Schönberger V., Cukier K., *Big Data: A Revolution That Will Transform How We Live, Work, and Think*, New York 2013

Mednis A., 'Cechy zgody na przetwarzanie danych osobowych w opinii Grupy Roboczej Art. 29 dyrektywy 95/46 No. 15/2011 (WP 187)', *Monitor Prawniczy* 2012, No. 7 – special appendix Ochrona danych osobowych 2012

Montjoye Y-A. de, Radaelli L., Singh V.K., Pentland A.S., 'Unique in the shopping mall: On the reidentifiability of credit card metadata', *Science* 30 January 2015, vol. 347, No. 6221

Motyka K., 'Prawo do prywatności', *Zeszyty Naukowe Akademii Podlaskiej w Siedlcach* 2010, No. 85

Osterwalder C., 'Cloud computing. Przetwarzanie na dużą skalę i bezpieczeństwo danych', in: *Internet. Cloud computing. Przetwarzanie w chmurach*, ed. by G. Szpor, Warszawa 2013

Parczewski R., 'Zbywanie wierzytelności przez banki – zagadnienia prawne', *Glosa* 2003, No. 1

Raab Ch.D., 'Different Processes, One Result: The Convergence of Data Protection Policy in Europe and the United States', *Governance* 1988, Vol. 1, No. 4

Raab Ch.D., 'Regulating the Computer: comparing policy instruments in Europe and the United States', *European Journal of Political Research* 1988, Vol. 16, No. 5

Reidenberg J.R., 'Resolving Conflicting International Data Privacy Rules in Cyberspace', *Stanford Law Review* 2000, vol. 52, http://reidenberg.home.sprynet.com/international_rules.pdf

Richards N.M., 'The Dangers of Surveillance', *Harvard Law Review*, 25.3.2013, http://papers. ssrn.com/sol3/papers.cfm?abstract_id = 2239412

Rodota S., 'Data Protection as a Fundamental Right', in: *Reinventing Data Protection?*, ed. by S. Gutwirth, Y. Poulet, P. de Hert, S. Nouwt, C. de Terwangne, Dordrecht 2009

Rosen J., 'The Right to Be Forgotten', in: *The Privacy Paradox. Privacy and Its Conflicting Values, Stanford Law Review*, 2.2.–12.4.2012, http://www.stanfordlawreview.org/online/privacy--paradox/right-to-be-forgotten

Rosen R.J., 'Stanford Researchers: It Is Trivially Easy to Match Metadata to Real People', *The Atlantic*, 24.12.2013, http://www.theatlantic.com/technology/archive/2013/12/stanfordresearchers-it-is-trivially-easy-to-match-metadata-to-real-people/282642/

Schmitz G.-P., 'SWIFT Suspension? EU Parliament Furious about NSA Bank Spying', *Spiegel Online International*, 8.9.2013, http://www.spiegel.de/international/europe/nsa-spyingeuropean-parliamentarians-call-for-swift-suspension-a-922920.html

Shattuck J.H.F., *Right of Privacy*, New York 1997

Sibiga G., *Przetwarzanie i ochrona danych osoby ubiegającej się o zatrudnienie w świetle przepisów prawa pracy*, Radca Prawny 2005, No. 2

Sibiga G., *Postępowanie w sprawach ochrony danych osobowych*, Warszawa 2003

Siegel E., *Predictive Analytics: The Power to Predict Who Will Click, Buy, Lie, or Die*, New Jersey 2013

Singleton S., *Data Protection: The New Law*, Bristol 1998

Smith G.J.H., *Internet Law and Regulation*, London 2007

Szpor G., 'Prawne aspekty dostępności chmur', in: *Internet. Cloud computing. Przetwarzanie w chmurach*, ed. by G. Szpor, Warszawa 2013

Szymielewicz K., Mazga A., 'Internet a prawa podstawowe. Ekspresowy przegląd problemów regulacyjnych', http://wolnyInternet.panoptykon.org/sites/default/files/raport_na_www.pdf

Tene O., Polonetsky J., 'Privacy in the Age of Big Data. A Time for Big Decisions', in: *The Privacy Paradox. Privacy and Its Conflicting Values, Stanford Law Review*, 2.2–12.4.2012, http://www.stanfordlawreview.org/online/privacy-paradox/big-data

Tinnefeld M.-T., 'Jak Internet zmienia prawne ramy prywatności?', in: *Internet. Prawno-informatyczne problemy sieci, portali i e-usług*, ed. by G. Szpor, W. Wiewiórowski, Warszawa 2012

Vamosi R., *When Gadgets Betray Us: The Dark Side of Our Infatuation With New Technologies*, New York 2011

Warren S.D., Brandeis L.D., 'The Right to Privacy', *Harvard Law Review* 1890, No. 4, http://groups.csail.mit.edu/mac/classes/6.805/articles/privacy/Privacy_brand_warr2.html

Westacott E., 'Does Surveillance Make Us Morally Better?', *Philosophy Now*, listopad-grudzień 2010, http://www.philosophynow.org/issue79/Does_Surveillance_Make_Us_Morally_Better

Wiewiórowski W.R., 'Nowe ramy ochrony danych osobowych w Unii Europejskiej', *Monitor Prawniczy* 2012, No. 7 – special appendix Ochrona danych osobowych 2012

Wiewiórowski W.R., 'Prawo do prywatności w systemie inteligentnych sieci', *Monitor Prawniczy* 2013, No. 8 – special appendix Aktualne problemy prawnej ochrony danych osobowych 2013

Witten I.H., Frank E., Hall M.A., *Data Mining: Practical Machine Learning Tools and Techniques*, Burlington 2011

Wright D., Hert P. de, in: *Privacy Impact Assessment*, ed. by D. Wright, P. de Hert, New York 2012

Wyka T., *Rola Kodeksu pracy w systemie przepisów dotyczących ochrony danych osobowych pracownika* (in:) *Internet. Prawno-informatyczne problemy sieci, portali i e-usług*, ed. G. Szpor, W. Wiewiórowski, *Warszawa* 2012

Zanfir G., *Tracing the Right to be Forgotten in the Short History of Data Protection Law: The 'New Clothes' of an Old Right*, in: *Reforming European Data Protection Law*, (ed.) S. Gutwirth, R. Leenes, P. de Hert, Springer 2015

Zinser A., 'European Data Protection Directive: the Determination of the Adequacy Requirement in International Data Transfers', *Tulane Journal of Technology & Intellectual Property* 2004, No. 16

Index

EUROPEAN MONOGRAPH SERIES

1. Lammy Betten (ed.), *The Future of European Social Policy,* 1991 (ISBN 90-654-4585-4).
2. Annemarie Loman, Kamiel Mortelmans, Harry H.G. Post & Stewart Watson, *Culture and Common Law: Before and After Maastricht,* 1992 (ISBN 90-654-4638-9).
3. John A.E. Vervaele, *Fraud against the Community: The Need for European Fraud Legislation,* 1994 (ISBN 90-654-4634-6).
4. Philip Raworth, *The Legislative Process in the European Community,* 1993 (ISBN 90-654-4690-7).
5. Jules Stuyck, *Financial and Monetary Integration in the European Economic Community,* 1993 (ISBN 90-654-4718-0).
6. Jules Stuyck & A.J. Vossestein (eds), *State Entrepreneurship, National Monopolies and European Community Law,* 1993 (ISBN 90-654-4773-3).
7. Jules Stuyck & A. Looijestijn-Clearie (eds), *The European Economic Area EC-EFTA,* 1994 (ISBN 90-654-4815-2).
8. Rosita B. Bouterse, *Competition and Integration: What Goals Count?,* 1995 (ISBN 90-654-4816-0).
9. René Barents, *The Agricultural Law of the EC: An Inquiry into the Administrative Law,* 1994 (ISBN 90-654-4867-5).
10. Nicholas Emiliou, *Principles of Proportionality in European Law: A Comparative Study,* 1996 (ISBN 90-411-0866-1).
11. Eivind Smith, *National Parliaments as Cornerstones of European Integration,* 1996 (ISBN 90-411-0898-X).
12. Jan H. Jans, *European Environmental Law,* 1996 (ISBN 90-411-0877-7).
13. Síofra O'Leary, *The Evolving Concept of Community Citizenship: From the Free Movement of Persons to Union Citizenship,* 1997 (ISBN 90-411-0878-5).
14. Laurence W. Gormley (ed.), *Current and Future Perspectives on EC Competition Law,* 1983 (ISBN 90-411-0691-X).
15. Simone White, *Protection of the Financial Interests of the European Communities: The Fight against Fraud and Corruption,* 1998 (ISBN 90-411-9647-1).
16. Morten P. Broberg, *Broberg on the European Commission's Jurisdiction to Scrutinise Mergers,* 4th Edition, 2013 (ISBN 978-90-411-3339-7).
17. Doris Hildebrand, *The Role of Economic Analysis in the EC Competition Rules: The European School,* 2nd Edition, 2002 (ISBN 90-411-1706-7).
18. Christof R.A. Swaak, *European Community Law and the Automobile Industry,* 1999 (ISBN 90-411-1140-9).

19. Dorthe Dahlgaard Dingel, *Public Procurement: A Harmonization of the National Judicial Review of the Application of European Community Law,* 1999 (ISBN 90-411-1161-1).
20. John A.E. Vervaele (ed.), *Compliance and Enforcement of European Community Law,* 1999 (ISBN 90-411-1151-4).
21. Martin Trybus, *European Defence Procurement Law: International and National Procurement Systems as Models for a Liberalized Defence Procurement Market in Europe,* 1999 (ISBN 90-411-1167-0).
22. Helen Staples, *The Legal Status of Third Country Nationals Resident in the European Union,* 1999 (ISBN 90-411-1277-4).
23. Damien Geradin (ed.), *The Liberalization of State Monopolies in the European Union and Beyond,* 1999 (ISBN 90-411-1264-2).
24. Katja Heede, *European Ombudsman: Redress and Control at Union Level,* 2000 (ISBN 90-411-1413-0).
25. Ulf Bernitz & Joakim Nergelius (eds), *General Principles of European Community Law,* 2000 (ISBN 90-411-1402-5).
26. Michaela Drahos, *Convergence of Competition Laws and Policies in the European Community,* 2002 (ISBN 90-411-1562-5).
27. Damien Geradin (ed.), *The Liberalization of Electricity and Natural Gas in the European Union,* 2001 (ISBN 90-411-1560-9).
28. Gisella Gori, *Towards an EU Right to Education,* 2001 (ISBN 90-411-1670-2).
29. Brendan P.G. Smith, *Constitution Building in the European Union,* 2001 (ISBN 90-411-1695-8).
30. Friedl Weiss & Frank Wooldridge, *Free Movement of Persons within the European Community,* 2nd Edition, 2007 (ISBN 978-90-411-2545-3).
31. Ingrid Boccardi, *Europe and Refugees: Towards an EU Asylum Policy,* 2002 (ISBN 90-411-1709-1).
32. John A.E. Vervaele & André Klip (eds), *European Cooperation Between Tax, Customs and Judicial Authorities,* 2001 (ISBN 90-411-1747-4).
33. Wouter P.J. Wils, *The Optimal Enforcement of EC Antitrust Law: Essays in Law and Economics,* 2002 (ISBN 90-411-1757-1).
34. Damien Geradin (ed.), *The Liberalization of Postal Services in the European Union,* 2002 (ISBN 90-411-1780-6).
35. Nick Bernard, *Multilevel Governance in the European Union,* 2002 (ISBN 90-411-1812-8).
36. Jill Wakefield, *Judicial Protection through the Use of Article 288(2) EC,* 2002 (ISBN 90-411-1823-3).
37. Sebastiaan Princen, *EU Regulation and Transatlantic Trade,* 2002 (ISBN 90-411-1871-3).
38. Amaryllis Verhoeven, *The European Union in Search of a Democratic and Constitutional Theory,* 2002 (ISBN 90-411-1872-1).
39. Paul L.C. Torremans, *Cross Border Insolvencies in EU, English and Belgian Law,* 2002 (ISBN 90-411-1888-8).

40. Malcolm Anderson & Joanna Apap (eds), *Police and Justice Cooperation and the New European Borders,* 2002 (ISBN 90-411-1893-4).
41. Christin M. Forstinger, *Takeover Law in EU and USA: A Comparative Analysis,* 2002 (ISBN 90-411-1919-1).
42. Antonio Bavasso, *Communications in EU Antitrust Law: Market Power and Public Interest,* 2003 (ISBN 90-411-1974-4).
43. Fiona G. Wishlade, *Regional State Aid and Competition Policy in the European Union,* 2003 (ISBN 90-411-1975-2).
44. Gareth Davies, *Nationality Discrimination in the European Internal Market,* 2003 (ISBN 90-411-1998-1).
45. René Barents, *The Autonomy of Community Law,* 2003 (ISBN 90-411-2251-6).
46. Gerhard Dannecker & Oswald Jansen (eds), *Competition Law Sanctioning in the European Union,* 2004 (ISBN 90-411-2100-5).
47. Nauta Dutilh (ed.), *Dealing with Dominance: The Experience of National Competition Authorities,* 2004 (ISBN 90-411-2211-7).
48. Stefaan van den Bogaert, *Practical Regulation of the Mobility of Sportsmen in the EU Post Bosman,* 2005 (ISBN 90-411-2327-X).
49. Katalin Judit Cseres, *Competition Law and Consumer Protection,* 2005 (ISBN 90-411-2380-6).
50. Philipp Kiiver, *The National Parliaments in the European Union: A Critical View on EU Constitution Building,* 2006 (ISBN 978-90-411-2452-4).
51. Alexander Turk, *The Concept of Legislation in European Community Law,* 2006 (ISBN 978-90-411-2472-2).
52. Dimitrios Sinaniotis, *The Interim Protection of Individuals before the European and National Courts,* 2006 (ISBN 978-90-411-2498-2).
53. M. Holoubek & D. Damjanovic, M. Traimer (eds), *Regulating Content: The European Regulatory Framework for the Media and Related Creative Sectors,* 2006 (ISBN 978-90-411-2597-2).
54. Anneli Albi & Jacques Ziller (eds), *The European Constitution and National Constitutions: Ratification and Beyond,* 2006 (ISBN 978-90-411-2524-8).
55. Gustavo E. Luengo, *Regulation of Subsidies and State Aids in WTO and EC Law: Conflicts in International Trade Law,* 2007 (ISBN 978-90-411-2547-7).
56. Eniko Horvath, *Mandating Identity: Citizenship, Kinship Laws and Plural Nationality in the European Union,* 2007 (ISBN 978-90-411-2662-7).
57. Rass Holdgaard, *External Relations Law of the European Community: Legal Reasoning and Legal Discourses,* 2007 (ISBN 978-90-411-2604-7).
58. Jill Wakefield, *The Right to Good Administration,* 2007 (ISBN 978-90-411-2697-9).
59. Dimitry Kochenov, *EU Enlargement and the Failure of Conditionality: Pre- accession Conditionality in the Fields of Democracy and the Rule of Law,* 2008 (ISBN 978-90-411-2696-2).
60. Despina Mavromati, *The Law of Payment Services in the EU: The EC Directive on Payment Services in the Internal Market,* 2008 (ISBN 978-90-411-2700-6).

61. Anne Meuwese, *Impact Assessment in EU Lawmaking,* 2008 (ISBN 978-90-411-2720-4).
62. Ulf Bernitz, Joakim Nergelius & Cecilia Cardner (eds), *General Principles of EC Law in a Process of Development,* 2008 (ISBN 978-90-411-2705-1).
63. Johan van de Gronden (ed.), *The EU and WTO Law on Services: Limits to the Realisation of General Interest Policies within the Services Markets?,* 2008 (ISBN 978-90-411-2809-6).
64. Alina Tryfonidou, *Reverse Discrimination in EC Law,* 2009 (ISBN 978-90-411-2751-8).
65. Mikael Berglund, *Cross-Border Enforcement of Claims in the EU: History Present Time and Future,* 2014 (ISBN 978-90-411-4564-2).
66. Theodore Konstadinides, *Division of Powers in European Union Law: The Delimitation of Internal Competence between the EU and the Member States,* 2009 (ISBN 978-90-411-2615-3).
67. Mattias Derlén, *Multilingual Interpretation of European Union Law,* 2009 (ISBN 978-90-411-2853-9).
68. René Barents, *Directory of EU Case Law on the Preliminary Ruling Procedure,* 2009 (ISBN 978-90-411-3150-8).
69. Yan Luo, *Anti-dumping in the WTO, the EU and China: The Rise of Legalization in the Trade Regime and Its Consequences,* 2010 (ISBN 978-90-411-3207-9).
70. Patrick Birkinshaw & Mike Varney (eds), *The European Union Legal Order after Lisbon,* 2010 (ISBN 978-90-411-3152-2).
71. Thomas Gr. Papadopoulos, *EU Law and Harmonization of Takeovers in the Internal Market,* 2010 (ISBN 978-90-411-3340-3).
72. Bas van Bockel, *The* Ne Bis In Idem *Principle in EU Law,* 2010 (ISBN 978-90-411-3156-0).
73. Veljko Milutinović, *The 'Right to Damages' under EU Competition Law: From* Courage v. Crehan *to the White Paper and Beyond,* 2010 (ISBN 978-90-411-3235-2).
74. Amandine Garde, *EU Law and Obesity Prevention,* 2010 (ISBN 978-90-411-2706-8).
75. Leonard Besselink, Frans Pennings & Sacha Prechal (eds), *The Eclipse of the Legality Principle in the European Union,* 2011 (ISBN 978-90-411-3262-8).
76. Sacha Garben, *EU Higher Education Law: The Bologna Process and Harmonization by Stealth,* 2011 (ISBN 978-90-411-3365-6).
77. Dimitry Kochenov (ed.), *EU Law of the Overseas: Outermost Regions, Associated Overseas Countries and Territories, Territories Sui Generis,* 2011 (ISBN 978-90-411-3445-5).
78. Pablo Ibáñez Colomo, *European Communications Law and Technological Convergence: Deregulation, Re-regulation and Regulatory Convergence in Television and Telecommunications,* 2012 (ISBN 978-90-411-3829-3).
79. Elise Muir, *EU Regulation of Access to Labour Markets: A Case Study of EU Constraints on Member State Competences,* 2012 (ISBN 978-90-411-3823-1).
80. Tim Corthaut, *EU Ordre Public,* 2012 (ISBN 978-90-411-3232-1).

81. Oana Ştefan, *Soft Law in Court: Competition Law, State Aid and the Court of Justice of the European Union*, 2013 (ISBN 978-90-411-3997-9).
82. Francesco Rossi dal Pozzo, *Citizenship Rights and Freedom of Movement in the European Union*, 2013 (ISBN 978-90-411-4660-1).
83. Jens Hartig Danielsen, *EU Agricultural Law*, 2013 (ISBN 978-90-411-3280-2).
84. Ulf Bernitz, Xavier Groussot & Felix Schulyok (eds), *General Principles of EU Law and European Private Law*, 2013 (ISBN 978-90-411-4683-0).
85. Michelle Everson, Cosimo Monda & Ellen Vos (eds), *European Agencies in between Institutions and Member States*, 2014 (ISBN 978-90-411-2843-0).
86. Stefan Leible & Matthias Lehmann (eds), *European Contract Law and German Law*, 2014 (ISBN 978-90-411-2588-0).
87. Piero Leanza & Ondrej Pridal, *The Right to a Fair Trial: Article 6 of the European Convention on Human Rights*, 2014 (ISBN 978-90-411-4855-1).
88. Patrick J. Birkinshaw, *European Public Law: The Achievement and the Challenge*, 2014 (ISBN 978-90-411-4744-8).
89. George Cumming, *Expert Evidence Deficiencies in the Judgments of the Courts of the European Union and the European Court of Human Rights*, 2014 (ISBN 978-90-411-4123-1).
90. Vesna Rijavec, Tomaž Keresteš & Tjaša Ivanc (eds), *Simplification of Debt Collection in the EU*, 2014 (ISBN 978-90-411-4854-4).
91. Nina Półtorak, *European Union Rights in National Courts*, 2015 (ISBN 978-90-411-5863-5).
92. Kyriaki-Korina Raptopoulou, *EU Law and Healthcare Services: Normative Approaches to Public Health Systems*, 2015 (ISBN 978-90-411-5013-4).
93. Torsten Frank Koschinka & Piero Leanza, *Preliminary Injunctions: Germany, England/Wales, Italy and France*, 2015 (ISBN 978-90-411-5833-8).
94. Vesna Rijavec, Tomaž Keresteš & Tjaša Ivanc (eds), *Dimensions of Evidence in European Civil Procedure*, 2016 (ISBN 978-90-411-6662-3).
95. Stefan Leible (ed.), *General Principles of European Private International Law*, 2016 (ISBN 978-90-411-5955-7).
96. Patrick J. Birkinshaw & Andrea Biondi (eds), *Britain Alone!: The Implications and Consequences of United Kingdom Exit from the EU*, 2016 (ISBN 978-90-411-5832-1).
97. René Barents, *Remedies and Procedures before the EU Courts*, 2016 (ISBN 978-90-411-6614-2).
98. Luca Prete, *Infringement Proceedings in EU Law*, 2017 (ISBN 978-90-411-6900-6).
99. Robert van den Hoven van Genderen, *Privacy Limitation Clauses: Trojan Horses under the Disguise of Democracy*, 2017 (ISBN 978-90-411-8599-0).
100. Mariusz Krzysztofek, *Post-Reform Personal Data Protection in the European Union: General Data Protection Regulation (EU) 2016/679*, 2017 (ISBN 978-90-411-6237-3).
101. Gianni Lo Schiavo, *The Role of Financial Stability in EU Law and Policy*, 2017 (ISBN 978-90-411-8230-2).

102. Emmanuel Guinchard & Marie-Pierre Granger (eds), *The New EU Judiciary: An Analysis of Current Judicial Reforms*, 2017 (ISBN 978-90-411-6834-4).
103. Kirsten Henckel, *Cross-Border Transfers of Undertakings: A European Perspective*, 2017 (ISBN 978-90-411-9227-1).
104. Vesna Rijavec, Wendy Kennett, Tomaž Keresteš & Tjaša Ivanc, *Remedies Concerning Enforcement of Foreign Judgements: Brussels I Recast*, 2018 (ISBN 978-90-411-9416-9).
105. Albert Sanchez-Graells & Constant De Koninck, *Shaping EU Public Procurement Law: A Critical Analysis of the CJEU Case Law 2015–2017*, 2018 (ISBN 978-94-035-0160-4).
106. Andrea Biondi, Patrick J. Birkinshaw & Maria Kendrick, *Brexit: The Legal Implications*, 2019 (ISBN 978-90-411-9540-1).
107. Mariusz Krzysztofek, *GDPR: General Data Protection Regulation (EU) 2016/679: Post-Reform Personal Data Protection in the European Union*, 2019 (ISBN 978-94-035-0594-7).